THE SON OF MAN TRADITION

THE SON
OF MAN
TRADITION

DOUGLAS R. A. HARE

FORTRESS PRESS   Minneapolis

THE SON OF MAN TRADITION

Scripture quotations, unless otherwise noted, are from the Revised Standard Version of the Bible, copyright © 1946, 1952, and 1972 by the Division of Christian Education of the National Council of Churches.

Book design by Publishers' WorkGroup
Jacket design by Publishers' WorkGroup

Library of Congress Cataloging-in-Publication Data

Hare, Douglas R.A.
  The Son of Man tradition / Douglas R.A. Hare.
    p. cm.
  Includes bibliographical references and index.
  ISBN 0-8006-2448-3 (alk. paper)
  1. Son of Man. 2. Bible. N.T. Gospels—Criticism,
interpretation, etc. 3. Bible. N.T. Acts—Criticism,
interpretation, etc. I. Title.
BT232.H37 1990   90–42907
226'.06—dc20   CIP

The paper used in this publication meets the minimum requirements of American National Standard for Information Sciences—Permanence of Paper for Printed Library Materials, ANSI Z329.48-1984. ∞™

Manufactured in the U.S.A.   AF 1–2448

94   93   92   91   90   1   2   3   4   5   6   7   8   9   10

In memory of
R. B. Hare and W. M. Mustard

CONTENTS

PREFACE

Since my days as a theological student, I have been intrigued by the mysterious phrase "the Son of man." One of my first papers as a doctoral student focused in large part on the meaning of this expression. At that time I assumed that the majority of New Testament scholars had good reasons for maintaining that the words constituted an apocalyptic title. Daniel 7:13f., I was assured, reflects a Jewish myth concerning an angelic champion who was expected to arrive "on the clouds of heaven" at the end of the age to liberate God's people and judge sinners. Rudolf Bultmann, the leading German *Neutestamentler*, confidently asserted that Jesus could not have identified himself as "the Son of man"; only those sayings are authentic in which Jesus points away from himself to a heavenly figure whose imminent arrival he announces.

Despite my assumption that these scholars were correct, I could not help having certain reservations because of the way the phrase is actually used in the Gospels. In Mark, for example, the motif of the messianic secret powerfully influences the way the story is told. The readers are informed that Jesus is Christ in the opening verse, but this knowledge is hidden from all narrative audiences except the demoniacs (who are promptly silenced) until Peter's confession. Yet Jesus is represented as referring to himself publicly as "the Son of man" early in the story (2:10, 28), without thereby divulging his identity to anyone. The scholars assured me that these passages are simply instances of Mark's clumsy inconsistency, but their explanation failed to satisfy, because the same phenomenon appears in connection with other sayings in Matthew and Luke.

The scholarly consensus was challenged linguistically by Geza Vermes. In a brief paper Vermes argued that the alleged title could not have been expressed in Aramaic, the language of Jesus and his earliest followers. Behind the gospel phrase lies the Aramaic expression *bar nash* or *bar nasha*, which can serve as an indefinite pronoun, "a man," or, in some contexts, as a circumlocution for "I." Authentic sayings of Jesus employed *bar nasha* as an indirect reference to the speaker. While it received a great deal of attention, Vermes's hypothesis was stoutly resisted, and for two good reasons: his linguistic evidence was not wholly satisfactory, and he seemed guilty of arranging the New Testament evidence to fit his hypothesis. While attracted by the proposal, I was not convinced that Vermes had proved his case.

For me the decisive turning point in modern study of "the Son of man" was effected by the Norwegian scholar Ragnar Leivestad. A short English version of Leivestad's study, provocatively entitled "Exit the Apocalyptic Son of Man," appeared in *New Testament Studies* in 1972. Leivestad's point was clear and unequivocal: nowhere in the literature of pre-Christian Judaism is there any evidence of a mythical figure bearing the title "the Son of man." The significance of the evangelists' use of the phrase must therefore be derived from the Gospels themselves, not from the alleged apocalyptic tradition.

My excitement over this proposal was tempered by the discovery that many of my peers were no more impressed by Leivestad's frontal attack on the Bultmannian consensus than by the linguistic argument of Vermes. It became increasingly clear to me that if the consensus was to be successfully challenged, a different methodology would be required. The wisest course, it seemed, would be to proceed from the known to the unknown. Rather than starting with Daniel 7:13f. or with the Aramaic *bar (e)nash(a)*, one should begin with the most recent understanding of the mysterious phrase and work backward through the various strata, just as an archaeologist begins at the top of the tell and moves down through its evidence to earlier occupations. Sound arguments regarding the meaning of the phrase in the Greek strata could alone provide a firm basis for inferring the use and meaning of the phrase in the Aramaic tradition and in Jesus' original sayings.

The working hypothesis I adopted was Leivestad's, namely, that "the Son of man" was not the title of a mythical figure but Jesus' self-designation, but I presupposed no specific proposal concerning the content of the phrase. My backward method required that Jesus' understanding of the term be determined only as the final step in the chain of inferences that would be developed. Much to my own surprise, this process led me to a position very close to that of Vermes. In chapter 7 I infer that Jesus did in fact employ the phrase but without attributing to it any theological content. In his use it constituted a modesty idiom that functioned in much the same fashion as the self-referring "one" in English. In the final chapter I make tentative proposals regarding what kinds of Son of man sayings may on this basis be regarded as probably authentic.

What importance can be attached to a study whose outcome is primarily negative? If the reasoning pursued in this book is justified, it will offer further support to the claim being made by a number of scholars that Christology centering on the study of titles, which has been so popular during the twentieth century, must now be replaced by one that pays greater attention to statements than to words and titles. As Donald Juel points out in a letter, "The death of the son of man clears the way to pose new questions about the [linguistic] resources available to Jesus' followers, how they employed them, and what the whole process tells us about the language of faith."

A subsidiary contribution of this book to future research may lie in the methodology employed. If the backward approach here employed is perceived as successful, it may prove fruitful in other studies.

The English translation of the Bible most frequently followed in this book is the Revised Standard Version. Where the renderings depart from this version, they are my own, unless otherwise specified.

Readers are advised that full publication data for sources cited are to be found in the Bibliography and are therefore omitted from the notes, where titles are frequently referred to in shortened form.

This extended study occupied most of my research time for fifteen years. I would like to record my gratitude to the administrators and directors of Pittsburgh Theological Seminary, who generously granted me several sabbatical leaves for work on the project. The staff of the Barbour Library were unfailingly gracious and efficient in their assistance. Portions of earlier drafts were read at various national and regional meetings of the Society of Biblical Literature; I am grateful to all who responded with criticisms and encouragement. I would like to express appreciation to my colleague Jared Jackson, for his persistent kindness over the years in supplying me with references to new articles on the Son of man. Special thanks are due to my colleagues Ulrich Mauser and George Kehm, for their careful reading of chapter 5, and to Jack Kingsbury and Ulrich Luz for their kind invitation to present a condensed form of this chapter to the Matthew Seminar of the Studiorum Novi Testamenti Societas at its Dublin meeting. An expanded version of a small section of the same chapter is to be published in a Festschrift for my retired colleague William F. Orr, under the title "The Mountain Where Jesus Laid Down Rules for Them." I am especially grateful to Donald Juel, who carefully read the whole manuscript and made several very helpful suggestions. John Hollar of Fortress Press, whose untimely death is deeply regretted by a host of theological writers, encouraged me from the project's earliest stages; I am grateful both to him and to his associate, Marshall D. Johnson, who has edited the manuscript for the press.

Finally I would like to thank my wife for her patience in supporting a project that took far more time than either of us anticipated. The book is dedicated to her father and mine, both of whom modeled for us their faith in the one who modestly referred to himself as "a son of man."

2 April 1990   DOUGLAS R. A. HARE
                                      Wm. F. Orr Professor of New Testament,
                                      Pittsburgh Theological Seminary

ABBREVIATIONS

AB	Anchor Bible
Adv. Haer.	Irenaeus, *Against Heresies*
ANCL	Ante-Nicene Christian Library
ANF	The Ante-Nicene Fathers
ASTI	*Annual of the Swedish Theological Institute*
Bib	*Biblica*
BJRL	*Bulletin of the John Rylands Library*
BZ	*Biblische Zeitschrift*
CBQ	*Catholic Biblical Quarterly*
CBQ MS	Catholic Biblical Quarterly Monograph Series
CuW	*Christentum und Wissenschaft*
Dial.	Justin Martyr, *The Dialogue with Trypho*
DR	*Downside Review*
Eccl. Hist.	Eusebius, *The Ecclesiastical History*
ETL	*Ephemerides Theologicae Lovanienses*
EvT	*Evangelische Theologie*
Ex.	*Exegetica*
ExpTim	*Expository Times*
GCS	Die Griechischen christlichen Schriftsteller der ersten drei Jahrhunderte
Greg	*Gregorianum*
Hom.	Pseudo-Clementine *Homilies*
HTR	*Harvard Theological Review*
HUCA	*Hebrew Union College Annual*
IB	*Interpreter's Bible*
IDB Suppl.	*Interpreter's Dictionary of the Bible,* supplementary volume
Int	*Interpretation*
JBL	*Journal of Biblical Literature*

JJS	*Journal of Jewish Studies*
JQR	*Jewish Quarterly Review*
JSNT	*Journal for the Study of the New Testament*
JTS	*Journal of Theological Studies*
LXX	Septuagint
MPG	Migne's *Patrologiae,* Series graeca
MPL	Migne's *Patrologiae,* Series latina
NCeB	New Century Bible
NEB	*New English Bible*
NIGTC	New International Greek Testament Commentary
NovT	*Novum Testamentum*
NTD	Das Neue Testament Deutsch
NTS	*New Testament Studies*
OTS	Oudtestamentische Studien
PGC	Pelican Gospel Commentaries
Rec.	Pseudo-Clementine *Recognitions*
Refut. Haer.	Hippolytus, *The Refutation of All Heresies*
RevQ	*Revue de Qumran*
RSV	*The Holy Bible: Revised Standard Version*
SBL MS	Society of Biblical Literature Monograph Series
SBT	Studies in Biblical Theology
ScEc	*Sciences Ecclèsiastiques*
ScrB	*Scripture Bulletin*
SNTS MS	Studiorum Novi Testamenti Societas Monograph Series
SPCIC	*Studiorum Paulinorum*
SST	*Studia Theologica*
StEv	*Studia Evangelica*
TBl	*Theologische Blätter*
TDNT	*Theological Dictionary of the New Testament*
Theol.	*Theology*
ThT	*Theologisch Tijdschrift*
TLZ	*Theologische Literaturzeitung*
TRu	*Theologische Rundschau*
TU	Texte und Untersuchungen
VC	*Vigiliae Christianae*
VD	*Verbum Domini*
ZNW	*Zeitschrift für die neutestamentliche Wissenschaft*
ZTK	*Zeitschrift für Theologie und Kirche*

THE SON OF MAN TRADITION

1 | INTRODUCTION

One of the most baffling problems confronting the New Testament scholar concerns the use and meaning of the phrase *ho huios tou anthrōpou*, "the Son of man." The semantic function of the phrase is most unusual. In *form* it appears to be an appellative, either a title comparable to "the Son of God" and "the king of Israel," or a nickname like the one Jesus is reported to have given James and John, "Sons of Thunder" (Mk. 3:17). In *function*, however, it serves neither as a title nor as a nickname; that is, it is not used by others, whether as a form of address or as a means of specifying his function in statements about Jesus. With only three exceptions, each of which is truly exceptional, the phrase is found only in direct discourse attributed to Jesus himself.[1] In most contexts it appears to function as a self-designation, yet this usage is implicit rather than explicit, since it is always employed in third-person speech, never in apposition to "I" or "me."[2] There are, indeed, passages where Jesus appears to be speaking of another person, a heavenly figure distinguishable from himself. It is clear, however, that the gospel writers intend the readers to understand all such instances as statements of Jesus concerning his own future role; our perception of the possible disjunction between Jesus and the Son of man must be contrasted with the apparent unconcern of the evangelists respecting the potential misunderstanding, which seems not to have occurred to them.[3]

It is truly puzzling that, despite all the Son of man sayings regarding Jesus' future role, no occasion is found by any of the Gospels to employ

---

1. Lk. 24:7, Jn. 12:34, and Acts 7:56.
2. The only exception is a dubious textual variant at Mt. 16:13, which introduces *me* in conformity with the parallels at Mk. 8:27 and Lk. 9:18.
3. This point has been forcefully made by Leivestad, "Exit the Apocalyptic Son of Man," p. 261.

1

the phrase as a way of speaking about the meaning of Jesus. John the Baptist does not query, "Are you the Son of man?" (cf. Mt. 11:3, "Are you the Coming One, or do we wait for another?"). No disciple confesses faith in Jesus as the Son of man, either before or after the resurrection. Indeed, the phrase is never used in the New Testament in a statement confessing faith in Jesus.[4] The missionary speeches of Acts do not employ it, and it is totally absent from the epistles. Even the Revelation of John, so thoroughly imbued as it is with the expectation of the imminent coming of Jesus as heavenly Lord, does not use the phrase.[5]

It is obvious that any proposal concerning the *meaning* of the phrase must deal with the peculiarities of its *function* in the Gospels. No suggestion regarding signification can claim to be more than conjectural that does not adequately account for these related phenomena: (1) Jesus alone employs the phrase; (2) he employs it as a self-designation but only by implication, using third-person speech; and (3) the evangelists and other New Testament authors do not use it as a way of articulating the meaning of Jesus.

Associated with this semantic problem is a historical one. While nothing might seem more obvious to the nonspecialist than the fact that this strange usage must have derived from Jesus himself, scholars have been seriously divided over its origin. Some have found reason to deny that Jesus ever used the phrase, either as a self-designation or as a title connoting a heavenly messianic figure.[6] Many have maintained that Jesus spoke only of a heavenly figure distinct from himself when employing the term.[7] Still others have argued that authentic Son of man sayings appear only among those that speak of Jesus' earthly ministry, suffering, and death.[8] A few

4. Jn. 9:35–38 is not an exception; see below, chapter 4.
5. In Rev. 1:13 and 14:14 we find the phrase *homoion huion anthrōpou*, "one like a son of man," but this use of Danielic imagery must not be confused with the phrase attributed to Jesus, which is distinguished by the presence of two Greek articles. Indeed, some scholars have argued that the use of the simile instead of the phrase with the articles by this apocalyptist should be construed as evidence that he was unaware of the title "the Son of man"; cf. Lietzmann, *Der Menschensohn*, pp. 56f.
6. In recent years this view has been represented most notably by Vielhauer, "Gottesreich und Menschensohn"; cf. also his later "Jesus und der Menschensohn." A similar position has been argued by Teeple, "The Origin of the Son of Man Christology," and Perrin, *A Modern Pilgrimage*.
7. No attempt will be made here to list all the recent advocates of this view, but the following deserve special attention: Bultmann, *Theology*, vol. 1, pp. 29–33; Tödt, *Son of Man*; Hahn, *Titles of Jesus*, pp. 23–26; Fuller, *Foundations*, pp. 34–43, 119–25. Both Tödt and Fuller leave room for some form of covert identification on Jesus' part of himself and the apocalyptic Son of man whose coming he prophesied.
8. Notably Schweizer, ("Der Menschensohn," pp. 185–209; "The Son of Man," pp. 119–29; "The Son of Man Again," pp. 256–61) and Leivestad ("Der apokalyptische Menschensohn," pp. 49–105, and the article cited in n. 3).

assert that Jesus spoke both of his present humility and future glory by means of this self-designation.[9]

The great disparity in the conclusions reached may seem even more astonishing to the nonspecialist when it is observed how broad a consensus exists among those who have engaged in the great debate. The participants all subscribe to the necessity of historical criticism, which in this instance means the necessity of discriminating between earlier and later forms of the traditions concerning Jesus. It is further agreed that: (1) Jesus' primary language was Aramaic, with perhaps an occasional use of Hebrew; (2) the traditions about his words and deeds circulated orally for an extended period before being written down; (3) none of the extant Gospels was written by an eyewitness; (4) of the Synoptic Gospels, Mark is probably the first, and Matthew and Luke made independent use of Mark;[10] and (5) the Fourth Gospel shows the greatest amount of development and can be used for reconstructing the teaching of Jesus only with the greatest caution. Why, then, are such very different results obtained? Because of diversity in method, including prior assumptions, working hypotheses, starting points, and divergent uses of the criteria for establishing authentic Jesus material. Tradition criticism as practiced by New Testament scholars is clearly more art than science, and there is yet no generally accepted method capable of overcoming the current impasse regarding the Son of man traditions. The ultimate cause of the impasse, however, is not the methodological disagreement but the stubborn complexity of the problem.

In sum, the problem to be solved is this: Did Jesus himself employ a phrase in Aramaic or Hebrew roughly comparable to "the Son of man," and, if so, did he use the phrase as a self-designation, as the designation of a figure distinct from himself, or, in some paradoxical way, as the designation of a heavenly figure with whom he identified himself? What did he intend to connote by the phrase? On the other hand, if all instances derive from the post-Easter church, what did the phrase mean to those who first employed it, why did they so rigorously restrict it to sayings attributed to Jesus, why was it not used elsewhere in the New Testament to explicate the meaning of Jesus for faith, and why did it later serve as a means of referring to the humanity of Jesus?

9. Bammel, "Erwägungen zur Eschatologie Jesu," pp. 22f.; Jeremias, *New Testament Theology*, p. 276.

10. This consensus has been vigorously challenged in recent years by proponents of the Griesbach hypothesis, according to which Matthew is the earliest Gospel, followed by Luke and later by Mark; cf. Farmer, *The Synoptic Problem*. The challenge, however, has not yet succeeded in overturning the established consensus.

The Hypothesis to Be Tested

As will be explained at the end of this chapter, the method to be followed in this book will be inductive rather than deductive. It is only fair, however, to point out at the beginning that one of the intentions of the study is to test a hypothesis that Leivestad and others have employed.

Despite the diversity of conclusions mentioned above, the dominant view of critical scholarship for the past half-century has been that espoused by Bultmann, who insisted that Jesus announced the coming of a transcendent, heavenly judge called "the Son of man," a figure distinct from himself, and that only after the resurrection did Christian theology appropriate this apocalyptic conception as a tool for interpreting the meaning of Jesus.[11] Vielhauer modified this position only to the extent of denying to Jesus any role in announcing the Parousia of the Son of man; he retained only the second half of the Bultmannian hypothesis.[12] Schweizer attacked this dominant view head-on by arguing that, while the material concerning the Parousia of the Son of man was indeed of postresurrection origin, it was rooted in authentic Son of man sayings in which Jesus spoke of his earthly activity.[13] Leivestad's attack came from a different direction. He argued that since the extant Jewish material is inadequate to prove the existence of a pre-Christian tradition about a heavenly Son of man, the New Testament ought not to be used to bolster up a flimsy history-of-religions hypothesis but should be examined in its own right; on this basis we see that the New Testament writers do not treat the phrase as an apocalyptic title.[14]

N. Perrin, apparently independent of Leivestad, came to the same conclusion concerning the nonexistence of any such titular usage in pre-Christian Judaism. There was no established concept, only diverse uses of the imagery of Dan. 7:13. Agreeing with Vielhauer that Jesus did not speak of a coming Son of man, Perrin developed the argument that all christological use of the phrase in the New Testament derives from the postresurrection employment of Dan. 7:13 to supplement Ps. 110:1 and Zech. 12:10 as tools for giving shape and content to the expectation that Jesus had been exalted to the right hand of God and would return in glory at the end of the age.[15]

Leivestad's view that "the Son of man" was used by Jesus as a self-designation and not as an apocalyptic title has much to commend it, but it

---

11. In addition to Bultmann's work cited in n. 7, see his "Die Frage nach der Echtheit von Mt. 16:17–19," pp. 277f., and *History*, pp. 112, 128, 152.
12. See n. 6.
13. See n. 8.
14. See n. 8.
15. See n. 6.

has not succeeded in displacing the Bultmannian position, largely because of the above-mentioned disagreements over method. This book will test Leivestad's hypothesis, employing a method that, it is hoped, will meet with fewer objections from those who have not found his view convincing.

The Methodological Problem: Finding the Right Starting Point

Bultmann's Use of Form Criticism

For six decades gospel research has been dominated by Bultmann's *History of the Synoptic Tradition*, which adapted Gunkel's form-critical study of the Old Testament to the study of the gospel tradition. Bultmann's influence has been far more pervasive than that of his fellow form critics, M. Dibelius and K. L. Schmidt in particular, because of his different intention.[16] All three believed it possible to identify the units of oral tradition behind the Synoptic Gospels, sort them by genre, and attribute each genre to a specific context (*Sitz im Leben*) in the life of the early church (preaching, liturgy, catechetical instruction, polemical disputes, etc.). Convinced that *function shapes form*, the form critics maintained that they could use this method to distinguish between the original units of tradition and the later accretions that had resulted from the process of transcribing the units into collections and editing them for inclusion in the Gospels.

What made Bultmann's work so much more influential than that of Dibelius and Schmidt was that he was not content thus to distinguish between tradition and redaction but pressed on to deal with the question of the authenticity of the material. Assuming that the traditions were transmitted precisely because they were *useful* in their specific contexts, Bultmann expanded the basic form-critical principle to read: *function shapes both form and content.* He was convinced that many of the traditions were not in any sense authentic recollections of Jesus' words and actions but were created de novo to provide material *useful* for preaching, catechetical instruction, polemical disputes, and so forth. He could confidently attribute to Jesus only those units (sayings, parables, etc.) that, for him, had no specifically Christian features and contrasted sharply with contemporary Jewish morality and piety.[17]

---

16. The first edition of Bultmann's *Die Geschichte der synoptischen Tradition* (1921) was preceded by Dibelius, *Die Formgeschichte des Evangeliums*, and Schmidt, *Der Rahmen der Geschichte Jesu*, both published in 1919.

17. Bultmann, *History*, p. 205.

It is important to observe that when Bultmann was engaged in assessing the authenticity of traditions, he was not doing form criticism but historical criticism. Form-critical principles and procedures as such make no contribution to the determination of the historicity of the tradition.[18] At this point in the discussion a different set of principles and procedures comes into play.

A thorough examination of the principles and procedures underlying Bultmann's historical-critical decisions would take us too far afield, but it will be helpful to consider those that pertain most directly to the subject of this study.

1. Thoroughgoing skepticism is indispensable if we are to obtain general agreement among scholars regarding the words of the historical Jesus, as distinct from sayings that early Christian prophets may have delivered in the name of the risen Christ. Bultmann, it should be observed, was not the first to call for such a posture. W. Wrede had already pointed out that "it is better to have a little real knowledge, whether positive or 'negative,' than a great assortment of spurious knowledge."[19]

2. No christological statement can safely be attributed to Jesus. It must be assumed that such statements represent post-Easter reactions to the resurrection experience. Those teachings that can with confidence be traced to Jesus reflect not a messianic but a prophetic consciousness on Jesus' part. Here again Bultmann seems to be depending on Wrede.[20]

3. Most of Jesus' religious ideas have their origin in contemporary Judaism, particularly in Jewish apocalyptic.

4. The basic criterion for establishing the authenticity of a saying of Jesus is an absence of Christian features and a contrast with Jewish beliefs.

5. Authentic teachings of Jesus were preserved by the post-Easter church not because of any historical or biographical interest but simply because they were useful in various contexts.

It must be observed, in the first place, that a premium is placed by this method on *discontinuity*; "the critically assured minimum" (Nils Dahl's phrase) will unavoidably consist of the teachings that distinguish Jesus most sharply from contemporary Judaism and from the post-Easter church. Yet this rule is in conflict with the third principle, according to which Jesus derived most of his religious ideas, notably the Son of man conception, from his environment. It also ignores the assumption underlying the fifth

18. Cf. Fuller, *Critical Introduction*, p. 93; J. M. Robinson, *New Quest*, pp. 36f.
19. Wrede, *Messianic Secret*, p. 7; cf. pp. 8f.
20. Cf. ibid., pp. 5, 211–23. Presumably Bultmann was also influenced by W. Bousset; cf. Bousset, *Kyrios Christos*, pp. 72f.

principle, namely, that *continuity* is presupposed by the claim that authentic traditions were in fact preserved and found useful by the early church. It is surely obvious that the usefulness of a tradition about Jesus is no criterion for inauthenticity.

Regarding the second principle, it must be remarked that, while statements attributed to Jesus that deal with his religious significance must be subjected to careful historical scrutiny, they must not be ruled out of order on a priori grounds. Specifically, our preconceived ideas about Jesus' self-understanding must not be allowed to dictate in advance whether or not he employed an Aramaic or Hebrew phrase roughly equivalent to "the Son of man" as a way of speaking about himself.

It is clearly impossible for Bultmann to pursue critically questions concerning the function and meaning of "the Son of man" because his principles dictate the conclusions in advance. Although his argumentation is not laid out in detail in the *History* and only briefly referred to elsewhere, we can reconstruct it as follows.[21]

- If Jesus used the term "the Son of man," he took it from Jewish apocalyptic, where it designated a heavenly figure who was expected to serve as God's chief agent in the last judgment (principle 3).
- Jesus, as eschatological prophet, can have announced the imminent appearance of the Son of man for this judicial function, but he cannot have uttered a christological statement in which he identified himself as this heavenly figure (principle 2).
- Consequently, authentic Son of man sayings are not to be found among those that speak of Jesus' earthly ministry, suffering, and death.

This implicit argumentation was buttressed by Bultmann's exegesis of Lk. 12:8f. and Mk. 8:38, which he could without difficulty attribute to Jesus because he saw in these related sayings an explicit distinction between Jesus and the Son of man.[22] It would probably be erroneous, however, to assume that for Bultmann this exegesis was the starting point of the argumentation rather than its confirmation.

The trichotomizing of the Son of man sayings into "future," "suffering," and "earthly" groupings, which is often attributed to Bultmann but is actually much older, is again a result and not a cause of the argumentation.[23] There is clearly a danger in such a division, because classifying the sayings

---

21. See n. 11.
22. Bultmann, *History*, pp. 151f.
23. Cf. Bultmann, *Theology*, vol. 1, p. 30. The perception that the Son of man sayings can be so categorized appears frequently in the older literature, e.g., Baldensperger, "Die neueste Forschung über den Menschensohn," p. 207. Also prior to Bultmann's treatment is that of Foakes Jackson and Lake, *The Beginnings of Christianity*, vol. 1, p. 376.

in this way predisposes us to regard one *group* as possessing a greater claim to authenticity than another, whereas it is just as possible that authentic and inauthentic sayings appear in each. The division, it must be observed, is a natural consequence of the prior decision that identified "the Son of man" as a Jewish apocalyptic title. Since the earthly and suffering sayings do not fit easily with such a construction, they very naturally fall away as secondary.

It should be further observed that Bultmann pays almost no attention to the linguistic debate that so exercised H. Lietzmann, J. Wellhausen, G. Dalman, and P. Fiebig concerning which Aramaic expression, if any, could have functioned as the alleged apocalyptic title.[24] Bultmann appeals to the linguistic issue only when he wishes to show that the appearance of "the Son of man" in a saying concerning Jesus' earthly ministry may have resulted from mistranslation.[25] He apparently regarded Lietzmann's challenge as adequately silenced by Dalman.

It would be difficult to exaggerate the influence of Bultmann on the understanding of the Son of man sayings that has prevailed in critical circles in the past fifty years. A number of British scholars have followed an independent path, continuing to treat the phrase as Jesus' self-designation, but historical-critical scholarship on the Continent and elsewhere has generally followed the Bultmannian position. This was assisted in no small degree by monographs and christological studies that gave fuller presentation to Bultmann's view. No attempt will be made here to review the flood of publications that have appeared, but brief mention must be made of the classic in the field, H. E. Tödt's *The Son of Man in the Synoptic Tradition*.[26] In this very helpful study Tödt takes over Bultmann's principles and starting point, as indicated in the opening sentence of the first chapter: "The intimate connection of the synoptic presentation of the Son of man with that of Jewish apocalyptic literature can no longer be seriously contested."[27] From the point of view of the challengers, such a statement seriously begs the question, since it assumes that which must be demonstrated. Tödt is no more to be faulted for beginning his study at this point than for assuming the two-document hypothesis. Since he wrote, however, the "critically assured result" from which he begins *has* been seriously contested and can no longer be treated as axiomatic.

---

24. Lietzmann, *Der Menschensohn*; Wellhausen, "Des Menschen Sohn"; Dalman, *Die Worte Jesu*, pp. 191–219, and *The Words of Jesus*, pp. 234–67; Fiebig, *Der Menschensohn*.

25. Bultmann, *Theology*, vol. 1, p. 30, and *History*, pp. 15–17, commenting on Mk. 2:10, 28.

26. The first German edition of *Der Menschensohn in der synoptischen Überlieferung* was published in 1959.

27. Tödt, *Son of Man*, p. 22.

Tödt evidently believed that proof of this connection had already been provided by Bousset, Wrede, and Bultmann, whose tradition-critical studies had demonstrated that "the different groups of sayings concerning the Son of man are located in different strata in the history of the synoptic tradition."[28] The linchpin in this particular argument, for Tödt as for Bultmann, lies in the absence of the suffering Son of man sayings from Q, the hypothetical sayings source behind Matthew and Luke.[29] The inadequacy of the linchpin lies in the fact that the Q material contains a significant number of earthly sayings; thus the absence of suffering sayings cannot logically be construed as demonstrating the priority of the future over the earthly sayings. It was therefore necessary for Bultmann to take the further step of explaining away the earthly sayings as the unfortunate result of mistranslation (without seriously attending to the linguistic problem inherent in his hypothesis). Bultmann's justification for making this move was his perception that the two kinds of sayings in Q are incompatible, and therefore only one kind can be authentic; but this *perception* was based on the prior assumption that the phrase derives from Jewish apocalyptic and connotes a heavenly being. The hypothesis of mistranslation is thus for Bultmann accidental, not essential. It would be a matter of indifference to Bultmann whether the apocalyptic title appeared in an earthly saying because of mistranslation, because of secondary insertion by the post-Easter community, or because the saying as a whole was created after the resurrection.

Must the History-of-Religions Origin of "The Son of Man" Be Settled in Advance?

Bultmann, Tödt, and others of a similar persuasion begin with the assumption that behind the Greek phrase *ho huios tou anthrōpou* lies an Aramaic expression that was current in Jesus' day as the designation of a supernatural figure whose advent was awaited in Jewish apocalyptic circles. Tödt, like Bultmann, regards it as unnecessary to argue this point. It is assumed that any proper treatment of the Son of man tradition in the Gospels must presuppose the results of the history-of-religions investigation of the phrase's background and commence at that point.[30] It is important to remember that this was not always the case and that the legitimacy of this starting point has recently been seriously called into question.

---

28. Ibid., p. 17.
29. Ibid. Cf. Bultmann, *History*, p. 152, and *Theology*, vol. 1, p. 30.
30. The same point of departure is taken by Higgins, *Jesus and the Son of Man*, p. 15.

Until the discovery of Jewish eschatology and apocalyptic in the mid-nineteenth century, it was generally assumed by the church's scholars that "the Son of man" was an expression used by Jesus to refer to his real humanity as distinct from his divinity. (A brief history of this understanding appears in the next chapter.) With the Enlightenment, however, came a search for the sources of Christian dogma in pre-Christian Judaism.[31] One of the earliest to explicate the phrase as a messianic title was D. F. Strauss in 1838.[32] This affirmation becomes more frequent, despite protestations by opposing scholars, as we traverse the nineteenth century. E. Schürer appears to have articulated an emerging consensus in his much-respected *A History of the Jewish People in the Time of Jesus Christ*: the title "the Son of man" clearly represents a supernatural Messiah in 2 Enoch and was probably current in Jesus' day.[33] Despite the linguistic objections of Wellhausen and Lietzmann, this point of view quickly became regarded as an assured result of research and was asserted without argument by many subsequent scholars.[34] By the time Bultmann wrote his *History,* he could treat the identification of the phrase as an apocalyptic title as axiomatic.[35]

This is no longer possible. The challenges that have been presented to the original history-of-religions investigation are too impressive to be dismissed.

To begin with, no unambiguous evidence of the conception can be drawn from Dan. 7:13. Although v. 27 clearly interprets the "one like a son of man" as a symbol for "the people of the saints of the Most High," that is, a purified Israel,[36] a number of scholars have insisted that this interpretation is secondary and that behind the present text of Daniel lies the mythic picture of a supernatural being to whom God delegates divine authority.[37]

It must be insisted, in the first place, that the appearance of the manlike figure is *not* theophanic; the fact that gods are sometimes described as

---

31. Cf. Appel, *Die Selbstbezeichnung Jesu*, p. 8.

32. So ibid., p. 19, citing the 3d ed. of Strauss, *Das Leben Jesu kritisch bearbeitet*, vol. 1, pp. 526ff. Available to me was the 4th ed. of 1840, where the matter is treated on p. 491 of vol. 4; cf. *The Life of Jesus Critically Examined* (1860), vol. 1, p. 294.

33. The English version reproduces the second German edition of 1886–90. See especially div. 2, vol. 2, pp. 160f., and vol. 3, p. 69.

34. See n. 7 above.

35. Cf. also "Die Frage nach der Echtheit von Mt 16, 17–19" [*Exegetica*], pp. 273f.

36. The proposal that "the saints of the Most High" designates angels rather than humans, made first by Procksch, "Der Menschensohn als Gottessohn," p. 429, has attracted a number of supporters, including recently J. J. Collins, "The Son of Man and the Saints of the Most High in the Book of Daniel," pp. 50–66. For a review of the literature and a careful critique, see now Casey, *Son of Man*, pp. 40–45. Cf. also Mertens, *Das Buch Daniel*, pp. 53–55.

37. E.g., Colpe, "Ho huios tou anthrōpou," TDNT 8, pp. 420–23. For a recent survey of literary-critical attempts to discover an earlier source behind Daniel 7, see Casey, *Son of Man*, pp. 11–17.

traveling upon clouds is interesting but irrelevant.[38] There is ample evidence that the use of clouds as a means of transport was not reserved for God in Jewish tradition, and it is entirely unlikely that a second god was here portrayed by the Jewish apocalyptist.[39] As M. Casey wryly remarks, "The author of Daniel 7 was a traditionalist defending the ancient Israelite faith against foreign encroachment; nothing he says leads one to the improbable notion that he chose a time of desperate persecution for his faith to introduce a second deity into the monotheistic faith of Israel."[40]

Second, there is no reason to believe that the author regards the figure as an angelic being, the archangel Michael perhaps.[41] In Jewish apocalyptic thought angelic beings are not presented to God, nor is authority bestowed upon an angel; such beings are treated rather as extensions of the divine authority (cf. Dan. 12:1). It is very doubtful that the alleged redactor responsible for v. 27 would have dared to provide a corporate interpretation of the heavenly figure had he been employing a source in which reference was clearly made to a supernatural being such as Michael. Had his religious environment presented him with the expectation of a heavenly judge with an established title, "the Son of man," his interpretation would make even less sense. Since the various attempts to distinguish an earlier source from later redaction have not proved convincing, it is better to concur with Casey that the chapter is a unity and that the author introduces the manlike figure as a pure symbol, representing the saints of Israel.[42]

Evidence of a messianizing interpretation of Dan. 7:13 is indisputably present in 4 Ezra 13. In 13:2f. we read: "And this wind brought a human figure rising from the depths, and as I watched, this man came flying with the clouds of heaven." The New English Bible, the source of this translation, refrains from capitalizing the word "man," which is not treated as a title in 4 Ezra. It is unlikely that the original Hebrew or Aramaic version of

38. Emerton, "The Origin of the Son of Man Imagery," p. 232, derives the Danielic manlike figure from the Canaanite storm god Baal, who comes on the clouds. Colpe, "Ho huios tou anthrōpou," TDNT 8, pp. 417–19, regards this as the best hypothesis concerning the history-of-religions background of the scene in Daniel 7.

39. In the Test. Ab. (Rec. A, 10:1; B, 8:3), Abraham travels on a cloud; in Rev. 11:12 the two prophets go up to heaven "in the cloud"; cf. also 1 Thess. 4:16f. This evidence is admittedly later than Daniel, but support for an earlier use of the motif has been found by Boobyer, St. Mark, pp. 82f., in the fact that a distinction can be drawn between Old Testament passages where clouds are employed theophanically and others where clouds serve simply as a means of transport for God. For rabbinic uses of the motif, cf. G. Vermes's excursus "The Cloud, a Means of Heavenly Transport," in his Jesus the Jew, pp. 186–88.

40. Casey, Son of Man, p. 37.

41. The most recent advocate of this view is J. J. Collins, "The Son of Man," pp. 63–66 who is opposed by Casey, Son of Man, pp. 31f.

42. Casey, Son of Man, p. 39. Cf. also Moule, "Neglected Features," p. 419.

this apocalypse employed "son of man" here.[43] Even if this had been the case, however, the way the expression is used (it is regularly defined by a demonstrative, relative clause, or other defining phrase that relates the man to the first appearance of the figure in 13:3) indicates that the author does not regard it as a title.[44] In the subsequent interpretation (13:25–53) the man from the sea is treated as a symbol for an eschatological rescuer whom God calls "my Son" (or perhaps "my servant") in vv. 32, 37, and 52; although the term "Messiah" is not used, the functions attributed to this figure correspond closely with those of the Messiah.

There is not the slightest suggestion that the person so described is an angelic being. Would pagan armies assemble to fight against Michael (v. 3)? Would it occur to the apocalyptist to mention that Michael carried no spear (v. 9)? Is it likely that Michael would be described as being joined by many humans (v. 13)? It is clear that this messianic figure is endowed with supernatural power, but so is the Davidic Messiah of Psalms of Solomon 17 (both 4 Ezra 13:10 and Ps. Sol. 17:27 are presumably exegeses of Isa. 11:4). Even if it could be demonstrated that the interpretation is secondary and that the original version portrayed a heavenly Son of man, the extant chapter no longer perceives the figure in this way.[45] Those special characteristics that scholars have traditionally ascribed to the Son of man are missing! As M. Stone has pointed out, this is virtually inconceivable if the Son of man conception was well established and the author intended to evoke it by his figurative language.[46] Thus, while 4 Ezra clearly witnesses to the existence of a messianizing interpretation of Dan. 7:13 in Jewish

43. Casey, *Son of Man*, pp. 124–26.

44. Ibid., pp. 125f. Cf. Tödt, *Son of Man*, p. 27 n. 1, and U. B. Müller, *Messias und Menschensohn*, p. 122.

45. U. B. Müller, *Messias und Menschensohn*, pp. 108–20, following earlier studies, attempts to distinguish between the vision and the interpretation in terms of content and diction. Cf. also Kearns, *Vorfragen*, vol. 2, pp. 52–82. Both Müller and Kearns argue that the vision is not a unity, but neither satisfactorily explains why these disparate elements were assembled as a dream vision by a previous apocalyptist and circulated without an interpretation until finally one was provided by the redactor of 4 Ezra. Müller acknowledges: (1) the traditions of a transcendent Son of man and a nationalistic Messiah have been combined in the vision; (2) there is little parallel between the functions of the Son of man of 2 Enoch and those of the "Man" of Ezra's vision; (3) closer parallels are provided by Psalms of Solomon 17; yet he cannot concede that the vision simply represents a messianizing interpretation of Dan. 7:13 (pp. 117–22). His chief objections are that, whereas the Messiah of Psalms of Solomon 17 receives his supernatural power from God, the "Man" of 4 Ezra 13 acts autonomously and that therefore there is no reference to the continuing rule of the "Man." But this is true only if one separates the dream from the interpretation that its genre requires! In any event, Müller agrees that the tradition of the transcendent Son of man plays no role in the work of the final redactor who supplied the interpretation (p. 124).

46. Stone, "The Concept of the Messiah in IV Ezra," p. 308.

circles in the late first century, it cannot be invoked as evidence of the alleged conception of a supernatural Son of man with clearly defined functions.

Those who claim that there existed such a notion in Judaism usually base their case primarily on the Similitudes of Enoch (1 Enoch 37–71). It is for this reason that the nonoccurrence of the Similitudes among the large number of Enoch fragments at Qumran has caused such a flurry. Although Milik's late dating of the Similitudes (third century C.E.) has received little support, it can no longer be assumed without question that the document is pre-Christian in origin.[47] The actual date of origin, however, is of secondary importance once it is recognized that, regardless of date, the Similitudes and the Gospels are mutually independent.[48] The real issue is whether or not the Similitudes witness to an earlier conception that could also explain the Gospels' use of "the Son of man."

Two observations are pertinent. In the first place, it has been demonstrated that the Similitudes do not employ "the Son of man" as a fixed title. U. Müller, a vigorous champion of the view that the Similitudes evince the notion of an apocalyptic judge entitled "the Son of man," grants that this is not the dominant appellation for the figure depicted.[49] Clearly more important to the author, Müller suggests, is the title "the Elect One"; it is the first designation employed (39:6; Müller regards 38:2 as textually uncertain), and it is used again in the important passage (45:3f.) that precedes the first appearance of "the Son of man" in chapter 46.[50] More important still is Müller's observation that when "the Son of man" is introduced by way of allusion to Dan. 7:13, it is not a known figure who is merged with the Elect One previously depicted; "the Son of man" is a cipher requiring interpretation.[51] The interpretation provided by the angel points back to the Elect One who has righteousness (39:6), whose function it is to judge the wicked (45:3), and who will live in the midst of the community (45:4). Thus 1 Enoch 46 simply affirms that the Elect One is identical with the manlike figure of Dan. 7:13. No positive content is added to "the Elect One" by means of this biblical imagery; Daniel, Müller argues, merely provided the possibility of attributing a new name to the Elect One.[52]

---

47. Milik, "Problèmes de la littérature Hénochique à la lumière des fragments Araméens de Qumran," pp. 333–78.
48. Cf. Black, "The Throne-Theophany Prophetic Commission and the 'Son of Man,' " p. 66. See also Sanders, *Paul and Palestinian Judaism*, pp. 347f.
49. U. B. Müller, *Messias und Menschensohn*, pp. 38f.
50. Ibid.
51. Ibid., p. 41.
52. Ibid., p. 46. Cf. also Theisohn, *Der auserwählte Richter*, pp. 51, 203.

Casey has extended the investigation by showing that it is hazardous to regard this appellation as a name. At its first appearance in 46:2 it is accompanied by a demonstrative, and in every subsequent occurrence of the phrase a demonstrative is used unless the context or another modifier supplies the necessary reference to chapter 46 and its allusion to Dan. 7:13. In each instance we can translate the phrase without capitalization, referring the reader to the one like a son of man of Daniel's vision.[53]

The second observation is equally important. The Elect One to whom judgment is committed is not portrayed as an angelic being. His body is not described with light imagery. The glory he possesses is not his because of his nature but is bestowed upon him by God (51:3; cf. 61:8; 62:2). If there is any suggestion of an angelic nature in the clause "whose countenance had the appearance of a man" (46:1; in Dan. 8:15 "one with the semblance of a man" is an angel), this is offset by the following clause, "And his face was full of graciousness, like one of the holy angels," where the description is much more appropriate for a human being. And whereas Daniel uses the term "man" freely for angels (9:21; 10:5; 12:6f.), in the Similitudes it is employed only for the Elect One, not for angels. While it was possible to use the term "elect" with reference to angels (e.g., Tob. 8:15; 1 En. 39:1; 1 Tim. 5:21, always plural), this usage was rare. By reason of its theological history it was far more suitable as an epithet for Israel and Israel's leaders.

Especially in the Similitudes do we find a heavy emphasis placed on "the elect" as the favored designation for members of the eschatological community. There is therefore a greater probability that "the Elect One" designates a human being who represents the chosen people in some way. The solidarity of the Elect One with the elect ones is indicated by the many parallels between the two. In 40:5 the Elect One and the elect ones are recipients of a common blessing from Raphael. Twice it is promised that the Elect One will dwell among them; indeed, they will *eat with him* (45:4; 62:14). Müller concedes that the Elect One can thus have a relationship with human beings that is otherwise open only to humans, a relationship analogous to that of a patriarch to his posterity.[54] In this connection we may also observe that the author does *not* promise that God will dwell with humans (contrast Rev. 21:3); the Lord of Spirits will abide *over* them (62:14).

The third appellation employed for the Elect One—"the Righteous One" (53:6)—likewise serves to link him closely to human believers, who are so often referred to in the Similitudes as "the righteous." It is, of course, conceivable that this term could be used of an angelic being (in contrast to

53. Casey, *Son of Man*, pp. 100–106.
54. U. B. Müller, *Messias und Menschensohn*, p. 45 and n. 36.

fallen angels, who are wicked), but the history of the term as involving the relationship between God and humans suggests that the Righteous One is more closely aligned with humans than with angels. The righteousness of this heavenly judge parallels, naturally, the righteousness of God, who is ultimately responsible for the judgment (50:4), but there is no suggestion in the Similitudes that the Righteous One is more closely aligned with God than with humanity. The dangerously ambiguous term "my Son" employed in 4 Ezra 13 finds no parallel here! The nature of the righteousness that he shares with the righteous is nowhere defined. It is never hinted that righteousness is obedience to Torah.[55] It is possible that a somewhat secularized understanding of righteousness is implied; the unrighteous par excellence are political and economic oppressors, the kings and mighty of this earth (53:5), although religious persecutors are also included among the wicked (46:8). It would appear, therefore, that the righteousness of the Righteous One consists primarily in the impartial, supernaturally wise dispensation of justice.

With respect to his supernatural attributes what was said above concerning his "glory" must now be repeated more generally: he possesses none of them by virtue of his nature (as would an angel). While he *possesses* righteousness, a quality appropriate for humans (46:3), he *receives* supernatural wisdom (51:3; cf. 49:3) and supernatural knowledge (49:3; cf. 46:3), in precisely the same way as does David's successor in Isa. 11:1–5 and Ps. Sol. 17:42.[56] Similarly, he *receives* his eschatological functions by God's commission as do all God's human servants (61:8; 62:2; 69:27), whereas angelic servants function more nearly automatically as expressions of the divine will (cf. the angels of punishment, 53:5; 54:6; 56:1; 62:11; 63:4). Likewise the statement that annihilation of the metal mountains will take place "when the Elect One shall appear before the face of the Lord of Spirits" (52:9) is to be contrasted with statements that view angels as continually before the face of God (cf. Mt. 18:10).

The primary argument against the humanity of the Elect One, of course, is the fact that he has no human birth or earthly life, and his preexistence is asserted: "Even before the sun and the constellations were created, before the stars of heaven were made, his name was named before the Lord of

55. The problematic nature of the statement in 60:6 encouraged Charles, *Apocrypha and Pseudepigrapha*, vol. 2, p. 224, to discover here an allusion to the law. The solution proposed by Knibb, *The Ethiopic Book of Enoch*, p. 143, is to be preferred: "judgment" is a mistaken rendering of the Aramaic *din*, which should have been translated "judge."

56. In 62:2 the "spirit of righteousness" is "poured out upon him"; here there may be a slightly different understanding of righteousness, possibly an allusion to God's saving righteousness (cf. 71:14).

Spirits."[57] References to the preexistence and heavenly domicile of the Elect One may, however, be due merely to the symbolic extravagance of apocalyptic; the author may intend nothing more than that which is conveyed in less exuberant writings by the motif of the hiddenness of the Messiah, which asserts that the eschatological champion of the righteous is safe from the attacks of the wicked and his coming is determined by God alone.

A proper estimate of the preexistence attributed to the Elect One is dependent upon a solution to the difficult literary-critical problem presented by chapters 70f., which identify the patriarch Enoch with the heavenly figure revealed to him in his visions: "You are the Son of man who was born to righteousness, and righteousness remains over you, and the righteousness of the Head of Days will not leave you" (71:14, Knibb's translation). No attempt will be made here to solve that problem. Suffice it to say that it is now generally agreed that at some stage or other in the history of the Enoch tradition, this identification was made. This is not in itself surprising, in view of the heavenly role attributed to Enoch in 1 Enoch 12–16. Further support for M. Black's hypothesis that this identification preceded rather than followed the writing of the Similitudes is to be seen in the fact that the eschatological judge is portrayed not as an archangel but in language more appropriate for a human being.[58] It is, moreover, increasingly clear that Jewish eschatological thought entertained the possibility that one or more human beings would share the role of judge in some phase of God's judgment. In the Testament of Abraham it is Abel who sits on the throne of judgment.[59] The Lives of the Prophets attributes such a role to Elijah.[60] The New Testament itself reflects the belief that Christians will participate as judges (Mt. 19:28; Lk. 22:30; 1 Cor. 6:2f.). There is therefore no reason to doubt the evidence provided by the Similitudes that at least some Jews regarded the translated Enoch as the human being to whom judgment had been delegated by God and that they viewed Daniel 7 as a prophecy of this eschatological event.

Seen in this light, the references to Enoch's existence prior to the creation of the world (48:3, 6; 62:7) seem to stay within the bounds of Jewish thought regarding significant humans. The Prayer of Joseph (ii.31), cited in Origen's commentary on John, speaks of the preexistence of Abraham,

---

57. 48:3, as trans. by Knibb, *The Ethiopic Book of Enoch*, pp. 133f.; cf. 48:6, 62:7.
58. Black, "The Eschatology of the Similitudes of Enoch," pp. 1–10.
59. Stone, *The Testament of Abraham*, pp. 32f., 78f. (Rec. A, 13:2-4; B, 11:2).
60. Cf. Hare, "The Lives of the Prophets," p. 396.

Isaac, and Jacob.[61] Similarly, preexistence was often attributed to the Messiah, but not in such a way as to jeopardize the genuine humanity of this figure. In 4 Ezra 12:32, for example, the Messiah is described both as preexistent and as born of David's seed. It is significant that in such portrayals the preexistent Messiah does nothing except wait passively for the time of his human existence.[62] It is this feature that so sharply distinguishes the early Christian understanding of Jesus as the preexistent Son of God from the Jewish belief in the preexistent Messiah; the preexistent Christ is given a divine role in creation.

In each of the three sources examined (Daniel 7; 4 Ezra 13; 1 Enoch 37–71), it is at least *possible* that behind the extant text lies a conception of a supernatural judge distinct from but assistant to the God of Israel, but this conjectural possibility has not been raised to the level of probability by the intense research that has focused on the question for the past century. In each case the manlike figure can be adequately interpreted without resort to this hypothesis.

What, then, are we to do with Colpe's suggestion that the oldest stratum of the Synoptic tradition itself constitutes a fourth source that must be placed beside these in our effort to reconstruct the original myth?[63] Again, it must be granted as an a priori possibility that the Gospels contain the fossil remains of such a myth. In terms of proper historical method, however, this hypothesis must not be made the starting point of the investigation, since this is precisely the question at issue. The "earliest stratum of the Synoptic tradition" has been identified on the basis of this hypothesis and then presented as proof of the correctness of the hypothesis, all contrary evidence being discarded as secondary![64]

Other fragments of evidence for the existence of the notion of the supernatural Son of man have been presented by scholars. Bousset pointed to Septuagintal texts reading *hōs* instead of *heōs* in Dan. 7:13 as evidence that this textual tradition regarded the Son of man *as* the Ancient of Days, that is, as a preexistent, supernatural messiah.[65] The difficulty of this

---

61. An English translation is provided by Smith, "The Prayer of Joseph," p. 256.

62. Colpe, "Ho huios tou anthrōpou," TDNT 8, p. 426: "His functions define him wholly and utterly as an eschatological figure." Cf. Jeremias, *New Testament Theology*, p. 271.

63. Colpe, "Ho huios tou anthrōpou," TDNT 8, p. 429.

64. Tuckett, "Recent Work on the Son of Man," pp. 14–18, compares the circularity involved in this reasoning with that evident in Bultmann's hypothesis of a gnostic background for John, where the Gospel is the main source for reconstructing the background, and the background then becomes the main source for interpreting the Gospel.

65. Bousset, *Die Religion des Judentums*, pp. 264f. This view has recently been revived by F. F. Bruce, "The Oldest Greek Version of Daniel," pp. 25f.

reading, however, is no guarantee of its originality; it is a slender reed that cannot bear the weight placed on it.[66]

The Targum to Psalm 80 has been cited, since the phrase *bar nash* is employed in a messianic context, but there is no evidence that the psalm was messianized by the targumist *because* it contained *ben adam*.[67]

The rabbinic literature has also been quarried for evidence of the super-natural Son of man. A favorite text is the tradition about R. Akiba, who, commenting on Dan. 7:9, is reported to have declared, "One for Him [God] and one for David."[68] The angry response of his colleagues, how-ever, is no proof that Akiba was suggesting that "David" was his designa-tion for the Son of man. Indeed, the tradition that assigns to Akiba the pronouncement that Simeon ben Kosiba was Messiah strongly suggests that he held a more traditional view of the eschatological redeemer. Whether "David" is to be taken here literally or not is moot.[69] As Casey points out, the talmudic tradition provides no evidence that Akiba's exegesis of Dan. 7:9 implies that he also interpreted 7:13 messianically.[70] In any event, the tradition by no means demonstrates the existence of a Jewish belief in a supernatural Son of man.

Still more ambiguous is the oft-discussed declaration of R. Abbahu: "If a man says to you, 'I am God,' he is lying; 'I am Son of man (*ben adam*),' he will repent it in the end; if he says, 'I am going up to heaven,' he has said it but he will not fulfill it."[71] There is general agreement on two matters: Abbahu is commenting on Num. 23:19, not Dan. 7:13; and his statement is to be regarded as a piece of anti-Christian polemic. Beyond this it is diffi-cult to secure consensus because of the very enigmatic use of the Hebrew phrase *ben adam*. Clearly *ben adam* is not a title in Num. 23:19, but on first glance Abbahu's statement appears to employ the phrase as a title. This does not mean, however, that Abbahu himself or non-Christian Jews of his acquaintance awaited the arrival of a supernatural judge bearing this title.

66. Cf. Casey, *Son of Man*, p. 132.

67. Cf. ibid., pp. 90f. Casey is opposed by Moloney, "The End of the Son of Man?" pp. 284–86.

68. *B. Sanh*. 38b, *Ḥag*. 14a. Segal, *Two Powers in Heaven*, pp 35f., argues that Dan. 7:9f. describes the enthronement of the Son of man.

69. So Casey, *Son of Man*, p. 87.

70. Ibid. Casey assembles evidence (pp. 80–84) of the persistence in rabbinic tradition of the corporate understanding of Dan. 7:13. It is therefore possible that Akiba interpreted the manlike figure corporately, while taking v. 9 as an allusion to David. Furthermore, K. Müller, "Menschensohn und Messias," pp. 57f., regards this passage as witnessing to the combination of the Son of man and Messiah traditions, a combination in which the notion of the Son of David predominated, thus permitting Akiba to hail Bar Kosiba as the Messiah.

71. *J. Taʿan*. 65b, as translated by Casey, *Son of Man*, p. 91. For a study of Abbahu's po-lemical stance toward Christianity in Caesarea, see Lachs, "Rabbi Abbahu and the Minim."

Indeed, it is most improbable that the anarthrous phrase, which occurs frequently in the Hebrew Scriptures as a poetic synonym for *adam* and *enosh*, could function as a title. Other traditions concerning this rabbi render it probable that Abbahu was in contact with Christians of Caesarea in the third century. As we shall see in the next chapter, it had become customary by that time for Christians to interpret occurrences of "the Son of man" in the New Testament as references to the incarnate state of the divine Son of God. It is reasonable to assume, therefore, that if this is anti-Christian polemic, it is an attack on the Christology of the gentile church, which attributed to Jesus the dual claim that he was God in virtue of his eternal being but son of man in virtue of his incarnation.[72]

Frequently cited also is the statement attributed to R. Joshua b. Levi (third century) concerning the coming of the Messiah: "If they are meritorious, 'with the clouds of heaven'; if not 'lowly and riding upon an ass.' "[73] It is remarkable that scholars have found here evidence of the alleged conception of a supernatural judge. Does the tradition really suggest that God has *two* Messiahs in readiness, a supernatural being who will be allowed to function only if Israel is worthy, and a human who will perform the messianic tasks if such is not the case? It is best to take the two biblical allusions as descriptions of alternative modes of arrival of the one Messiah. The context clearly indicates that Joshua was discussing the timing of the Messiah's advent, not his nature.

In some Targum texts of Exod. 12:42 we read: "Moses shall go forth from the wilderness and the King Messiah from Rome. The one shall lead the way on top of a cloud and the other shall lead the way on top of a cloud, and the Memra of the Lord shall lead the way between the two of them, and they shall proceed together."[74] Whatever the date of this tradition, the Messiah who leads the way on top of a cloud is clearly human; he arrives from Rome, and his means of transport is shared by Moses.

---

72. Kearns, *Vorfragen*, vol. 1, p. 87, regards Abbahu's allusion to *ben adam* as better explained by reference to the use of *bar adam* in Jewish magical texts such as the Sword of Moses, published by Moses Gaster, *Studies and Texts*, vol. 3, p. 72, lines 12 and 16. If Kearns is right, Abbahu's statement refers neither to Jesus nor to an eschatological judge. Another remote possibility is that, while Abbahu is attacking gentile Christianity in the first clause, in the second he is reacting to a form of Jewish Christianity that preached that Jesus as True Prophet was in a sense the reincarnation of Adam; for a discussion of the relevant texts, cf. Schoeps, *Theologie*, pp. 98–116, summarized in his *Jewish Christianity*, pp. 68–73. I am not aware, however, of any Jewish Christian text that uses "Son of Adam" in a titular sense.

73. *B. Sanh.* 98a, as translated by H. Freedman, *Sanhedrin*, vol. 2, p. 663, in *The Babylonian Talmud,* ed. I. Epstein (London: Soncino Press, 1935).

74. The translation is that of Levey, *The Messiah*, pp. 12f. Cf. Klein, "The Messiah 'That Leadeth upon a Cloud' in the Fragment Targum to the Pentateuch," pp. 137–39.

Finally, there are rabbinic passages that refer to the Messiah as Anani (the last-named descendant of David in 1 Chron. 3:24) and find allusion to this figure in Dan. 7:13. As Casey points out, the citation of the Danielic text makes sense only if Anani is identified with the Hebrew word for "clouds," and not with the manlike figure, so that the verse is translated, ". . . and behold with Anani of heaven one like a son of man was coming," thus preserving the corporate interpretation of the manlike figure proffered by v. 27.[75] There is no relationship between the Anani-tradition and the figure Bar Naphali, according to Casey, because the alleged connection between Naphali and the Greek word for "cloud," *nephelē*, has not been demonstrated and is intrinsically improbable.[76] The tradition in question indicates that Bar Naphali was a most unusual title for the Messiah; R. Isaac, the interlocutor, must ask the declarer, R. Nachman, what is meant by such a strange term, "Son of a fallen one." No hint is given by the passage that Dan. 7:13 is in mind at all.[77] There was no Jewish messianic title based upon the clouds of Dan. 7:13.

In sum, there is ample evidence that Dan. 7:13 was in fact interpreted messianically by Jews. Although it cannot be certainly demonstrated that this interpretation was prevalent before Jesus' death, such a possibility must not be ruled out. Without stronger evidence than we now possess, however, it must not be assumed that Jewish exegesis of the passage frequently treated the figure as an angelic judge, much less that behind this verse and subsequent allusions to it lay a well-known myth about a supernatural judge with a fixed title—"the Son of man." Historical method does not permit a dogmatic denial that such a concept existed and that it was evoked by the postulated title, but no positive evidence of this has yet been uncovered. It is therefore methodologically unsound to *begin* an investigation of the Christian use of *ho huios tou anthrōpou* with this hypothesis.[78] The New Testament evidence must be considered in a way that does not predetermine the conclusion that only this hypothesis can make sense of the data. At the same time, care must be taken to ensure that such a conclusion is not excluded.

Still another possibility should be constantly kept in mind. It is entirely possible that belief in an angelic judge entitled "the Son of man" was cherished by some Jews before the time of Jesus but had not yet become

75. Casey, *Son of Man*, p. 82, citing *Tanh. Toledoth* 20.
76. Casey, *Son of Man*, pp. 91f. For a different view, cf. Kearns, *Vorfragen*, vol. 2, pp. 97ff.
77. Casey, *Son of Man*, pp. 91f.
78. Higgins, *The Son of Man in the Teaching of Jesus*, p. 52, acknowledges that it is an unproven hypothesis; but his entire investigation is predicated upon its legitimacy!

dominant; it was possible for Jesus or his disciples to make independent use of whatever Aramaic or Hebrew phrase lay behind the Greek expression *ho huios tou anthrōpou*. That is to say, even if it could be demonstrated that (1) the Similitudes of Enoch were extant at Qumran at the beginning of the first century, (2) in the earliest version of that document there was no attempt to identify Enoch with the heavenly figure, and (3) the phrase normally translated "the Son of man" occurred there in a linguistically defensible form, constituting a recognizable title, it would still by no means follow axiomatically that that usage determined the significance of the phrase in the New Testament. In this sense the date and interpretation of the Similitudes are irrelevant for an impartial investigation of the gospel material. No scholar can fairly claim on the basis of the extant evidence that "the Son of man" had become a widespread, universally recognized title for a supernatural figure who was expected to function as God's deputy in the last judgment. We must not begin the investigation with this assumption as our starting point.

Must the Linguistic Problem Be Settled in Advance?

At first glance the phrase *ho huios tou anthrōpou* appears to be a title. In form it is precisely parallel to *ho huios tou theou*, "the Son of God," which clearly functions as a title in the New Testament. The uninitiated Greek reader would probably have taken the phrase to mean either "the son par excellence of the human genus" or, understanding the first article as specifying one member of a class, "the son of the human genus here referred to."[79]

The problem is that no extant evidence proves the existence of such a title in Aramaic or Hebrew. Should research proceed on the assumption of mistranslation and deduce the function and meaning of the earliest use by Jesus or Palestinian Christians on the basis of known Aramaic or Hebrew expressions? Should an Aramaic or Hebrew phrase be constructed hypothetically as a retroversion from the Greek, and the history of the tradition be reconstructed on that basis? Or is the linguistic problem so severe that we should attribute all instances of the phrase to Greek-speaking Christians?

No attempt will be made here to review the intricacies of the linguistic debate that involved H. Lietzmann, G. Dalman, J. Wellhausen, and

---

79. For pagan parallels, see Martitz, "*Huios* in Greek," pp. 336f. The phrase "the man of God" is rendered in the LXX without the first article whenever the context does not require it, i.e., where it is not needed to specify the man of God in question (e.g., 1 Sam. 9:6–10).

P. Fiebig at the turn of the century.[80] It is sufficient to note that despite the most recent round of discussion by competent Semitists, the issue is still unresolved.[81] The discovery of Aramaic documents contemporaneous with the New Testament at Qumran and elsewhere has significantly enlarged the empirical base on which the discussion can proceed, but the new finds have not greatly altered the parameters of the debate. The consensus now, as in 1900, is that behind the Greek phrase lies some form of the Aramaic *bar enasha*. It is now generally recognized that the second member of the phrase probably had an initial aleph, and possibly a final aleph, but the latter may not have affected the meaning, since the absolute (without final aleph) and emphatic (with final aleph) states were sometimes used interchangeably in the first century.[82] It is also generally agreed that this phrase functioned as an everyday expression for "man" and consequently was used indefinitely to mean "a man," "anybody," or "someone."

It has been argued by G. Vermes that this usage made possible a special idiom whereby a male speaker could refer to himself exclusively. The evidence that he has adduced, however, proves only that in certain contexts the reference is primarily or exclusively to the speaker, not that the phrase bears this as one of several connotations.[83] That is, in itself the phrase in its extant instances never means "this man" but only "a man." In a limited number of situations it may be rendered obvious to the audience that the

---

80. Lietzmann, *Der Menschensohn*; Dalman, *Die Worte Jesu*; Wellhausen, "Des Menschen Sohn," pp. 187–215; Fiebig, *Der Menschensohn*. A helpful summary of the debate is provided by Vermes, "The Use of *bar nash/bar nasha* in Jewish Aramaic," pp. 311–13. Cf. also Colpe, "Ho huios tou anthrōpou," TDNT 8, pp. 401–5.

81. In addition to the article by Vermes cited in the previous note, see his *Jesus the Jew*, pp. 160–91, and "The 'Son of Man' Debate," pp. 19–32. Other participants in the debate are Black ("Jesus and the 'Son of Man' " and "Aramaic Barnasha and the 'Son of Man' "), Bowker ("The Son of Man"), Casey ("The Son of Man Problem," pp. 147–54, and *Son of Man*, pp. 224–39), Fitzmyer ("Methodology in the Study of the Aramaic Substratum of Jesus' Sayings in the New Testament," pp. 92–94; "The New Testament Title 'Son of Man' Philologically Considered"; "Another View of the 'Son of Man' Debate," pp. 58–68), Formesyn ("Was There a Pronominal Connection for the 'Bar Nasha' Self-Designation?"), Jeremias (*New Testament Theology*, pp. 260–62), and Kearns (*Vorfragen*, vols. 1 and 2).

82. Fitzmyer has emphasized that no instance of the phrase without an initial aleph has yet been found in documents earlier than the Second Revolt ("The New Testament Title 'Son of Man,' " p. 149). For the breakdown in the distinction between the absolute and emphatic states, cf. Casey, *Son of Man*, p. 228. Muraoka, "Notes on the Aramaic of the Genesis Apocryphon," pp. 12f., is not convinced that the breakdown was so complete; cf. also his later study "The Aramaic of the Old Targum of Job from Qumran Cave XI," p. 432; likewise Black, "Aramaic Barnasha and the 'Son of Man,' " p. 202. Colpe, "Ho huios tou anthrōpou," TDNT 8, p. 404, presupposes that the Greek phrase renders the emphatic *bar enasha*.

83. Vermes, "The Use of *bar nash/bar nasha* in Jewish Aramaic," pp. 320–26. Vermes has been criticized by Jeremias, *New Testament Theology*, p. 261; Fitzmyer, "The New Testament Title 'Son of Man,' " pp. 152f.; Bowker, "The Son of Man," p. 32; Casey, *Son of Man*, pp. 224–27; R. Le Déaut, "Le substrat araméen des Évangiles," pp. 398f.; Kearns, *Vorfragen*, vol. 1, p. 96.

speaker intends to refer to himself (cf. the English idiom "Can't a man have any privacy?"). Casey insists that the idiom implies that the statement has potentially a wider reference, even when the context suggests that the speaker means to apply it particularly to himself. Conversely, argues Casey, it would not have been possible to make a unique claim for oneself by means of this idiom, as, for example, "A man is going to be raised from the dead on the third day." In such a statement the self-reference is lost unless a demonstrative is used.[84]

If this idiom is taken as the Aramaic antecedent of "the Son of man" in the Gospels, it would appear that the phrase has been mistranslated into Greek in the phrase *ho huios tou anthrōpou*, which uses definite articles. At Mk. 2:10, for example, Casey postulates a *Vorlage* in which Jesus declared, "A man has power to forgive sins on earth."[85] This general statement had pertinence, however, only because at issue was *Jesus'* right to forgive sins. In the Greek translation this half of the communication was preserved, but only at the cost of eclipsing the general statement.[86] The translator is too quickly exonerated by Casey, who argues that there was no way to represent both the general and specific references of the Aramaic idiom in Greek translation: "He could omit the articles, but that would produce a general statement which would not clearly refer to Jesus."[87] Casey's difficulty seems to be that he regards the Aramaic expression as sui generis, without linguistic parallel. The fact is that the idiom is potentially if not actually present in every conceivable language.[88]

A correct Greek translation, then, would have used the anarthrous *anthrōpos*, or the more poetic *huios anthrōpou*, leaving it to the *context* to indicate that Jesus made the statement in order to justify his own behavior. Is the Aramaic idiom unique because extant instances indicate that it is most often used in contexts alluding to death, danger, or humiliation and when claims are made that require modesty or reserve?[89] At issue here is

84. Casey, *Son of Man*, p. 232. Lindars, *Jesus Son of Man*, p. 24, attempts to mediate between the positions of Vermes and Casey, proposing that the generic article is used when a speaker wishes to refer to "a class of persons, with whom he identifies himself." See chapter 7 below.

85. Casey, *Son of Man*, p. 228.

86. Ibid., p. 229.

87. Ibid., p. 231. It is ironic that Casey excuses the translator, while himself supplying an English translation that is very close to the Greek translation he rejects!

88. This point has been made recently by O'Neill, *Messiah*, p. 106, who cites Wellhausen, "Des Menschen Sohn," p. 200.

89. Casey, *Son of Man*, pp. 227, 230, following Vermes, "The Use of *bar nash/bar nasha* in Jewish Aramaic," p. 327. Bowker, "The Son of Man," p. 36, believes he can trace a proclivity to employ *bar nash* in preference to other words for "man" in contexts suggesting "man born to die" but concedes that this is a tendency only.

the validity of frequency studies in establishing the range of usage. Some of the Son of man sayings in the Gospels that are treated as authentic by Vermes and Casey do not fit nicely under these rubrics (e.g., Mt. 8:20; 11:19). Even if such restrictions were to prove valid, however, they would not render the idiom as Casey understands it so unique that translation into Greek by an anarthrous expression would be totally inappropriate, thus justifying the translator in the creation of an appellative with two articles. If the Aramaic expression was an established circumlocution for "I" ("a man such as I"), as Vermes has argued without adequate evidence, the Greek translator could have used *egō, houtos ho anthrōpos*, or even *tis anthrōpos*. If, on the other hand, it was a term of general reference in which the speaker was included only by implication, as Casey proposes, the translator made a serious error in introducing the Greek articles. In either case, we have what appears to be egregious mistranslation, obscuring the sense of the original by the creation of an appellative.

Mistranslation is certainly a factor to be considered in the study of the Gospels, and it is to be hoped that research into the Aramaic origins of our faith will continue to ferret out problems of this kind. It is important to remember, however, that the hypothesis of mistranslation, like conjectural emendation of a problematic text, is a hypothesis of last resort. Mistranslation presupposes (1) ignorance of the donor or receptor language, (2) genuine ambiguity in the original, which cannot be reproduced in the translation, (3) the absence of equivalent terms in the receptor language, or (4) intentional alteration. Here equivalent terms are available. Ambiguity is not the problem; according to Vermes and Casey, the idiom was clear enough in Aramaic. In view of the large number of passages involved and the large number of tradents that must be presupposed on the hypothesis of Vermes and Casey that most of the earthly sayings and perhaps some of the suffering sayings derive from Jesus, it is exceedingly improbable that mistranslation was due to ignorance.

That leaves us with intentional alteration as the probable cause. We can then speculate that the appellative was created by Greek-speaking Christians after the resurrection who wished to identify Jesus as the "one like a son of man" in Dan. 7:13 and employed two Greek articles for this purpose. The appellative became so popular in secondary sayings concerning Jesus' return in glory, it could be argued, that authentic sayings about Jesus' earthly life and suffering that employed *bar enasha* were gradually conformed to this usage. While this seems to be the most likely of various explanations of the alleged mistranslation, it is entirely conjectural. It remains to be demonstrated that the earliest sayings containing the Greek phrase *ho huios tou anthrōpou* are future sayings deriving from the Greek-speaking church. Such a conclusion must not be assumed in advance.

Still to be considered is the possibility that we are dealing not with a mistranslation at all but with a reasonably correct rendering of an underlying Aramaic or Hebrew phrase, representing an idiom that is no longer extant. Here, again, we enter the realm of pure speculation, finding no firm ground under our feet. All we have to go on is the well-established Greek phrase, now assumed to be legitimate. Certainly the absence of the postulated phrase from the scanty remains of first-century Hebrew and Aramaic literature cannot be construed as conclusive evidence of its nonexistence.[90] Hapax legomena are too common a feature of the study of ancient literature for us to be so misled. Modern experience, too, reminds us that creative persons frequently initiate neologisms that they are able to employ in effective communication. Unfortunately, we are seldom able to observe this process in ancient texts. In this case, however, supportive evidence is provided by the various early Syriac renderings of *ho huios tou anthrōpou*, all of which constitute neologisms (like the Greek phrase itself) and thereby demonstrate the *possibility* that such an expression was coined or borrowed by Jesus in either Aramaic or Hebrew.[91] Indeed, it is not impossible that the phrase employed by Jesus differed little if at all from the extant examples of *ben adam* and *bar enasha* uncovered at Qumran but that the reference to himself was made explicit by means of oral emphasis (compare the distinction between "*der* Mann and "der *Mann*" in German).

The point to be made here is not that a conjectural reconstruction of the *Vorlage* of *ho huios tou anthrōpou* is to be preferred to the hypothesis of mistranslation of *bar enasha*, but rather that *the investigation of the Son of man problem cannot begin with this question*. Vermes and Casey have proposed one hypothetical solution of the Son of man problem, but, like the earlier proposal of Bultmann and Tödt, it suffers from circularity by beginning with the solution and arranging the evidence to fit. If we are to avoid begging the question, an approach must be found that allows us to examine the data and infer the solution from the observed phenomena. That is, the linguistic antecedent of the Greek phrase can be fruitfully explored only

90. The youthful Lietzmann departed from sound historical method in his provocative statement "Jesus hat sich selbst nie den Titel 'Menschensohn' beigelegt, weil derselbe im Aramäischen nicht existiert und aus sprachlichen Gründen nicht existieren kann" (*Der Menschensohn,* p. 85).

91. Kearns, *Vorfragen*, vol. 1, pp. 74–77, treats the Greek phrase as a neologism that was created to serve as a technical term in the early Greek-speaking mission of the church and that was subsequently rendered by unusual phrases in Syriac; he finds no reason to postulate an Aramaic neologism behind the Greek.

after a careful study of the way or ways in which the phrase functions in the extant Greek literature. It can then be asked, What kind of expression in Hebrew or Aramaic must be postulated in order to explain adequately the phenomena that have been observed? This question must therefore be deferred to the end of the study.

Which Starting Point Begs the Fewest Questions?

In a murder trial it sometimes happens that the prosecutor presents a case against the accused that the prosecutor finds personally compelling, a complete scenario of the motivation of the killer and the means by which the murder was effected. She is frustrated, however, because she is unable to convince the jury. It turns out that while some of the jury members were convinced by her arguments, others felt that she too quickly dismissed evidence produced by the defense that pointed toward the innocence of the accused.

A similar frustration has no doubt been experienced by scholars who have proposed to their colleagues a firm solution of the Son of man problem. A plausible scenario has been presented, showing how Jesus did (or did not) use the term and tracing subsequent developments whereby earliest uses were gradually supplemented by different ones. Unfortunately, the plausibility depends upon a significant number of conjectures, without which the picture does not hold together, or upon the rejection of conflicting evidence. It is not surprising that the result is a hung jury.

The problem is to find a method that will have a better chance of treating the evidence in a way that will be convincing to the jury. The optimum method will be the one that begs the fewest questions, makes the least use of conjecture, and proceeds from the known to the unknown, that is, from propositions concerning which there will be general agreement to those that are more debatable. The method must be inductive rather than deductive.

This means that although this book, like its predecessors, hopes to demonstrate the correctness of a specific hypothesis, the investigation must not begin with the hypothesis and proceed to an arrangement of the data that will lend it plausibility. Rather, the data must be examined with a variety of possible results in mind. We begin with the candid acknowledgment that in fact *we do not know* what Semitic phrase, if any, lay behind *ho huios tou anthrōpou*, whether Jesus himself used such a phrase at all, and, if he did, what its connotation and denotation were.

In effect, the study of the Son of man tradition, like the search for the historical Jesus, the larger study of which this is one small piece, must proceed in backward fashion. It is conceded that the resurrection experience, as a result of which the Proclaimer became the Proclaimed, cast a halo over the entire gospel tradition. It is to be assumed that the Christology of the early church has been so commingled with the authentic Jesus material that it is almost impossible to separate the strands and recover the original teaching of Jesus in a way that will obtain general approval from rigorous scholars. The nature of the problem, therefore, requires that we begin with the Greek documents as we have them, carefully examine the way or ways in which the phrase is used in each of them, and on this basis work backward to hypothetical sources in Greek and Aramaic, watching intently for clues of possible earlier uses that have subsequently been abandoned. Finally, by means of appropriate criteria we will attempt to isolate Son of man sayings whose authenticity can be cogently defended as best explaining the later developments that have been traced retrogressively.

In this process the temptation to resort to conjecture will increase as we work further back in the tradition from the extant Gospels. It will probably turn out that at one point or another such speculation will alienate a segment of the jury, and it may have to be admitted in the end that the Son of man problem is in fact insoluble on the basis of extant evidence. That in itself, however, would be a positive achievement.

The study will begin not with the Gospels themselves but with the use of "the Son of man" in Christian literature from the second century to the twentieth, from Ignatius to Barth. The understanding of the phrase by the exegetical tradition of the church demands an explanation, and its relationship to the use in the Gospels needs to be investigated.

2 | FROM IGNATIUS TO BARTH

When undertaking to construct a christologically based anthropology in *Church Dogmatics* III/2, Karl Barth found it appropriate to discuss the significance of *ho huios tou anthrōpou* in the Gospels and the relationship of this phrase to *ho huios tou theou*. Both are messianic titles, Barth finds; both identify Jesus "as the embodiment of the coming kingdom of God," but "the Son of man" points to "the Son of God who as such has become man, and who as man has acted as the Son of God and proved himself to be such."[1] In what follows, Barth reminds us that he is fully aware of the various history-of-religions proposals concerning the background of the phrase but declares that we need not be detained by such questions. It is enough that we recognize that in the Gospels Jesus is identified as "the man" by means of this title.[2]

The significance of the term is addressed again by Barth when he considers "the exaltation of the Son of man" in section 64 of *Church Dogmatics* IV/2. God, he tells us, "was not content merely to be God," but for our sakes, without ceasing to be God, "he himself became man in his Son: an Israelite, this Israelite, the Son of Abraham, David and Mary, and therefore the Son of man, for the conversion of all men to himself."[3] The atoning event consists in the "going out of the Son of God" and the "coming in of the Son of man."[4] That Barth sees this phrase as a way of talking about the humanity of the Incarnate One becomes still clearer a few pages later, when he speaks of the exaltation of the Son of man: ". . . without ceasing to be true man, without being divinized, but in our nature and flesh, he is at the side of the Father in heaven, participating as man in his power and

1. K. Barth, *The Doctrine of Creation*, p. 45.
2. Ibid., pp. 45f.
3. K. Barth, *The Doctrine of Reconciliation*, p. 6.
4. Ibid., p. 21.

glory, in the exercise of his grace and mercy."[5] It does not occur to Barth to treat "the Son of man" as a way of speaking of the preexistence of the Incarnate One. He does not speak of Jesus as eternally the Son of man but as the one who *became* the Son of man when the Word became flesh.[6] In this Barth reflects the consensus of eighteen centuries of theological reflection: "The older christology gave us the right answer that he is the Son of God and Son of man who as such is of divine and human essence."[7]

In his brief review of previous scholarship, Lietzmann noted that, despite the recent appearance of the apocalyptic interpretation of the phrase, the majority still held to the traditional view that Jesus called himself the Son of man with reference to his human appearing, his identification with humanity, or his function as humanity's *Urbild*.[8] If Lietzmann had been interested in pressing his survey back still further, he would, of course, have found this to be the opinion of the Reformers. Typical is the statement of Calvin: "His task was so to restore us to God's grace as to make of the children of men, children of God. . . . Who could have done this had not the selfsame Son of God become the Son of man, and had not so taken what was ours as to impart what was his to us, and to make what was his by nature ours by grace?"[9] Writing of the Scriptures' use of these two names for Jesus, Calvin states what was axiomatic to him and his contemporaries: "For it is just as appropriate to refer the fact that he is called 'Son of God' to his divine nature, as it is to refer the fact that he is called 'Son of man' to his human nature."[10]

Calvin, however, is merely echoing a common patristic theme. More than a thousand years earlier, Augustine had written: "For there is but one Son of God by nature, who in his compassion became Son of man for our sakes, that we, by nature sons of men, might by grace become through him sons of God."[11] This was no theological novelty in Augustine's day, but an exegetical tradition deriving from the earliest fathers. In Irenaeus's *Against Heresies*, for example, we read: "For it was for this end that the Word of God was made man, and he who was the Son of God became the Son of man, that man, having been taken into the Word, and receiving the adoption, might become the son of God."[12]

---

5. Ibid., p. 24; cf. pp. 28, 30.
6. Ibid., p. 73.
7. Ibid., p. 108.
8. Lietzmann, *Der Menschensohn*, p. 2.
9. Calvin, *Institutes*, vol. 1, p. 465.
10. Ibid., p. 490.
11. Augustine, *The City of God* xxi.15, trans. by M. Dods, vol. 2, p. 441.
12. *Adv. Haer.* iii.19.1.

For the patristic authors generally, *huios anthrōpou* or *filius hominis* is not a synonym for "man" but a designation for Jesus that refers to the incarnation of the Word through Mary. This is shown in a passage where Irenaeus employs both terms in a discussion of Jesus' birth: "For if he did not receive the substance of flesh from a human being, he neither was made man nor the Son of man . . ." (*Adv. Haer.* iii.22.1). Synonymity is approximated, however, in one of Tertullian's discussions of the virgin birth of Christ: "It was not fit that the Son of God should be born of human seed, lest if he were wholly son of man he might not be Son of God, and he would be nothing more than Solomon and Jonah, as in Ebion's opinion one had to believe."[13]

The fathers are, of course, familiar with the fact that the Gospels associate this name for Jesus with Dan. 7:13. For Latin writers like Tertullian this was especially easy, since Latin, lacking a definite article, employed *filius hominis* for both *ho huios tou anthrōpou* and *huios anthrōpou*, the anarthrous phrase used in the Septuagint's rendering of Dan. 7:13. The presence or absence of Greek articles did not, however, deter the Greek fathers from making the same connection. Cyril of Jerusalem explicitly relates the Christian tradition of calling Jesus "Son of man" (*huios anthrōpou*, anarthrous) to the Danielic text: "He is called Son of man, not as each of us has been born of the earth, but (as) 'coming on the clouds' to judge the living and the dead."[14] This does not mean, however, that Cyril understood "Son of man," with or without the articles, as an apocalyptic title designating a heavenly being conceived as having no contact with earth until his doomsday appearance. That is to say, if behind the Gospels there is a Jewish conception of an angelic judge, such cannot be proved by Cyril's statement, which simply reflects the New Testament belief that Jesus' eschatological return was prophesied by Daniel.

In his work *Against Marcion* (iv.10), Tertullian argues that Jesus gave himself the appellation by which the Creator prophesied through Daniel the advent of the Christ. It apparently did not occur to Tertullian that Daniel's phrase might have designated an angel, whose incarnation was never contemplated. In the same chapter he clearly states his understanding of *filius hominis*: "Concerning the Son of man our rule is a twofold one: that Christ cannot lie, so as to declare himself the Son of man, if he be not truly so; nor can he be constituted the Son of man, unless he be born of a human parent, either father or mother." He can then turn with contempt to his opponent: "On what principle you, Marcion, can admit him Son of man

---

13. Tertullian, *De Carne Christi* xviii, in Klijn and Reinink, *Patristic Evidence*, pp. 109, 111.
14. Cyril of Jerusalem, *Catecheses* x.4 (MPG 33.664); my translation.

I cannot possibly see."[15] Lietzmann is probably justified in finding in this statement confirmation of the fact that Marcion's truncated gospel retained "the Son of man."[16] Since Marcion would certainly have expunged the phrase if he had understood it as a designation of Christ's humanity, Lietzmann argues, he must have been aware of its original apocalyptic meaning.[17]

Lietzmann's argument is deficient; he too quickly assumes that Marcion must have chosen between these two possibilities. Had Marcion understood the phrase as a messianic title (as Lietzmann does), he would have been as eager to delete it as if he had taken it as a designation for Christ's humanity, since it was his purpose to distinguish his Christ from the Messiah promised by the false god of the Jews. Lietzmann does not consider the possibility that Marcion saw no need to expunge the phrase because it had not yet been employed as a significant weapon in the war between the orthodox and the docetists. It does not seem likely that we shall ever recover Marcion's perception of the phrase. He apparently did not share the common gnostic view whereby "the Son of man" was taken as "Son of Anthropos"; Tertullian gibes that Marcion really ought to have followed Valentinus's example in this matter and named his god "Homo" (*Against Marcion* iv.10). In any event, *Tertullian* did not perceive in Marcion's use of the phrase the understanding Lietzmann assumes; if Tertullian had had any inkling that the phrase functioned as a messianic title in Marcion's gospel, we can be sure that he would have seized upon so great an inconsistency with delight. Nor is it likely that Marcion proposed that "the Son of man" designated a heavenly messenger (i.e., the Christ as Marcion conceived him); if Tertullian had been aware of such a proposal, he must surely have responded to it in his usual fashion, instead of simply expressing surprise that Marcion had inconsistently retained a phrase that in Tertullian's view connoted the humanity of Jesus.

Lietzmann was concerned to prove that *ho huios tou anthrōpou* was not the translation of an Aramaic phrase but a neologism created by Hellenistic Jews, probably in Alexandria, and subsequently adopted by Christians as a means of expressing their belief that the risen Jesus would return as heavenly Messiah.[18] We have seen how weak is the evidence he drew from Tertullian's treatment of Marcion. In addition to Marcion, Lietzmann appealed to

15. English translation in Roberts and Donaldson, *The Ante-Nicene Fathers*, vol. 3, p. 358. Cf. Eusebius, *Eccl. Hist.* i.2.26.
16. Lietzmann, *Der Menschensohn*, pp. 61, 79. In the reconstruction attempted by Harnack, *Marcion*, the phrase occurs frequently.
17. Lietzmann, *Der Menschensohn*, p. 62.
18. Ibid., pp. 85–95.

Justin Martyr, the gnostic Ophites, Jewish Christianity, and Ignatius. Let us examine each of these in turn.

Of the early Christian writers Justin makes greater use of *huios anthrōpou* than any other, but it is nonetheless of limited usefulness to him. In the *Apologies*, addressed to Gentiles, it occurs once in a citation of Dan. 7:13 (I.51) and once in a nontechnical use in a passage where Jesus' origin is in view (I.54).[19] It is rather in dialogue with Jews that Justin finds the phrase serviceable. This does not mean, however, that either Justin or his Jewish respondents regarded *huios anthrōpou* as an apocalyptic title.

The discussion is broached by Justin in *Dialogue with Trypho* 31, where he cites Dan. 7:13 as scriptural proof of Christ's glorious Parousia: "For like a son of man he will come upon clouds, as Daniel disclosed." Our English translations err when they perceive a title in Justin's anarthrous phrase ("For he shall come on the clouds as the Son of man"); he is simply employing the standard Greek translation of Daniel's Aramaic phrase, precisely the same translation that recurs a few lines later in a long quotation from Daniel 7.[20] In the following chapter Trypho is given his chance for a rebuttal: "These and similar scriptures compel us to await a glorious and great one who, 'like a son of man,' receives from 'the Ancient of Days' the eternal kingdom." It is clear that Trypho is simply alluding to the cited Scriptures; *huios anthrōpou* is again anarthrous and therefore not a title. There is no reason to argue that Justin's apologetic fervor here seduces him into attributing to his Jewish interlocutor the (Christian) belief in a supernatural Messiah.[21] All that Trypho concedes is that Jews, like Christians, regard Dan. 7:13 as a messianic prophecy. There is no hint in his response that he regarded the messianic figure as a preexistent, heavenly being.

When Justin turns again to Dan. 7:13 in *Dial.* 76, using the anarthrous phrase *hōs huios anthrōpou*, his intention is to show that Jesus only appeared to be the son of a *man* but was in fact the offspring of a virgin. A few lines later he contrasts the virgin-born Jesus with *anthrōpos ex anthrōpōn*.[22] No perceptible relationship can be seen between this citation

19. Lietzmann (ibid., p. 70) argues that since the cited scripture (Gen. 49:10f.) provided no reason for Justin's employment of *huios anthrōpou*, he must have introduced it here as a messianic title. *Non sequitur.* In the context, the issue is simply whether the prophesied figure is to have a human or a divine father.

20. The faulty rendering of Roberts and Donaldson in *The Ante-Nicene Fathers*, vol. 1, p. 209, seems to underlie the understanding of the passage presented by Higgins, "Jewish Messianic Belief in Justin Martyr's *Dialogue with Trypho*," p. 301.

21. This view is argued by Higgins, "Jewish Messianic Belief," p. 301.

22. Cf. *Dial.* 54. Justin's use of this phrase is examined by Trakatellis, *The Pre-existence of Christ in the Writings of Justin Martyr*, p. 155; cf. p. 149.

of Dan. 7:13 and his employment at the end of the same chapter of the passion prediction, "The Son of man must suffer many things and be rejected."[23] Justin's intention is to show that Jesus announced to his disciples prior to the crucifixion that his suffering would be in fulfillment of the predictions of Israel's prophets. Since it is improbable that Justin found any prediction of the suffering of Jesus in Daniel 7, there is no suggestion that "the Son of man" is for him an apocalyptic title derived from Dan. 7:13.[24]

This conclusion is confirmed by his subsequent appeal to the passion prediction in chapter 100.[25] Here Justin feels constrained to offer possible explanations of the strange phrase. "He said that he was the Son of man, either because of his birth by the Virgin, who was, as I said, of the family of David and Jacob and Isaac and Abraham; or because Adam was the father both of himself and of those who have been first enumerated from whom Mary derives her descent."[26] It is apparent that Justin finds Jesus' self-designation a little embarrassing.[27] Much more to his liking is the title "the Son of God," to which he appeals a few lines later. He can give no definitive interpretation of "the Son of man," but the two possibilities he proposes both assume that the phrase serves as a way of speaking of the incarnation of the eternal Son of God. He portrays no awareness of the possibility that *ho huios tou anthrōpou* might originally have been an apocalyptic title.

In the beliefs of the gnostic Ophites, Lietzmann also thought he found evidence of the persistence of the apocalyptic title. Concerning these Irenaeus reports:

> Others, again, portentously declare that there exists, in the power of Bythos, a certain primary light, blessed, incorruptible, and infinite: this is the Father of all, and is styled the first man. They also maintain that his Ennoia, going forth from him, produced a son, and that this is the son of man—the second man. Below these, again, is the Holy Spirit, and under this superior spirit the elements

23. Mk. 8:31 (Lk. 9:22) is quoted exactly up to this point but then is modified in subsequent details. Allusion to the passion prediction is also made in chap. 51, without "the Son of man," and less directly in chap. 106. See the discussion by Borsch, *The Christian and Gnostic Son of Man*, pp. 45–47.

24. Further allusions to Dan. 7:13 in chaps. 79 and 126 contribute nothing additional. Borsch (ibid., pp. 47f.) points to a number of passages where Justin might have used "the Son of man" and chose not to.

25. The same variant form is cited here as in chap. 76, the only change being a reversal of the order of "scribes" and "Pharisees."

26. Translation by Roberts and Donaldson, *The Ante-Nicene Fathers*, vol. 1, p. 249; it accepts the conjecture that *Adam* was intended by Justin instead of *Abraam*, which stands in the received text.

27. Borsch, *The Christian and Gnostic Son of Man*, p. 49, writes: "The plain fact of the matter is that Justin was not sure what this title did mean."

were separated from each other, namely water, darkness, the abyss, chaos, above which they declare the Spirit was borne, calling [it] the first woman. Afterwards, they maintain, the first man, with his son, delighting over the beauty of the Spirit—that is, of the woman—and shedding light upon her, begat by her an incorruptible light, the third male, whom they call Christ, the son of the first and second man, and of the Holy Spirit, the first woman.[28]

Lietzmann's argument was that this was one of the oldest components of the Ophite system, and that the highest god could be named First Man only as a reflex of belief in Jesus as the messianic Son of man, whose heavenly prototype was thus conceived as son of Man.[29] The argument is weak and has not won many followers. The Ophite system, as Colpe notes, is too confused to permit certainty on a matter of this kind.[30] All that can be clearly affirmed on the basis of Irenaeus's report cited above is that the figure identified as *filius hominis* (the Greek for this section is not extant) has nothing in common with the alleged Jewish conception of an apocalyptic judge apart from a heavenly origin, which is hardly sufficient to establish a genetic relationship between the two conceptions.[31]

It may be stated as a general rule that where *huios anthrōpou* appears in early gnostic works, there is some reference in the context to a higher deity called Anthropos. That is, whatever the origin of "son of Man" in the gnostic writings, the tendency is to understand the phrase as the designation of a heavenly aeon who is derived from and subordinate to another being called Man. In another report, concerning the followers of Ptolemy, Irenaeus happily notes the internal dissension in this school regarding the Savior's genetic relationship to the various aeons of their Pleroma: two factions insist on relating him to Anthropos, explaining that this is why the Savior called himself "son of Man" (*kai dia touto huion anthrōpou heauton legein ton Sōtēra, Adv. Haer.* i.12.4).

Scholars will continue to disagree regarding the ultimate origin of "Son of Anthropos" in gnostic literature. Colpe has argued that the Gospels must be seen as the stimulus behind the gnostic use of the phrase.[32] His arguments have been challenged by Borsch, who proposes that it is just as defensible to maintain that Jewish speculation about a heavenly Adam and

---

28. *Adv. Haer.* i.30.1; translation from Roberts and Donaldson, *Ante-Nicene Fathers*, vol. 5, p. 104.
29. Lietzmann, *Der Menschensohn*, p. 63.
30. Colpe, "Ho huios tou anthrōpou," TDNT 8, p. 475, n. 502.
31. Borsch, *The Christian and Gnostic Son of Man*, p. 64, emphasizes the contrast between the cosmogonic Son of man here presented and the figure identified by "the Son of man" in the Gospels.
32. Colpe, "New Testament and Gnostic Christology," pp. 238–40.

his son Seth underlies gnostic belief in Anthropos and Son of Anthropos.[33] Such a view appears in the *Apocryphon of John*: "And when Adam recognized the likeness of his own foreknowledge, he begat the likeness of the son of man. He called him Seth according to the way of the race in the aeons."[34] Since nothing further is reported here concerning Seth, and no function is attributed to him, we may be dealing with an element taken over from prior tradition and imperfectly assimilated. The same tradition, without specific reference to Seth, appears in *Eugnostos the Blessed* and in its parallel, *The Sophia of Jesus Christ*: "First-begetter Father is called 'Adam of the light.' And the kingdom of Son of Man is full of ineffable joy. . . ."[35] In neither version, however, is it intimated that "Son of Man" refers to Seth; it more probably serves as an additional title for Adam, who is thus represented as the offspring of Immortal Man.[36]

Support for Colpe's view that "Son of Man" constitutes a Christian element in gnostic systems can be seen in *Poimandres*, the first tractate of the *Corpus Hermeticum*, where Anthropos has a significant role in the cosmogony, but no reference is made to a son of Anthropos.[37] Borsch counters that since "Son of Anthropos" occurs in gnostic writings in contexts where Christian influence is otherwise not apparent, it can just as well be explained as due to Jewish speculation about the heavenly Adam as the image of God.[38]

In his very helpful survey of the use of "Son of Man" in gnostic literature, Borsch finds few instances where use of the phrase is inspired by the Gospels' usage.[39] Yet the phrase occurs with greater frequency in gnostic than in orthodox writings. Why? It seems unlikely, reasons Borsch, that gnostic interest in the phrase can be explained on the basis of the Son of

---

33. Borsch, *The Christian and Gnostic Son of Man*, pp. 118f.
34. Translation by F. Wisse, in J. M. Robinson, *Nag Hammadi Library*, p. 112. Cf. Giversen, *Apocryphon Johannis*, pp. 92–95; Borsch, *The Christian and Gnostic Son of Man*, pp. 103, 109.
35. Translation by D. M. Parrot, in J. M. Robinson, *Nag Hammadi Library*, p. 217.
36. The context in *Eugnostos* is very confused, but the basic sequence seems to be: from the Unnameable emanated Immortal Man or First Man, the highest form of deity that has been revealed and therefore can be named; from him emanated First-begotten, also known as First-Begetter and Son of Man. This sequence seems to be supported by the parallel in *Sophia of Jesus Christ*: First Man, the first manifestation of the Ineffable, "revealed his first-begotten, androgynous son. His male name is called 'First-Begetter Son of God.' . . . Now the First-begotten is called 'Christ.' . . . First-Begetter Father is called 'Adam, [the] Eye of the Light,' because he came from the shining light [with] his holy angels, who are ineffable (and) shadowless. They rejoice continually with joy in their reflecting, which they received from their Father. (This is) the whole kingdom of Son of Man, the one who is called 'Son of God' " (ibid., pp. 216f.).
37. Such a possibility is conceded by Borsch, *The Christian and Gnostic Son of Man*, p. 107.
38. Ibid., p. 108.
39. Ibid., p. 111.

man sayings in the Gospels, which appear even less frequently in gnostic writings than in those of the church fathers.[40] The infrequency of patristic use, together with the fact that orthodox writers used it primarily as a way of speaking about the humanity of Jesus, make it most improbable that gnostic interest in the phrase derived from orthodox Christianity, whether canonical or postcanonical. We must therefore assume a non-Christian source, probably Jewish sectarianism, where speculation concerning a heavenly Adam was rife.[41]

Here Borsch is reinforcing the conclusions reached by H.-M. Schenke in his research regarding the origin of the gnostic use of "Man" as the name for the highest deity: this peculiar usage derived not from Iran, as earlier researchers claimed, but from Jewish (and pagan) speculation about Gen. 1:26f.; the gnostic myth was developed on the basis of allegorizing exegesis of this passage.[42] Schenke, however, believed that the gnostic Son of Man represented a secondary combination of a Jewish conception of an eschatological king (either a returning Adam or Adam's heavenly *Urbild*) with the primary gnostic conception of the consubstantiality of humans with the highest god, who is therefore called Anthropos.[43] It is clear that Schenke's argument presupposes that "the Son of man" was extant in Jewish sources as the title for an apocalyptic judge. His argument about the use of "Man" in Gnosticism, however, does not depend upon this subordinate theme.

Do those few gnostic passages that seem to reflect New Testament usage suggest that memory of the postulated meaning of "the Son of man" as a Jewish apocalyptic title lived on in Gnosticism?

At first sight this might appear to be the case in a statement attributed to the Peratae by Hippolytus: "For the Son of man (*ho huios tou anthrōpou*) did not come into the world to destroy the world, but in order that the world might be saved through him."[44] "The Son of man" does seem here to be the title of a heavenly being. As Borsch points out, the statement is probably a conflation of Lk. 9:56 and Jn. 3:17.[45] Since the Peratae, like more orthodox Christians, regarded Christ as a preexistent divine being who entered the human realm to save humans, it is not surprising that they conflated these two texts and referred to the Savior by the name that appears in Lk. 9:56. It cannot properly be treated, however, as evidence of

---

40. Ibid., p. 114.
41. Ibid., p. 118.
42. Schenke, *Der Gott "Mensch" in der Gnosis.*
43. Ibid., pp. 151–54.
44. Hippolytus, *Refut. Haer.* v.12 (v.7 in Roberts and Donaldson, *Ante-Nicene Fathers*); my translation.
45. Borsch, *The Christian and Gnostic Son of Man*, p. 64.

a pre-Christian Jewish conception, nor can their use of the Johannine Son of man saying (3:14).[46]

The phrase with articles is also employed by Monoïmos, according to Hippolytus: "For the whole Pleroma was pleased to dwell upon the Son of man in a bodily way (*sōmatikōs*)."[47] Two texts in Colossians (1:19; 2:9) spring to mind, but, as Borsch suggests, we perhaps ought to see a reference here also to Lk. 3:22, since the baptism of Jesus was frequently treated by Gnostics as the "birth" of the Savior through the descent of a heavenly aeon.[48] In this case, however, "the Son of man" appears to designate the human Jesus, who was the recipient of the descending aeon.[49]

In Origen's *Commentary on John* a fragment of Heracleon is cited that seems to reflect Mt. 13:37, 39: "The Son of Man (*ho . . . huios anthrōpou*) above the Place sows; the Savior, who is himself also Son of man [anarthrous], reaps and sends as reapers the angels known through the disciples, each for his own soul."[50] Although the original context in Matthew is apocalyptic, the gnostic reinterpretation has individualized and thus de-eschatologized the passage.

The *Letter to Rheginos* appears in some respects to represent a Gnosticism that stands closer to orthodoxy than most gnostic systems. Being less inclined to docetism than others, it can refer to Christ as "existing in the flesh."[51] We are, therefore, not surprised to find "Son of man" used as it is in orthodox patristic writers:

> Now the Son of God, Rheginos,
> was Son of Man.
> He embraced both of them,
> possessing the humanity and the divinity,
> so that on the one hand he might conquer
> death through his being
> Son of God,
> and that on the other through the Son of
> Man the restoration to the Pleroma

---

46. *Refut. Haer.* v.16 (v.11 in *Ante-Nicene Fathers*). Cf. Borsch, *The Christian and Gnostic Son of Man*, pp. 65f.

47. *Refut. Haer.* viii.13 (viii.6 in *Ante-Nicene Fathers*); my translation.

48. Borsch, *The Christian and Gnostic Son of Man*, pp. 66f.

49. Ibid., p. 69. As in his earlier work, *The Son of Man in Myth and History*, pp. 278ff., Borsch argues that the tradition used by Monoïmos reflects a liturgical context celebrating Jesus' baptism as the moment when he was commissioned "to act as the Son of man."

50. At Jn. 4:37. For the GCS edition by E. Preuschen, see *Origenes Werke*, vol. 4, pp. 276f. The translation is that of Grant, *Gnosticism*, p. 203.

51. P. 44, lines 14f.; cf. Peel, *Epistle to Rheginos*, p. 29.

might occur because
originally he was from above,
a seed of Truth before
this structure had come into being.[52]

The association with the humanity of Jesus is reinforced two pages later:

For we have known the Son of
Man, and we have believed
that he arose from among the dead.[53]

The function of the phrase "the Son of Man" relative to the restoration to the Pleroma is not clear. Borsch maintains that "the author comprehended more than mere humanity when he used the Son of Man designation."[54] Because of the repeated contrast between Son of God and Son of Man, however, it is better to assume that "Son of man" functions here as a way of referring to the incarnate state of the Son of God; the restoration of human souls to the Pleroma for this author requires incarnation, not simply a docetic revealer.[55] The document as a whole indicates that "the Son of God" is, as in orthodox Christianity, a far more important christological tool. If the author was aware of gnostic speculation about "Son of Anthropos," it is clear that he has not allowed such thinking to influence this writing very profoundly.

In the Gospel of Mary there is a passage strongly reminiscent of Lk. 17:21 and Mt. 24:26. "Beware that no one lead you astray, saying 'Lo here!' or 'Lo there!' For the Son of man is within you. Follow after him! Those who seek him will find him."[56] It is not clear whether we are dealing here with gnostic ideas or simply with "realized eschatology" that celebrates Jesus' presence with believers (cf. Jn. 14:18–20, Gal. 2:20). In any event, "the Son of man" is used here as the designation of the heavenly Lord, not of the incarnate Savior. It may well reflect an awareness of the future Son of man sayings in the gospel tradition, where Jesus' return in glory is spoken of in third-person speech using this phrase. The same may be true of a statement that appears a few lines later in the same document: "How shall we go to the Gentiles and preach the gospel of the kingdom of the Son of man?"[57] It is more probable that we are dealing here with a remi-

52. P. 44, lines 21–36; Peel, *Epistle to Rheginos*, p. 30.
53. P. 46, lines 14–17; Peel, *Epistle to Rheginos*, pp. 31f.
54. Borsch, *The Christian and Gnostic Son of Man*, p. 86.
55. Compare the conclusion to Chapter 4 below.
56. Translation by G. W. MacRae and R. M. Wilson, in J. M. Robinson, *Nag Hammadi Library*, p. 472.
57. Ibid.

niscence of Mt. 16:28 and 28:16–20 than with a gnostic conception uninflu-
enced by Christian thought.[58] In this case we have a second allusion to the
gospel tradition concerning the Parousia of the Son of man, although this
tradition was probably radically reinterpreted by the author.

Let us return to Lietzmann's claim that the Ophites provide evidence
that "the Son of man" was known as the title of an apocalyptic Messiah.
We have seen that better explanations are available. It is not surprising
that Gnosticism was not particularly interested in Jewish apocalyptic
thought. When the Gospel of Mary provides reminiscences of Christian
traditions about Jesus' return in glory, traditions that employed third-person
speech when attributing to Jesus the self-designation "the Son of man,"
there is no evidence in the context that the author is aware that this is a
Jewish title for a heavenly Messiah who is expected to come from heaven
to earth without any prior human existence. That is, this gnostic gospel
provides no support for Lietzmann's hypothesis that early Christians derived
the title from Greek-speaking Jews who had created the phrase with articles
through a messianizing exegesis of Daniel 7.[59]

Since both orthodoxy and Gnosticism were little interested in apocalyptic
eschatology, such evidence was not to be expected. Perhaps an authentic
recollection of the earliest use of "the Son of man" persisted in Jewish
Christianity. Lietzmann found evidence of this retention in a tradition
concerning James the brother of Jesus transmitted by Hegesippus, as re-
corded by Eusebius. In his narrative about the martyrdom of James,
Hegesippus attributed to the martyr the declaration: "Why do you ask me
concerning the Son of man? He is sitting in heaven on the right hand of the
Great Power, and will come on the clouds of heaven."[60] Since this is represented as James's response to the request "Declare to us what is the door
of Jesus," it is obvious that "the Son of man" functions here as a name for
Jesus. Is it also a title, inasmuch as it is accompanied by an allusion to Dan.
7:13? Is this possibility reinforced by the report that some of the hearers,
convinced by James's testimony, voice their faith in the words "Hosanna to
the Son of David"? Lietzmann was sure that this was so.[61]

There is, however, another way of treating the evidence. Borsch convincingly argues that James's statement is a second-century creation, modeled on the declaration of Jesus before the Sanhedrin (Mk. 14:62; Mt.
26:64) and Stephen's confession before the same body (Acts 7:56). James

---

58. Cf. Borsch, *The Christian and Gnostic Son of Man*, pp. 92–94.
59. Ibid., pp. 92–95.
60. *Eccl. Hist.* ii.23.13.
61. Lietzmann, *Der Menschensohn*, pp. 71f.

does not confess faith in Jesus as the Son of man; in his statement "the Son of man" functions as a name for Jesus, not as a confessional title. Earlier in the report Hegesippus attributes to James a public affirmation that Jesus is the Savior (*Eccl. Hist.* ii.23.8). It is illegitimate to make the statement about the Son of man function in the same way; James does *not* say, "Jesus is the Son of man, and as such he is sitting in heaven on the right hand of the Great Power."[62]

The phrase is again associated with James in Jerome's citation from the Gospel of the Hebrews regarding an appearance of the risen Jesus: "He brought bread and blessed and broke it and gave it to James the Just and said to him: 'My brother, eat thy bread, for the Son of man is risen from among those who sleep (*quia resurrexit Filius hominis a dormientibus*).' "[63] Since "the Son of man" functions here as a self-designation, it seems to be modeled on the passion predictions of the Gospels, in which Jesus, referring to himself in this way, predicts his resurrection (Mk. 8:31; 9:31; 10:33f., and par.). Certainly this tradition, whatever its origins, provides no support for the allegation that "the Son of man" was remembered by Jewish Christianity as an apocalyptic title.

The Pseudo-Clementine *Homilies* and *Recognitions* likewise provide no such evidence. In *Rec.* i.60 a contrast is developed between John the Baptist, who was hailed by Jesus as the greatest of those born of women (Mt. 11:11; Lk. 7:28), and Jesus, who is still greater because he is *filius hominis*. From other passages, however, it is clear that the contrast here intended is not between a human figure and a divine one but between two classes of prophets, those with a "female" and those with a "male" nature. Adam, the only true prophet, has reappeared in subsequent times with different names (*Hom.* iii.20, 21). His companion, Eve, a female nature, was the first prophetess, and with her are associated those false prophets who are designated "among those born of women" (*Hom.* iii.22, an exact citation of the Greek of Mt. 11:11 par.). "But the other, as 'son of man,' being male, also prophesies the superior things respecting the age to come as [i.e., which is] male" (in contrast to the present age, which is female).[64] Because of this contrast we also find the plural expression "among the sons of men," *en huiois anthrōpōn*, modeled apparently on the Matthean phrase *en gennētois gynaikōn* (*Hom.* iii.26; cf. ii.17). "Son of man," *filius hominis*, does appear to function as an appellative in the listing of contrasting pairs

62. Borsch, *The Christian and Gnostic Son of Man*, pp. 51–54; cf. O'Neill, *Messiah*, pp. 114f.
63. Jerome, *De Viris illustribus* ii (MPL 23.643), translated by Klijn and Reinink, *Patristic Evidence*, p. 211.
64. Pseudo-Clementine *Hom.* iii.22; my translation.

in *Rec.* iii.61, where the Tempter and the Son of man are paired. From the context, however, we gather that *filius hominis* need not be taken here as the designation of a heavenly being, since all members of the pairs up to this point, apart from the Tempter, have been humans, starting with Cain and Abel.

Such are the results of a study of the *Homilies* and *Recognitions* (excluding *Rec.* iii.48, where *filius dei et hominis* seems to reflect the contrast we have found to be normal in orthodox Christianity). It must surely be conceded that we do not have here any evidence that "the Son of man" persisted in Jewish Christianity as an apocalyptic title. H.-J. Schoeps, one of the chief protagonists for this unsubstantiated position, was forced to concede that the Pseudo-Clementine writings, when speaking of the glorious second coming of Christ, do not employ the term![65] There is therefore no justification for Schoeps's proposal that "Ebionite usage appears to have finally rendered the title 'Son of man' unusable by the church."[66]

At the end of our retrospective survey, we come finally to the earliest uses of "Son of man" outside the New Testament—Barn. 12:10 and Ignatius, Eph. 20:2.

As far as Lietzmann was concerned, Barn. 12:10 constituted negative evidence, demonstrating that at the time and place of origin of this document there was no knowledge at all of the Gospels' use of the phrase "the Son of man."[67] The Greek text reads: *Ide palin Iēsous, ouchi huios anthrōpou, alla huios tou theou, typō de en sarki phanerōtheis.* The following paraphrase seems justified by the context: "Look, again in this text, Ex. 17:14, we have a prophecy concerning Jesus, not as son of man but as Son of God, yet manifested in Joshua as a type in the flesh." The intention of the author in the phrase "not as son of man" is, however, far from clear. The general intention is not difficult to grasp. The author wishes to show that statements in the Pentateuch about Joshua are really prophecies regarding Jesus (the names are identical in Greek). Accordingly, it can be argued that he means: "Now consider Joshua, not from the literal point of view, that is, as a normal man, but as the type of the Son of God." On the other hand, since Barnabas reads a variant text of Ex. 17:14, "Take a book in your hands and write what the Lord says, that the Son of God will tear out by the roots the

65. Schoeps, *Jewish Christianity*, p. 63, and *Theologie*, p. 79.

66. Schoeps, *Jewish Christianity*, p. 63, and *Theologie*, p. 80. Borsch, *The Christian and Gnostic Son of Man*, p. 77, suggests that, "though not demonstrable," the term was used in the Pseudo-Clementine writings "because it still had some currency among Jewish-gnostic-Christian sectarians."

67. Lietzmann, *Der Menschensohn*, p. 58. Casey, *Son of Man*, p. 96, agrees.

whole house of Amalek in the last days," it is just possible that he is contrasting the incarnate Jesus (Son of man) with the eschatological judgment of the Son of God, adding that this divine judge was manifested typologically in Joshua, who ravaged the Amalekites. The ambiguity, however, is such that there is no good reason to argue, as Lietzmann does, that Barnabas was totally unaware of the Gospels' tradition of employing "the Son of man" as Jesus' self-designation.[68] All that can be safely affirmed is that Barnabas does not find it useful or meaningful to refer to Jesus' eschatological function by means of *ho huios tou anthrōpou*; in 15:5 he employs "his Son" for this purpose.

The one occurrence of "Son of man" in the letters of Ignatius was regarded by Lietzmann as evidence that the term functioned as a messianic title, even though it was certainly of less importance to Ignatius than "Son of God."[69] It is most unlikely that this represents a correct reading of Eph. 20:2. Ignatius here expresses the hope that he will be permitted to write another little book for the Ephesians concerning "the new man Jesus Christ . . . the one who is Son of man and Son of God," *tō huiō anthrōpou kai huiō theou*. Since his primary concern in this sentence is with "the new man," it is unlikely that "Son of man" and "Son of God" are introduced, as Lietzmann suggests, as parallel *messianic* titles. They point rather to the two aspects of the new man who was God incarnate. A good parallel is provided by an earlier passage in the same letter: "There is one physician, fleshly and spiritual, begotten and unbegotten, God and man, true life in death, both of Mary and of God, first subject to suffering and then impassible, Jesus Christ our Lord" (7:2).[70] From the brief reference in 20:2 it is not possible to determine whether or not Ignatius is drawing upon the evangelical tradition that Jesus called himself "the Son of man," especially since the phrase, as Ignatius uses it, omits the articles.[71] The most that can be said is that if Ignatius intends that his readers here recall the use of *ho huios tou anthrōpou* in the gospel tradition, he understands that phrase as referring to Jesus' humanity.

In conclusion, it must be noted how seldom "Son of man" appears in early Christian writings. In the collection known as "the Apostolic Fathers," it occurs only twice, Barn. 12:10 and Ignatius, Eph. 20:2. Still

---

68. Lietzmann, *Der Menschensohn*, p. 58.
69. Ibid., p. 69.
70. My translation.
71. The article, which governs both *huiō anthrōpou* and *huiō theou*, serves rather as a substitute for the relative pronoun; cf. Moule, "Neglected Features," p. 425.

more significant, perhaps, is the fact that it is *absent* precisely from those apocalyptic contexts where, according to the current scholarly consensus, one should expect to find it. If "the Son of man" connoted "the angelic figure appointed by God to function as judge at the last judgment," it is indeed surprising that no use was made of the term when authors addressed the belief that Jesus would return to perform this function. The avoidance of the term is particularly striking in the eschatological chapter of the Didache, where even an allusion to Dan. 7:13 is not sufficient to induce the author to use the phrase. Instead we read: "Then will the world see the Lord coming on the clouds of heaven" (16:8). In the unlikely event that the author does not depend here on the Synoptic tradition but on a pre-Christian Jewish apocalypse, as proposed by H. Koester, the absence of "the Son of man" is all the more instructive.[72] Koester's suggestion that the author replaced an original *ton huion tou anthrōpou* with *ton kurion* because he did not find "the Son of man" serviceable ignores the question why this should have been so, *if* the phrase was regarded by the early Christian author and his readers, as well as by his source, as an established apocalyptic title.[73] The conclusion seems obvious: it was not so regarded.

None of the early Christian writings uses the term "the Son of man" kerygmatically. It is never used in a confession of faith or vocatively in a prayer addressed to Jesus. No texts promise that Jesus will return *as* the Son of man, thereby indicating that "the Son of man" functioned as an independent concept with its own distinctive content. In the patristic period it survives primarily as an anarthrous phrase that is interpreted literally, "Son of a human being," and is thus employed in affirmations of the real humanity of the incarnate Word.

These findings prompt a question that must not be quickly dismissed. Is it probable that in the brief period separating Ignatius and his contemporaries (including, perhaps, the authors of the Didache and Barnabas) from the authors of the Gospels the connotation of "the Son of man" was totally forgotten? Conversely, is it possible that Ignatius had a better understanding than modern scholars of the way the phrase was used in the Gospels and therefore felt justified in employing it, without the articles, not as a title but as a descriptive phrase, to affirm the humanity of Jesus?

72. Koester, *Synoptische Überlieferung*, pp. 188f. This omission is "corrected" in the Georgian version of the Didache, which inserts "the Son of man who (at the same time) is Son of God"; cited by P. Vielhauer in Hennecke and Schneemelcher, *New Testament Apocrypha*, vol. 2, p. 628.

73. Koester, *Synoptische Überlieferung*, p. 187.

This question compels us to take a fresh look at the way "the Son of man" actually functions in each of the Gospels. We will begin with Luke and John, which are generally regarded as further removed than Matthew and Mark from the apocalyptic enthusiasm of early Christianity, and in this sense closer to the thought of the second-century church.

3 | LUKE-ACTS

Our task in this chapter is to discover, if possible, what the phrase "the Son of man" meant to the author of the Third Gospel and Acts. This task is complicated by the fact that most of the Son of man sayings in these writings are drawn by Luke from his sources. We must not assume, however, that he adopted the meaning attributed to the phrase by his predecessors. It is possible that he gave the term a different connotation, whether through misunderstanding or reinterpretation. We must therefore begin with the assumption that we do not know how Luke understood "the Son of man." Was it for him an apocalyptic title, a phrase designating the humanity of the Incarnate One, a self-designation employed by Jesus without specific content, or something else? Did he inconsistently employ the term in two different ways? To answer these questions we must leave behind our assumptions about what it meant to others (Jewish apocalyptists, Jesus, Mark, etc.) and focus on Luke's own appropriation of the phrase by examining how it functions in his writings.

The normal redaction-critical approach will be unsatisfactory. It has become customary for redaction criticism to proceed on the basis of source criticism. The peculiarities of the Lukan perspective are to be identified, it is averred, by concentrating on those passages where Luke's source is either extant (Mark) or can be inferred (the Q passages in Matthew) and noting the changes that Luke introduces. Where no change has been made, the passage must remain mute respecting Luke's own theology. This, as many scholars have observed, is a dubious procedure. The fact that the material has been selected for inclusion must surely be taken as evidence that Luke found it meaningful. The absence of alteration merely makes it more difficult to determine his understanding. Such a determination must be attempted on the basis of composition criticism, which attempts to relate each part of the Gospel to the whole, thus establishing the meaning contextually.

A thorough composition-critical study of Luke would exceed the limits of this volume. We must be satisfied with something far less complete, while maintaining the necessity of treating the Son of man sayings in their Lukan context rather than in relationship to their putative sources. The sayings will therefore be examined in the order in which they appear in the Lukan writings.

> **Lk. 5:24** But that you may know that the Son of man has authority on earth to forgive sins—

This first instance of the term must be seen in the context of the first five chapters of the Gospel. It is preceded by the birth narratives, which recount the birth of a unique human being through the intervention of the Holy Spirit (1:35), a human being who is destined to sit on the throne of David his ancestor (1:32) and who can therefore be referred to by the titles *Christos* (2:11, 26), *huios theou* (1:35), and *kyrios* (2:11), and who, for the same reason, appropriately calls God "my Father" (2:49). It is prophesied of him that he will rule and judge Israel (1:33; cf. 3:16f.); that is, he will perform functions traditionally assigned to Israel's eschatological king. It must be noted that there is no suggestion in these opening narratives about Jesus' birth and youth that Luke regards him as the incarnation of a heavenly being. This conclusion has been confirmed for Luke-Acts as a whole by J. D. G. Dunn's recent study.[1] It appears that Luke was either unaware of or unsympathetic to an incarnational Christology.[2]

Our text is preceded also by the temptation narrative, in which the Messiah is tempted by the devil. Nothing in this story suggests that two transcendent figures are here opposed. The narrative makes little sense if it is assumed that Jesus is a heavenly personage who has recently left his glorious home to sojourn among humans in fleshly disguise. All three questions addressed to Jesus by the tempter assume that Jesus is a human being who can be tempted. The basis for Jesus' victory over the temptations is his genuine piety and his being empowered by the Holy Spirit (notice how 4:1 and 4:14 bracket the narrative).

Although Jesus' central function is understood in terms of the category *Christos*, his public ministry does not fulfill this function except in some

---

1. Dunn, *Christology in the Making*, pp. 50f.
2. Tödt, *Son of Man*, pp. 284ff., attributes the absence of the idea of preexistence from the Synoptic Son of man sayings to the fidelity with which Jesus' teaching was transmitted. He regards Luke as responsible for introducing the motif of the exaltation of the Son of man at 22:69 but does not consider the significance of the fact that Luke does not similarly inject the preexistence motif.

anticipatory ways, and to that extent he is the hidden Messiah. The ministry is presented by Luke primarily in prophetic terms. After his encounter with Satan, Jesus returns to Galilee "in the power of the Spirit"; that is, he is empowered in the same way as other prophets (4:14; cf. 1:15, 41, 67; 2:25–27). At Nazareth Jesus speaks of himself as a prophet and compares his miraculous activity with that of Elijah and Elisha (4:24–27; cf. 13:33). W. Wrede is surely incorrect in regarding the Nazareth story as functioning as a messianic self-proclamation as Luke presents it.[3] He ignores the fact that in Luke's narrative the angry reaction of the crowd is prompted not by Jesus' application to himself of what Wrede regards as a messianic text (Isa. 61:1f.) but by Jesus' subsequent remarks about Israel's rejection of its prophets (cf. 13:33). Even in this programmatic scene Jesus remains the hidden Messiah.[4]

The prophetic category is, of course, transcended in the first miracle story, where the unclean spirit reminds the readers that the miracle-worker is not just another prophet like Elijah and Elisha but "the Holy One of God" (4:34; cf. Jn. 6:69). *Hagios* is not one of Luke's favorite designations for Jesus, and one suspects that in each occurrence it derives from a source (1:35, neuter; Acts 3:14; 4:27, 30). It is perhaps Luke's own hand that explicates the term at its first appearance in 1:35 by the somewhat awkward apposition *huios theou*. That Luke understood *ho hagios tou theou* to be a messianic designation is confirmed by the parallel demonic ejaculation in 4:41, "You are the Son of God!" which is immediately interpreted by Luke in the following redactional statement: "But he rebuked them, and would not allow them to speak, because they knew that he was *the Christ*" (the Markan parallel, 1:34, has only "because they knew him"). In these first narratives of Jesus' miraculous activity, the motif of the messianic secret appears without explication. It is indicated only that Jesus is acting as Messiah and that this fact is not to be revealed. Nor is there the slightest suggestion in the following narrative of the call of the first disciples that Peter and his colleagues have left everything to follow Jesus because they perceived the secret of his identity (contrast Jn. 1:35–42).

The question of Jesus' identity is raised again in the story of the healing of the paralytic, in which Luke's first Son of man text appears. It is anticipated by the introduction of "Pharisees and teachers of the law" who have come "from every village of Galilee and Judea, and from Jerusalem" (5:17). The parallels in Matthew and Mark make no mention at this point of the

---

3. Wrede, *Messianic Secret*, p. 178. Cf. Bultmann, *History*, p. 363.
4. Two recent commentators stress that for Luke the anointing of 4:18 (Isa. 61:1) is prophetic rather than messianic; cf. Fitzmyer, *Luke I–IX*, p. 529; Marshall, *Luke*, p. 183.

presence of the opponents; Luke's introduction gives the narrative more weight and allows it to function as a parallel to the rejection at Nazareth. The narrative assumes that the readers already know that the Pharisees and teachers of the law represent the leadership of contemporary Judaism and that this Judaism is opposed to Christianity. Their appearance, therefore, prepares the readers to expect a significant challenge to Jesus, one that will in some sense represent the distinction between Judaism and Christianity as perceived by Luke and like-minded Christians. It is therefore not surprising that the challenge, when it occurs in v. 21, is more explicitly christological in its orientation than in the Synoptic parallels, where the narrative apparently bears less weight. Whereas Mark reads "*Why* does this man speak thus? He blasphemes!" Luke has "*Who* is this who speaks blasphemies?" (cf. 7:49; Matthew has simply "This man blasphemes"). To Luke and his community the one who made forgiveness of sins available is the Christ; to their Jewish contemporaries he is a blasphemer and the occasion of blasphemy by Christians (Acts 7:57; cf. Acts 6:11).

Although the question of Jesus' identity is thus directly raised by Luke, it is not answered. It is rather the premise on which the question was based that is addressed: "Who can forgive sins but God alone?" That is, the narrative by no means concurs with the premise, so as to agree that the charge of blasphemy is indeed justified from the opponents' point of view. It is not the intention of the narrative to declare: "Yes, no one can forgive sins except God, and therefore Jesus who forgives sins is God." Instead, the premise is challenged; the opponents are presented with a new fact that will effectively negate the premise: "But that you may know that the Son of man has authority on earth to forgive sins. . . ." Whereas the opponents insist that God does not delegate to any human being the right to grant forgiveness, Jesus' response claims that right for himself: "To the Son of man has been granted authority to communicate divine forgiveness."[5]

There is no need to discuss at this point the question of the origin of this Son of man saying and whether or not it was inserted secondarily into the miracle story. We will simply assume that Luke received the saying in its present setting and regarded it as a legitimate part of the tradition of Jesus' words and deeds. This means that he understood "the Son of man" to function as Jesus' peculiar way of referring to himself, although, as we shall see, Luke is responsible for later broadening this usage when he allows Stephen to use the phrase as a way of speaking about Jesus (Acts 7:55f.).

5. Montefiore, *Synoptic Gospels*, vol. 1, p. 47, in his comments on the parallel at Mk. 2:10, notes that Jesus, as a prophet, could have appealed to the precedent established by Nathan (2 Sam. 12:13).

What did Luke think Jesus intended to convey by this self-designation? Many commentators believe that for Luke, as for the earliest tradition, the phrase designated the apocalyptic figure whose arrival from heaven would signal the end of history.[6] Is such an understanding supported by the context? The answer is clearly no. In the flow of the narrative Jesus' use of the self-designation awakens no response whatsoever from any segment of the audience; in *function* it is purely denotative, designating Jesus as one who possesses authority to forgive *on earth*.

It has sometimes been argued that the phrase *epi tēs gēs* requires that "the Son of man" be understood as connoting a transcendent figure who normally functions in heaven rather than on earth.[7] Since it is most unlikely that Luke intended to present Jesus as the incarnation of a heavenly being, it is also improbable that he understood "on earth" in this way. In view of the opponents' question, *epi tēs gēs* is readily intelligible as a response to the implication of the Pharisees' claim that only God *in heaven* can forgive. There is not the slightest hint in the Lukan redaction of the narrative that the evangelist understood Jesus' statement as a revelation of his heavenly glory. The conclusion created by Luke, "We have seen strange things today," serves as a response to the miracle and the accompanying act of forgiveness, not to any christological revelation. Apparently for Luke "the Son of man" is here equivalent simply to "I, Jesus."

This conclusion is confirmed by the presence of the strange question, "Which is easier, to say, 'Your sins are forgiven you,' or to say, 'Rise and walk'?" (5:23). The significance of *eukopōteron* is not clear, but in any event the authority to forgive is here conjoined to the authority to heal. For Luke the authority to heal does not reveal the future heavenly glory of Jesus, because it is an authority that Jesus will share with his followers (9:1; 10:9; Acts 3:6, etc.). The authority to heal is derived from God (5:17, "And the power of the Lord was with him to heal"); it ought, therefore, to be clear to the opponents that the authority to forgive, which is about to be demonstrated in the healing, is derived from the same source. Although it is not here made explicit that the authority to forgive was also shared by Jesus with his followers (cf. Mt. 9:8; 16:19; 18:18), it is surely implicit in Acts

6. Marshall, *Luke*, p. 216; Plummer, *S. Luke*, pp. 156f.; Schürmann, *Lukasevangelium*, p. 284. Ellis, *Luke*, p. 105, urges that there is no certain evidence that "the Son of man" constituted a title in pre-Christian Judaism, but in his comments on 12:8 he suggests that the "mysterious distinction between 'me' and the Son of man reserves the latter title to Messiah's role in the last judgment" (p. 174). Does Ellis mean to imply that *for Luke* the phrase functions as a title for the eschatological Messiah?

7. Cf. Thompson, "The Son of Man—Some Further Considerations," p. 205; Marshall, *Luke*, p. 216.

2:38–40 and ought to be assumed for the early church generally (cf. Jn. 20:23). Thus the narrative opposes the stance of the opponents ("Who can forgive sins but God only?") by suggesting that the Christian practice of declaring forgiveness of sins is justified by the empirical evidence provided by the miracles effected by Jesus and his followers.

There remains the possibility that for Luke "the Son of man" functions here as a *secret* title connoting "heavenly judge," that is, that Luke and his readers know that the phrase was used in this way in esoteric Jewish circles prior to its application to Jesus, but the pericope's audience is assumed to be totally ignorant of this eschatological conception, and thus the secret is not broken by Jesus' public claim to be the Son of man. It is certainly clear that for Luke "the Son of man" designates Jesus, who will function as eschatological judge (Acts 10:42; 17:31). It is not at all clear in any Lukan passage that he understood the term as possessing this meaning in itself, independently of its application to Jesus. This is surely the most adequate explanation of the curious fact that Luke, who retains many primitive christological expressions in the speeches of Acts, finds no occasion to use "the Son of man" kerygmatically, not even in those passages where Jesus' role as future judge is proclaimed.[8]

Those who maintain that for Luke "the Son of man" connoted "heavenly judge" or "transcendent Messiah" have proposed two explanations for its allegedly inappropriate use here. The most common proposal is that its presence is due to carelessness on Luke's part respecting the messianic secret. On this view the phrase is taken as a well-known messianic title, so that Jesus' use of it as a self-designation in public reveals the secret of his identity. This ought not to surprise us, it is alleged, since Luke is inconsistent in his treatment of the secrecy theme.[9]

This explanation is not in the least convincing. Luke is very careful in his use of those titles that he regards as messianic. Jesus never accepts the title *Christos* in public until the trial scene. The same holds true for "the Son of God." Demented persons who address Jesus with such titles are rebuked and silenced. The title "king" is apparently accepted by Jesus in Luke's version of the triumphal entry (19:38–40). This public application of the title to Jesus is probably treated by Luke as one of the events precipitating the Passion; the intention to destroy Jesus reported in 19:47b finds little

8. Leivestad, "Exit the Apocalyptic Son of Man," pp. 248ff., deals with the avoidance of the term in Christian confessions of faith; he makes no explicit reference, however, to the speeches of Acts.

9. Cf. Wrede, *Messianic Secret,* pp. 164–80; Sjöberg, *Der verborgene Menschensohn,* pp. 142ff.

motivation in Luke's abbreviated narrative of the temple cleansing and is best understood as referring back to 19:39 and forward to 22:67 and 23:2. "Son of David" is used publicly without rebuke in 18:38f., but the anarthrous phrase is properly ambiguous, as indicated by Matthew's application of it to Joseph (1:20).

On the other hand, we must observe that no demon addresses Jesus as Son of man. Neither Satan nor an opponent at the cross challenges Jesus with the words, "If you are the Son of man. . . ." It is surely an injustice to accuse Luke of using "the Son of man" in so careless a manner, when it is evident that he is careful with respect to the unambiguous titles. Furthermore, while the argument appears to have some force at first sight when applied to Mark (Mk. 2:10, 28 provide the only public uses of the term until the trial, excluding 8:38, whose audience is uncertain), the problem of inconsistency is greatly intensified in Luke, where the number of public uses of the term increases. The simplest and most satisfactory explanation of the alleged inconsistency is that *for Luke* the phrase does not function as a messianic title.

The second proposal may be quickly dismissed. It has been suggested that, because of the strange syntax found in Lk. 5:24 and the Synoptic parallels, we may regard the *hina* clause as addressed not to the narrative audience (the Pharisees and neutral observers) but to Luke's readers, as in the parenthetical remark "Let the reader understand" at Mk. 13:14 and Mt. 24:15.[10] While the syntactic problem of the verse as it stands must be admitted, the problem is not solved by treating this clause as a parenthetical remark comparable to a gloss. An even more awkward disjunction occurs when the clause is removed from the syntax by being placed within parentheses. Second, it makes little sense to argue that *hina de eidēte* is addressed to the readers, who as Christians already know this fact; it is the opponents who do not know it. Third, it is very unlikely that a glossator (pre-Synoptic or one of the Synoptists) would have referred to Jesus as the Son of man in this way; one of the established kerygmatic titles would be expected. Fourth, such an aside to the readers would more appropriately employ the past tense of the verb: "But in order that you may know that the Son of man *had* authority while on earth to forgive sins. . . ."

10. Cf. Boobyer, "Mark II,10a and the Interpretation of the Healing of the Paralytic"; Ceroke, "Is Mk 2,10 a Saying of Jesus?"; L. S. Hay, "The Son of Man in Mark 2:10 and 2:28"; Fitzmyer, *Luke I–IX*, p. 579. Boobyer, p. 120, correctly notes that his proposal requires the further conjecture that a connective word or phrase was excised when the interpolation was inserted.

There is thus no evidence that "the Son of man" is treated as a messianic title at its first appearance in Luke's Gospel. It functions as Jesus' self-designation without betraying to the audience the secret of his identity. If it was nonetheless a messianic title for Luke and was used here in a public setting because of carelessness, evidence supporting such an assumption must be drawn from other passages.

> **Lk. 6:5** And he said to them, "The Son of man is lord of the Sabbath."

This verse functions as a close parallel to the one just examined; both employ "the Son of man" in public statements addressed by Jesus to opponents in defense of his actions. From the perspective of Luke's narrative, Jesus' claim to be able to set aside the Sabbath commandment as normally interpreted was almost as reprehensible to his Jewish opponents as his claim to mediate divine forgiveness. While Luke may intend an implicit Christology in these two passages, neither is explicitly christological. The allusion to David in the second pericope does, of course, raise the possibility that Jesus is being presented as the eschatological Messiah, for which David is the prototype. The narrative, however, does not develop this possibility. The logic is not: "Just as David, possessing the authority of God's anointed king, stood above the law in his day, so David's eschatological successor stands above the law now." It is rather: "Just as a human being, David, transgressed the ritual requirement when he and his associates were in genuine need, so can the human Jesus and his followers do so now."

Both this narrative and its sequel (6:6–11) imply that Jesus does not violate the Sabbath commandment in an arbitrary fashion simply because it is a source of inconvenience but because he follows a higher law, the law that gives precedence to human needs over ritual requirements. Nothing in the narrative suggests that Jesus' response to his critics is presented, anachronistically, as a christological declaration: "I, the incarnate, heavenly Messiah, am lord of the Sabbath, even though you are unable to recognize my divine dignity." It is rather a sequel to 5:24: "I, who have authority to announce the breaking in of the kingdom of God, to cast out demons, to heal the sick, and to forgive sins, have also the authority to elevate human need over ritual prescription." It is a bold claim, but not overtly christological, as far as we can tell from Luke's incorporation of the narrative into his Gospel. The messianic secret is not divulged. The following narrative presents the opponents as infuriated by what is presented as antinomian behavior, not by any messianic claim on Jesus' part.

> **Lk. 6:22** Blessed are you when people hate you, and when they exclude you and revile you, and cast out your name as evil, on account of the Son of man!

"The Son of man" does not occur in the parallel beatitude at Mt. 5:11, where we read instead *heneken emou*. It will not be profitable at this point to pursue the question concerning which version has the greater claim to originality. Nor is there any certain way of determining whether Luke found "the Son of man" in his source or added it himself. Our concern is rather to discover, if possible, what force the term had for Luke in this setting.

As intimated both in the introduction (6:17–19) and in the conclusion (7:1), Luke conceives the "sermon" containing this saying to be addressed directly to the disciples and indirectly to the crowd. It is also clear that Luke understands *ho huios tou anthrōpou* as a self-designation of Jesus here as in 5:24 and 6:5, where the context excludes any ambiguity. Thus Luke's presentation again assumes that nondisciples hear Jesus referring to himself as the Son of man, and yet the messianic secret is not revealed.

It is a mistake to argue that this verse teaches that the disciples will be persecuted "for the sake of the coming Son of man."[11] The Jewish disciples are persecuted in Acts because they proclaim Jesus as the Christ, not because they proclaim that Jesus is the Son of man.[12]

> **Lk. 7:34** The Son of man has come eating and drinking; and you say, "Behold, a glutton and a drunkard, a friend of tax collectors and sinners."

This saying is set in a public discourse concerning John the Baptist. Here again "the Son of man" is unambiguously employed as the self-designation of Jesus in the hearing of "the crowds" without revealing the secret of his identity. Notice that the following pericope is concerned with whether or not Jesus is a *prophet* (7:39), a question that would fade into

11. Tödt, *Son of Man*, p. 123, properly insists that the reference is to the Son of man's activity on earth.
12. Stephen is not martyred because he proclaims that Jesus is the Son of man; see below, under discussion of Acts 7:55f.

insignificance if Jesus had just openly claimed to be the heavenly Son of man.

The saying occurs in a unit of tradition that rebukes Jesus' contemporaries for their failure to respond positively to two messengers ("children") of Wisdom. Of each messenger it is stated that he "has come"; that is, no distinction is made between the nature of John's coming and that of Jesus, so as to suggest that, while John has come as a prophet, Jesus is the incarnation of a heavenly being.[13] Jesus who calls himself the Son of man is here presented as a human messenger comparable to John.

> **Lk.9:21f.** But he charged and commanded them to tell this to no one, saying, "The Son of man must suffer many things, and be rejected by the elders and chief priests and scribes, and be killed, and on the third day be raised."

This first reference to the suffering, death, and resurrection of the Son of man must be considered in terms of its Lukan context. The secret of Jesus' identity, again recognized by demons at 8:28, is still hidden from the disciples, who, in response to the stilling of the storm, ask, "Who then is this, that he commands even wind and water, and they obey him?" (8:25). According to Luke's presentation, they still do not perceive that he is the Messiah. Not until after the miraculous feeding of the five thousand is Peter able to make the correct identification—*ton Christon tou theou* (9:20; cf. 2:26, *ton Christon Kuriou*). The immediate response by Jesus to Peter's confession is the command that the messianic secret not be divulged to anyone. Note that Luke is here more explicit than Mark, using *touto* instead of *peri autou*.

Luke connects Peter's confession and the first passion prediction more closely than do the other Synoptic writers, by linking the injunction to silence with the prediction by a participial construction, thereby suggesting a causal relationship: "You must not announce that I am the Christ, because I must suffer." By omitting Peter's rebuke and Jesus' counterrebuke, Luke removes any suggestion that Jesus did not fully accept Peter's confession. There is not the slightest basis for arguing that, from Luke's perspective, the title *Christos* was seen as a misleading or inadequate title by Jesus (cf. 24:26).[14] In the Lukan presentation Jesus' response declares in effect: "Yes,

---

13. Arens, *The **ēlthon**-Sayings*, p. 242, argues against Hamerton-Kelly, *Pre-existence, Wisdom, and the Son of Man*, pp. 42f.

14. Pace Fitzmyer, *Luke I–IX*, p. 780, who maintains that "the Son of man" occurs here "precisely as a corrective of a messianic title, of that used by Peter."

I am the Christ, but before I bring eschatological salvation I must die and be raised." There is therefore no reason for supposing that Luke regards "the Son of man" as a title used by Jesus in this context to correct a nationalistic conception of the Messiah. Nowhere in either the Gospel or Acts is there any hint that Luke perceived any such problem. The term functions here, as in the passages already examined, simply as a self-designation; it brings no content to the matter under discussion, namely, that the Messiah must suffer, die, and be resurrected. There is nothing in Luke's editing to suggest that the use of the term here heightens the paradox so as to suggest: "Not only must the Messiah suffer; the heavenly Son of man incarnate in this human body must suffer."[15]

> **Lk. 9:26** For whoever is ashamed of me and of my words, of him will the Son of man be ashamed when he comes in his glory and the glory of the Father and of the holy angels.

At first sight this verse seems to distinguish between Jesus, the eschatological prophet who announces the arrival of the kingdom of God, and another figure, the Son of man, who will come in glory to judge the living and the dead. As we have seen in chapter 1, this apparent disjunction encouraged Bultmann to treat this and other sayings concerning the future coming Son of man as genuine utterances of Jesus. Even if Bultmann were proved correct relative to the earliest stage of the transmission of this saying, his interpretation is clearly not relevant to its function in the extant Gospels, as Bultmann himself clearly recognized.[16] None of the gospel writers betrays the slightest awareness of dangerous ambiguity in sayings of this kind; they uniformly assume that it will be self-evident to their readers that Jesus is speaking of himself whenever "the Son of man" occurs.[17] In each of the Synoptic Gospels the term is used as a self-designation in sayings about Jesus' earthly activity *prior to* its appearance in a saying that speaks of the future coming of the Son of man. There is therefore no cause for the evangelists to fear misunderstanding. Just as Jesus refers to himself in the third person when justifying his exercise of a God-given authority to forgive sins (5:24) and to place human need above the ritual requirements of the Sabbath (6:5), and when prophesying his death and

---

15. Tödt, *Son of Man*, p. 178, properly insists that the suffering sayings must not be interpreted by means of the Danielic conception; the paradox relates not to the heavenly origin but to the *exousia* of the Son of man (cf. pp. 200, 230).

16. Bultmann, *History*, p. 112.

17. Cf. Leivestad, "Exit the Apocalyptic Son of Man," pp. 261–63.

resurrection as Messiah (9:21f.), so now he uses this strange third-person idiom to speak of his future glory and judicial activity.[18] It would strike Luke and his contemporaries as immaterial that Jesus uses a first-person form in v. 26a and a third-person form in v. 26b. This abrupt alternation in idiom has already been employed by Luke at 5:24 and in successive verses at 9:22f.

Thus understood, 9:26 announces that Jesus will play an eschatological role in an otherworldly sphere: Jesus will "come" in glory. Since this first announcement of the future coming of Jesus follows the first prophecy of the Son of man's resurrection in 9:22, it would not occur to Luke that his readers would take "the Son of man" in 9:26 as anything but a name for Jesus. The one who prophesies his own resurrection on the third day prophesies also his return in glory.

Does 9:26 divulge the messianic secret to nondisciples? The answer depends upon the reference of *pantas* in v. 23. Does Luke intend by this word to expand the audience from the narrow circle of disciples to include the crowd (as does the Markan parallel, 8:34)? Or does he intend the *pantas* to mean simply "all his disciples" (cf. Mt. 16:24)? It seems impossible to answer this question with any degree of certainty. In any event, if the secret is inconsistently divulged at this point, it is not by a public use of "the Son of man" (since this occurred already at 5:24) but by the content of the saying.

Nothing in Luke's presentation of this first announcement of Jesus' future glory suggests that Jesus will return *as* the Son of man, that is, that the human Jesus will *become* the divine figure known by this title. Whatever Luke understood to be the connotation of the phrase, he evidently believed that Jesus could appropriately call himself the Son of man during his earthly ministry. As we have already seen, Luke could do this without resorting to incarnational Christology. Certainly, no incarnational thinking is perceptible in the following pericope concerning the transfiguration. Two other humans, Moses and Elijah, share Jesus' anticipatory participation in divine glory on the mountain. Whatever Luke may have understood by Peter's reference to "three tabernacles" (9:33), this close association of Jesus with two preceding human messengers is not radically corrected by the *bat qol*

18. Whether Jesus is here conceived as eschatological advocate or as judge is not clear. Tödt, *Son of Man,* p. 98, argues for the former on the basis of Luke's omission of the motif of the Son of man's dispatch of angels (understood as emissaries of the heavenly court). In the light of Acts 10:42 and 17:31, however, the latter is more likely. Still more probable is the hypothesis that Luke and other early Christians would have sensed little tension between these two views, since God for them always remained the ultimate judge. See below, chapter 7.

that declares: "This is my Son, the Elect, listen to him" (9:35). Luke has already made it perfectly clear that for him "Son of God" is an alternative way of saying *Christos*.[19] Furthermore, in his second volume he indicates his familiarity with the important passage in Dt. 18:15–18, which predicts the coming of a prophet like Moses, to whom the people must listen carefully (Acts 3:22; 7:37). In alluding to this prophecy at Lk. 9:35 he employs a word order (*autou akouete*) that reflects the Septuagint version of Dt. 18:15 more closely than do Matthew and Mark. Thus it would appear that for Luke the Christ is both a prophet and more than a prophet, yet the "more than" is not conceived in terms of incarnation.

> **Lk. 9:44** Let these words sink into your ears; for the Son of man is to be delivered into the hands of men.

This second passion prediction is preceded in Matthew and Mark by two Son of man sayings not found in Luke (Mt. 17:9 // Mk. 9:9; Mt. 17:12 and Mk. 9:12 are similar but not identical). There seems to be no theological motivation for Luke's omission of these sayings, which fit well with his own point of view.[20]

The use of "the Son of man" in this passage coincides exactly with that of 9:22. The motif of the failure of the disciples to understand the prophecy, which did not occur at 9:22 but is developed in some detail both here and following Luke's fourth passion prediction at 18:31–34, is apparently associated in Luke's mind with the motif that the Scriptures predict in a veiled way the sufferings of Christ (24:25–27). We should therefore assume that for Luke *paradidosthai eis cheiras anthrōpōn* is a matter of scriptural prophecy. It is clearly not prophesied of the "one like a son of man" of Dan. 7:13. That is to say, for Luke the Scriptures predict the suffering of the Christ; they do not predict the suffering of the Son of man as a figure independent of Jesus, with whom Jesus then identifies himself.

The misunderstanding of the disciples, therefore, has nothing to do with the alleged paradox that the heavenly Son of man must experience human suffering. The disciples are simply represented as failing to comprehend how the one they have confessed as the Christ, the eschatological Savior, should be "delivered into the hands of men" and experience death prior to victory.

---

19. See the comment on 4:41 earlier in this chapter. For a different opinion, cf. Fitzmyer, *Luke I–IX*, p. 793.
20. Cf. ibid., p. 805.

Lk. 9:58 Foxes have holes, and birds of the air have nests; but the
Son of man has nowhere to lay his head.

Whereas this saying is placed in a very early context in Matthew,
where it constitutes the first Son of man saying in the Gospel (8:20), Luke
locates it in the context of the final journey to Jerusalem. Scholars have
sometimes argued that the saying originally referred to the condition of
humans as contrasted with animals and have postulated a mistranslation
from Aramaic.[21] In this connection it has been observed that the saying
does not accurately describe Jesus' condition.[22] However this matter may
be resolved relative to a possible setting in the life of Jesus, it is obvious
that in the Lukan setting it *does* accurately describe Jesus' condition as
understood by Luke. It occurs in a section on discipleship that follows
immediately upon the commencement of the final journey (upon the
abandonment of the Galilean "home") and the refusal of a Samaritan
village to offer hospitality to Jesus and his company.

Since the saying constitutes a response to a would-be disciple, the emphasis lies on the human condition of Jesus that must be shared by those
who follow him. That is, the saying in this context does not hint at any
supposed paradox involving the preexistent glory of the Son of man and
his present humiliation. Here again "the Son of man" has no connotative
force, only denotative effect.[23]

Lk. 11:30 For as Jonah became a sign to the people of Nineveh, so
will the Son of man be to this generation.

In both Matthew and Luke this saying is set in the general context
of the controversy narrative concerning the charge that Jesus exorcizes by
the authority of Beelzebul. Whereas Matthew links the Jonah saying with
the Beelzebul material by means of a temporal connective (*tote*, 12:38), Luke
anticipates it by placing the request for a sign right in the middle of the
controversy narrative (11:16), where it fits very poorly but functions well as
the explicit anticipation of the Jonah saying. It is those who cannot see the
significance of Jesus' expulsion of demons who demand a sign.

The only sign that God will give to this generation will be the sign of
Jonah. While Matthew and Luke provide different interpretations of this

21. Bultmann, *History*, p. 28.
22. Vielhauer, "Jesus und der Menschensohn," p. 162; Teeple, "The Origin of the Son of
Man Christology," p. 235.
23. Fitzmyer, *Luke I–IX*, p. 835, suggests that the term is here simply a surrogate for "I."

saying, both reflect the future tense of *dothēsetai* in the use of *estai*. That is to say, neither evangelist suggests that Jesus, in his prophetic and exorcistic ministry, is already the sign of Jonah; both believe that the saying points forward to a future activity of Jesus. For Matthew the parallel with Jonah is at the point of Jonah's sojourn in the sea monster: the sign that will be provided in Jesus will be his death and resurrection (seen as a single event).

Luke's *estai* is far more ambiguous. He may understand it to refer to Jesus' prophetic ministry in Jerusalem; he places the saying in the context of the journey to Jerusalem, and at a number of points it represents a parallel to 13:32–35 and the preceding allusion to the participation of Gentiles in the kingdom of God, 13:29f.[24] Like Matthew, Luke may refer the saying to the paradox and miracle of the death and resurrection of the Christ.[25] A third possibility is that he is thinking of the "coming" of the Son of man (cf. 17:24 and Mt. 24:30).[26] It might be urged that the reference to the judgment in vv. 31f. favors the third proposal, but this understanding would misconstrue the relationship between v. 30 and v. 32; in this context the sign of Jonah, whether the reference is to Jonah's miraculous deliverance from the sea monster, his preaching of repentance, or both, is the occasion of repentance for Nineveh's inhabitants, whereby they will be able to condemn those who were granted a similar opportunity by the preaching and/or resurrection of Jesus and yet failed to repent.[27]

Regardless of the saying's origin in the tradition, "the Son of man" here functions for Luke as a self-designation: "Just as Jonah was God's 'sign' calling the Ninevites to repentance, so will I be to this generation, even though this generation will not respond positively as the Ninevites did" (cf. 13:32–35).

> **Lk. 12:8** And I tell you, every one who acknowledges me before other people, the Son of man also will acknowledge him or her before the angels of God.

Israel's subsequent failure to respond to the "sign of Jonah" provides the theme for the following material about the "evil eye" and the

---

24. Edwards, *The Sign of Jonah*, pp. 95, 106, suggests that Luke applies the saying to Jesus' preaching activity but does not note the parallel with 13:32–35.

25. Marshall, *Luke*, p. 485.

26. Rengstorf, *Das Evangelium nach Lukas*, p. 151; Higgins, *Jesus and the Son of Man*, p. 138.

27. Contra Lührmann, *Die Redaktion der Logienquelle*, pp. 40f.; see n. 24 in chapter 7 below. Edwards, *The Sign of Jonah*, p. 95, regards Jesus' resurrection as included with his prophetic preaching in Luke's understanding of the saying.

Pharisees (11:33—12:3). The antagonism of Israel's religious leaders will eventually be turned against Jesus' followers, who will then be pressed to confess or deny Jesus publicly (12:4–12).

This verse adds nothing to Luke's christological material, since it so closely parallels 9:26. As in the earlier passage, "the Son of man" functions for Luke as a surrogate for "I." Jesus' future role of "confessing" before angels those who have confessed him before others is not explicitly defined; we do not know whether this saying, or, more precisely, Luke's use of this saying, conceives the role as that of a judge or that of a heavenly witness.[28] A similar ambiguity is present at 13:25–27, where the eschatological "master of the house" refuses to open the door to evildoers who claim his acquaintance, saying, "I do not know you, where you are from." In both passages, as E. Schweizer has argued, we may be dealing with a tradition that viewed Jesus as a heavenly witness, ascribing to God the function of Judge.[29] In any event, there can be no doubt that Luke, in taking the saying from his source, understood "the Son of man" here, as everywhere, as Jesus' self-designation. He has not used it primarily as a way of referring to Jesus' future heavenly glory. It sharpens the contrast between present humility and future glory as little here as does the emphatic "I" (*kagō*) in the Matthean parallel (Mt. 10:32).[30] The saying declares: "Be faithful to me when you are persecuted, because I am the one who will testify on behalf of my followers in the heavenly court."

> **Lk. 12:10** And every one who speaks a word against the Son of man will be forgiven; but he who blasphemes against the Holy Spirit will not be forgiven.

The earlier history of this saying and its relationship to the parallels in Mt. 12:32 and Mk. 3:28f. have been the subject of much discussion, to which reference will be made in later chapters.[31] At this point it is sufficient to note that, whatever its original location in Luke's source, it now immediately follows the saying that promises that Jesus, who calls himself the Son of man, will acknowledge before angels those who acknowledge him before other people. That is to say, whether or not Luke was the one

---

28. See above, n. 18.
29. Schweizer, "Der Menschensohn," p. 194.
30. For a different view, cf. Marshall, "The Synoptic Son of Man Sayings in Recent Discussion," p. 345.
31. For a recent review of the discussion, see Marshall, *Luke*, pp. 516–19.

who brought these sayings together, as they now stand in his Gospel they interpret each other.[32]

Accordingly, if one is tempted to assume that an earlier view that treated "the Son of man" as a title of heavenly dignity persisted in Luke's appropriation of 12:8, this assumption should be dispelled by 12:10, where "the Son of man," as is generally conceded, must refer to the earthly Jesus.[33] I. H. Marshall, adhering to the view that for Luke "the Son of man" was a recognizable title of dignity, finds it inconceivable that Luke could have understood the saying as proclaiming that slander against Jesus "as the 'Son of man' " was forgivable because his glory was hidden.[34] But this is precisely Luke's view, as expressed in Acts 3:17ff., 13:27ff., and in Luke 23:34a, if this belongs in Luke's original text: it is possible for those who have opposed Jesus (whether they have encountered the historical Jesus or not) to repent and receive forgiveness in his name.[35] It is not at all likely that Luke understood "the Son of man" as here referring to Jesus' heavenly glory. First, it is improbable that blasphemy against the Lord sitting at the right hand of God would appear to Luke as more excusable than blasphemy against the Holy Spirit, especially since the Spirit is linked so closely with the glorified Christ in Acts (2:33; 16:6f.). Second, from Luke's point of view it is unlikely that the opponents would be tempted to blaspheme the exalted Christ (much less the heavenly Son of man conceived as distinct from Christ!), since for them Jesus was nothing more than a dead human being. No, we must concur with Bultmann that in this saying, whatever its origin, "the Son of man" is a way of referring to the human Jesus.[36]

Because both Matthew and Mark place the saying in the context of the Beelzebul controversy, we are apt to regard it even in Luke as alluding to the failure to perceive that the Holy Spirit is active in Jesus' ministry. In view of the persecution context in which Luke places the saying, however, it is more likely that he takes it as referring to the failure of the persecutors to perceive that the Holy Spirit empowers Jesus' followers to confess him boldly before hostile audiences. The opponents can be forgiven for making derogatory remarks about Jesus, whom they have probably never met

32. According to Tödt, *Son of Man,* p. 272 n. 1, it was Luke who transferred the saying to this location because of his failure to perceive its original meaning.
33. Ibid., p. 119.
34. Marshall, *Luke,* pp. 517f.; he concedes, however, that "the tension between v. 8 and v. 10a may not have appeared so great to Luke" (p. 519).
35. Cf. Tödt, *Son of Man,* p. 119 n. 5. An excellent discussion of the text-critical problems regarding Lk. 23:34a is provided by Marshall, *Luke,* pp. 467f., who favors its inclusion on the basis of internal evidence.
36. Bultmann, *History,* pp. 131, 149.

(note the future tense *erei*); such ignorance is forgivable. If, however, they speak blasphemously by denying the Spirit's manifestation in the charismatic *apologia* presented by the Christian defendants and attempt to dissuade others from being convicted by the truth of the kerygma, they will render account.

If this analysis correctly perceives Luke's intention in placing (or retaining) the saying in this context, further confirmation is provided that he understood "the Son of man" in 12:8 as a way of referring to *Jesus*, not as the designation of a heavenly figure whose role Jesus would fulfill.

> **Lk. 12:40** You also must be ready; for the Son of man is coming at an hour you do not expect.

This saying is placed by Luke in the midst of extensive material concerning preparing oneself for the kingdom (12:13–48). As in Matthew (24:43f.), it is attached to the saying about the unanticipated thief. In Luke, however, these conjoined sayings serve jointly as the interpretation of the parable of the expectant servants who stay awake to welcome their master (*kyrios*) as he returns from a wedding feast. As in 9:26f., the coming of the kingdom is here signaled by the coming of the Son of man, and, as in the earlier passage, Luke's context makes it clear that this is not the first appearance of the Son of man but his *return*. For Luke the saying speaks not of the advent of a heavenly figure never before experienced but of the return of Jesus of Nazareth.[37]

> **Lk. 17:22** The days are coming when you will desire to see one of the days of the Son of man, and you will not see it.
>
> **Lk. 17:24** For as the lightning flashes and lights up the sky from one side to the other, so will the Son of man be in his day.
>
> **Lk. 17:26** As it was in the days of Noah, so will it be in the days of the Son of man.
>
> **Lk. 17:30** So will it be on the day when the Son of man is revealed.

Luke places these sayings in a private discourse to the disciples that is prompted by a question of the Pharisees concerning when the kingdom of God will come (17:20). No attempt will be made here to deal with

---

37. Jeremias, *Parables*, p. 55, finds evidence that the parable has been allegorized so as to apply it to Jesus' return.

the thorny problem of which segments of this discourse derive from the source common to Matthew and Luke, which from a special source (or perhaps an expanded form of Q unknown to Matthew), and which from Lukan redaction.[38] For our purposes it is sufficient to observe that in Luke's context all four refer to Jesus' return in apocalyptic glory. In this eschatological discourse there is not the slightest redactional hint that Luke was aware of the possibility that "the Son of man" had once connoted a heavenly figure distinct from Jesus, with whom Jesus had been identified by Christian faith after the resurrection. On the contrary, Lukan redaction assumes that "the Son of man" was the self-designation of the earthly Jesus and recognizable as such to friend and foe.

This conclusion is evidenced by the careful way in which Luke guards the messianic secret in this context. The Pharisees ask about the time of the kingdom's arrival and are told only that it will be a public event, not a hidden manifestation requiring investigation or precise identification (17:20f.).[39] Nothing is said to the opponents about the coming of the Son of man, although this information would have been fully appropriate had Luke conceived the term as a well-known designation for a future heavenly judge distinct from Jesus. Since, however, Luke has employed the term from 5:24 on as Jesus' public self-designation, uttered in the hearing of Pharisees as well as of disciples and neutral observers, it is important for Luke's presentation that sayings referring to *Jesus'* return in glory not be heard by unbelieving ears. Thus a careful note of the change of audience is made in v. 22a before Jesus speaks of the coming Son of man.

This understanding is then reinforced redactionally by Luke's insertion of his third passion prediction between two future Son of man sayings. Verse 25 is peculiar to the Third Gospel and is probably Luke's own creation, based on the first prediction at 9:22.[40] It employs "the Son of man" indirectly by means of a pronominal reference to the preceding verse. Had Luke intended to distinguish the earthly Jesus from his future role "as the Son of man," he could have done so by switching to first-person language

38. Cf. Marshall, *Luke*, pp. 652–64.

39. Klostermann, *Das Lukasevangelium*, p. 175; Schmid, *Das Evangelium nach Lukas*, p. 274. Marshall, *Luke*, p. 655, prefers to take the saying as referring to the presence of the kingdom of God in the ministry of Jesus, as in 11:20. This is certainly a more natural reading of 17:20f. taken in isolation, but since Luke employs these verses as the introduction to an eschatological discourse, a future reference is more probable. Cf. Conzelmann, *The Theology of St. Luke*, pp. 122f.; Noack, *Das Gottesreich bei Lukas*, p. 41; Schnackenburg, "Der eschatologische Abschnitt Lk. 17,20–37," pp. 214f.

40. Bultmann, *History*, p. 122; Tödt, *Son of Man*, p. 107; Schnackenburg, "Der eschatologische Abschnitt Lk 17,20–37," p. 222; G. Schneider, " 'Der Menschensohn' in der lukanischen Christologie," p. 275.

for the passion prediction, saying in effect: "But before the glorious Son of man can come, *I* must suffer many things." By electing instead to employ the third-person pronoun, Luke makes it abundantly clear to his readers that the one who will come in glory is none other than the one who must first die. For Luke "the Son of man" is not an apocalyptic title that has been appropriated for Jesus but a name for the earthly Jesus that can then be used of the returning Lord.

In this context v. 22 does not look backward to the time of Jesus' earthly ministry, when repentance was a possibility for the Pharisees; in Luke's presentation it is not addressed to the opponents.[41] Nor does it speak of a wistful remembering of the earthly life of Jesus on the part of his disciples.[42] It refers rather to the yearning of the faithful in the midst of trials and afflictions, as they earnestly desire that their salvation appear. This understanding is indicated not only by the future orientation of the Pharisees' question but also by the allusions to the future coming of the Son of man in the following verses. For Luke the purpose of the saying is to prepare Jesus' followers for an extended period of waiting, during which there will be false alarms concerning the arrival of the Messiah. They are not to be seduced by their fervent hope into being deluded by false prophets who proclaim that the Messiah has already arrived and is in hiding. When Jesus returns with full messianic glory, there will be no hiddenness. It will be a public event, fully visible and recognizable to opponents and believers alike.

"In the days of the Son of man" in v. 26 has not the same reference as the comparable phrase in v. 22. Although the saying may perhaps have originally referred to the days of Jesus' prophetic ministry, for Luke the reference is unmistakably to the future.[43] The time alluded to, however, is not the days after Jesus' return, the days of salvation (as in v. 22), but rather the days just before the glorious return (a similarly inexact use of the plural "days" is found in 9:51). The inexactitude is corrected in v. 30, where the singular *hēmera* is used for the time of the revealing of the Son

41. Schweizer, "Der Menschensohn," p. 190, suggests the possibility that 17:22 originally referred to the time of Jesus' ministry.

42. Grundmann, *Das Evangelium nach Lukas*, p. 343, alludes to the disciples' remembrance of their experiences with Jesus but correctly perceives that the reference here is to the future. Leaney, *A Commentary on the Gospel according to St. Luke*, pp. 68–72, argues that "the days of the Son of man" are occasions of special revelations of Jesus, such as the transfiguration and the appearances to Stephen and Paul. He apparently assumes, nonetheless, that the desire of the disciples to which v. 22 alludes is directed to a future rather than a past revelation.

43. Schweizer, "Der Menschensohn," p. 190, argues that v. 26, like v. 22, referred originally to Jesus' ministry.

of man.[44] It is to be noted that the use of the passive *apokalyptetai* ("is revealed") does not in itself imply that the subject is a divine being. Paul speaks of the future revelation of the sons of God (Rom. 8:19). In 2 Thess. 2:3, 6, 8 there is reference to the revealing of the "man of lawlessness," who, despite his apocalyptic significance, is apparently conceived as a historical figure. The use of this verb in Lk. 17:30, therefore, says nothing about the nature or function of the one who will be revealed but implies only that the revealing event belongs to the apocalyptic denouement.

Lk. 18:8b Nevertheless, when the Son of man comes, will he find faith on earth?

Despite determined efforts on the part of scholars to understand this saying in its context, it is difficult to suppress the suspicion that it is a gloss that was added by a pessimistic scribe at a later date.[45] In its present form and context the question appears to be concerned not with the faith or faithfulness of individuals but with faith as a corporate, worldwide phenomenon (*tēn pistin epi tēs gēs*). The question implies, first, that such faith is currently extant and, second, that there will be sufficient time before the Son of man comes for this faith to be eroded to the vanishing point; because of persecution, heresy, or simply "the cares of this world," the faithful church may disappear. Such pessimism seems far removed from Luke's sources and from Luke-Acts itself, which throbs with the triumphalism of the gentile expansion of the church. It is possible that the reference to the crying out of the elect in v. 7 may have suggested the

---

44. Tödt, *Son of Man,* p. 52, sees a relationship between the day of the Son of man and the day of Yahweh announced by the prophets; cf. Catchpole, "The Son of Man's Search for Faith (Luke XVIII 8b)," p. 85. It is to be noted, however, that the phrase "the day of the Son of man" does not occur here or elsewhere in the New Testament, whereas the phrase "the day of the Lord" is found (1 Thess. 5:2; 2 Thess. 2:2). We must not assume, therefore, that "the day" of the Son of man's appearing is primarily judicial in connotation; a nonjudicial view is presented in 1 Thess. 4:16f.

45. The view that v. 8b is a Lukan creation has claimed a host of adherents; cf. Bultmann, *History,* p. 175. Jeremias, who espoused this position in the earlier editions of his *Parables,* more recently urged its authenticity as a saying of Jesus (Eng. rev. ed., p. 155). Jeremias is supported by Catchpole (see preceding note) and opposed by G. Schneider, *Parusiegleichnisse im Lukas-Evangelium,* pp. 75f. Creed, *The Gospel according to St. Luke,* p. 224, taking *tēn pistin* as the faith of the Christian church, proposes that the saying "echoes the anxiety of a church leader distressed at the inroads of strange teachings." If such anxiety can be ascribed to Luke, the sole supporting evidence, as far as I can see, is Acts 20:29f. (a more optimistic perspective on the threat of heresy is provided in the treatment of Simon of Samaria, Acts 8:18–24); Schmid, *Das Evangelium nach Lukas,* p. 280, points to the parallel in Mt. 24:12. That a delayed Parousia is implied by v. 8b is cogently argued by Grässer, *Parusieverzögerung,* p. 38.

primitive ejaculation *maranatha* to the mind of Luke or the glossator and thus have occasioned this allusion to Jesus' return. These suggestions, however, do not adequately account for the pessimism.

In any event, "the Son of man" does not here function differently than in 17:22–30; it serves as a recognized way of referring to Jesus, who will return from heaven to earth. No allusion to Jewish apocalyptic as such is here discernible; it can be adequately understood as the expression of Christian apocalyptic.

> **Lk. 18:31–33** Behold, we are going up to Jerusalem, and everything that is written of the Son of man by the prophets will be accomplished. For he will be delivered to the Gentiles and will be mocked and shamefully treated and spit upon, they will scourge him and kill him, and on the third day he will rise.

This fourth passion prediction, paralleling the third in Matthew (20:17–19) and Mark (10:32–34), departs from the parallels not only by omitting all reference to the Jewish opponents but also, more significantly, by two additions expressive of Lukan theology: (1) "and everything that is written of the Son of man by the prophets will be accomplished"; (2) "But they understood none of these things; this saying was hid from them, and they did not grasp what was said" (v. 34). The second addition is, of course, the amplification of a Markan theme (Mk. 9:32) that Luke has already developed at 9:45. It is reiterated here because it belongs with the theme expressed by the first addition concerning the prophetic predictions of the sufferings of the Son of man. As was noted above in the discussion of 9:44, it is clearly not Dan. 7:13 that Luke has here in mind. He is alluding rather to that great body of proof texts to which reference is made twice in his final chapter: "'Was it not necessary that the Christ should suffer these things and enter into his glory?' And beginning with Moses and all the prophets, he interpreted to them in all the scriptures the things concerning himself" (24:26f.; cf. vv. 44–46). In Luke's view the disciples' inability to understand Jesus' passion predictions was predestined; only through the testimony of the *risen* Christ could their eyes be opened to understand the scriptural prophecies of Christ's sufferings.

Here it is unmistakably transparent that for Luke "the Son of man" is not an apocalyptic title that has been transferred to Jesus but a name that Jesus uses of himself in a variety of contexts, including sayings that speak of the sufferings of the Christ.

Lk. 19:10 For the Son of man came to seek and to save the lost.

Whatever the origin of this verse, Luke obviously means it to be understood as a statement of Jesus about his own ministry.[46] It is a public statement and, like 5:24, apparently bears no relationship to the messianic secret. The *ēlthen* by no means implies the preexistence of the Son of man; Luke has used it in 7:33 of John's prophetic activity. If the words "and to save" are attributable to Lukan redaction, the addition suggests that the evangelist wishes to indicate that Jesus' soteriological role marks him as far more than a prophet.[47] This does not mean, however, that Luke is here explicating the content of "the Son of man." In Luke's usage the term *denotes* Jesus without *connoting* anything regarding Jesus' nature and functions. It is apparently as empty of specific content for Luke as the simple name "Jesus."

Lk. 21:27 And then they will see the Son of man coming in a cloud with power and great glory.

This is the only passage in Luke's Gospel about which it can be said with any degree of plausibility that the term "the Son of man" occurs in association with an allusion to Dan. 7:13. As we shall see presently, the allusion to Daniel found in Matthew and Mark in Jesus' reply to the high priest is missing from Luke's version. Even respecting 21:27, however, one must raise questions concerning the alleged reference to Daniel. Whereas the Synoptic parallels have the plural "clouds" as found in Daniel, Luke employs the singular, a variant that apparently reflects no extant text of Dan. 7:13. The singular does, however, correspond to the *nephelē* of the ascension of Jesus as depicted by Luke in Acts 1:9, and thus to the promise attributed to the two men in white robes: "This Jesus who was taken up from you into heaven will come in the same way as you saw him go into heaven" (1:11). Apparently following Mark, Luke employs *en* (the Greek texts of Daniel have either *epi* or *meta*; cf. Mt. 24:30) and omits *tou ouranou* (contrast Mt. 24:30). It must also be observed that there is not a single quotation from Daniel in either Luke or Acts. The proposed allusions to

46. The Son of man saying that appears in many manuscripts at Lk. 9:56 is undoubtedly a gloss formulated on the basis of 19:10; it manifests no independent perception of the meaning of "the Son of man."

47. Cf. Arens, *The ēlthon-Sayings,* p. 168.

Daniel listed in the Nestle text are so remote that they cannot be used to demonstrate that Luke was influenced by this apocalypse. It is therefore by no means certain that in this saying Luke intended that it be perceived by his readers as prophesying the fulfillment of the Danielic text. Indeed, it is not impossible that Luke, like some modern scholars, believed that Dan. 7:13 made more sense as a prophecy of the exaltation of Jesus than as a statement about the Parousia.[48]

As we have seen in chapter 1, the use of a cloud as a means of transport in Jewish and Christian literature says nothing about the nature of the person so conveyed. We must not assume, therefore, that in taking over this saying Luke is suggesting that Jesus will *become* the Son of man, who, as a preexistent, heavenly figure, has the right to travel on a cloud. And despite Luke's use of *nephelē* as a symbol of the divine presence at 9:34, his use of the same word in Acts 1:9 gives no hint of a theophany. Consequently, if we are justified in perceiving here an allusion to the numinous presence of Deity, it is because of the associations invoked by "power" and "great glory" rather than the use of "cloud" in isolation from these other motifs.[49]

Although the reason for the omission is obscure, Luke's pericope makes no reference to the function to be performed by the Son of man at his coming, whereas the Synoptic parallels (Mt. 24:31; Mk. 13:27) state that he will send out the (Matthew: his) angels to gather the elect. Perhaps Luke's mention of the "redemption" of Jesus' followers in the next verse is simply his way of summarizing this element of the prediction. At any rate Luke, in agreement with Matthew and Mark, makes not the slightest suggestion in this context that the Son of man comes for judgment. Contra Tödt, it is most unlikely that Luke suppresses the reference to the angels because he wishes to present the Son of man as advocate and intercessor instead of judge.[50] Luke elsewhere makes it perfectly clear that he regards Jesus as the eschatological judge (Acts 10:42; 17:31). In view of Luke's adherence to this belief, it is especially noteworthy that in this most apocalyptic of all his Son of man passages the alleged Jewish apocalyptic tradition of the heavenly judge known as the Son of man leaves no mark! Here as always in Luke "the Son of man" is simply Jesus' self-designation. The reference is to Jesus' return as glorified Messiah, as initially predicted at 9:26.

---

48. Glasson, *The Second Advent*, pp. 63–68; J. A. T. Robinson, *Jesus and His Coming*, p. 45.
49. For a different opinion, see Marshall, *Luke*, p. 776.
50. Tödt, *Son of Man*, p. 98.

Lk. 21:36 But watch at all times, praying that you may have strength to escape all these things that will take place, and to stand before the Son of man.

If Tödt is correct in his view that this saying is the evangelist's own creation, it may be especially significant for a proper understanding of Luke's use of "the Son of man."[51] It is obvious that the verb "stand" can be employed in a judicial context with reference to the posture of those who must appear before a judge (regardless of whether the eventual verdict will be condemnation or acquittal).[52] It has been argued that the verb should be so construed here: the saying identifies the Son of man as the eschatological judge as conceived by the Similitudes of Enoch.[53]

Before this possibility is elevated to the status of probability, opposing evidence must be considered. In eschatological contexts "stand" often has a very different meaning. Mal. 3:2, "But who can endure the day of his coming, and who can stand when he appears?" was surely more significant in early Christian thinking than is evidenced by extant allusions, since it is contiguous with 3:1, which is cited in the Synoptic tradition (Mt. 11:10; Mk. 1:2; Lk. 7:27). This text undoubtedly underlies Rev. 6:17, "For the great day of their wrath has come, and who is able to stand?"[54] The use of "stand" for survival or persistence is, of course, well established for the Old Testament.[55]

Particularly instructive is the use of the verb in the Similitudes of Enoch. In several passages it denotes the posture of the angels, who stand before the Lord of Spirits (1 En. 40:1; 47:3; 60:2). The wicked, on the other hand, will not be able to stand in his presence: "And on the day of their trouble there will be rest on the earth, and they will fall down before him and not rise; and there will be no one who will take them with his hands and raise them, for they denied the Lord of Spirits and his Messiah" (48:10, Knibb's translation). In Knibb's rendering of 50:4 it is explicitly stated: ". . . and before his glory iniquity will not (be able to) stand at his judgment: he who

---

51. Ibid. p. 97; similarly G. Schneider, "'Der Menschensohn' in der lukanischen Christologie," pp. 269f. The saying is accepted as genuine by Colpe, "Ho huios tou anthrōpou," TDNT 8, pp. 434f., and Marshall, *Luke*, p. 783.
52. Cf. Mt. 27:11 and Colpe, "Ho huios tou anthrōpou," TDNT 8, p. 434 n. 260.
53. Schweizer, "Der Menschensohn," p. 192; Marshall, *Luke*, p. 783.
54. Plummer, *S. Luke*, p. 487, cites Rev. 6:17 in his comments on 21:36, and suggests that *stathēnai* should be rendered "to hold your place." Schmid, *Das Evangelium nach Lukas*, p. 315, also rejects the judicial interpretation of "stand before."
55. Pss. 76:7; 130:3; 147:17; Nah. 1:6. For a positive use of the verb in connection with standing before a king, cf. Dan. 1:5, 19. Cf. also Rom. 14:4.

does not repent before him will be destroyed."[56] In the judgment scene of chapter 62, it is indeed declared that the wicked rulers of the earth will "stand up" and will behold how the Elect One sits on the throne of his glory, but it is not explicitly stated that they will stand before the judge. A few lines later, however, we read: ". . . and all the chosen will stand before him on that day. And all the mighty kings, and the exalted, and those who rule the dry ground, will fall down before him on their faces and worship; and they will set their hope upon that Son of man, and will entreat him, and will petition for mercy from him" (62:8f., Knibb's translation).

Does this mean that Lk. 21:36 reflects the same apocalyptic conception as the Similitudes, according to which God's deputy at the last judgment is a preexistent figure entitled "the Son of man"? This conclusion is dubious. Luke, as we have seen, shows no interest in the preexistence of Jesus. We may assume that he would have been more sympathetic to the view that regarded "that son of man" as a human being (Enoch) who had been appointed to fulfill this eschatological role (1 Enoch 70f.). Had he been aware of such thinking, however, he must surely have polemicized against it, arguing that Jesus, not Enoch, would function "as the Son of man." Nowhere in Luke is there the slightest hint of such a concern.

In his discussion of this verse Tödt argues that Luke does not regard the Son of man as judge but rather as advocate and intercessor for Christians before God, noting that in none of the Lukan Son of man sayings is the judicial function (condemning or acquitting) mentioned.[57] This comment is helpful insofar as it reminds us that in none of the Lukan sayings does "the Son of man" unambiguously connote "eschatological judge." It is not strictly accurate, however, inasmuch as Luke indisputably regards Jesus, who calls himself the Son of man, as the man appointed by God to be judge of the living and the dead (Acts 10:42; 17:31). What Tödt's observation demonstrates is that Luke does not regard Jesus as the eschatological judge on the basis of a prior conviction that "Jesus is the Son of man."

Whether or not Luke had Jesus' judicial role in mind in 21:36, the emphasis surely lies elsewhere. It is unlikely that he would urge believers to pray for the privilege of being defendants at the divine bar. They are to pray rather for strength to remain faithful throughout the messianic woes and thus receive the privilege of enjoying the presence of their glorified Lord.

56. Knibb, *The Ethiopic Book of Enoch*, p. 135. Charles's translation does not employ "stand."
57. Tödt, *Son of Man*, p. 98.

Lk. 22:22 For the Son of man goes as it has been determined; but woe to that man by whom he is betrayed!

This pronouncement of woe upon the betrayer is found in all three Synoptic Gospels, but Luke's version is shorter, omitting the second occurrence of "the Son of man." Whereas Mt. 26:24 and Mk. 14:21 contain the clause *kathōs gegraptai peri autou*, Luke has instead *kata to hōrismenon*, which more closely resembles his formulation in Acts 2:23. There is no change in meaning, however; for Luke the sufferings foreordained for the Christ are prophesied in the Scriptures (24:25–27).

This passion saying belongs with the others we have examined as far as the use of "the Son of man" is concerned. Nothing in the text hints at a heavenly origin for the one so designated.

Lk. 22:48 Judas, would you betray the Son of man with a kiss?

Whether this statement comes from Luke's special source or is his own creation, it belongs with the passion sayings.[58] It witnesses to the fact that at this point in the gospel story the fulfillment of the passion predictions is initiated. We are probably to regard it as a public statement, not as a private communication heard only by Judas. As such it belongs with the other public Son of man sayings in Luke that appear to have no bearing on the messianic secret. It does not occur to Luke to have Jesus' enemies report at the trial before the council that Jesus had claimed messianic status by applying to himself the title "the Son of man." Neither here nor elsewhere does the term bear such a meaning for Luke.

Lk. 22:69 But from now on the Son of man shall be seated at the right hand of the power of God.

The source-critical problems encountered in this passage are profound. The earlier consensus that Luke's account of the trial before the Sanhedrin is a redacted version of Mark's trial narrative has been chal-

---

58. Rehkopf, *Die lukanische Sonderquelle*, pp. 40–56, argues that this saying derives from Luke's special source. More probably it represents Lukan redaction of Mk. 14:41, 45; cf. Tödt, *Son of Man*, p. 152, and G. Schneider, " 'Der Menschensohn' in der lukanischen Christologie," p. 271.

lenged at a number of points.[59] It is not impossible that Luke was here following a source independent of Mark. On either hypothesis, however, it remains true that Luke's version of this Son of man saying omits any allusion to Daniel. If we postulate dependence on Mark, he has intentionally deleted the allusion to Daniel here as in 21:27. In this case, as Conzelmann proposes, Luke may have wished to correct what he perceived as a mistaken prophecy in Mark: the members of the Sanhedrin had died without seeing the Parousia of Jesus.[60] If his source did not contain the allusion to Daniel, we have the possibility to reckon with that the earliest church did not derive its use of "the Son of man" from an exegesis of Daniel 7.[61] In any event, it cannot be argued that Luke perceived a primary relationship between Jesus' self-designation and the Danielic text.

In all three Synoptic Gospels an affirmative answer is given by Jesus to the question, "Are you the Christ?"[62] In Luke, however, the indirect acceptance of the title (*humeis legete hoti egō eimi*, v. 70) is not immediately forthcoming but is preceded by a statement that implies a messianic claim without directly stating it: "If I tell you, you will not believe, and if I ask you [whence my authority derives, as in 20:3–7], you will refuse to respond."[63] At this point the crucial testimony is introduced: "But from now on the Son of man shall be seated at the right hand of the power of God." The context makes it perfectly clear that for Luke "the Son of man" is *not* a messianic title designating a heavenly figure with whom Jesus identifies himself. In this case a simple statement *about* the Son of man would not suffice to convict Jesus; it would be necessary for him to confess, "I am the Son of man." This the Lukan text does not do.

On the assumption of the currency of "the Son of man" as a messianic title, the members of the Sanhedrin would have heard from Jesus the innocent statement that the Son of man, whom his opponents might also have expected as heavenly redeemer, was to be enthroned at God's right

59. Tyson, "The Lukan Version of the Trial of Jesus," pp. 250–58; Taylor, *The Passion Narrative of St. Luke*; Catchpole, "The Problem of the Historicity of the Sanhedrin Trial," pp. 64f. While Catchpole regards it as demonstrable that Luke is following a special source for most of the trial scene, he nevertheless believes that 22:69 is simply a redacted version of Mk. 14:62.

60. Conzelmann, *Theology of St. Luke*, p. 116; cf. pp. 56f.

61. Cf. Perrin, "Mark 14:62: The End Product of a Christian Pesher Tradition?" pp. 150–55; reprinted in his *Modern Pilgrimage*, pp. 10–18, supplemented with a postscript, pp. 18–22.

62. Cf. Catchpole, "The Answer of Jesus to Caiaphas (Matt. xxvi.64)," pp. 213–26, and literature there cited.

63. Flender, *St. Luke: Theologian of Redemptive History*, pp. 45f., urges that Luke here wished to present a two-stage Christology distinguishing between "Christ" and "Son of God." This separation is most unlikely in view of 4:41 and the positive use of *Christos* in Acts.

hand. At most this could be taken as a pronouncement of the prophet from Nazareth that God was about to initiate the eschatological judgment (cf. 1 En. 69:26–29). Such is clearly not the force of the passage. The narrative assumes that Jesus is speaking about himself, not about some other figure, and that this self-reference is obvious to the members of the council. That is, the audience does not hear Jesus say, "From now on the eschatological judge will be at God's right hand," but rather, "From now on I, Jesus of Nazareth, will be at God's right hand." Just as the term served as Jesus' self-designation throughout Luke's Gospel without betraying the messianic secret, so now. Only such a perception of Jesus' response can be intended by Luke in view of the next question he attributes to the interrogators. They do not immediately respond, "What further testimony do we need? We have heard it ourselves from his own lips" (v. 71), because *in applying the term "the Son of man" to himself Jesus has made no explicit claim to messiahship*: the *implicit* claim lies not here but in the prophecy that he will sit at God's right hand. Consequently the hearers must still ask, "Are *you* [note the emphatic *su*] accordingly the Son of God, that is, the Messiah?"[64] Only on the basis of his affirmative answer to this question does the council determine that it has a case against Jesus that can be brought to the governor (23:2).

> **Lk. 24:6f.** Remember how he told you, while he was still in Galilee, that the Son of man must be delivered into the hands of sinful men, and be crucified, and on the third day rise.

Because this verse is simply an echoing of the passion predictions, nothing new is added relative to Luke's use of "the Son of man" except for the fact that the statement is here attributed to someone other than Jesus.[65] Since *ton huion tou anthrōpou* precedes the *hoti* clause, its syntactic connection is ambiguous; it may be simply the accusative subject of the infinitive in the *hoti* clause, presented in anticipatory fashion for emphasis, or it may be an accusative of respect to be taken with the participle that precedes it. If the latter suggestion, which proposes a more natural syntax, were accepted, the translation of v. 7 would be: "saying concerning the Son of man, 'It is necessary to be delivered into the hands of sinful men. . . .' "[66] In this case *ho huios tou anthrōpou* has made a first

---

64. Cf. Conzelmann, *Theology of St. Luke*, p. 84: "These verses are meant to set out explicitly the fundamental identity of the current eschatological titles.'" Cf. pp. 170f. Conzelmann is opposed by Tödt, *Son of Man*, p. 103.
65. The only addition is the specific reference to the crucifixion.
66. Cf. Rengstorf, *Das Evangelium nach Lukas*, p. 278.

step in the transition from being strictly limited to Jesus' lips to being a name for Jesus that can be used by others.

This suggests that, while Luke is thoroughly conversant with the well-established tradition that "the Son of man" is a name that Jesus used of himself and not a title that others could use in addressing him or in speaking of his significance to others, he is either not familiar with the peculiarities of the underlying Semitic expression that dictated this restriction, or, working with the phrase in the Greek medium, he feels no longer bound by this tradition. Luke's readiness for a less restricted usage is indicated by the one instance of the phrase in Acts.

> **Acts 7:55f.** But he, full of the Holy Spirit, gazed into heaven and saw the glory of God, and Jesus standing at the right hand of God; and he said, "Behold, I see the heavens opened, and the Son of man standing at the right hand of God."

Stephen's statement, with its allusion to Jesus' position at God's right hand, may reflect the Lukan version of Jesus' response to the council (Lk. 22:69).[67] It is unique, however, in its assumption that it is linguistically possible for Stephen to speak of Jesus in this way.

That "the Son of man" is here simply a name for Jesus is made clear by the context. Stephen is not perceived as making the statement, "Behold, I see the heavenly judge at God's right hand." Such a declaration of Enochian theology would not provide adequate motivation—from Luke's perspective—for the murderous attack that follows.[68] Nor is it possible to twist the words of Stephen so as to make them say, "Jesus is the Son of man!" The words attributed to the martyr simply repeat what the narrator has already stated in v. 55: "But he . . . gazed into heaven and saw . . . *Jesus* at the right hand of God." The author intends that Stephen's audience hear him say precisely this: "I see Jesus at God's right hand." Whatever may have been the actual historical circumstances, the narrator (whether Luke or his source) regards the murder as provoked by Stephen's public confession that Jesus of Nazareth has been exalted through death and resurrection to be God's right-hand man, that is, the Messiah.

The fact that in this verse "the Son of man" is used by someone other than Jesus, completing the transition to which Lk. 24:7 perhaps witnesses,

---

67. Cf. Conzelmann, *Die Apostelgeschichte*, p. 51. Tödt, *Son of Man,* pp. 303–5, argues that Acts 7:56 is "predominantly a pre-Lukan formulation."

68. Contra Teeple, "The Origin of the Son of Man Christology," pp. 214, 216, 242. Cf. Leivestad, "Exit the Apocalyptic Son of Man," p. 253.

thus does not give any support to the argument that Luke perceived the term as a meaningful title. It is precisely because it does not function for Luke as a traditional Jewish title comparable to "the Messiah" but rather serves consistently as a recognizable name for Jesus that it can be used so unambiguously in this narrative.

Conclusion

Our examination of all instances of "the Son of man" in Luke-Acts has now been completed. The results fully corroborate Bultmann's view of Luke's understanding of the phrase: ". . . it is significant that for these later evangelists [Matthew and Luke] the original meaning of the title is lost. . . ."[69] Bultmann here explicitly acknowledges that his hypothesis concerning the original meaning of the phrase as an apocalyptic title cannot be demonstrated on the basis of Luke's use but only by peering behind Luke and the other evangelists to the earliest stage of the tradition.

If we are justified in concluding that Luke-Acts shows no awareness of the alleged apocalyptic connotation, we are bound to ask: What content did "the Son of man" possess for Luke? The examination undertaken above has, regrettably, produced no answer to this question. There is, for example, no evidence in Lukan redaction that for him "the Son of man" connotes divine authority.[70] While Lk. 5:24 explicitly introduces the question of authority, the text and context by no means require that the phrase "the Son of man" in and of itself connote "One possessing divine authority." What the passage declares is that *Jesus* possesses divine authority. For Luke, Jesus possesses this authority whenever he speaks and acts; it underlies his "I" statements (e.g., 11:20) no less than his Son of man sayings. There is therefore no justification for arguing that "the Son of man" connotes authority in the Third Gospel.

In Luke's use the phrase shines like the moon with no light of its own but only the reflection of its various contexts. Thus the phrase appears in some sayings to speak of the humanity of Jesus (e.g., 9:58), but since Luke shows no interest in the preexistence of the Christ, there is no reason to argue that the term here designates the humanity of the Incarnate One as in patristic usage. Similarly, in apocalyptic sayings it appears to connote "the apocalyptic redeemer," but, as this chapter has attempted to demonstrate, this is again to read the meaning too directly from the immediate context

---

69. Bultmann, *Theology*, vol. 1, p. 30.
70. Contra Tödt, *Son of Man*, pp. 274f.

instead of from Luke-Acts as a whole. None of the Lukan Son of man sayings requires this connotation; all are fully comprehensible in their present context when the phrase is taken simply as a well-known self-designation of Jesus. Conversely, to ascribe such a connotation to the apocalyptic sayings is to freight Luke's Gospel with grievous inconsistency, since he employs the phrase in nonapocalyptic contexts in more than half the instances without betraying any awareness of paradox.

If "the Son of man" had some specific content in Luke's understanding, it seems impossible to retrieve this from his usage. What is demonstrable is that he did not find the term's content of great significance for the communication of the gospel; he did not appropriate it to articulate the soteriological or eschatological meaning of Jesus in the missionary speeches of Acts. Like the proper name "Jesus," the phrase is for Luke completely denotative in function: it points to Jesus without saying anything specific about him.

If this is a correct representation of Luke's use of "the Son of man," we can well understand why his successors in the second century made so little employment of the term. As we saw in chapter 2, it was not because they were so uninterested in apocalyptic that they ignored this phrase; the Didache, for example, concludes with a striking apocalyptic passage, from which "the Son of man" is significantly missing. There is no reason to believe that they found the phrase particularly distasteful either in linguistic form or in its associations. Their avoidance is best understood as the natural result of what we have discovered in Luke-Acts: no significant content was associated with the term, and its denotative function was not needed. We can also understand why, later in the second century, Justin Martyr was able to propose several possible connotations, indicating thereby that there was no established Christian tradition in his day regarding the term's content.[71]

There is thus no sharp discontinuity between Luke and the Apostolic Fathers. If radical discontinuity is to be discovered between an apocalyptic and a nonapocalyptic understanding of the term, that gulf must be sought further back in the tradition. There is no chasm between Ignatius and Luke.

71. See chapter 2 above.

4 | JOHN

The investigation of the meaning of "the Son of man" in the Fourth Gospel is impeded by many problems. Prominent among these is the problem of the Gospel's literary history. Various inconsistencies and abrupt breaks have suggested to scholars that this Gospel took shape in a series of steps or successive editions involving two or more authors.[1] If the disunity is real rather than simply the product of the idiosyncratic literary habits of a single author, we are confronted with the possibility that "the Son of man" does not bear the same significance in every instance because of diverse authorship.

For the purposes of this study it will be necessary to forgo a fresh investigation of the Gospel's literary origins and concentrate instead upon the Gospel as we now have it. Our question is this: Regardless of the prior history of the Johannine material, how does "the Son of man" function in the extant Gospel?

There is general agreement among scholars that, regardless of the literary problem, the predominant Christology of the Fourth Gospel as we now have it is incarnational. That is to say, despite any conjectures we may wish to make about the Christology of earlier strands or stages, the Gospel in its final form intends to present Jesus as the incarnation of God's Word or Son. Various linguistic expressions are adopted in order to give expression to this idea, among which is the motif of descent/ascent. The consensus breaks down, however, as soon as a question is raised concerning the relationship between "the Son of man" and John's incarnational Christology in general and the motif of descent/ascent in particular. Does "the Son of man" serve to point to the preexistence of Jesus?

---

1. The most notable proposals of the last two decades have been those of R. E. Brown, *The Gospel according to John I–XII*, pp. xxxiv–xxxix, and Lindars, *The Gospel of John*, pp. 46–54. For a careful review of these and other recent theories about the composition of John, cf. Kysar, *The Fourth Evangelist and His Gospel*, pp. 10–81.

When we examine recent studies of the Johannine Son of man passages
we find many different suggestions.

1. Many assume that the phrase connotes the same meaning here as it is
alleged to bear in the Similitudes of Enoch—that it designates a preexistent,
transcendent figure whom God appoints to act as eschatological judge.
Some scholars believe that John has taken the phrase from early Christian
tradition with little modification.[2] Others argue that John has radically
transformed it in terms of his realized eschatology.[3]

2. Also widespread is the view that the Johannine Son of man has little
to do with Jewish apocalyptic but derives rather from the conception of
the heavenly Man found in Hellenistic syncretism.[4] Variations of this view
arise in connection with an allegedly apocalyptic saying such as 5:27, which,
according to Bultmann, derives not from John's gnostic source but from
the evangelist or the redactor.[5] Others suggest that John combines wisdom
speculation of Hellenistic Judaism with the Son of man conception of
Jewish apocalyptic.[6]

3. A third view maintains that the Fourth Gospel took the term from
Hellenistic Christianity, in which the phrase had entirely lost its original
eschatological content. In this non-Aramaic environment the term had
already become simply a self-designation of Jesus and was well on its way
to becoming an expression for the humanity of the Son of God.[7]

---

2. See, e.g., Coppens, "Le Fils de l'homme dans l'évangile johannique," pp. 71f., 77; Maddox,
"The Function of the Son of Man in the Gospel of John," pp. 203f.

3. This appears to be the view of R. E. Brown, *John*, pp. cxvii, 220, but cf. p. 345. Perhaps
the most impressive presentation of this position is that of Martyn, *History and Theology in
the Fourth Gospel*, pp. 132f. See also Lindars, "The Son of Man in the Johannine Christology," pp. 58f.; Kinniburgh, "The Johannine 'Son of Man,'" pp. 64–71.

4. Bultmann, *John*, p. 8, maintains that John's Christology has been profoundly influenced
by the myth of the gnostic Redeemer who descends from heaven to bring humans the
saving message. On p. 261, commenting on 5:27, Bultmann writes: "For to the Evangelist, to
whom the title 'Son of Man' is the title of the Revealer who walks this earth in human
form, Jesus, as the 'Son of Man,' who is 'exalted,' is of course also the Judge; but this
statement itself would have to be justified, and could not be advanced as an explanation
of something else." For C. H. Dodd the origins of the Johannine Son of man lay not in
Gnosticism but in Hermetism and other developments from Platonism that speculated on a
divine Anthropos; cf. his *Interpretation of the Fourth Gospel*, pp. 241–49. Among the many
recent adherents of this second view are Barrett, *John*, pp. 60f., and Meeks, *The Prophet-King*,
p. 297. Borgen, "God's Agent in the Fourth Gospel," argues that the sources of the Johannine Son of man are to be found rather in Jewish *merkabah* mysticism than in Hellenistic
syncretism.

5. Bultmann, *John*, p. 260.

6. Braun, "Messie, Logos, et Fils de l'homme," pp. 133–47; Schnackenburg, "Der
Menschensohn im Johannesevangelium," pp. 123–37, especially p. 136; Hamerton-Kelly,
Pre-existence, Wisdom, and the Son of Man, p. 241.

7. C. J. Wright, in Major, Manson, and Wright, *The Mission and Message of Jesus*, p. 683;
Hoskyns, *The Fourth Gospel*, p. 184.

4. A development from this third view is the interpretation that in the Fourth Gospel "the Son of man" has no distinctive content of its own but functions simply as a synonym for "Son of God" and "Son," being employed in place of these for purely stylistic reasons.[8]

5. Another variation of the third option suggests that "the Son of man" is used by John as an ambiguous synonym for "Son of God," "Messiah," and "Christ." There is, it is argued, a kind of messianic secret in the Fourth Gospel also; "the Son of man" is a messianic title whose meaning is hidden from Jesus' audience.[9]

6. Yet another variation maintains that the Fourth Gospel employs the term as a way of referring to the incarnational existence of the Preexistent One. It refers to the humanity of Jesus, but not in the way the simpler *anthrōpos* does; it points to the unique humanity of the Logos-become-flesh.[10]

Because of the complexity of Johannine literary history, none of these six views may do full justice to the phenomenon under investigation. And because John is continually involved in the theological paradox that the man Jesus of Nazareth is the Word-become-flesh, affirmations concerning his divinity and humanity inevitably overlap to some extent. The "I" of Jesus represents at the same time a historical man and a preexistent divine being. There is, therefore, the a priori possibility that a name for this unique one, such as "the Son of God" or "the Son of man," will not refer exclusively to his divinity or his humanity. It is possible that "the Son of man" is for John primarily a way of referring to the transcendent origin of Jesus and yet is used paradoxically in some contexts to refer to the man of flesh and blood, as is argued by some scholars respecting 6:53.[11] The reverse, however, is just as possible. Since, as Tödt has pointed out, the Son of man tradition is never drawn upon in the Synoptic Gospels as a way of referring to the preexistence of Jesus, it cannot be assumed that the author or redactor of John regarded the term as useful in this connection, especially if Bultmann is correct in his claim that the Hellenistic church quickly

8. Freed, "The Son of Man in the Fourth Gospel." According to Dion, "Quelques traits originaux de la conception johannique du Fils de l'homme," in John "the Son of man" has been assimilated to the author's Logos Christology.

9. Smalley, "The Johannine Son of Man Sayings," pp. 298f.

10. Leivestad, "Exit the Apocalyptic Son of Man," pp. 252f.; Ruckstuhl, "Die johanneische Menschensohnforschung, 1957–1969"; Moloney, *The Johannine Son of Man*. Ruckstuhl and Moloney provide valuable surveys and assessments of recent studies of the Johannine Son of man passages.

11. E.g., Higgins, *Jesus and the Son of Man*, p. 174.

forgot the apocalyptic origin of the phrase.[12] In this case the normal use of "son of man" and "sons of men" in the Old Testament would incline a Hellenistic Christian to treat the phrase as a useful way of referring to the humanity of Jesus. Only a careful examination of the Son of man sayings in their contexts will show which of these two possibilities has a better claim to probability.

In view of the danger of prejudicing the case by singling out certain texts as "keys" to the problem, we will again deal with the passages seriatim.

> **Jn. 1:51** Truly, truly, I say to you, you will see the heaven opened, and the angels of God ascending and descending upon the Son of man.

When we consider this first Son of man logion in isolation from the rest of the gospel tradition, it is possible to argue that Jesus is here presented as speaking of a figure other than himself (as has been argued by Bultmann and others respecting Lk. 12:8 and Mk. 8:38).[13] From this perspective Nathanael is given no additional information concerning the significance of Jesus, whom he has just confessed as Son of God and King of Israel, but is promised that he and his fellow disciples will see the Son of man (apocalyptic Son of man or Hellenistic heavenly Man?) in the midst of the angels of God. In view of the way that christological terms are clearly applied to Jesus in John's opening chapter, however, it is surely more probable that "the Son of man" is here intended to be perceived by Nathanael and any other auditors as Jesus' self-designation, as proved to be the case in Luke's use. At the conclusion of this long chapter that introduces the disciples (and the readers) to the significance of Jesus, Jesus himself makes a pronouncement regarding his significance, using "the Son of man" as a recognizable self-designation.

This first Son of man utterance, as we shall see, is characteristic of the instances in John in two respects: it is attributed to Jesus (12:34, as we shall see, is no exception), and is used in a nonkerygmatic way (9:35 is likewise no exception). That is to say, Jesus is not represented in 1:51 as declaring, "You will come to recognize that I am not only the Messiah but also the Son of man." Our tendency to read the statement as if this were its intent derives from the assumption that "the Son of man" functioned for John as

---

12. Tödt, *Son of Man*, pp. 284f. Bultmann's view (*Theology*, vol. 1, p. 30) is shared by Fuller, *Foundations*, p. 229.

13. Bultmann, *History*, pp. 112, 151f. Bultmann is opposed by Leivestad, "Exit the Apocalyptic Son of Man," pp. 261ff.

a messianic title, an assumption that remains to be justified. Until it has been demonstrated that "the Son of man" serves in the Fourth Gospel as a "higher" title than those just employed by Nathanael, it is safer to assume that the focus of revelation in this logion lies not in the application of "the Son of man" to Jesus but in the statement made about the one who calls himself by this name: it will be revealed to Nathanael and others that Jesus of Nazareth is uniquely related to the heavenly world.

Most interpreters approach this verse with the assumption that it is formulated on the basis of Gen. 28:12, which reports Jacob's dream of a ladder extending to heaven, with angels of God ascending and descending upon it. A parting of the exegetical ways then occurs regarding the preposition *epi*. Those who regard the preposition as consciously taken from the Septuagint version of Jacob's dream perceive it as meaning "upon."[14] Accordingly "the Son of man" replaces the ladder and is seen as a bridge joining heaven and earth.

Despite its popularity, there are significant objections to this interpretation. In the first place, the use of such grotesque, apocalyptic imagery as this is not characteristic of the Fourth Gospel.[15] Second, if John had intended this image, it is probable that he would have employed the genitive following *epi* as in the Greek version of Gen. 28:12 (cf. 6:19, where Jesus walks *epi tēs thalassēs*).[16] If it is maintained, despite these objections, that John wishes to present Jesus as Jacob's ladder, the logion nonetheless makes no significant statement about the *nature* of the one so described but focuses rather on a *function* to be performed. It must also be noted that, if this is John's intention, there is not the remotest connection of John's Son of man with the Enochian figure at this initial presentation of the term.

Other interpreters choose to take the *epi* as meaning not "upon" but rather "to," "toward," or "at." In this case the Son of man is not identified with the ladder. He may, however, be identified with Jacob as true Israel, taken in either an individual or a corporate sense. There is also the possibility that the "Jacob" with whom the Son of man is here identified is not

14. Cf. Barrett, *John*, p. 61: "In 1:51 the Son of man himself is the way of angelic traffic between heaven and earth. . . ." A similar opinion is expressed by Hamerton-Kelly, *Preexistence, Wisdom, and the Son of Man*, pp. 228f.

15. Contrast the exuberant imagery of the Gospel of Peter, which describes the resurrected Christ as so tall that his head surpasses the heavens (see Hennecke and Schneemelcher, *New Testament Apocrypha*, vol. 1, p. 186). According to Odeberg, *Third Enoch*, "Introduction," p. 123, Metatron is presented in certain mystical texts as the ladder on which angels are ascending and descending.

16. Cf. Michaelis, "Joh 1,51, Gen 28,12, und das Menschensohn-Problem," col. 572.

the earthly patriarch or the people Israel but Jacob's heavenly alter ego, as
conceived in mystical Judaism.[17] Others propose that the Son of man is to
be related neither to the ladder nor to Jacob but rather to some other
entity mentioned in the context of Gen. 28:12: the Bethel stone, the sanc-
tuary at Bethel, or the *kabod* of God that appeared to Jacob (28:13).[18]

W. Michaelis has argued that exegesis of this verse has gone astray
because it has been too quickly assumed that the logion represents a midrashic use of the Genesis passage; he points to significant motifs of the
Pentateuchal narrative that are missing from our verse.[19] Few exegetes have
shown any inclination to agree with Michaelis, yet a number of scholars
have in fact proceeded as if he were correct. That is, while claiming to be
interpreting the verse on the basis of the Genesis passage, they have not
related the Son of man to the ladder, Jacob, or anything else in the context! It must be noticed that this interpretation leaves all the options open
concerning (1) the nature of the Son of man (human, divine, or incarnate
divine being), (2) the locus of the Son of man at the time of the promised
vision (earth or heaven), and (3) the time of the vision (during Jesus'
earthly life, at the time of the resurrection/exaltation, or at the Parousia).

This is not the place to treat in detail the plethora of proposals that have
been made on the basis of these various options. When the logion is treated
in abstraction, no firm decision is possible concerning the nature of the
figure here identified as the Son of man. It is interesting to note, however,
that some scholars who derive John's use of the term from Jewish apocalyptic or Hellenistic syncretism (whether gnostic or pregnostic), that is,
who regard "the Son of man" as the designation for a heavenly being,
nonetheless believe that this verse speaks of something that happens in
connection with the earthly life of Jesus. Bultmann describes the verse as
presenting "a mythological picture of the uninterrupted communion between Jesus and the Father," that is, between the Father in heaven and
Jesus on earth, a communion that will be manifested in particular in the
working of miracles.[20] Brown similarly sees the point of the logion as

17. Cf. Dodd, *Interpretation*, pp. 245f.; Dahl, "The Johannine Church and History," p. 136;
Borgen, "God's Agent in the Fourth Gospel," pp. 145f.
18. According to Jeremias, "Die Berufung des Nathanael," pp. 2–5, the Son of man is
identified with the Bethel stone. Fritsch, " '. . . videbitis . . . angelos Dei ascendentes et
descendentes . . .' (Io. 1,51)," pp. 1–11, argues that Bethel as the house of God has been
replaced by Jesus, who is the real temple; similarly Davies, *The Gospel and the Land*,
pp. 296–98. Quispel, "Nathanael und der Menschensohn (Joh 1,51)," pp. 281–83, maintains
that in John's midrashic use of Gen. 28:12, the Son of man takes the place of God's *kabod* at
the top of the ladder.
19. See n. 16.
20. Bultmann, *John*, pp. 105f.

describing Jesus as "the locus of divine glory, the point of contact between heaven and earth. The disciples are promised figuratively that they will come to see this; and indeed, at Cana they do see his glory."[21] Michaelis, sharing the view that "the Son of man" was an eschatological title, maintains that it does not function eschatologically in this verse but refers rather to the earthly Jesus: the logion promises a revelation of glory in Jesus' earthly life.[22]

The intuition of these scholars, which at this point opposes the meaning they normally attribute to the phrase, is surely justified contextually. In the context of the first chapter of John, the logion promises Nathanael and his fellow disciples that they will come to a profounder understanding of Jesus' significance as one uniquely related to God and his purpose. It is thus the opened heaven and the movement of the angels that express the point of the verse, not the name "the Son of man"; the latter merely serves to identify Jesus as the person who is related to heaven in this way.

> **Jn. 3:13** And no one has ascended into heaven except he who descended from heaven, the Son of man.

Interpreters commonly take this verse as indicating that John regarded "the Son of man" as the designation of a preexistent divine being.[23] Grammatically, it is natural to take *ho huios tou anthrōpou* as an epexegetical identification of *ho ek tou ouranou katabas*, and in such a way that one might paraphrase: "And no one has ascended into heaven except the Son of man, who previously descended from heaven." It is not surprising that this paraphrase represents the most frequent interpretation. Is there another possibility?

There can be little doubt that this verse has polemical import, comparable probably to that of 1:18. It asserts than no human being has ascended to heaven. Heavenly beings are presumably not in mind; the angels of 1:51 and 20:12 are not restricted in their movements between heaven and earth. Enoch, Moses, and Elijah are not denied a heavenly residence, because in this context the denial is implicitly directed against humans who claim to have ascended to heaven and to have returned with heavenly information—

21. R. E. Brown, *John*, p. 91.
22. Michaelis, "Joh 1,51," cols. 576–78.
23. E.g., Barrett, *John*, pp. 61, 177; Schnackenburg, *John*, vol. 1, pp. 392–94; Marsh, *The Gospel of St. John*, p. 180. Coppens, "Le Fils de l'homme," pp. 66f., insists, contra Ruckstuhl, that this verse affirms the preexistence of the Son of man but then concedes: "Toutefois le Sauveur n'apparaît vraiment comme Fils de l'homme qu' à partir du moment où il est incarné."

the claim asserted by many apocalyptists and by *merkabah* mysticism.[24] Given the polemical intention of the verse, the function of *ei mē* is to contrast the one who descended from heaven as sharply as possible with those humans who claim direct access to heavenly knowledge. A strong argument against treating "the Son of man" as the designation of a heavenly being would thus be provided if we were to take *ei mē* in its normal meaning "except," since the individual so designated represents a true exception to the rule only if he is considered a real human: "No member of the human race except the Son of man has ascended to heaven." If "the Son of man" were here the name for a heavenly being, so that we might substitute "the Logos" or "the heavenly Man," the ascent to heaven would not be in the least distinctive or significant, since angels follow the same itinerary, and the "except" would be meaningless.

There is, however, a serious difficulty with this interpretation. Although John clearly shares the Christian belief that the resurrection of Jesus represents an exaltation to the presence of God, the emphasis in the context is not on the ascension; the heavenly knowledge that Jesus offers Nicodemus derives not from his ascension but from his descent.[25] A reference to Jesus' postmortem ascension would be not only anachronistic at this juncture but pointless, since John presumably does not wish to deny that Enoch, Moses, and Elijah ascended to heaven at the conclusion of their earthly lives.[26]

It is necessary, therefore, to consider an alternative meaning for *ei mē*. E. M. Sidebottom argues that the phrase should be construed as expressing opposition but not exception: "No one has ascended to heaven but one has descended."[27] C. F. D. Moule, while concurring that *ei mē* need not mean "except," objects to Sidebottom's paraphrase on the grounds that *ho katabas* is illegitimately turned into an indicative clause.[28] Ruckstuhl concedes that this is a valid objection according to the strict rules of grammar but maintains that we are here dealing with an elliptical statement.[29] If Sidebottom, Ruckstuhl, and Moloney are correct in seeing here no allusion to the ascension of Jesus, then an ellipsis of some kind must be assumed. In view of v. 12 the ellipsis may be filled out as follows: "No human has

24. Cf. Odeberg, *The Fourth Gospel*, pp. 72ff.; Meeks, "The Man from Heaven in Johannine Sectarianism," p. 52; Moloney, *The Johannine Son of Man*, p. 54.

25. Cf. Sidebottom, *The Christ of the Fourth Gospel*, p. 120; Ruckstuhl, "Die johanneische Menschensohnforschung," p. 210; Moloney, *The Johannine Son of Man*, pp. 54f.

26. Cf. Sidebottom, *The Christ of the Fourth Gospel*, p. 119; Moloney, *The Johannine Son of Man*, p. 54.

27. Sidebottom, *The Christ of the Fourth Gospel*, p. 120.

28. Moule, "The Individualism of the Fourth Gospel," p. 176 n. 1.

29. Ruckstuhl, "Die johanneische Menschensohnforschung," p. 209 n. 25. Cf. Moloney, *The Johannine Son of Man*, p. 55.

ever ascended to heaven (and returned with knowledge of *ta epourania*), but the one who descended from heaven (is the one who reveals *ta epourania*)." Indeed, if we are justified in placing the emphasis on the unstated but implied reference to the possession of heavenly knowledge, we could retain the exceptive meaning of *ei mē*: "No one can claim to have returned from heaven with supernatural knowledge except the one who came from heaven in the first place." A similarly inexact use of the exceptive *ei mē* can be claimed for Gal. 1:19.

If the contrast is between humans who falsely claim to be able to reveal heavenly secrets and the one who came from heaven, must we not take "the Son of man" as the title of a preexistent divine being? Not necessarily. It is possible that the phrase refers not to the heavenly origin but to the incarnate status of the Word-become-flesh. The contrast John wishes to develop opposes not angels and humans but the one unique human being and all other members of the species. John has already alluded to his belief in angels who descend from heaven at 1:51, but their descent is not at all comparable to that of the Word, who descends into flesh; it is incarnation that distinguishes the Son of man from Gabriel, Michael, and other angels whose itinerary is superficially the same as his. *Ho katabas ek tou ouranou* is thus John's shorthand way of referring to the incarnation. Consequently we must reckon with the possibility that "the Son of man" has been added precisely to make this reference more explicit, *if* John perceives the phrase as Jesus' way of referring to his humanity.

On the basis of this verse alone, therefore, no certain conclusion can be drawn concerning John's understanding of "the Son of man"; it may designate a heavenly being who has visited earth, or it may refer to the humanity of the Incarnate One. Our decision can be made only on the basis of subsequent uses of the phrase in the Fourth Gospel.

One further question must be addressed before we move on to the next verse. Does John here treat "the Son of man" as Jesus' self-designation, or is it used as a name for Jesus in a theological statement that the author does not attribute to Jesus? Schnackenburg argues that the dialogue with Nicodemus ends with v. 12, and that vv. 31–36, 13–21 constitute a kerygmatic discourse of the evangelist.[30] Ruckstuhl properly objects that this breaks the close connection of v. 13 and vv. 11f.[31] We may add that such a punctuation of the text ignores the present tense of v. 14, which, like the Synoptic passion predictions, looks forward to the crucifixion and therefore

---

30. Schnackenburg, *John*, vol. 1, pp. 380f.
31. Ruckstuhl, "Die johanneische Menschensohnforschung," pp. 235f.

belongs in direct discourse attributed to the earthly Jesus and not in a post-Easter kerygmatic discourse of the evangelist.[32]

Does John assume that Jesus' self-designation is recognizable as such to the narrative audience, or is it presented as a mysterious title that may induce Nicodemus to think that Jesus is speaking of someone else? Since John does not make Nicodemus the mouthpiece of further misunderstanding, it is clearly not his intention to emphasize the ambiguity of the phrase's denotation. Indeed, the close connection between vv. 12 and 13 argues against such a proposal. The one who speaks of his capacity to reveal *ta epourania* in v. 12 reveals the basis of this capacity in v. 13, referring to himself as the Son of man.

> **Jn. 3:14f.** And as Moses lifted up the serpent in the wilderness,
> so must the Son of man be lifted up, in order that every one who
> believes may have eternal life in him.

There is good reason for regarding this logion as a Johannine version of the Synoptic passion predictions (Mk. 8:31; 9:31; 10:33f.; and par.).[33] Just as the Synoptic Jesus speaks of his impending, violent death, using the self-designation "the Son of man" and the impersonal *dei* to indicate divine necessity, so here too the Johannine Jesus. The Johannine version differs from the Synoptic parallels chiefly in terms of the function it serves in its context.

The first passion prediction in the Synoptic Gospels occurs after Peter's confession, where it supplies an interpretation of the messianic role; Jesus accepts Peter's confession but proceeds to instruct the disciples that as Messiah he must suffer and die. There is little theological development of the theme at its first appearance; no answer is given to the question: Why must the Messiah suffer? Following the third passion prediction in Matthew and Mark, there is the unamplified statement that the Son of man came to give his life as a ransom for many (Mt. 20:28; Mk. 10:45).

This first instance of a passion prediction in John thus differs from the Synoptic parallels in terms of both context and content. It is not addressed to disciples as instruction relative to messiahship but is directed to a semi-believer as a soteriological answer to the question: "How can these things

---

32. Cf. Moloney, *The Johannine Son of Man*, p. 54.

33. Windisch, "Angelophanien um den Menschensohn auf Erden," p. 230, proposed that 3:14 is an *Umbildung* of Mk. 8:31. This view is shared by many recent interpreters, including Brown (*John*, p. 146), Schnackenburg ("Der Menschensohn," p. 130), and Moloney (*The Johannine Son of Man*, p. 61). Although the allusion to death is ambiguous at this point, the intention of "lifted up" is made explicit at 12:33.

[i.e., birth from above] be?" (v. 9). It should be noted that Nicodemus's question is not What must I do to be saved? but What is the soteriological basis of birth from above? The soteriological question prompts a christological answer, in two parts. In v. 13 it is stated that only Jesus, because of his heavenly origin, can provide an answer to the question; only he has knowledge of *ta epourania*, which includes knowledge of God's plan for salvation. Since the Johannine Christ is not a gnostic redeemer who provides a way of salvation by revealing heavenly secrets, v. 13 must be supplemented by vv. 14f.: Jesus makes salvation available only by means of his death. It is the death of a human being (divine beings cannot be crucified!), but it is not for that reason to be regarded as a propitiatory act performed by the human race on its own behalf; the lamb that takes away the sin of the world is *God's* lamb (1:29, 36).

In 3:16 different language is used to make the same theological point. Because of his unfathomable love for the human race, God gave his unique Son, so that humans might enjoy eternal life by appropriating for themselves the results of God's saving act in Jesus.[34] This text focuses in a single statement the entire incarnational Christology of the Fourth Gospel. Primitive adoptionism's unreflected affirmation that Messiah Jesus had been crucified because it was God's will that he suffer as a prelude to exaltation (Lk. 24:26) was no longer satisfactory. A more adequate soteriology required a profounder Christology. The pre-Pauline tradition that "Christ died for our sins in accordance with the Scriptures" (1 Cor. 15:3) needed to be grounded in Jesus' relationship to God. John apparently perceived the insufficiency of articulating this relationship merely in terms of Jesus' obedience to God, which would make it possible to regard the saving event as a human act. Bultmann correctly observes that John does not present Jesus' conformity to the Father's will as an act of human obedience; his doing nothing from himself marks him not as the most moral of humans but as the one who has his origin outside the realm of humanity.[35] It is God who gives and sends. Consequently those who really "see" Jesus "see" the Father (14:9), because Jesus is God's act.

In order to communicate this profound theological truth, John employs the concept of preexistence, articulated by means of the motif of descent in v. 13 and that of "sending" in v. 17. We must now ask whether "the Son

---

34. Meeks, "The Man from Heaven in Johannine Sectarianism," p. 63, concurs with Barrett (*John*, p. 180), Brown (*John*, p. 147), and Dahl, "The Atonement—an Adequate Reward for the Akedah? (Ro 8:32)," p. 28, in seeing here an allusion to the binding of Isaac in Genesis 22.

35. Bultmann, *John*, p. 249.

of man" as used in v. 14 serves the same purpose or not. Is it a title of heavenly glory employed paradoxically here, so that we may paraphrase: "And as Moses lifted up the serpent in the wilderness, so must the pre-existent heavenly Man be lifted up in crucifixion, so that every one who believes may have life in him"? This meaning does not seem probable. In this context as elsewhere in the Gospel, "the Son of man" is not simply a synonym for "the only begotten Son" or "the Logos."[36] It is the Son who is sent into the world, not the Son of man (v. 17).[37] Conversely, when crucifixion is the theme John employs "the Son of man," never "the Son" (cf. 8:28; 12:23).[38] There is just as little evidence here as at Mk. 8:31 that paradox is intended. It is a statement concerning the forthcoming execution of a historical person, the man who refers to himself as "the Son of man." Unless subsequent instances of the phrase point in the opposite direction, it would appear that John employs it as a way of speaking of the humanity of the incarnate Son of God.

> **Jn. 5:27** . . . and he has given him authority to execute judgment, because he is "son of man."

This is not a normal Son of man logion, for three reasons: (1) the phrase *huios anthrōpou* lacks the articles; (2) it serves as the predicate of a declaratory statement employing the copula; (3) it cannot be construed as a self-designation of Jesus. Scholars who have found here evidence of the alleged pre-Christian conception of a heavenly judge called "the Son of man" have been constrained to explain the absence of the articles as due either to the inversion of the predicate and copula or to John's desire to recall Dan. 7:13. Insufficient attention, however, has been paid to the other two irregularities, which may be interrelated with the first. This statement is utterly unique in the New Testament in making *(ho) huios (tou) anthrōpou* the predicate of the copula in a clause in which the implied subject is Jesus; for that reason it cannot be treated as a purely denotative term.[39]

Modern translations tend to follow Luther and the English Authorized Version in rendering the anarthrous phrase as if it were the normal *ho*

---

36. See n. 8 above.
37. Cf. Lindars, "The Son of Man in the Johannine Christology," p. 48 n. 16.
38. Moloney, *The Johannine Son of Man*, p. 66.
39. In Acts 7:56 (perhaps also Lk. 24:6), "the Son of man" is not a self-designation. This may or may not be the case in Jn. 12:34. In all three passages, however, the term functions as a name for Jesus rather than as the identifier of a concept. In Mt. 13:37 it is the predicate of a copula but functions nonetheless as the self-designation of Jesus. In Jn. 9:35–38 it functions as Jesus' self-designation but is not perceived as such by the interlocutor.

huios tou anthrōpou. Since the modern rediscovery of the Similitudes of Enoch, it has been customary to justify this procedure by claiming that the allusion to judgment is intended to recall the conception of a heavenly judge identified by the title "the Son of man."[40] Earlier scholars, understanding the phrase as referring to the humanity of the Savior whether used with the articles or not, felt no compunction in rendering the phrase as definite in this instance.[41] It is now generally agreed that this is entirely permissible in terms of the rules of Greek grammar. An anarthrous predicate noun that precedes the copula may nonetheless be definite. Indeed, E. C. Colwell would take the matter a step further: define predicate nouns preceding the copula regularly omit the article.[42] Colwell has been followed by a number of scholars in regarding Jn. 5:27 as a clear instance of this rule.[43] Leivestad objects, noting that although Colwell's rule explains the omission of the first article, it does not justify the absence of the second, and points to parallel instances in the Fourth Gospel where the second article is retained (1:49; 19:21).[44] Leivestad's examples are not entirely apposite, inasmuch as the genitive noun with its article follows the copula in both instances. An exact parallel, however, is provided at 10:36, where we read *huios tou theou eimi*; the entire genitive phrase precedes the copula, but only the first article is omitted.

Also neglected in the debate is Colwell's concession that the New Testament contains fifteen exceptions to his rule, three of which are found in John; in 1:21, 6:51, and 15:1 a predicate noun preceding the copula retains the article. The first of these exceptions is particularly instructive; the article was surely added precisely because its omission would have led to misunderstanding ("Are you *a* prophet?"). It must also be stressed that Colwell's rule by no means prevents *indefinite* nouns from preceding the copula—of this practice John affords numerous examples.[45] There is thus no grammatical necessity for regarding *huios anthrōpou* as definite simply

40. Cf. Bernard, *St. John*, vol. 1, p. 244; Bultmann, *John*, pp. 257, 261; Schulz, *Untersuchungen zur Menschensohn-Christologie im Johannesevangelium*, pp. 111f., 132; Higgins, *Jesus and the Son of Man*, pp. 165–68; Colpe, "Ho huios tou anthrōpou," TDNT 8, pp. 464f.

41. Alford, *The Greek Testament*, vol. 1, p. 742; Schlatter, *Der Evangelist Johannes*, p. 151.

42. Colwell, "A Definite Rule for the Use of the Article in the Greek New Testament."

43. Ibid., p. 14; Higgins, *Jesus and the Son of Man*, p. 166; Moloney, *The Johannine Son of Man*, p. 82. Although Moule cites Colwell's article with approval in *An Idiom Book*, pp. 115f., he himself seems inclined to take *huios anthrōpou* as indefinite or qualitative in Jn. 5:27; see his "Neglected Features," p. 420.

44. Leivestad, "Exit the Apocalyptic Son of Man," p. 252 n. 3. Moule, "Neglected Features," p. 420, notes, however, that the absence of the second article is not particularly significant, because its presence in the genitive construction is due to the first article: *ho huios anthrōpou* does not accord with Greek idiom.

45. E.g., 4:19; 8:48; 9:8, 17, 24, 25, 28; 10:1, 13, 34; 12:6.

because it precedes the copula. In view of the contrast between 1:21 and 9:17, where *prophētēs* precedes the verb in both cases but is marked as a title in the first instance by the presence of the article, there is reason to argue that John would have similarly employed the article at 5:27 to guard against misunderstanding, had he wished his readers to take *huios anthrōpou* as the exact equivalent of *ho huios tou anthrōpou*.

It has been argued that the omission of the articles was motivated by a desire to recall the anarthrous phrase of Dan. 7:13.[46] Higgins and Borsch have quite properly attacked this proposal, pointing out how very weak is the evidence for conscious allusion in this case.[47] Indeed, no passage in the Fourth Gospel can be cited as proof that the author ever depends upon Daniel. The nonapocalyptic nature of John's vision of truth suggests that he would not have found the Danielic apocalypse particularly congenial.

Since John chose to omit the articles in this instance, and it is improbable that he did so in order to recall Dan. 7:13, what was his intention? We can best approach this question by returning to the observation that the clause is utterly unique in presenting (*ho*) *huios* (*tou*) *anthrōpou* as the predicate of a copula in which the implied subject is Jesus. Nowhere in the gospel tradition does Jesus declare, "I am the Son of man." Nowhere in the New Testament do we read, "Jesus is the Son of man." The complete absence of the phrase from the missionary speeches of Acts, Paul's christological discussions, and the Revelation of John reminds us that "the Son of man" was not perceived as a useful way of talking about the meaning of Jesus.[48] We should be properly cautious, therefore, in ascribing kerygmatic status to this statement, the content of which would then be: "Jesus is the Son of man, and as such he will judge the living and the dead."

Elsewhere in John the phrase with the articles is employed as Jesus' self-designation and is perceived as such by his listeners except at 9:35. The fact that this is not the case here compels us to assume that the absence of the articles is indicative of a change in semantic function; whereas the phrase with the articles is strongly denotative, the anarthrous *huios anthrōpou* is primarily connotative. That is, while "the Son of man" points

46. Schulz, *Untersuchungen*, pp. 111–13; Barrett, *John*, p. 218; Sidebottom, *The Christ of the Fourth Gospel*, pp. 92f.; Lindars, *John*, p. 226.

47. Higgins, *Jesus and the Son of Man*, p. 166; Borsch, *The Son of Man in Myth and History*, p. 294. Reim, *Studien zum alttestamentlichen Hintergrund des Johannesevangeliums*, p. 186, finds no evidence of John's use of Daniel here or elsewhere in the Gospel.

48. Neither in Rev. 1:13 nor in 14:14 does *huios anthrōpou* function as a name or title; cf. Lietzmann, *Der Menschensohn*, p. 56; Lindars, "Re-enter the Apocalyptic Son of Man," p. 63; Dunn, *Christology*, p. 91.

to a figure, whether Jesus himself or another figure with whom he may be identified, the anarthrous phrase refers to a quality or status.[49]

If it could be demonstrated that John regarded "the Son of man" as the established title of an apocalyptic figure destined to function as eschatological judge, *huios anthrōpou* would likely refer to the quality or status of this mysterious figure. Because this is precisely the question at issue, we must seek to uncover the connotative value of the phrase from the context.

Jesus' role as future judge is referred to with some frequency in the New Testament, but why he should so function is nowhere the subject of much reflection. It is simply stated that Jesus will judge the living and the dead because God has so ordained (Acts 10:42; 17:31; cf. 2 Cor. 5:10; Mt. 25:31–46). If we were able to ask the author of Luke-Acts, "Why did God appoint Jesus as judge?" the answer would undoubtedly involve messianism. There are passages in earlier and later Jewish literature that ascribe to the Messiah a role as judge in virtue of the fact that he is the eschatological king who implements divine justice.[50] This human being functions as judge under the mandate of the supreme Judge.

But why should a human being be selected for this responsibility? The roots of this conception undoubtedly lie in an earlier age when the implementation of divine justice was conceived of in this-worldly terms: God would raise up a powerful king like David who would punish Israel's foreign enemies and oppressors within Israel and thus introduce a golden age for the pious. When pessimism altered this picture and transformed judgment within history into a judgment terminating history, the image of the eschatological king did not entirely disappear. Possibly one reason for this persistence was the inconsistency that permitted this-worldly and other-worldly views of the new age to coexist.[51] For Christians, for whom messianism was far more important than it was to many other Jewish groups, the doctrine of the judging Messiah presumably had a *soteriological* base. To say that Jesus was the man appointed by God as humankind's apocalyptic judge was to employ eschatological imagery as a means of communicating Jesus' soteriological significance.

49. Harner, "Qualitative Anarthrous Predicate Nouns: Mark 15:39 and John 1:1," argues that anarthrous predicate nouns preceding the verb may be primarily qualitative in force, yet without thereby excluding any hint of definiteness. Moloney chooses to follow both Colwell and Harner: "It appears that 'Son of Man' in its present context is definite, i.e. titular, but it may well retain a 'qualitative' sense" (*The Johannine Son of Man*, p. 82).

50. Psalm of Solomon 17; 2 Bar. 40:1; 4 Ezra 12:32. Akiba's exegesis of "thrones" in Dan. 7:9f., "One for him and one for David" (*b. Sanh.* 38b, *Ḥag.* 14a), seems to imply some kind of judicial role for "David."

51. Cf. Klausner, *The Messianic Idea in Israel*, pp. 408ff. Cf. Revelation 20f.

John shows his insight into this theological situation when he writes in 5:22f., "For the Father judges no one, but has committed all judgment to the Son, in order that all may honor the Son just as they honor the Father." This is reminiscent of the Christ hymn of Phil. 2:5–11: God has exalted Jesus so that all may honor him. Why is this honoring necessary? Because "the one who does not honor the Son does not honor the Father who sent him" (Jn. 5:23). If genuine reconciliation between humankind and God has occurred in the Christ event, Jesus must be God's act, and thus to honor him is to honor God.

John is not satisfied, however, with the traditional Christian eschatology that honors Jesus by ascribing to him a future eschatological role. Forging his own variety of realized eschatology, John transfers the judgment from the end of history to the present and then employs apparently conflicting statements to indicate the strange relationship between the two roles played by Jesus as savior and judge (contrast 9:39 with 12:47). At the same time judgment on the basis of works is transmuted into a judgment on the basis of faith: "Amen, amen, I say to you that the one who hears my word and believes in the one who sent me has eternal life, and does not come into judgment but has moved from death into life" (5:24). The basis of acquittal is acceptance of Jesus as God's act! In the following verse John employs more traditional language about the resurrection for final judgment, but the future has been brought into the present: the dead who hear the Messiah's voice and "live" are not the deceased but those who have been living in the darkness of sinful alienation from God (cf. 12:35, 46). Just as the Father has the power to raise the dead, so also the Son (5:21). In v. 26 this is expressed as "having life in himself"; but we are reminded that the Son does not have this life-giving power in and of himself (i.e., for metaphysical reasons—because of consubstantiality with the Father), but because the Father has conferred this power upon him. John does not tell us when this conferral took place, because he is not interested in mythological narrative. His concern is entirely soteriological. He chooses the language of conferral (which functions in precisely the same way as "send") to reiterate that in the man Jesus, God's redemptive intentions found actualization.

In view of this context, which is the more likely connotation of *huios anthrōpou* in v. 27: angelic status or the unique humanity of the Word that became flesh? The older commentators were surely on firm exegetical ground when they insisted that this verse alludes to the incarnation.[52] In

---

52. In addition to the works cited in n. 41, cf. Meyer, *John*, vol. 1, pp. 251–53; Westcott, *St. John*, vol. 1, pp. 6, 194.

terms of Johannine Christology it would be superfluous to declare that the Son has been granted authority to execute judgment because he is the heavenly Messiah ordained for this task. For John "the Son" is a profounder term than "the Christ," but it includes the latter in its field of meaning: the Son is both the Word and "the Christ, the Son of God" (20:31). A certain redundancy is thus attributed to the evangelist by those who find a reference to the apocalyptic Son of man in this verse. When we consider how John has de-eschatologized the judgment by relating it to acceptance or rejection of the revelation of God's saving intention in the life and death of the Word-become-flesh, the causal clause is no longer superfluous but a significant theological affirmation regarding the relationship between incarnation and judgment.

There is no need to attribute the verse or the clause to pre-Johannine tradition or to a post-Johannine redactor, because it simply reiterates the fundamental affirmation of 5:24: those who accept Jesus as the Word-become-flesh in whom salvation is actualized have been acquitted.[53] The same thought was expressed earlier in 3:13–21, which speaks of the saving incarnation and the resultant judgment: "The one who believes in him is not judged; the one who does not believe has been judged already, because he has not believed in the name of the only begotten Son of God" (v. 18). The theme reappears at 9:39: "For judgment I came into this world, that those who do not see may see, and those who see may become blind." Here "seeing" is clearly a matter of accepting the revelation of God's saving action in the incarnate Son. In view of the importance of this theme, it is unlikely that John is here using *huios anthrōpou* as the poetic equivalent of *anthrōpos*, so as to express the idea found in the later Testament of Abraham regarding the appointment of Abel as apocalyptic judge: "For this reason God said, 'I do not judge you, but every man will be judged by a man.' "[54] It is not John's thought that the Son is qualified to become the judge of humans by sharing their lot, as in the Epistle to the Hebrews he is

53. The verse is derived from earlier tradition by a number of scholars, including Schulz, *Untersuchungen*, p. 112; Higgins, *Jesus and the Son of Man*, p. 168; Martyn, *History and Theology in the Fourth Gospel*, p. 131; Smalley, "The Johannine Son of Man Sayings," p. 292. Bultmann, on the other hand, proposed that the verse was added by the evangelist or, more probably, by the redactor who inserted vv. 28f. in order to correct the realized eschatology of vv. 24f. (*John*, pp. 260f.).

54. Rec. A, chap. 13; cf. Sidebottom, *The Christ of the Fourth Gospel*, pp. 92–94; Casey, *Son of Man*, pp. 198f. The same opinion was expressed half a century earlier by Badham, "The Title 'Son of Man,' " pp. 445f. Ruckstuhl, "Die johanneische Menschensohnforschung," pp. 207f., rightly objects, contra Sidebottom, that the Johannine context prohibits the translation "a man"; it is not Jesus' humanity as such that qualifies him for judgment but rather the fact that he is the unique man who is the incarnation of the Son of God.

accredited to serve as expiatory high priest by sharing the mortality and temptations of humanity (Heb. 2:17f.; 4:15).

While John seems not to have repudiated the traditional Christian belief that Jesus will function as the man appointed by God to judge the living and the dead, for him the emphasis is at a very different point: the quintessence of the response required of humans by God is not ethical behavior, important as this is (cf. 13:34f.), but acceptance of God's saving act in the incarnate Word. Consequently, judgment occurs whenever a man or woman is confronted with the gospel of the incarnation; to accept it is to be acquitted, to reject it is to be condemned. It is in this sense that all judgment has been committed to the Son: the incarnation is the locus of judgment. We might paraphrase v. 27: ". . . and he has given him authority to execute judgment, because he is the incarnation of the Word."

Does John intend by this anarthrous phrase to recall the self-designation of Jesus, *ho huios tou anthrōpou*? Indubitably. The two are not identical; *huios anthrōpou* does not serve as a name but expresses a quality or status, yet its connotative force appears to be the same as that of the fuller appellative. Both forms of the phrase can refer to the humanity of the Word that became flesh for our salvation.

It would be foolish to claim that it has been irrefutably demonstrated that *huios anthrōpou* connotes the incarnate status of the Son. It is to be hoped, however, that this investigation will convince the reader that the case for this interpretation is at least as strong as that which has been presented (often with little or no argument) in support of the view that allusion is here made to a pre-Christian conception of an angelic judge. If there is no evidence elsewhere for the alleged tradition, this verse, because of its several ambiguities, cannot be used for its reconstruction.

> **Jn. 6:27** Do not work for the food which perishes but for the food which persists into eternal life, which the Son of man will give you; for on this one the Father, God, has set his seal.

No attempt can here be made to discuss hypothetical earlier stages of the Bread of Life discourse, which in its extant form contains three Son of man statements.[55] Regardless of the conjectural relationship of these statements to earlier tradition, none of them in its present context suggests that *ho huios tou anthrōpou* is the designation for an apocalyptic, heavenly judge.

---

55. A helpful survey of scholarly opinion is provided by Moloney, *The Johannine Son of Man*, pp. 87–107.

Taken in isolation, 6:27 could conceivably be taken as referring to an apocalyptic Messiah expected to function as host at a great messianic banquet.[56] There is nothing in the context, however, to support such an interpretation. Conversely, there is important evidence against it. The request of v. 34, "Lord, at all times give us this bread," is completely unmotivated and inexplicable unless Jesus' hearers understand v. 27 as a statement made by Jesus *about himself*: "Work . . . for the food . . . which *I* will give you." So understood, these verses constitute a very close parallel to the declaration and response of 4:13–15.

Convinced that the evangelist intended this parallel, Bultmann argues that v. 27 originally used this first-person language, for which the ecclesiastical redactor substituted "the Son of man" and a third-person verb.[57] This conjecture seems necessary to Bultmann, for two reasons: (1) the present statement requires that the hearers perceive that "the Son of man" refers to Jesus, which he regards as improbable in view of 12:34; (2) he takes v. 27 as referring to the activity of the exalted Lord in the Eucharist and regards this idea as deriving, like v. 53, from the redactor. As we shall see below, there is a way of looking at 12:34 that removes the first of these problems.

Regarding the second, it must be objected that v. 27 does *not* clearly refer to the activity of the exalted Lord in the Eucharist. A reference to the Eucharist may well be intended at a secondary, "contemporizing" level of meaning, but at the primary level the statement refers to the incarnation. If we are justified in reading the future *dōsei* (following the Bodmer papyrus, Codex Vaticanus, et al.), the statement focuses on Jesus' death on the cross as the climax of the incarnational event.[58] This meaning is not immediately apparent, of course. In typically Johannine fashion the initial statement must first be misunderstood by the hearers (v. 34) and subsequently reinterpreted progressively: (1) *I* am the bread of life (v. 35); (2) the bread that I shall give is *my flesh* (v. 51). In the course of the discourse it becomes clear that believing in the one whom God has sent (v. 29) and "eating" the living bread that came down from heaven (v. 51) are alternative descriptions of the same spiritual event: faith's appropriation of the miracle of the incarnation.[59]

56. Cf. 2 En. 62:14, Lk. 22:30, Rev. 19:9, and the article by J. F. Priest, "Messianic Banquet," in IDB Suppl., pp. 591f.

57. Bultmann, *John*, p. 225 n.1.

58. Cf. Moloney, *The Johannine Son of Man*, pp. 112, 119. Lindars, *John*, p. 255, takes the future as referring to the Son of man's eschatological function of feeding his people with manna. The present tense, *didōsin*, found in Sinaiticus, Bezae, et al., is preferred by Wikenhauser, *Das Evangelium nach Johannes*, p. 124.

59. Cf. Schürmann, "Joh 6,51c—ein Schlüssel zur grossen johanneischen Brotrede," pp. 244–62; Dunn, "John VI—A Eucharistic Discourse?" pp. 328–38.

In v. 27, accordingly, "the Son of man" functions as Jesus' self-designation and is clearly perceived as such by the narrative audience. Its theological content is unclear, but this much can be affirmed with some assurance: in this statement the term refers not to the preincarnate activity of the Word or the postincarnate work of the risen Lord but to the incarnate status of the one who became flesh and gave that flesh for the world. Because of the close relationship between v. 27 and v. 51, it is possible to see this Son of man statement as a Johannine parallel to Mk. 10:45, which declares that the Son of man came to give his life as a ransom for many. While at first sight the parallel may seem remote, its pertinency becomes more apparent as we follow the development of the theme in v. 53.

> **Jn. 6:53** Amen, amen, I say to you, unless you eat the flesh of the Son of man and drink his blood, you do not have life in yourselves.

Many interpreters are certain that vv. 51c–58 are intended to refer primarily to the Eucharist. For Bultmann the tone of these verses is so crudely sacramentalist, reminiscent of Ignatius's "medicine of immortality" (Eph. 20:2), that he cannot ascribe them to the evangelist.[60] Brown is convinced that, while the Eucharist is alluded to at a number of points earlier in the chapter, it becomes the exclusive theme of these verses.[61] Schweizer concurs that the Lord's Supper must be in mind here, but not directly or exclusively, he suggests; the *sarx* of v. 51c has reference not to the Eucharist but to Jesus' death and is antidocetic in intent, signifying not so much a substance as an event.[62] Accordingly, the fundamental demand of these verses is for faith in the incarnation and for the consequent recognition that to participate in the Eucharist is to affirm this faith.[63] Dunn limits the eucharistic reference more severely. Arguing for the unity of the chapter, he insists that the language reminiscent of the Eucharist in vv. 51c–58 is used not realistically but metaphorically, so that the focus of thought is not on the Eucharist as such but on the reality to which the Eucharist itself points, namely, the soteriological significance of the incarnation, death, resurrection, and Spirit giving of Jesus.[64]

---

60. Bultmann, *John*, pp. 218–20, 234f.
61. R. E. Brown, *John*, pp. 284–91.
62. Schweizer, "Das johanneische Zeugnis vom Herrenmahl," pp. 341–63, reprinted in *Neotestamentica*, pp. 371–96, especially pp. 391f., 394.
63. *Neotestamentica*, p. 395. A very similar conclusion is reached by Schürmann, "Joh 6,51c," p. 261.
64. Dunn, "John VI—a Eucharistic Discourse?" p. 336.

Critical to a proper understanding of the function of vv. 51c–58 in the discourse as a whole is the interpretation of vv. 60–63. Bornkamm finds here the strongest support for Bultmann's thesis that vv. 51c–58 constitute a redactional insertion: v. 63 contradicts the assertion that eternal life is to be obtained through the Eucharist; if the interpolation is removed, vv. 60–63 connect very naturally with v. 51ab.[65] Dunn objects that this is to misunderstand the force of *sarx* in v. 63, which has reference not to the material bread of the Eucharist but to the human condition of the Incarnate One; in and of itself Jesus' *sarx* accomplishes nothing: "Jesus in his earthly life belongs to the realm of *sarx* and is *sarx*, and so cannot effect or give eternal life (3:6; 6:63). But Jesus lifted up and glorified becomes a source of life to all who believe (3:14–15; 7:37–9)."[66] In support of Dunn it should also be pointed out that the author of vv. 51c–58, whether evangelist or redactor, does not conceive of the Eucharist crudely as a "medicine of immortality"; in v. 54 the final clause indicates that eating and drinking are intended metaphorically: "He who eats my flesh and drinks my blood has eternal life, *and I will raise him up at the last day.*" That is, those who "eat" and "drink" will nonetheless die as mortals and remain in their graves until the final resurrection.[67]

Whether we follow Bultmann and Bornkamm or Schweizer and Dunn regarding the origin of vv. 51c–58, it is clear that in either case "the Son of man" functions as a name for the earthly Jesus. Verse 53 picks up the misunderstanding of v. 52, "How can *this man* give us his flesh to eat?" which in turn is a response to v. 51, "*I* am the living bread which came down from heaven; if any one eats of this bread he will live for ever; and the bread which I will give for the life of the world is my flesh." In this context "the Son of man" points unambiguously to Jesus and is perceived as such by the auditors. If v. 53 refers directly to the Eucharist, as Bultmann and Brown believe, the designation refers most naturally to the human Jesus, whose sacrificial death is celebrated in the ritual. If, on the other hand, we follow Dunn in taking the verbs "eat" and "drink" metaphorically, these

65. Bornkamm, "Die eucharistische Rede im Johannes-Evangelium," pp. 161–69. Bornkamm continues the discussion in "Vorjohanneische Tradition oder nachjohanneische Bearbeitung in der eucharistischen Rede Johannes 6?" pp. 51–64.

66. Dunn, "John VI—a Eucharistic Discourse?" p. 332. A similar conclusion was reached independently by Johnston, *The Spirit-Paraclete in the Gospel of John*, p. 22, who paraphrases v. 63, "His spirit it is that is life-giver; his flesh is of no value."

67. Cf. Schweizer, "Das johanneische Zeugnis vom Herrenmahl" (*Neotestamentica*), p. 393 n. 72. Bultmann, *John*, pp. 235f., maintains that the presence of *en heautois* proves that the reference is to actual participation in the Lord's Supper, but he ignores the force of v. 54b.

metaphors point to the appropriation of the meaning of the incarnation, so that again "the Son of man" must refer to the earthly Jesus.[68]

If there is justification for seeing in v. 51 a remote parallel to the suffering Son of man saying of Mk. 10:45, it is possible that the use of "the Son of man" in v. 53 was prompted by the tradition of such sayings.[69] Theological interpretation of the passion predictions, which found one of its earliest expressions in Mk. 10:45, here receives another, profounder presentation: eternal life is granted to those who through faith appropriate the whole incarnational event, an event that climaxes in the death of Jesus but includes the consequent exaltation and the gift of the Spirit.[70]

Jn. 6:62 What then if you were to see the Son of man ascending where he was before?

When this verse is treated in isolation from its context in chapter 6 and its relationship to the Johannine Son of man sayings as a group, it is very easily regarded, in conjunction with 3:13, as evidence for a tradition that spoke of a preexistent Son of man, with whom the Christian community had identified Jesus.[71]

It must be conceded immediately that the verse speaks of the heavenly preexistence of someone, and that this person is identified by the name "the Son of man." This by no means requires, however, that we see here a reference to a pre-Christian tradition concerning a heavenly Man. The logion simply reflects the Johannine incarnational Christology, which employs the descent/ascent motif as well as the motif of the Father sending the Son. The verse cannot have existed in a pre-Johannine source; its elliptical form makes it unusable as an independent saying. It can have been created only for this particular context, where it serves as a further response to the disbelief of v. 60. Like v. 61, it is concerned with the scandal of the incarnation and the exclusivist claim implied therein. We may paraphrase the two verses as follows: "Are you scandalized by the

68. Barrett, *John*, p. 247, insists that "the Son of man" here designates the heavenly Man. Since the heavenly Man as such does not possess flesh and blood, however, Barrett must assume that v. 53 presents a startling paradox. While this is not impossible, there is no hint in this verse or its context that paradox is intended, so that Barrett's interpretation is extrinsic, deriving rather from his understanding of 3:13 and 6:62. This point is conceded in effect by Barrett on p. 60, where he lists 6:53 as one of the Johannine Son of man sayings that parallel in some degree the Synoptic passion sayings.

69. Cf. Moloney, *The Johannine Son of Man*, p. 120.

70. Cf. Dunn, "John VI—a Eucharistic Discourse?" p. 336.

71. Cf. Barrett, *John*, pp. 60f., 250f.; Schulz, *Untersuchungen*, pp. 117f. Ruckstuhl, "Die johanneische Menschensohnforschung," p. 276, opposes this understanding of 3:13 and 6:62.

exclusivist claim that only through faith in the Word-become-flesh you can have life eternal? Are you offended by the assertion that this man of flesh and blood is the immanent love and judgment of God? Would it be of any help to you if you were to see this man of flesh and blood returning to the Father who sent him?"

Is the elliptical question intended negatively or positively? The obscurity of the text is underscored by the inability of scholars to reach any consensus on the issue. Bultmann argues for the negative, because he associates "ascending" with the "lifting up" on the cross, which will simply intensify, or reveal more fully, the scandal inherent in Jesus' claim to be God's Revealer.[72] E. C. Hoskyns, on the other hand, regards the question as having a positive intent: the vision of the ascension will "provide the solution to the riddle of the Eucharistic terminology."[73] It is difficult to see how any certain determination of intention can be made on the basis of the preceding verses. The following verse, however, may provide the necessary clue. The declaratory statement of v. 63 implies that v. 62 is intended negatively; beholding the ascent of the Son of man would be of no help in overcoming the scandal, if this were a merely human beholding, that is, *kata sarka* (cf. 2 Cor. 5:16).[74] It must necessarily remain a human beholding, however, unless it is informed by the Spirit that is conveyed by Jesus. The *sarx* of v. 63 refers to the realm of the human and to everything that is seen or treated as purely human. Even the fleshly Jesus (the Word become *sarx*) is of no advantage to us if we see him as purely human. His testimony is simply a scandal to us unless it is received as life-giving Spirit.[75]

Regardless of what force we ascribe to v. 62, however, in its context it can refer only to Jesus. The Johannine Jesus has already used first-person language to speak of his coming from heaven (vv. 38, 51); we should, therefore, assume that the author intends the narrative audience to perceive the self-reference of v. 62. In this verse "the Son of man" points not to an angel but to a human being. His origin was in heaven, and he is destined to return thither, but his anticipated ascent will be meaningful only because the incarnation is real.

Does "the Son of man" nonetheless refer here primarily to the preexistence of Jesus rather than to his incarnate state? Because of the great

---

72. Bultmann, *John*, p. 445.
73. Hoskyns, *The Fourth Gospel*, p. 301.
74. Schweizer, *Neotestamentica*, p. 390, cites 8:15 in this connection: to behold *kata sarka* is to see only the *sarx*—but the *sarx* cannot save.
75. Cf. Johnston, *The Spirit-Paraclete in the Gospel of John*, p. 22; Dunn, *Jesus and the Spirit*, p. 350, and *Baptism in the Holy Spirit*, p. 184.

influence exerted on contemporary scholars by the Similitudes of Enoch, the consensus favors a preincarnate connotation. It cannot be pretended that this view has been conclusively refuted here, but it must be insisted that nothing in the verse or its context requires such a view. The text and its context speak of the Incarnate One, and of the offense provoked by the claim that Jesus is uniquely the one sent by God. It is concerned neither with his preexistent activity nor with his postincarnate functions but rather with the completion of his earthly mission, the point at which he returns to his place of origin. One can cogently argue, therefore, that here "the Son of man" designates the eternal Son not respecting his eternity but his temporality, not his divinity but his humanity.

> **Jn. 8:28** When you lift up the Son of man, then you will know that I am what I am, and that I do nothing on my own authority, but speak just as the Father instructed me.

The translation of *egō eimi* as "I am what I am" is taken from the New English Bible, whose translators were undoubtedly influenced by C. H. Dodd's insistence that this phrase reflects the divine *egō eimi* of the Septuagint and the *ani hu* of the Hebrew Scriptures (as, e.g., at Isa. 43:10).[76] In his use of the *egō eimi* formula, the Johannine Jesus presents himself as the one uniquely related to God, the one who in some sense is the bearer or manifestation of the sacred Name.[77]

In true Johannine style, however, this mysterious revelation is veiled in ambiguous language, so that it is not immediately apparent to the narrative audience.[78] In response to the first use of the absolute *egō eimi* in 8:24, the hearers do not pick up stones in order to punish Jesus for blasphemy (cf. 8:59) but instead express unsatisfied curiosity—"Who are you?" (v. 25). In response to the second use of the formula, greater understanding is manifested: "As he was speaking these things, many believed in him" (v. 30).

In both instances the English Authorized Version, followed by the Revised Standard Version, translated *egō eimi* as "I am he." Although this rendering is merely puzzling in v. 24, it is positively misleading in v. 28, because it suggests to the English reader that "he" refers to "the Son of

76. Dodd, *Interpretation*, pp. 93–96. Cf. Bernard, *St. John*, vol. 1, pp. cxxf.

77. Daube, *The New Testament and Rabbinic Judaism*, pp. 325–29, favors taking *egō eimi* in the sense "the Messiah is present," supporting a suggestion made by T. W. Manson in an unpublished paper.

78. It is possible that John intends the *hoti* to have two meanings, both "that" and "what" (*ho ti*; cf. 8:25), so that the obtuse hearers miss the allusion to the divine *egō eimi*, hearing only "what I am."

man," so that the meaning is: ". . . then you will know that I am the Son of man." This is in fact the interpretation adopted by a number of commentators, on the assumption that "the Son of man" was an established title for an expected eschatological figure with whom Jesus was identified in Christian faith.[79]

For this assumption to be justified in the present instance, it is necessary to assume further, as Bultmann does, that Jesus' hearers understand the term as designating the Messiah, that is, that the alleged distinctions between the heavenly judge of the Similitudes of Enoch and the human Messiah have disappeared, so that it is now understood as designating a human figure who can be crucified.[80] Bultmann correctly perceives that "lift up," while a double entendre for the evangelist, is intended to be heard by the narrative audience as a reference to crucifixion.[81] According to this interpretation, then, the audience hears Jesus say, "When you crucify the Messiah, then you will recognize that I am he." But this is not how Bultmann himself really understands the verse! His exposition indicates that he takes the meaning to be: "When you crucify me, then you will realize, too late, that I am your judge."[82] This is surely a more satisfactory understanding (apart from the reference to judgment, which derives from Bultmann's belief that "the Son of man" connotes "heavenly judge"). It makes no sense to assume that this logion predicts that Jesus' hearers will think that they are crucifying the Messiah and then come to recognize that the person they are crucifying is none other than Jesus. It is far more natural to take v. 28, like 3:14, as a Johannine variation on the theme of the Synoptic passion predictions, where "the Son of man" serves as a recognizable self-designation of Jesus.

There is thus no justification for Bultmann's claim: "Thus everything that he is can be referred to by the mysterious title 'Son of man.' "[83] Brown correctly objects that "it does not fit John's thought that the ultimate insight into the exalted Jesus would be that he is Son of Man," especially since the confessional titles "Lord" and "God" are used in 20:28.[84] As in the earlier logia, "the Son of man" seems here to refer not to the heavenly glory of the Son of God but to his incarnate weakness and humility, which render him subject to crucifixion.

---

79. E.g., Bernard, *St. John*, vol. 2, p. 303, who is followed by Lindars, *John*, p. 322.
80. Bultmann, *John*, p. 354.
81. Ibid., p. 350.
82. I am paraphrasing Bultmann's exposition in his *John*, pp. 349f.
83. Ibid., p. 349.
84. R. E. Brown, *John*, p. 348.

Is the prediction intended positively or negatively, as a promise of salvation or of judgment? The commentators divide on this issue, partly on the
basis of whether or not they understand the unexpressed predicate of *egō
eimi* to be "heavenly judge."[85] Since Jesus' relationship with God involves
him in both salvation and judgment, it is possible that both are in mind
here. Those who are drawn to Jesus following his death and exaltation (cf.
12:32) will find salvation through the Word that became flesh, while those
who refuse to believe in the gospel will eventually acknowledge that he is
their judge. In this case the logion parallels in a distant way both the
soteriological Son of man logion of Mk. 10:45 addressed to believing disciples and the word of judgment addressed to the Sanhedrin in Mk. 14:62.[86]

Jn. 9:35 Do you believe in the Son of man?

This verse is seen by some as sure evidence of a primitive Christology in which Jesus was publicly confessed as the Son of man.[87] On first
impression the passage certainly suggests this. It is natural to assume that
when the man confesses in v. 38, "I believe, Lord," he is really declaring, "I
believe that you, Jesus, are the Son of man" (whatever be the content
attributed to the predicate). A careful examination, however, shows that
this cannot be the force of the passage.

Leivestad correctly observes that we cannot substitute either "me" or
"the Messiah" for the ambiguous "the Son of man" in Jesus' question.[88]
The man's answering question makes it clear that he does not perceive *ho
huios tou anthrōpou* to be Jesus' self-designation.[89] Nor does he hear Jesus
say, "Do you believe in the Messiah?" In this case the answer should be a
simple yes or no, not a question concerning the identity of the Messiah.
The situation is not made easier if we take "the Son of man" as the title for
a transcendent figure, waiting in heaven for the last day; in this case, as

85. Bultmann, *John*, p. 353, emphasizes judgment, since this is for him the connotation of
"the Son of man." Moloney, *The Johannine Son of Man*, p. 137, argues for a positive interpretation. Schnackenburg, *Das Johannesevangelium*, part 2, p. 257 (English ed., vol. 2,
pp. 202f.), proposes that both are in view.
86. See the discussion of these verses in chapter 6 below. Accordingly, Bultmann is incorrect not in his exposition but only in his exegetical basis.
87. The most vigorous proponent of this view is Higgins, *Jesus and the Son of Man*, p. 175,
who suggests that 9:35 records the question addressed to baptismal candidates in John's
church; cf. also p. 155.
88. Leivestad, "Exit the Apocalyptic Son of Man," p. 251.
89. This exchange suggests that John is not aware of any peculiarity of the underlying
Semitic expression (whether Hebrew or Aramaic) that would *restrict* the expression to service as a self-designation equivalent to "this man" (comparable to the English self-referring
idiom "yours truly").

Bultmann points out, the man's response makes no sense at all.[90] The responding question presupposes that the initial question has to do with a historical figure whose identity can be a matter of inquiry.

When we approach v. 35 in this way, we are able to perceive that the exegetical problem relates to John's peculiar use of the verb "believe."[91] The verb is not used by John with reference to the act of giving assent to various religious beliefs. When Mary expresses her belief in the final resurrection of the dead, she does so with the verb *oida*, not *pisteuō* (11:24); Jesus' response to her proposes that such beliefs are not in themselves wrong but inadequate, since what is required is believing in him (11:26). Both the absolute use of the verb and its use with a prepositional phrase ("in me," etc.) are heavily loaded with content, which must be unpacked. This conclusion is forced upon us especially by instances where *pisteuein* is followed by a *hoti* clause that contains only *egō eimi* (8:24, 28; 13:19), but it is valid also for those instances where the *hoti* clause contains traditional christological titles (6:69; 11:27; 20:31) or refers to the fact that Jesus has been sent by God (16:27, 30; 17:8, 21).

The believing that is a precondition for receiving the gift of eternal life involves acceptance of the mystery of the incarnation: to believe in Jesus is to accept him as the Word become flesh for our salvation. John's entire Christology and soteriology are thus implied in his use of *pisteuein*. (There are, of course, levels of believing in the Fourth Gospel; those who "believe" because of Jesus' miracles have not yet attained to full faith; cf. 2:23–25.) Various shorthand ways of referring to this full faith are employed by John, including the use of traditional titles as in 11:27 and 20:31. It cannot be satisfactorily indicated, however, by using such titles with a preposition, such as, "We believe in the Messiah."[92] When a prepositional phrase employing *eis* or *en* is used with *pisteuein*, the verb implies the Johannine doctrine of salvation through incarnation, and the prepositional phrase identifies the historical person to whom this faith is related.

When we unpack the question of v. 35 in this fashion, we may paraphrase as follows: "Do you believe that the one who calls himself the Son of man is the incarnate Son of God, the Savior of the world?" Seen in this way, the question does not seek information about the man's religious beliefs but challenges him to become a believer in the Johannine sense (cf. the similar

90. Bultmann, *John*, p. 338.
91. See Bultmann's treatment, "*Pisteuō* in John" TDNT 6, pp. 222–28. In addition to John's theological use of the verb, it is also used nontechnically in the everyday sense of "accept as true," e.g., at 9:18, where "the Jews" do not believe that the beggar was previously blind.
92. "(You) believe in God" (14:1) is also a packed expression; in a Johannine context it can by no means be reduced to a banal affirmation of the existence of God.

question and response at 11:26f.). Not knowing the identity of the Savior whom the prophet from God (9:17, 33) has offered him, the man asks, "Who is the man who calls himself the Son of man, whom I am to accept as my Savior?" When Jesus identifies himself as the one in whom the saving purposes of God are fulfilled, the man immediately accepts him as Savior and Lord.[93]

It is surprising that so many have been misled into regarding 9:35 as the relic of an early Christian practice of confessing Jesus as the Son of man. The text does not do this! Just as we nowhere find (nor expect to find) a Christian confession "I believe in the Messiah," but rather a formula conforming to the pattern "I believe that Jesus is the Messiah," so we have no reason to assume that the confessional statement "I believe in the Son of man" would be used by Christians at any time or place in Christian history. It could be so employed *only if "the Son of man" was a name for Jesus*, thus making the statement equivalent to the shorthand confession "I believe in Jesus."

Because "the Son of man" does not here function as a recognizable self-designation of Jesus (although it is revealed to be such in Jesus' response to the man's question), we must reckon with the possibility that in this passage the phrase is not merely a name but the bearer of theological content. That content, however, is not to be derived from contemporary eschatology, so that the man is being asked whether or not he accepts the promise of the prophets concerning the advent of a redeemer. The man's response indicates that he understands Jesus' question as challenging him to commit himself in faith in the one human being who is uniquely related to God, the one in whom the Word became flesh. By thus employing Jesus' self-designation as a means for speaking of the human status of the incarnate Word, John prepares for the usage we found in the early church fathers, where "Son of God" refers to Jesus' divinity and "Son of man" to his humanity.

Jn. 12:23 The hour has come for the Son of man to be glorified.

If it were not for the hypotheses that the Johannine Son of man sayings are based upon the heavenly Man of Hellenistic syncretism or the transcendent judge of Jewish apocalyptic, there would be no attempt to

---

93. This conclusion is probably to be inferred, even if we were to omit vv. 38–39a, with Codex Sinaiticus, P75, and other early witnesses. See the discussion by Brown, *John*, p. 375; Lindars, *John*, p. 351. The authenticity of vv. 38–39a is defended by Metzger, *A Textual Commentary*, p. 229.

discover either of these conceptions here.[94] As the following verse makes perfectly clear, this logion announces that the prediction of the passion of the Son of man (3:14; cf. 6:53; 8:28) is now to receive fulfillment.[95] Higgins describes this as a Son of man saying of non-Synoptic type because of the peculiarly Johannine use of *doxazein*, but in function it forms a close parallel to the passion saying of Mk. 14:41 (as Higgins himself observes): "The hour has come; behold, the Son of man is betrayed into the hands of sinners."[96] Nor is there here, any more than in the Synoptic parallels, any hint of an overwhelming paradox that the preexistent Logos should suffer the death of an ordinary mortal. Where the death of Jesus is concerned, his genuine humanity is always in view. It is most natural to take "the Son of man" as referring here not to Jesus' heavenly glory but to his incarnate status.

Is the audience expected to perceive that Jesus is using the term as a self-designation? Yes, since vv. 27–34 make it clear that Jesus is speaking not of the death of someone else but of his own imminent death, and that this is perceived by his audience.[97] There is therefore no basis for speaking of a titular use of the phrase here. It functions as a name used by Jesus of himself and is recognized as such by the narrative audience.

Jn. 12:34 We have heard from the Law that the Christ remains for ever. How can you say, "The Son of man must be lifted up"? What is this, "the Son of man"?

This verse is frequently cited as evidence that John did not intend "the Son of man" to be taken as a recognized self-designation of Jesus but rather as the title for a heavenly or earthly eschatological figure with whom Jesus was to be identified by faith.[98] The verse is consequently interpreted as employing "the Christ" and "the Son of man" as synonyms.[99] Reflective of this understanding is the following paraphrase: "We have

---

94. Schulz, *Untersuchungen*, p. 119, treats the verse as deriving from the apocalyptic tradition concerning the enthronement of the heavenly Son of man.

95. "The hour" and "glorify" are used by John primarily with reference to the crucifixion; cf. G. Kittel's treatment of *doxazein* in the Fourth Gospel, TDNT 2, p. 249, and J. Schneider, *Doxa*, pp. 120ff.

96. Higgins, *Jesus and the Son of Man*, pp. 52f.

97. On the basis of his understanding of 12:34, Bultmann is convinced that the crowd does not perceive that Jesus uses "the Son of man" as a self-designation (*John*, p. 225 n. 1), but he does not address the question relative to 12:23.

98. E.g., Lietzmann, *Der Menschensohn*, p. 55; Potterie, "L'exaltation du Fils de l'homme (Jn 12,31–36)," p. 475.

99. Barrett, *John*, p. 356; Lindars, *John*, pp. 434f.; Sidebottom, *The Christ of the Fourth Gospel*, p. 72; Thompson, "The Son of Man—Some Further Considerations," pp. 206f.

heard from the Law that the Messiah does not die, and how then do you say that the Son of man, that is, the Messiah, must be crucified? What kind of a Messiah is this that you are proclaiming to us?"[100] If we remove the verse from its present context, as Bultmann does, then it is possible to ascribe such meaning to it; but the excision creates more problems than it solves.[101] When we examine the verse in context, it becomes clear that "the Christ" and "the Son of man" are not synonymous. What brings these terms together is not their connotations but their common application to Jesus.[102]

In v. 34 the crowd attributes to Jesus the statement "The Son of man must be lifted up," which, of course, is inaccurate (assuming that the crowd has not learned from Nicodemus what was said at 3:14!). What they have heard according to the narrative context is that Jesus, who calls himself "the Son of man," is to die (12:23f.) and that this can be expressed by the passive verb "be lifted up" (v. 32). The statement that the crowd attributes to Jesus is thus not so much a glaring inaccuracy as a compounding of vv. 23f. and v. 32, adding an explicit reference to (divine) necessity that was only implicit in the earlier verses.[103]

What, then, prompts the crowd's allusion to the Messiah, if it is not Jesus' use of "the Son of man"? We are apparently to remember that Jesus was publicly hailed as the king of Israel at 12:13 (cf. 6:15; 7:41) and that it will be on the charge of claiming to be "King of the Jews" that he will be executed (18:33; 19:19–21). The crowd's second question is thus not a rhetorical one, challenging Jesus' scriptural orthodoxy, but a puzzled inquiry concerning the identity of Jesus: Is he or is he not the Christ? Since the Messiah, according to the Scriptures, will not die, how can Jesus be the Messiah if, as he claims, he must die?

The second question, therefore, cannot be translated, "What kind of a Son of man is this?" as if the crowd regards "the Son of man" as merely

100. Cf. Barrett, *John*, p. 357; Brown, *John*, pp. 478f.; Bultmann, *John*, p. 354; Blank, *Krisis*, p. 293.

101. Bultmann, *John*, pp. 347ff., transfers 12:34–36a to a position following 8:21–29, insisting that 12:34 "clearly assumes that Jesus has just been speaking about the exaltation of the Son of man (in the third person). Yet this is not the case, for in the immediately preceding verses there is no mention whatsoever of the Son of man" (p. 313); in n. 7 on the same page he adds that 12:34 cannot depend upon 12:23, where reference is made to the glorification of the Son of man, not to his being lifted up. This approach treats the texts atomistically, as if 12:23 did not in its context speak of the death of the Son of man. Regardless of what possible context 12:34 may have had in an earlier edition of the Gospel, its final editor, if not the evangelist, has placed the verse in this context, apparently believing that it makes sense here. It is the responsibility of the exegete to recover a plausible meaning from this context, not to attribute to the verse a meaning derived from a purely hypothetical connection.

102. Cf. Leivestad, "Exit the Apocalyptic Son of Man," pp. 250f.; Vermes, *Jesus the Jew*, p. 162; Maddox, "The Function of the Son of Man," p. 200; O'Neill, *Messiah*, p. 114.

103. Schnackenburg, *Das Johannesevangelium*, part 2, p. 495. (Engl. ed., vol. 2, pp. 394f.)

another way of identifying the Messiah.[104] The context requires that we regard the question as seeking semantic clarification of the phrase "the Son of man" relative to the salvation-historical function of Jesus. To paraphrase broadly, the crowd asks: "If we have been mistaken in regarding you as the Messiah, what then are you? What are you telling us when you call yourself 'the Son of man'?" Such an understanding of the question receives strong support from 7:36, where the content of the question is very different but the structural similarity striking: *tis estin ho logos houtos*, "What is the meaning of this statement?"[105] In both instances *tis estin houtos* is employed to raise a question about the meaning of a semantic unit.

If this represents a correct understanding of the crowd's second question, it becomes apparent that the first question does not mean "How can you be so heretical as to suggest that the Messiah must be crucified?" Certain that Jesus employs "the Son of man" as a self-designation but totally uncertain as to its content, the crowd asks, "How can you be the Messiah, in view of your statement, 'I must be crucified'?"

Modern scholars may perhaps be disappointed that the Johannine Jesus does not answer the crowd's semantic question; judgment, not clarification, is the essence of his response. For John it is a matter of unbelief to constrict Jesus' significance to the channels provided by traditional titles and expectations, none of which are adequate to convey the new theological reality. Those traditional titles and expectations are indeed employed in John's dramatic portrait of Jesus, but faith has so transformed them that they function not as constrictors of meaning but as shorthand symbols for the miracle of the incarnation. It would be pointless, therefore, for the Johannine Jesus to explicate "the Son of man" to the unbelieving crowd, which cannot rise above traditional theological expectations to faith in the Word-become-flesh. Jesus' self-designation is employed by John, we may guess, precisely because it is *not* a traditional title with misleading meanings. Pointing to the uniqueness of Jesus (*the* son of man), it calls for faith without divulging the content of faith. To unbelievers it must remain opaque.

Jn. 13:31 Now is the Son of man glorified, and God is glorified in him.

Whatever grammatical specification is employed to describe the use of the aorist in *edoxasthē* (proleptic, dramatic, or prophetic), the presence of *nun* makes it obvious that the present tense is intended rather than

---

104. Cf. NEB: "What Son of Man is this?"
105. Bernard, *St. John*, vol. 2, p. 443, points to the parallel but nonetheless translates *tis* as "who" in 12:34.

the past.[106] The wider context, however, indicates that the *nun* itself is proleptic; the act of glorification has its focal point in the moment of Jesus' death on the cross.[107] It is here considered as contemporaneous, inasmuch as the traitor's departure initiates the process that brings Jesus to Golgotha.

It is important to stress the fact that the focal point of the glorification of Jesus is for John the crucifixion and not the subsequent return to heavenly glory. It would be erroneous to understand 13:31 as referring *primarily* to the return of the Logos to his proper home.[108] As J. Schneider correctly observes, to place the emphasis here, thus rendering the flesh little more than a veil covering the uninterrupted glory of the Logos, would be far too docetic for John.[109] In the Fourth Gospel everything hinges on the reality and significance of the incarnation. As eternal Son of God, Jesus possesses glory before, during, and following his life on earth (2:11; 12:41; 17:5, 24). The verb "glorify," however, refers not to status but activity. The glorification of the Son of man is related to a historical event.

The meaning of this event can be understood only by reference to the glorification of God to which it is reciprocally related ("and God is glorified in him").[110] It is a common New Testament theme that God is glorified by the faithful obedience of his saints (Mt. 5:16; Jn. 15:8; 20:19; 1 Cor. 6:20; 2 Cor. 9:13; 1 Pe. 2:12; cf. Isa. 49:3). Accordingly, when Jesus prays, "Father, glorify thy name" (12:28), the force is the same as that of the Gethsemane prayer of the Synoptic Gospels, "Abba, Father . . . not what I will, but what thou wilt" (Mk. 14:36 par.). The whole of Jesus' life has been a glorification of God, because in his words and deeds he has manifested the Name of God (17:6, 26; cf. 10:25), but his conformity with the Father's will reaches its ultimate manifestion in willing acceptance of a criminal's death. The divine intention of the incarnation is not fully accomplished until Jesus draws his last breath (19:30), for only in the lifting up of the Son of man is the saving love of God actualized in human history (3:13–17). Thus the acme of Jesus' glorification of the Father occurs on the

106. Neither Burton, *Moods and Tenses*, nor Zerwick, *Biblical Greek*, treats the aorist in Jn. 13:31.

107. Cf. Bultmann, *John*, p. 524; Dodd, *Interpretation*, p. 208; Moloney, *The Johannine Son of Man*, pp. 178, 196; J. Schneider, *Doxa*, pp. 120ff.

108. Schulz, *Untersuchungen*, pp. 121f., argues that the logion originally referred to the enthronement of the apocalyptic Son of man. Hamerton-Kelly, *Pre-existence, Wisdom, and the Son of Man*, p. 235, objects to so precise a determination but concurs with Schulz that the logion is concerned primarily with "the return of Christ to the pre-existent unity with God."

109. J. Schneider, *Doxa*, pp. 120f.

110. Schulz, *Untersuchungen*, p. 122, notes that God is glorified by placing the apocalyptic Son of man on this throne but does not explain why this should be so.

cross, and correspondingly it is there that Jesus is glorified by the Father: he is manifested as the unique human being in and through whom salvation takes place, the incarnate Son of God. While the anticipated glorification of Jesus includes the return to the Father, the emphasis for John, as for Paul (Phil. 2:10f.), lies in the death.[111]

Like 12:23, therefore, 13:31 reflects the same tradition as the Synoptic passion predictions (cf. especially Mk. 14:41 par.). It presupposes that the disciples know that Jesus uses the phrase "the Son of man" as a self-designation and that he is speaking of his forthcoming passion, as at 12:23ff. There is no justification for finding here evidence that "the Son of man" is the title of a preexistent, heavenly being.[112] Wherever the Passion is the focus of attention, it is the genuine humanity of the Son of man that is in view.

Conclusion

It is now time to recapitulate. How does "the Son of man" function in the Fourth Gospel? Of the six options listed at the beginning of this chapter, the sixth appears to have the best support in the texts. The term refers to the incarnational existence of the Logos. It points to the unique humanity of the Incarnate One.

It must be conceded, of course, that this option has not been conclusively demonstrated. John's use of double entendre and paradox makes it impossible to attain certainty in such matters. What has been shown, however, is that this understanding of the Johannine use of "the Son of man" is *possible in every instance*, even those that on first impression appear to point in a different direction (3:13; 5:27; 6:62). Moreover, this possibility is enhanced by the fact that a larger number of texts refer to the death of the Son of man (3:14; 6:53; 8:28; 12:23, 34; 13:31), thus emphasizing the real humanity of the Word-become-flesh. There is thus good reason to believe that John stands in close proximity to the Christian writers of the second and succeeding centuries, who employ *huios anthrōpou* as a way of speaking of the genuine humanity of Jesus in their battle against the docetists.

111. Cf. J. Schneider, *Doxa*, p. 120; Higgins, *Jesus and the Son of Man*, pp. 179–81. It is entirely possible that the Johannine use of "lift up" and "glorify" with reference to the death of Jesus represents a midrashic appropriation of Isa. 52:13 LXX; cf. Dodd, *Interpretation*, p. 247; Sidebottom, *The Christ of the Fourth Gospel*, p. 80; Blank, *Krisis*, p. 271.

112. See n. 108.

5 | MATTHEW

Even if readers of the foregoing chapters generously concede that a substantial case has been made for the thesis that the Gospels of Luke and John stand closer to Ignatius than to the Similitudes of Enoch in their use of "the Son of man," we may expect greater resistance to the presentation of a similar thesis with respect to the Gospel of Matthew. This is true despite the fact that Bultmann himself, rightly regarded as one of the stoutest advocates of the view that "the Son of man" was originally an apocalyptic title, did not believe that Matthew was aware of its proper meaning.

> The secondary material peculiar to Matthew or Luke does not need to be taken into account here; it is significant that for these later evangelists the original meaning of the title is lost and Son of Man has become so completely a self-designation of Jesus that Matthew can either substitute "I" for a traditional Son of Man (Mt. 10:32f. against Lk. 12:8f. . . .), or, vice versa, Son of Man for an "I" (Mt. 16:13 against Mk. 8:27).[1]

Following Bultmann, R. H. Fuller came to a similar conclusion.

> The title itself sank in the Hellenistic Jewish stage of the tradition to the level of a mysterious self-designation of Jesus devoid of any specifically christological color (cf. Mt. 16:13). Thus it was on its way to become, as in post-NT writers, a designation for Jesus' humanity, contrasted with "Son of God" as a designation for his divinity. Any idea that it was originally a title of majesty is completely lost.[2]

Bultmann's perception, however, has been strongly challenged by many who nonetheless share his starting point, namely, the conviction that at the earliest stage of the tradition the phrase functioned as an apocalyptic title.

1. Bultmann, *Theology*, vol. 1, p. 30; cf. his *History*, p. 155.
2. Fuller, *Foundations*, p. 229.

And with good reason. It is indisputable that Matthew not only uses the term more frequently than any other Gospel writer but uses it more often in an apocalyptic context. Of the Son of man sayings peculiar to Matthew, the majority are apocalyptic in orientation.[3] Recognition of these facts has led many scholars to adopt the position of Tödt, who argues that Matthew was fully aware of the Jewish apocalyptic tradition concerning the heavenly figure appointed by God as eschatological judge—that is, the Son of man described by the Similitudes of Enoch (1 Enoch 37–71). In this respect Matthew is for Tödt more primitive than either of his primary sources, Mark and Q. "The first evangelist often reaches back behind the Son of Man sayings from Mark and Q to elements of the concept in Jewish apocalyptic tradition which he employs independently to modify and expand the concept of the Son of Man."[4] He insists that elements in the Son of man sayings peculiar to Matthew "refer repeatedly to 1 Enoch."[5]

It is not surprising, therefore, that some have argued that "the Son of man" is Matthew's most important christological term and that, regardless of its use elsewhere, for Matthew it is an apocalyptic title of majesty referring to Jesus' role as eschatological judge.[6] If this view has been firmly substantiated, Matthew can be regarded as providing valid evidence of an early Son of man Christology of which Luke, John, Ignatius, and subsequent Christian writers were no longer aware.

It is possible, however, that this understanding of Matthew rests upon a faulty method and unproven assumptions. To begin with, it must be insisted that the frequency of Son of man sayings alluding to Jesus' future role does not in itself constitute proof that Matthew regarded *ho huios tou anthrōpou* as an apocalyptic title. That Matthew is especially interested in statements about Jesus' future role is incontestable, and most (but not all) of these employ "the Son of man," but it remains to be demonstrated that for Matthew the term functions as a "title of majesty." That is to say, since Matthew contains significant statements in which Jesus speaks about his future role using "I" (e.g., 7:21–23; 10:32f.; 28:18–20) or "your Lord" (24:42) instead of "the Son of man," it can just as reasonably be maintained that Matthew is more interested in the future role as such than in the concept of the Son of man.[7]

3. Cf. Kingsbury, *Matthew: Structure, Christology, Kingdom*, p. 114; Luz, *Matthew 1—7*, p. 74.
4. Tödt, *Son of Man*, p. 108.
5. Ibid., p. 223.
6. E.g., Blair, *Jesus in the Gospel of Matthew*, p. 83.
7. Cf. Lindars, *Jesus Son of Man*, p. 130.

If we begin with the assumption underlying this book that we do not in fact know whether or not "the Son of man" served as an apocalyptic title *at any stage of the tradition*, then we must be very careful to examine the Matthean evidence in a way that does not prejudice the investigation. Whatever solution to the Synoptic problem is adopted, clearly Matthew incorporates Son of man sayings in every category; his understanding of the term cannot logically be inferred by concentrating, as Tödt does, on the apocalyptic sayings. The truth of this assertion would be particularly obvious if one were to adopt the Griesbachian view of Matthew as the earliest Gospel.[8] The same objection holds on the two-document hypothesis, however; comparison with Mark and Luke suggests that Matthew has *added* "the Son of man" to materials referring to the earthly Jesus (16:13; 17:12; 26:2) as well as *deleting* the phrase from apocalyptic material (10:32f). In view of this state of affairs, then, it must be insisted that Matthew's understanding of the term can be obtained, if at all, only through careful observation of how he places Son of man sayings in context. An unprejudiced investigation must depend heavily on composition and redaction criticism.

Preliminary Considerations

Before we begin the study proper, some observations are in order concerning the way the messianic secret suffers from Matthew's rearrangement of his material, the possibility that "the Son of man" has multiple uses in this Gospel, and the function of the Son of man material within the overall structure of the Gospel.

Matthew's Use and Abuse of the Messianic Secret Motif

Two different organizational principles are employed by the First Evangelist, and the tension between them produces inconsistencies and anachronisms relative to the messianic secret. On the one hand, Matthew, like the other evangelists, presents his material in accordance with a story line, giving the "biography" of Jesus in chronological order. The messianic secret is a constituent part of this story. On the other hand, Matthew likes to arrange Jesus' teachings topically, grouping the sayings and parables according to theme. In chapter 10, for example, he brings together from various sources material dealing with discipleship, including sayings that

---

8. See Walker, "The Son of Man Question and the Synoptic Problem."

are found in Mark's "little apocalypse" (Mark 13). As a result of this
topical ordering, the Matthean Jesus speaks prematurely of his future
heavenly role (10:23, 32f.), before the disciples confess their faith in him as
the Son of God (14:33; 16:16). Inconsistencies of this kind convinced Wrede
that the idea of a messianic secret no longer had the importance for
Matthew that it had for Mark: "The idea of a hiddenness of the Messiah
on earth such as Mark shows us had already worn very thin in Matthew."[9]

Not all of the tensions and inconsistencies can be explained as the result
of the thematic ordering of material, however. It is obvious that 23:2 stands
in unresolved tension with subsequent statements in the same discourse
that warn against the teaching as well as the behavior of "the scribes and
Pharisees" (e.g., vv. 4, 13, 15f.). Kenzo Tagawa is fully justified in maintaining that these contradictions must not be superficially harmonized.[10] Yet
Tagawa's own assessment that "the evangelist Matthew is a writer who
blithely makes such contradictory utterances" must not be applied incau-
tiously to Matthew's treatment of the Son of man material.[11] Even if we
agree with Tagawa that Matthew is not a theologian for whom consistency
is the foremost virtue, it must be urged that Matthew's mind is not so
disordered that we should expect "the Son of man" to be used without any
consistency.

Matthew's seeming indifference to inconsistency and anachronism
becomes particularly troublesome when we attempt to relate the Son of
man sayings to the messianic secret motif. Scholars who are sure that "the
Son of man" connoted a transcendent heavenly being treat the two occurrences of the term in Mark that occur prior to Peter's confession (2:10, 28)
as Markan anachronisms, resulting perhaps from topical arrangement.[12] In
the First Gospel, however, there are no fewer than ten instances of the
phrase before Peter's confession. Can Matthew really have been so careless
about premature disclosures of Jesus' transcendent status?

It can readily be conceded that Matthew is indeed inconsistent with
respect to the messianic secret. Although the Matthean narrative of Jesus
walking on the sea is climaxed with the disciples' confession "Truly, it is
God's Son" (14:33), Peter's confession in 16:16 is treated more solemnly
than in the Synoptic parallels, as if it were the first and foundational
expression of the church's faith (". . . on this rock I will build my church,"

---

9. Wrede, *Messianic Secret*, p. 161; cf. pp. 154, 163.
10. Tagawa, "People and Community in the Gospel of Matthew," p. 151.
11. Ibid.
12. Cf. Wrede, *Messianic Secret*, p. 18.

v. 18).[13] Yet it is not fair to say that there is no messianic secret in Matthew.[14] Matthew is more explicit than the other Synoptists regarding the command to silence issued by Jesus following Peter's confession: "Then he ordered the disciples not to tell anyone that *he was the Christ*," v. 20 (the italicized words are not represented in Mark and Luke). Matthew, however, allows the climactic disclosure of Peter to be liberally foreshadowed in prior material. Just as Mark allows the confession to be anticipated by the ecstatic cries of demoniacs (1:24; 5:7), which are ignored by the narrative audience, so Matthew includes numerous "premature" foreshadowings of Jesus' messianic status (e.g., 5:17; 7:21; 10:32f., 34) as well as the explicit confession of 14:33.

It must be noted, however, that Matthew's violation of the messianic secret is strictly limited in extent. The christological titles that unambiguously identify Jesus as the Messiah are "the Christ," "the Son of God," "the Son of David," and "the King of the Jews/Israel." Matthew can speak narratively of "the deeds of the Christ" (11:2), but not until the trial before the high priest does the Matthean Jesus publicly identify himself as the Messiah by applying one of these titles to himself (Mt. 11:27, where "the Son" is probably understood by Matthew as an abbreviated form of "the Son of God," is a strong foreshadowing of 16:16f. and 28:18 but falls short of articulating an explicit claim to messiahship). That is to say, although Matthew clearly presents Jesus as functioning in a messianic way in the early chapters (the Sermon on the Mount constitutes the Messiah's reinterpretation of Torah)[15] and allows Jesus to allude to his role in the imminent eschatological drama (7:21–23; 10:32f.), he shrinks from attributing to Jesus any saying employing one of the unambiguous messianic titles in self-reference. Consequently we must not be too quick to assume that when Matthew ascribes to Jesus a public Son of man saying claiming special authority as in 9:6 ("But in order that you may know that the Son of man has authority on earth to forgive sins—"), he is showing total indifference to the messianic secret. We cannot imagine that Matthew could have substituted one of the unambiguous messianic titles in this saying and then have concluded as he does in v. 8, "And seeing this the crowds were struck with awe, and they glorified God *for giving such authority to humans*" (Mark and Luke have nothing corresponding to the italicized words).

Clearly Matthew distinguished between hints and open statements about messiahship. Hints such as "my Father" and "I have come" are freely

13. Cf. Vögtle, "Messiasbekenntnis und Petrusverheissung," especially p. 262.
14. E.g., Meier, *The Vision of Matthew*, p. 94 n. 80.
15. Cf. Davies, *Setting*, pp. 106–8.

employed without divulging the secret to the narrative audience, whereas explicit messianic titles are used with the greatest reserve. It would appear, therefore, that if Matthew regarded "the Son of man" as having a messianic connotation of some kind, his frequent use of the term in public contexts indicates that he included it among the hints rather than among the explicit titles.

Does "The Son of Man" Have More Than One Meaning for Matthew?

Does this state of affairs suggest that Matthew regarded the phrase as possessing more than one connotation? Considerable confusion surrounds this issue, as can be observed in a number of commentaries. Not even writers of such impeccable scholarship as F. W. Beare are immune. In the introduction to his commentary Beare refers to the "communal symbol" presented by the manlike figure of Dan. 7:13f., then adds: "In Matthew, as in the usage of the Gospels generally, it has become a symbol of Jesus, peculiarly fused with the notion of 'Messiah.' "[16]

That is, the Danielic figure—not the title—has become a symbol representing Jesus' messianic role. The title itself, he observes, is used by Matthew in a variety of contexts, and "in a few instances it seems to be no more than a surrogate for the personal pronoun and is occasionally equivalent to the generic 'man.' "[17] On a later page he refers to the eschatological judgment as "unquestionably the principal function of Jesus—not indeed in his earthly ministry, but in his glorious coming *as Son of man*."[18] It must be observed that three different entities are here discussed by the commentator: (1) a Danielic symbol, "one like a son of man"; (2) a Greek phrase, *ho huios tou anthrōpou*, rendered in English as "the Son of man"; and (3) an eschatological figure called "Son of man." It is the interrelationship of these three entities that is confused.

Beare probably represents a consensus of contemporary scholars in his uncertainty regarding whether or not the Greek phrase consistently refers to the Danielic symbol and/or the eschatological figure. In his comment on the first instance of the phrase at 8:20, he notes that it functions in the Gospels as a title "developed out of the apocalyptic figure of 'one like a son of man,' " but a few pages later, commenting on 9:6, he suggests that it is here "virtually a substitute for the pronoun 'I,' with an overtone of 'I, as

---

16. Beare, *The Gospel according to Matthew*, p. 39.
17. Ibid., p. 40.
18. Ibid., p. 43 (my italics).

man' (a man commissioned by God)."[19] This understanding of the phrase reappears in the discussion of 11:19, but at 12:8 Beare sees a messianic claim implicit in the use of the title, and at 16:13 he is greatly puzzled because Matthew's insertion of the phrase suggests that it is *not* a messianic title: "If they know him *as 'Son of Man*,' what point is there in asking them who he is taken to be by them?"[20] Beare apparently regards Matthew as inconsistent in his use of the phrase: it is sometimes simply a surrogate for "I," and at other times it is a christological title alluding to Jesus' eschatological role.

It is entirely conceivable that a phrase such as "the Son of man" could have had very different uses at different stages of the tradition or in different writers. It is quite another matter to maintain that this important phrase was used in such varied ways by the same author.

A still bolder presentation of the hypothesis of multiple uses is provided by J. P. Meier, who argues that for Matthew "the Son of man" is a "multifaceted title" with three main meanings: "lowly yet powerful servant on earth, dying and rising savior, eschatological judge who returns to save his own."[21] Even more expansive language is employed on a later page, where it is claimed that

> . . . Son of Man has the widest conceivable span of meanings: humble servant of the public ministry, possessor of the divine power to forgive sins during the public ministry, friend of sinners who is exposed to reproach, mockery, and blasphemy, Lord of the Sabbath, the suffering, dying, and rising servant, the cosmocrator, the judge of the last day, coming in his glory and accompanied by his angels.[22]

There is serious confusion here concerning the semantic function of a linguistic unit. Does the word "God" *connote* the whole of Christian theology? Certainly, the use of the word can trigger the recollection of a wide variety of beliefs about the Deity, but it is linguistically inaccurate to suggest that the word (whether name or title) *contains* all these as *meanings*.

We are all indebted to James Barr for bringing clarity to a much confused topic. In his criticism of the word studies contributed to Kittel's *Theological Dictionary of the New Testament,* Barr points out:

> . . . The attempt to relate the individual word directly to the theological thought leads to the distortion of the semantic contribution made by words in contexts; the value of the context comes to be seen as something contributed

19. Ibid., pp. 213, 223.
20. Ibid., pp. 262, 272, 353 (my italics).
21. Meier, *Vision*, pp. 68, 77.
22. Ibid., pp. 217f.

by the word, and then it is read into the word as its contribution where the context is in fact different. Thus the word becomes overloaded with interpretative suggestion. . . .[23]

Barr is here referring to common nouns, especially those that function as technical terms in some contexts and not in others, but his point is surely just as valid with respect to the word combination *ho huios tou anthrōpou*. If all statements employing the phrase "the Son of man" are read back into the phrase as its implicit content or meaning, then the sentences in question are treated as tautological: "The Son of man who has no place to lay his head has no place to lay his head." Worse still, the interpreter may be tempted to commit the exegetical sin of "illegitimate totality transfer," where other contexts employing the phrase are superimposed upon the sentence in question: "The Son of man who is lord of the sabbath, who must be delivered into the hands of men and be killed, but who will come on the clouds of heaven with his holy angels, has nowhere to lay his head."[24] To read all other Matthean statements containing the phrase into its use at 8:20 is totally to obscure its semantic function.

A more reasonable way of speaking of the alleged multiple uses of the phrase in the First Gospel is represented by David Hill. Commenting on 11:19, Hill proposes that here "the Son of man" is "used ambiguously as messianic title *and* as 'a man' denoting the speaker."[25] There is no further explication, but apparently Hill believes that the evangelist Matthew (as distinct from the Aramaic tradition behind the Gospel) regards the phrase as possessing two distinct linguistic functions, both of which are known to his Greek readers. There is, accordingly, a double entendre for the readers, who perceive that the narrative audience takes the phrase as a simple self-reference without significant content, whereas they, the readers, realize that Jesus is employing the phrase as a means of alluding to his messianic status and glory.

This is a very reasonable proposal. Language does indeed often function in this way. The issue is simply whether or not the hypothesis is justified here. Is there compelling evidence that the First Evangelist understands the phrase as possessing these two very different connotations? Does he treat it as a *secret* messianic title well known to his readers, the significance of which is hidden from the disciples until 16:13 and from the opponents until 26:64? Hill does not propose this state of affairs in his comments on the two passages. It must be asked, however, why we should infer ambigu-

23. Barr, *The Semantics of Biblical Language*, pp. 233f.
24. Cf. ibid., pp. 218, 222.
25. Hill, *The Gospel of Matthew*, p. 202.

ity if no note is taken by the Gospel's narrator of the discrepancy between the perception of the narrative audience and that of Jesus, the primary actor. Hill's rationale, presumably, is that he (like many other scholars) believes that Matthew must have understood the phrase as functioning as a messianic title, and yet he recognizes that this understanding does not suit all instances equally well.

A fascinating variant of this third view is provided by Jack Kingsbury.[26] At first glance, Kingsbury's view seems very different from Hill's, because he argues that the significance of "the Son of man" is to be found not in its content but in its narrative function. Whereas "the Son of God" is a confessional term with theological content, "the Son of man" has no such christological function. It serves rather to identify "the people in view of whom it is used as being unbelievers or opponents of Jesus."[27]

> As to its nature, "Son of Man" is the "public" title by which Jesus refers to himself as he interacts in Israel with the crowds and the leaders of the people (also Judas) or tells his disciples of what his enemies will do to him or what his death will mean for the world. From their standpoint, however, the people of Israel think of Jesus Son of Man simply as a man (cf. 9:6; 16:13). . . .[28]

Does this mean that Matthew regards the phrase as purely denotative, a name pointing to Jesus without conveying any distinctive connotation? Not at all. For Matthew it is indeed a christological title, not merely a substitute for the personal pronoun, for at the Parousia Jesus "will be unveiled before all as the Son of Man, the Judge of all."[29]

In a subsequent essay Kingsbury modifies his view in part. While still insisting that Matthew "would have the reader construe it as a technical term, or title," he notes that Jesus' application of the title to himself "appears to convey virtually nothing to those who hear it."[30] He proposes that "for purposes of translation, one can perhaps capture its force by rendering it as 'this man,' or 'this human being.' "[31] Nonetheless, while this is its ostensible meaning, the one assumed by the narrative audience who hear the "public title" without discerning its significance, its *real* meaning is discovered from the contexts in which it is used.

> The purpose for which the Matthean Jesus employs this title is multiple: to assert his divine authority in the face of public opposition, to tell his disciples

---

26. See especially Kingsbury, *Matthew: Structure*, pp. 113–27.
27. Ibid., p. 115.
28. Ibid., pp. 119f.
29. Ibid., p. 127 (italicized in the original).
30. Kingsbury, "The Figure of Jesus in Matthew's Story," pp. 24, 27.
31. Ibid., pp. 27f.

what the "public," or "world" (Jews and Gentiles), is about to do to him, and
to predict that he whom the world puts to death God will raise and that,
exalted to universal rule, he will return in splendor as judge and consequently
be seen by all as having been vindicated by God. Through Jesus' use of the
public title of the Son of man, therefore, Matthew calls the reader's attention
to the twin elements of "conflict" and "vindication."[32]

This statement apparently indicates that Kingsbury has not really abandoned the view that "the Son of man" is a title with christological content;
it connotes divine authority (even if it does not denote an apocalyptic
figure of pre-Christian eschatological thinking). Thus, despite his careful
attention to the narrative function of the phrase, Kingsbury concurs with
Hill and others that the term is for Matthew truly ambiguous: it is a secret
messianic title that the narrative audience perceives as nothing more than
a colorless self-designation.

It is notoriously difficult to prove or disprove the presence of double
entendre in a piece of literature, unless the author provides the necessary
clues (as in Jn. 3:3–8; 14:4–8). It is particularly difficult in the present
instance, where the proposed ambiguity relates to a term whose meaning
or meanings cannot be presupposed on the basis of prior usage but must
be discovered by examining the Matthean texts. On a priori grounds, however, I regard it as distinctly more probable that a phrase of such limited
circulation should have been employed by Matthew with a single semantic
function.

The denotative function clearly is single. The term is unambiguously
and consistently used as Jesus' idiosyncratic way of referring to himself.
There is never the slightest suggestion that the narrative audience believes
that Jesus is speaking of someone else. This is true not only of the sayings
referring to Jesus' present activities and anticipated sufferings but also of
those that speak of his future glory and "coming." Whatever such sayings
may have meant at an earlier stage of the tradition, in Matthew's use they
are statements of Jesus about himself, not about a figure distinct from
himself. This is particularly obvious in chapter 24. Here we find three
statements regarding the *parousia* of the Son of man (vv. 27, 37, 39) that,
read in isolation, could be taken as referring to someone other than the
speaker, but these are set by Matthew in the context of a discourse prompted
by the disciples' request, "Tell us, when will this be, and what will be the
sign of your coming (*parousia*) and of the close of the age?" (v. 3).

Matthew's use of the term thus corresponds completely with the eighth
thesis of Ragnar Leivestad: "In cases where it is formally possible to take

32. Ibid., pp. 31f.

'Son of man' as a designation of someone different from Jesus, such a possibility has apparently never occurred to anyone. No precautions have been taken to prevent misunderstanding."[33] For Matthew and his first Christian readers, the Parousia sayings referred unambiguously to the "coming" of *Jesus*, whatever their connotation of "the Son of man."

Is there any basis for postulating that the connotation also is single? Matthew's readers, we may safely assume, knew the Greek phrase only in sayings attributed to Jesus. Not one scrap of evidence has come to light in support of the hypothesis that the Greek phrase employing two articles was extant outside of Christian circles. Even if one were to conjecture that his readers were already familiar with Luke's attribution of the phrase to Stephen in Acts 7:56, this would not affect the point in question, since, as we have seen in chapter 3, the Lukan passage clearly uses the term as a name for Jesus. That is to say, the phrase was *strange* to them; they had no prior acquaintance with it in secular language or any other religious context.

As far as I can see, Matthew gives us not the slightest reason to believe that either he or his readers were aware of any connection between the Greek phrase and the indefinite Aramaic phrase *bar enasha,* which meant "a man," and thus in some contexts could by implication point to the speaker, "a man such as I." That is, even if Vermes and others are correct in hypothesizing that at the origin of the entire corpus of Son of man sayings in the Gospels is Jesus' use of the colorless *bar enasha* as a self-reference, there is no basis for maintaining that *for Matthew's readers* the phrase possessed as one of its two connotations the meaning "this man," as Hill and Kingsbury propose. Nothing in their prior linguistic experience would incline them to the inference that in certain contexts *ho huios tou anthrōpou* could function recognizably as a synonym for *houtos ho anthrōpos*. In this respect their situation is not very different from that of modern readers of the First Gospel in translation; uncontaminated by the strange suggestions of scholars, such readers perceive very naturally that the phrase, whatever its meaning, functions as a name for *Jesus*, not as the equivalent of a demonstrative pronoun that could, at least theoretically, be used by any human male with reference to himself.[34] Matthew's readers probably inferred that *ho huios tou anthrōpou* was a peculiar name that

---

33. Leivestad, "Exit the Apocalyptic Son of Man," p. 261.
34. It must be conceded that in one respect the modern reader's situation is different; in modern Western languages it is customary to capitalize the phrase or at least the first word, indicating thereby that it is a name or title.

Jesus had coined for himself (just as, according to Mk. 3:17, he had nick-named James and John "Sons of Thunder").[35]

In what follows, then, it will be assumed that for Matthew "the Son of man" functions *unambiguously* as a name or title applied by Jesus to himself, whose connotation (if any) remains to be determined. The hypothesis that the phrase is in some sense a messianic title must be carefully tested, but in the process it will be insisted that, while this significance can reasonably be conceived as *unknown* to the narrative audience, or (less reasonably) as *ignored*, for Matthew and his readers the narrative opponents of Jesus in the First Gospel do not hear him saying anything so mundane as "this man."

The Distribution of Son of Man Material in Relation to Matthew's Structure

A number of proposals have been made concerning the structure of the First Gospel. In his recent commentary U. Luz has assigned these to three main groups: (1) those concurring with Bacon's suggestion regarding five "books" related to five major discourses; (2) those arguing for a chiastic structure, in which the parables discourse of chapter 13 functions at the center of the Gospel; (3) those urging a narrative structure based on Mark, where Peter's confession provides the major turning point.[36]

The first two of these three models focus on the five discourses marked by the transition formula "and when Jesus had finished . . ." (Mt. chaps. 5–7, 10, 13:1–52, 18, 24–25, or 23–25). If one considers these five segments the heart of the Gospel, however, it is clear that "the Son of man" does not play a major role structurally. The phrase occurs not at all in the Sermon on the Mount or in the discourse on church discipline (chap. 18), once only in the discourse on discipleship (10:23), and only twice in the parables discourse (13:37, 41). A high density of instances is observed in the eschatological discourse, where the phrase is used seven times in material speaking of Jesus' future role. We notice, however, that occurrences of the term *outside* the five discourses outnumber these by a ratio of 20 to 10. It is obvious, therefore, that the first two models do not help very much in identifying Matthew's understanding of the phrase—unless, of course, the

---

35. Observant readers in the first century, as in the twentieth, were probably also aware of the difference between the name Jesus gives himself and those he applies to others: "the Son of man" is not a name that others can use in addressing Jesus or speaking of him, except at Acts 7:56 and possibly Luke 24:7.

36. Luz, *Matthew 1–7*, pp. 35f. Luz raises objections to all three, but the third seems closest to his own view of Matthew as a connected *narrative* (p. 37).

concentration of instances in the eschatological discourse is taken as sufficient in itself to establish an apocalyptic meaning. This is the assumption
we are testing here.

The most satisfactory presentation of the third model is that of Kingsbury, who urges that the formula "From that time Jesus began . . . ," while
occurring only twice (4:17; 16:21), nonetheless serves to demarcate the
three major divisions of the Gospel, concerned respectively with (1) the
person of Jesus Messiah (1:1—4:16); (2) the proclamation of Jesus Messiah (4:17—16:20); (3) the suffering, death, and resurrection of Jesus
Messiah (16:21—28:20).[37]

In relation to this third model it will be observed, first, that "the Son of
man" does not appear in the first section at all and, second, that no distinctive pattern is perceptible that would distinguish the use of the term in the
third section from that of the second. "The Son of man" occurs in part 2
in material dealing with Jesus' present activity, anticipated suffering, and
future "coming," and the same is true of part 3, except that the phrase
does not occur in statements about Jesus' present activity, and the number
of instances in the other two categories significantly increases—nine
instances in "suffering" sayings as against one (12:40) in part 2; eleven
occurrences in "future" material, compared with three in part 2. It is
noteworthy that in the third section, despite the heavy concentration of
instances in the eschatological discourse, "future" Son of man sayings do
not greatly predominate over those dealing with Jesus' anticipated suffering; the ratio is 10 to 8 (the phrase occurs twice each in 24:30, a "future"
saying, and in 26:24, a "suffering" saying). Those who too quickly assume
that "the Son of man" is an apocalyptic title for Matthew should also
observe that in the Gospel as a whole the term occurs more frequently in
nonapocalyptic contexts (sixteen instances, compared with fourteen uses
in "future" material, including the problematic statement of 13:37).

Kingsbury argues persuasively that the major intention of the first section is to define who Jesus is.[38] The climax is thus reached in the utterance
from heaven at Jesus' baptism: "This is my Son" (3:17). Kingsbury comments: "God himself declares Jesus to be his beloved Son and in so doing
gives expression to the evaluative point of view concerning Jesus' identity
which the reader is to regard as being normative for Matthew's story."[39] In
view of this state of affairs, Kingsbury notes, it is surely significant that

37. Kingsbury, *Matthew: Structure*, p. 9, building on prior work by E. Krentz and N. B.
Stonehouse.
38. Kingsbury, "The Figure of Jesus," pp. 26f.
39. Ibid., p. 26.

"the Son of man" plays no role at all in part 1, that is, in defining who Jesus is. The phrase does not appear until 8:20, and this initial instance is very unobtrusive in terms of its setting: "The reader does not anticipate its sudden use and the focus of the text is neither on the term itself nor on the topic of Jesus' identity but on the theme of discipleship. Literarily, it is difficult to see from the way in which Matthew first acquaints the reader with 'the Son of man' that it is calculated to inform the reader of 'who Jesus is.' "[40]

These helpful comments concerning the late and casual appearance of the term at 8:20 may be supplemented by some further structural considerations. It has been remarked that Luke's long Nazareth pericope in 4:16–30, his first major departure from the Markan order, constitutes the "frontispiece" of Luke-Acts. In the same way, the Sermon on the Mount, Matthew's first major departure from Mark, is the frontispiece of his Gospel, serving to define its fundamental thrust.[41] Substituted for an exorcism, which for Mark demonstrates Jesus' authority as a teacher (Mk. 1:21–28), the Sermon on the Mount functions for Matthew as "the Messiah's inaugural address." The one identified by the voice from heaven as "my Son" is here presented as the Messiah who does not annul Torah but provides it with a divinely authorized interpretation.[42]

The importance of this block of material is reinforced by the final pericope of the Gospel, which constitutes an *inclusio* with the Sermon on the Mount by means of the phrase "to the mountain" (*eis to oros*, 5:1 and 28:16).[43] Since this phrase occurs elsewhere (14:23; 15:29), its occurrence at 28:16 does not point unambiguously back to 5:1 if one assumes that the adverb *hou* is here used loosely with the meaning "to which, whither" rather than in the more correct sense "in which place." The Greek clause as it stands, however, is not readily comprehensible if the adverb is taken in the second way (as is done in most modern translations); something must be added if the clause is to make sense. Perhaps the best suggestion is that of Walter Bauer, who proposes that the infinitive *poreuesthai* be understood as completing the verb *etaxato*; we should thus take the clause as meaning "to the mountain to which Jesus had directed them (to go)."[44] It is a little strange to take the words in this way, since, as A. B. Bruce

40. Ibid., pp. 26f.
41. This analysis will hold true even for those who regard Matthew from a Griesbachian perspective.
42. Davies, *Setting*, p. 102.
43. Ibid., p. 85; cf. Fenton, *Saint Matthew*, p. 453.
44. Bauer, *A Greek-English Lexicon*, p. 594.

noted, one would expect to find an earlier statement in the Gospel to which this would refer (just as Mk. 16:7, "as he told you," refers back to 14:28).[45] Although this is not a major problem, it and the fact that an infinitive must be supplied suggest that it would be better to take the adverb in its normal sense (as Matthew uses it in both other instances, 2:9 and 18:20) and seek another meaning for the verb.

It is used twice in the Septuagint in exactly the same form (aorist middle) with the meaning "issue orders, command" (Ex. 8:8; 1 Sam. 20:35). Furthermore, it is used in the aorist active by Josephus with reference to what the Torah does, following a usage well established in Plato.[46] It is therefore possible to take *etaxato* in 28:16 as meaning "issue orders, lay down rules, legislate." If this is correct, 28:16 was intended to say: "And the eleven disciples went to Galilee to the mountain where Jesus had commanded them (i.e., had given rules for living to them)."[47] In this case *etaxato autois* anticipates *eneteilamēn humin* in v. 20; the latter, however, looks back not only to the Sermon on the Mount but to all the dominical instruction that Matthew has included in his Gospel. If the perception is correct that Matthew places special emphasis upon the importance of doing the will of the Father by living in accordance with Jesus' words, it is surely true that 28:16-20 does intend to take the reader back to the Sermon on the Mount, the first major statement of what this means.[48]

With this in mind, let us consider the significance of the *nonappearance* of "the Son of man" in the Sermon on the Mount. Assuming the two-document hypothesis, we notice that Matthew has greatly expanded the Q sermon, whose compass is probably more nearly represented by Luke's Sermon on the Plain (Lk. 6:20–49). Like the underlying Q version, Matthew's sermon ends with the theme of judgment, represented in the parable of the two builders (7:24–27; cf. Lk. 6:47–49). If Luke's brief introduction to the parable, "Why do you call me 'Lord, Lord,' and not do what I tell you?" (Lk. 6:46), represents the original, it appears that Matthew has considerably amplified it because of his special interest in the judgment (as the ultimate sanction for doing the will of the Father, 7:21). He does

45. A. B. Bruce, "The Synoptic Gospels," p. 338.

46. Josephus, *Apion* 2:203, 214; Plato, *Leges* 772C. Bauer, *A Greek-English Lexicon,* p. 813, notes that at Mt. 28:16 the middle is equivalent to the active.

47. Chevasse, "Not the Mountain Appointed," p. 478, following the rendering of the Revised Version, argues that, despite the dative *autois,* the pronoun should be taken as the object of the verb "appointed." This is illegitimate, since the verb regularly takes objects in the accusative.

48. It can be argued that in some respects the conclusion of the Sermon on the Mount, 7:21-27, is more "programmatic" than 5:17-20, the section to which this adjective is usually applied.

this by picking up another pericope from Q, which is placed by Luke at a much later point in his narrative framework (13:25–27). The Lukan version is generally regarded as the more primitive; Matthew's looks very much like a free rewriting of Luke's parable of the closed door, redrafted in the interest of making the significance of the Q introduction to the parable of the two builders (Lk. 6:46) more explicit.[49]

If we are justified in seeing any relationship between Mt. 7:22f. and Lk. 13:25–27, it is surely more probable that Luke's third-person language represents the earlier form; it is easy to understand how this form of speech gave rise to the first-person language of Matthew's version, whereas the reverse appears most improbable. Given this state of affairs, we must observe how easy it would have been for Matthew in his liberal editing of the Q material to have inserted "the Son of man" instead of introducing first-person forms. Since Matthew clearly regards Jesus as the future judge and finds it appropriate for Jesus to speak of his eschatological function in third-person language employing "the Son of man" (16:27), this first reference to Jesus' role at the last judgment provided him with an excellent opportunity to introduce Jesus to his readers as "the Son of man whose primary function is that of eschatological judge"—if that were indeed his understanding of the term. If it is objected that Matthew was too conservative to add "the Son of man" to traditional material, the example of 16:28 presents strong evidence to the contrary; most commentators would concede that in all probability Matthew has here edited Mk. 9:1 so as to substitute "the Son of man" for "the kingdom of God."[50] Furthermore, Matthew's use of *homologēsō*, "I will confess," in 7:23 clearly anticipates its occurrence in 10:32, another judgment saying, where Matthew has apparently *deleted* "the Son of man."[51]

These remarks concerning the absence of "the Son of man" from the juridical climax of the structurally important Sermon on the Mount constitute an argument from silence, which is necessarily of limited probative force. Matthew's avoidance of the term at this important juncture should, however, at least cause us to ponder whether he regards "the Son of man" as an apocalyptic title whose *primary* linguistic function is to identify Jesus as the eschatological judge.

49. Cf. Gundry, *Matthew*, pp. 130f.; Marshall, *Luke*, p. 566.
50. It cannot be objected that the vocative use of *Kyrie* with reference to Jesus in the Q *Vorlage* (Lk. 6:46) deterred Matthew from employing "the Son of man"; in Matthew's edited form of the judgment scene in 25:31–46, the one who calls himself "the Son of man" is addressed as *Kyrie*.
51. Pace Jeremias, "Die älteste Schicht," p. 170 (reiterated in his *New Testament Theology*, p. 275).

A similar observation can be made respecting 28:16–20. No one doubts the importance to the author of this final passage, and most scholars will probably agree that in its present form it reflects Matthean editing.[52] It presents the resurrected Jesus as a transcendent figure who claims, "All authority in heaven and on earth has been given to me." It is not surprising that scholars have proposed that Matthew, in creating or editing this pericope, consciously alludes to Dan. 7:13f., where the "one like a son of man" receives authority.[53] Some go further and claim that for Matthew Jesus here speaks *as* the Son of man, that is, as the transcendent figure anticipated in Jewish apocalyptic.[54] The allusion to Daniel is hard to prove or disprove.[55] If it is granted, however, that such an allusion is intended, it is all the more significant that this statement concerning Jesus' vindication and "divine authority" is not couched by Matthew in the form of a Son of man saying.

Returning to the third model, we observe that "the Son of man" appears at a critical point in the structure, namely, the transitional pericope that links the second and third sections (16:13–20). Perhaps the Matthean insertion of the phrase at 16:13, like his avoidance of the term at other structurally important locations, will reveal his understanding of the phrase.

The structural significance of 16:13 is questioned by some of Bacon's followers. In response to Kingsbury's proposal that 16:21 marks the beginning of a new section, Meier comments: "Such a view simply takes over the main division of Mark with too little consideration of the restructuring activity of Matthew."[56] It is true that the passion prediction of 16:21 has been anticipated by a public announcement concerning the three-day sojourn of the Son of man in the heart of the earth (12:40), just as Peter's confession has been foreshadowed by the corporate confession of the disciples (14:33). This fact, however, does not prevent Matthew from treating the announcement of 16:21 with special solemnity (just as he gives Peter's confession far more weight than Mark does), which can be seen by com-

---

52. Cf. Gundry, *Matthew*, pp. 593–97.

53. E.g., Michel, "Der Abschluss des Matthäusevangeliums," p. 22; Schniewind, *Matthäus*, p. 279.

54. J. P. Meier, *Vision*, pp. 37f. Meier is followed by Geist, *Menschensohn und Gemeinde*, pp. 117f.

55. The presence of two words in common between 28:18 and Dan. 7:14 LXX (*edothē, exousia*) is hardly sufficient to establish an allusion. It is noteworthy that the older editions of Nestle's text, where Old Testament allusions are printed in bold type, find no allusion here. Tödt, *Son of Man*, p. 288, concedes the possibility of an allusion but asks, "But what is alluded to? It is enthronement alone, not the concept of the Son of Man; for if an allusion to this concept had been intended, it would not have been possible to omit the name Son of Man."

56. Meier, *Vision*, p. 95 n. 80.

paring his version with Mark's. He adds not only the important temporal formula "from that time" (*apo tote*) but also the formal subject "Jesus Christ" and the explicit object "his disciples" (in place of Mark's "them").[57]

The significance of this first explicit passion prediction (since 12:40 must be reckoned as a "foreshadowing") is further enhanced by the sequel. Where Mark provides only a brief narrative statement, "And Peter took him, and began to rebuke him" (Mk. 8:32), Matthew supplies direct discourse for Peter, "God forbid, Lord! This shall never happen to you" (Mt. 16:22). Furthermore, Matthew subsequently adds two passion predictions to material he takes over from Mark (17:12; 26:2), both of which, like the Markan model (Mk. 8:21), employ "the Son of man."[58] These additions reinforce the significance of the first formal announcement of the Passion at 16:21.[59]

Assuming, then, the pivotal importance of 16:21 in Matthew's narrative structure, what is the significance of the fact that he has *deleted* "the Son of man" from this verse (cf. Mk. 8:21) and *added* it at 16:13? It has frequently been said that Matthew has "moved" the phrase from v. 21 to v. 13.[60] This view seems to suggest that, while Matthew was motivated to insert the phrase at the beginning of the pericope, he did not wish to repeat it as soon as v. 21, because this would offend his sense of good literary style.[61] This may, indeed, have been his reason for omitting the phrase at v. 21, but we should note that stylistic considerations did not prevent him from repeating the phrase in successive verses at the end of this pericope (vv. 27f., where Matthew has apparently added the phrase in the second saying; cf. Mk. 9:1), and he uses the phrase twice within the same sentence on two different occasions (24:30; 26:24). It should be conceded, therefore, that, if the evangelist had felt that the phrase was indispensable in v. 21, he would surely have retained it without stylistic compunction. Even though he finds it appropriate to use "the Son of man" in passion predictions and, as we have seen, adds two of his own (17:12; 26:2), he apparently did not regard it as improper for Jesus to speak of his suffering and death in more direct language. Matthew was not mastered by a "mystery of the Son of

---

57. Adopting the original reading of Sinaiticus and Vaticanus.

58. Assuming that 17:12 is not simply a greatly reformulated version of Mk. 9:12; see below.

59. Kingsbury, *Matthew: Structure*, p. 114, suggests that since Matthew adds six "future" and only two "suffering" sayings, it is clear that "Matthew's primary interest in the term Son of Man has to do with its association with the parousia." It would perhaps be more accurate to say that Matthew has a primary interest in the Parousia and finds it appropriate for Jesus to speak of it in third-person language just as in sayings about his destined suffering.

60. E.g., Tödt, *Son of Man*, p. 150.

61. Ibid., p. 90.

man" that demanded that Jesus invariably speak of his death and resurrection in this way.[62]

A possible motive for the omission of the phrase at 16:21 is proffered by Lindars: Matthew wants to impress upon the reader that it is *as Messiah* that Jesus must suffer. "Precisely because the Son of Man was not a messianic title, it could not resume 'the Christ' of the preceding verse. Rather, being a self-designation, it would appear to introduce a new subject, so spoiling the close connection which Matthew wishes to maintain."[63] Scholars who are certain that "the Son of man" was for Matthew a messianic title will not be convinced by Lindars's argument, but those willing to follow the method here employed by assuming an agnostic position will be able to see the force of his remarks. Whatever Matthew's understanding of "the Son of man," his omission of it here suggests that he did not regard it as simply synonymous with "the Christ, the Son of the living God" (v. 16), an affirmation that is emphatically praised by the Matthean narrative (vv. 17–19).

More important for this investigation, however, is Matthew's motivation for adding the phrase at v. 13. Inevitably interpreters bring to their examination of this verse their own preunderstanding of the phrase's meaning. M.-J. Lagrange suggests: " 'The Son of man' indicates here the human nature of Jesus, and prepares by way of contrast for the revelation of his divine nature."[64] S. E. Johnson, on the other hand, maintains: "Matthew adds 'Son of man' here in order to make it clear that Jesus is both celestial Son of man and the Messiah. . . ."[65] Which of these exegetical comments is better supported by the context?

Those who stress the narrative function of gospel language are inclined to align themselves more nearly with Lagrange than with Johnson. Numerous scholars have pointed out that if "the Son of man" is understood by Matthew to function as a recognizable title for the "heavenly Messiah," the narrative makes no sense; there is no room for the bestowal of a divine revelation upon Peter, because Jesus discloses his status in the initial question.[66] Those whose position is closer to Johnson's must therefore treat Matthew's language as transcending the narrative in some sense. For them

---

62. This is observed by Tödt (ibid., p. 85 n. 2). See also the comments on 26:64 below.

63. Lindars, *Jesus Son of Man*, p. 116.

64. Lagrange, *Évangile selon Saint Matthieu*, p. 322: "Le fils de l'homme indiquait ici la nature humaine de Jésus, et préparait par contraste la révélation de sa nature divine."

65. Johnson, "The Gospel according to St. Matthew: Introduction and Exegesis," p. 449.

66. E.g., Klostermann, *Matthäus*, p. 271; Leivestad, "Exit the Apocalyptic Son of Man," pp. 256f.; Lindars, *Jesus Son of Man*, p. 115.

"the Son of man" as used here (and everywhere?) by Matthew is not heard by the narrative audience.

Perhaps the least confused statement of this point of view is Tödt's. In response to the argument that the narrative excludes the possibility that "the Son of man" serves Matthew as a messianic title, Tödt protests: "But obviously Matthew does not wish to put a *genuine* question at the beginning."[67] Its function is different from that of the parallel question in Mark, because the passage as a whole has a different purpose. Whereas in Mark the pericope deals with the fact and meaning of Jesus' messiahship, in Matthew it treats the founding of the church. "The sovereignty of the one who announces the period of his church is solemnly enunciated at the beginning of the section. This is done by using the name Son of Man as an emphatic heading."[68] Tödt then attempts to buttress this proposal by reference to 26:2, where, as we have seen, Matthew adds a Son of man passion prediction to Markan material; this, too, is a "heading," set over the whole passion narrative.[69]

If one begins the study of Matthew's use of "the Son of man" with the assumption that one does not yet know what the phrase means to Matthew, it is not likely that Tödt's response will be convincing.[70] Whereas Bultmann, Fuller, Klostermann, and others assume that Matthew is using language in normal ways, Tödt must attribute to the First Evangelist an abnormal use of language for which parallels in the Gospels are difficult if not impossible to find. On what basis can Tödt argue that the words attributed to Jesus transcend the narrative setting (i.e., they do not constitute a "genuine" question), apart from his prior conviction that Matthew employs the phrase as an apocalyptic title? One cannot dismiss the function of a literary genre (here, *question*) by providing it with the name of another genre (*heading*), without supplying more evidence than Tödt does.

Tödt would be on safer ground if he were to argue that Matthew's use of the apocalyptic title at 16:13 does not compromise the narrative because the true meaning of the appellation is hidden from the narrative audience here and at its prior appearances in the Gospel. This argument is plausible, however, only if it can be shown that at some point the secret connotation

---

67. Tödt, *Son of Man,* p. 150.
68. Ibid.
69. Ibid. Cf. Senior, *Passion Narrative,* p. 21.
70. While 26:2 inaugurates the passion and thus can metaphorically be referred to as a "heading," this is because of the content of the statement, not because of the presence of "the Son of man." The initial question of 16:13 is a "heading" for the brief passage dealing with the identity of Jesus, but no more so than in the Synoptic parallels, where "the Son of man" is not used.

is disclosed to one or more segments of the narrative audience. Such a proposal is made by Meier, who locates the disclosure in Peter's confession. "Peter identifies the Son of Man mentioned in Jesus' question with both the Messiah and the Son of the living God. . . . The question was: What is the precise sense and range of the title as applied to Jesus? Peter's reply delineates some aspects of Son of Man by explaining it with two other titles, now drawn together for the first time in the gospel."[71] "The Son of man," Meier continues, nevertheless brings a content of its own to this collocation, so that henceforth "Messiah" and "Son of God" are expanded to include connotations proper to the "the Son of man": they become associated with "the mystery of the powerful transcendent One hidden in the deprivation and service of the public ministry," "the mystery of the dying and rising servant," and "the mystery of the judge who will come in glory."[72]

This thesis is hard to disprove. It is equally hard to prove. All that can be demonstrated from the context is that "the Son of man" functions here, as elsewhere in Matthew, as Jesus' peculiar self-designation. Peter's response to the two questions does not define the Son of man but *Jesus*; it cannot logically be inferred from the passage that because Jesus has called himself the Son of man and Peter calls him the Messiah, the Son of the living God, that these various names have all been assigned the same connotative force. This can be illustrated by substituting "the Son of the carpenter" for "the Son of man" in v. 13; Peter's confession does not change the meaning of the appellation but merely affirms that the one who so designates himself is to be regarded as the Son of the living God.

If a disclosure cannot be demonstrated for 16:13, perhaps it occurs in Jesus' declaration before the Sanhedrin at 26:64, by reason of an allusion to Dan. 7:13f. Does Matthew intend the narrative audience to hear Jesus saying, in effect: "You have heard me call myself the Son of man, and this did not anger you because you did not perceive my meaning; now I disclose to you that I meant thereby that I am the 'one like a son of man' of whom Daniel prophesied, the heavenly Messiah who will sit at God's right hand and come on the clouds to judge the world"? This seems to be Meier's understanding: "Now his own explanation of what he means by Son of Man calls down upon him the final charge of blasphemy. . . ."[73]

This is more easily asserted than established. That Matthew intends an allusion to Dan. 7:13f. is unmistakable—his version conforms more closely

71. Meier, *Vision*, p. 109.
72. Ibid., p. 110.
73. Ibid., p. 193.

to the Septuagint than Mark's—but this need not mean that he understands Jesus' statement as disclosing the hitherto concealed meaning of *ho huios tou anthrōpou*. Undoubtedly Matthew saw a connection between Jesus' customary self-designation and the Danielic phrase *hōs huios anthrōpou*, but it must not be assumed without demonstration that he saw the former as derived from and dependent on the latter (just as it cannot be assumed that he regarded *ho huios tou theou* as exhaustively defined by the reference to *ton huion mou* in Hos. 11:1 at Mt. 2:15). Matthew assuredly accepted as authentic the tradition that Jesus had spoken of his future role by means of an allusion to Daniel, but he also regarded it as indisputable that Jesus had called himself the Son of man in sayings referring to his present activity and anticipated suffering. That is, the term's function for Matthew is not dictated by the eschatological reference of the Danielic text. He shows no embarrassment about incorporating non-eschatological Son of man sayings and, as we have seen, increases their number through redactional insertions. Matthew's interest in Dan. 7:13f. does not mean that he has apocalypticized the self-designation; there is nothing about the way he employs the term in apocalyptic sayings, including 26:64, that would rule out the connotation "the Human Being par excellence." If evidence could be found that this was indeed Matthew's understanding, we would then conclude without difficulty that he found in Dan. 7:13f. a relevant prophecy concerning the one who regarded himself as the Human Being par excellence.

We must address the question, How does "the Son of man" actually function in the trial narrative? Rhetorically, it serves as Jesus' self-designation and nothing more. Not the slightest hint in the succeeding narrative suggests that the charge of blasphemy is related to Jesus' use of the phrase. This conclusion can be tested (as at 16:13) by substituting some other possible self-designation such as "the Son of the carpenter." The narrative effect of Jesus' declaration is not altered by such a substitution; the charge of blasphemy is based not on the self-designation but on the outrageous claim that Jesus makes, namely, that he, a human being, will be the kind of Christ that even David must call Lord because he will be seated at God's right hand (cf. 22:43–45) and, armed with the authority this implies (cf. 28:18), will come for judgment (cf. 24:30).[74] As Kingsbury points out, the self-designation apparently conveys nothing to the hearers, for it is totally ignored in the sequel, where Jesus is mocked not because of his self-

74. Although the narrative assumes that a formal charge of blasphemy was sustained against Jesus by a competent Jewish court, this is historically improbable; cf. Hare, *Persecution in Matthew*, pp. 23–30.

designation as the Son of man but because he has claimed to be "the Christ, the Son of God" (26:28; cf. 27:40, 43); "in this crucial pericope, therefore, Matthew once again shows that he does not employ 'the Son of man' to explain 'who Jesus is.' "[75]

Still one other possibility concerning 16:13 must be considered briefly before we move on. It is theoretically possible that Matthew's use of "the Son of man" as an apocalyptic title in Jesus' question does not compromise the narrative because of a peculiar language game, according to which its force is consistently ignored by all narrative audiences. I have not come across any extensive argument in support of such a view, but it seems to be assumed by a number of commentators who take the phrase as alluding to Jesus' heavenly status in 16:13 but appear to see no problem therein for the subsequent narrative. This differs from the preceding view in its assumption that the phrase contains not a secret that must subsequently be disclosed but rather a frank claim to celestial status that is totally without narrative effect. The perception that the phrase has no effect on the narrative constitutes, as we shall see, a valid observation not only for this but for all contexts in which it occurs in the First Gospel. What the adherents of this view do not notice, however, is that now there is no possible way of validating their claim that "the Son of man" serves Matthew as an apocalyptic title. It can just as well be assigned a nonapocalyptic meaning, or be treated as a mysterious name without specific content.

What has emerged from this examination of Matthew's addition of "the Son of man" to 16:13 and his corresponding omission of it at 16:21 is that it is not possible to determine Matthew's perception of the phrase's connotation on the basis of composition criticism alone. Indeed, it is possible to conduct an extensive investigation of the structure that Matthew has imposed on his inherited material and pay very little attention, if any, to occurrences of the phrase. It is noteworthy that Kingsbury, who devotes so much attention to the "title" later in the same book, finds no occasion to speak of "the Son of man" in his excellent discussion of the *christological* basis of Matthew's structure and the understanding of salvation history implicit therein! This is not surprising, however, since, as Kingsbury acknowledges, "the Son of man" is not a confessional term for Matthew.[76]

The one negative conclusion to which this preliminary study has led is not without importance. It has been demonstrated that at this critical junc-

75. Kingsbury, "The Figure of Jesus," p. 25. Cf. Senior, *Passion Narrative*, p. 178 n. 2.
76. Kingsbury, *Matthew: Structure*, pp. 1–39. "The Son of man" is alluded to tangentially on pp. 10, 27, and 30, but not in relation to structure and salvation history as such. The nonconfessional nature of the term is affirmed on p. 114.

ture in Matthew's narrative (16:13–20), "the Son of man" does not *function* as an apocalyptic title. If it nonetheless possesses such a meaning for the author (as a secret or ignored title), this must be determined from other contexts. With this as our agenda we turn now to a seriatim study of the relevant passages.

> **Mt. 8:20** Foxes have holes, and birds of the air have nests; but the Son of man has nowhere to lay his head.

An investigation of this saying's earliest form and content must be postponed until the final chapter. What is relevant at the moment is its function in Matthew. As in the Lukan parallel (9:58), it is clearly presented as a discipleship saying; in his response to a would-be follower, Jesus refers to his homelessness, implying that any disciple of his must be willing to share this condition.

Since the First Gospel seems to have been written for a settled community, the saying may have been understood by Matthew as applicable only to the wandering prophets alluded to in 7:15 or to the itinerant missionaries whose efforts to preach Christ in the synagogues frequently resulted in judicial flogging and informal expulsion.[77] It is interesting that the disciple whose declaration of allegiance provokes the saying is identified by Matthew as a *scribe* (where Luke has only the indefinite pronoun *tis*). This allusion to a Christian scribe anticipates 13:52 and 23:34 and underscores Matthew's interest in the exegetical and catechetical functions of Christian missionaries (cf. 28:19).[78] The scribe who here promises to follow Jesus is to be seen as an educated man, one accustomed to being respected and well received in a Jewish community, who here learns that he must face deprivation and homelessness, as symbolized in the following storm scene.

On the other hand, Matthew may well regard this discipleship saying as applicable to the rank-and-file members of a settled community through an allegorization of the homelessness to which Jesus here summons his followers. G. Bornkamm correctly emphasizes that Matthew has deftly

77. Cf. Luz, *Matthew 1—7*, p. 83; Hare, *Persecution in Matthew*, pp. 46, 56.
78. Pace Kingsbury (*Matthew: Structure*, p. 115), Matthew does not treat the scribe as an opponent by having him address Jesus as "Teacher." Although *Didaskale* is a form of address often attributed to opponents and never to the Twelve, this fact is offset by a more significant one: Matthew introduces the accompanying saying with the phrase "another *of the disciples*" (where the Lukan parallel has only "another"). Matthew thus gives us no reason to exclude either of these from the group of disciples who follow Jesus into the boat in v. 23. Although Matthew undoubtedly regards *Kyrie* as a more adequate form of address than *Didaskale*, it is to be noted that the Matthean Jesus refers to himself as teacher at 23:8, 26:18, and, by implication, 10:24f.

integrated the discipleship sayings of vv. 19–22 with the story of the stilling of the storm by placing the introduction to the latter (v. 18) before the former and by using the verb "follow" in both segments of the integrated pericope.[79] In this way the sea miracle becomes an allegory about the precarious existence of the church in a hostile world, where its sole defense is its Lord (vv. 25f.).

Does this new context in which Matthew has placed the Son of man saying tell us anything about what the phrase meant to him? First, we must ask what the saying, *apart* from the self-designation, says about Jesus for Matthew. It has often been pointed out that in its most literal sense the saying is untrue to the Matthean picture of Jesus, who is represented as having a home in Capernaum (4:13; 9:1, 10; 17:25). It is probable, there-fore, that Matthew understands the saying as referring figuratively to the rejection Jesus experienced at the hands of his people. In context, then, the saying suggests that, as Jesus was rejected, so will his followers be.[80]

If a common source lies behind 8:20 and Lk. 9:58, we can assume that Matthew simply takes "the Son of man" from that source, and conse-quently it may have no particular importance to him. We shall here presuppose, however, that Matthew's decision not to delete the phrase constitutes sufficient evidence that he regarded it as an appropriate self-designation for Jesus to employ in the context in which he has located the saying. What, then, is its connotation here?

It has been proposed that Matthew is aware that this is a transformed wisdom saying that originally referred to the myth of Wisdom's sojourn on earth and her rejection by humans.[81] According to Hamerton-Kelly, the saying was transferable to Jesus because in calling himself "the Son of man," Jesus implied his preexistence and thus presented himself as compa-rable to preexistent Wisdom.[82] Indeed, for Matthew Jesus was Wisdom Incarnate.[83] Hamerton-Kelly's argument presupposes the view that pre-existence is an essential characteristic of the Enochian Son of man and that consequently the term implies preexistence when applied to Jesus. We have examined the weak links in this chain of reasoning in chapter 1, and need not repeat those observations here. It must be noted, however, that Hamerton-Kelly is by no means alone in interpreting 8:20 from this per-

---

79. Bornkamm, Barth, and Held, *Tradition and Interpretation in Matthew*, pp. 54f.
80. Higgins, *Jesus and the Son of Man*, p. 126.
81. This seems to be the view of Hamerton-Kelly, *Pre-existence, Wisdom, and the Son of Man*, pp. 29, 43, 67–83. Cf. Tuckett, "The Present Son of Man," p. 69.
82. Hamerton-Kelly, *Pre-existence, Wisdom, and the Son of Man*, pp. 100f.
83. Hamerton-Kelly (ibid., p. 67 n. 2) cites Suggs, *Wisdom*, p. 71: "Jesus is Wisdom incarnate."

spective. Johnson, for example, suggests that for Matthew and Luke this saying presents a sharp paradox: "The heavenly Son of man is homeless."[84] Dibelius regarded this verse as giving expression to the stark contrast "between the obscurity of his indigent, earthly existence and the glory of the 'Man' from heaven—the contrast and at the same time the connection—for the needy life belongs to the concealment of the Son of man and points to the future."[85]

This view is opposed by Tödt, who correctly insists that there is no evidence of a concealment motif in the Synoptic material concerning the present activity of the Son of man; indeed, the Gospels never associate the term with the notion of preexistence.[86] Hamerton-Kelly concedes that there is no explicit reference to concealment here but insists, contra Tödt, that "when this saying is read along with the other Son of Man sayings in Q, the theme of rejection and humiliation, which is tantamount to concealment of his heavenly dignity, becomes apparent."[87] There is here, regrettably, a confusion of the motifs of rejection and humiliation. The rejection of the prophets or envoys of Wisdom is a common theme in Judaism, but "humiliation" is by no means implied in the texts containing this theme. Humiliation can be discovered in texts dealing with the rejection of Jesus only by those who *on other grounds* are convinced that Matthew believed in the preexistence of Jesus.

It is not possible in this chapter to engage in a full-scale treatment of Matthew's Christology. Here it must suffice to say that there is no compelling evidence that Matthew conceived Jesus as the incarnation of a preexistent heavenly being. James Dunn is fully justified in insisting, on the basis of a meticulous examination of the pertinent material, "There is no real indication that Matthew had attained a concept of incarnation, had come to think of Christ as a pre-existent being who became incarnate in Mary's womb or in Christ's ministry (as incarnate Wisdom)."[88]

Tödt has his own explanation of the function of the term in the "earthly" Son of man sayings such as 8:20: "Jesus is acting as the one who with full authority summons men to follow him. The name Son of Man is thus used to designate his sovereignty, his supreme authority."[89] Unfortunately, Tödt's proposal also goes beyond the evidence. Every statement Jesus makes in

84. Johnson, "The Gospel according to St. Matthew," p. 344.
85. Dibelius, *Jesus*, p. 98.
86. Tödt, *Son of Man*, p. 121; cf. pp. 284ff.
87. Hamerton-Kelly, *Pre-existence, Wisdom, and the Son of Man*, p. 43.
88. Dunn, *Christology*, p. 257.
89. Tödt, *Son of Man*, p. 123.

the First Gospel is made with authority as far as the author and his readers are concerned, whether or not "the Son of man" is employed. There is no suggestion that special authority is claimed where the term appears.

Another proposal, reflecting T. W. Manson's well-known thesis, urges that "the Son of man" here serves Matthew as a corporate designation. H. Waetjen declares that, although it is clearly a self-designation, "it reaches beyond him [Jesus] to include others, specifically his disciples, who share his life style. It is an epithet for a community as well as for an individual."[90] A similar suggestion is made by Margaret Pamment; whereas christological terms such as "the Son of God" distinguish Jesus from his disciples, "the Son of man" "draws Jesus and his disciples together into a shared destiny. In other words, terms like *ho huios tou theou* and *ho Christos* define who Jesus is, but the term *ho huios tou anthrōpou* defines who man is."[91] Although Pamment's observation fits 8:20 taken in isolation, her argument is less persuasive for 11:19 and 16:13 and is not at all convincing for the apocalyptic sayings. It seems a bit procrustean to urge that the Son of man is consistently presented by Matthew as "a representative and exemplary figure" when 16:27 so sharply distinguishes Jesus from the disciples by describing him as the one who is to come in the glory of his Father with his holy angels.[92] It is hardly true that here "the Son of man" serves to define "who man is" (Pamment) or functions as "an epithet for a community" (Waetjen).

Are Waetjen and Pamment at least pointing in the right direction by suggesting that for Matthew "the Son of man" is used in material that speaks of Jesus' humanity? This, of course, is the understanding that ruled exegesis for centuries.[93] Metaphysical speculation concerning the "two natures" of Christ does not appear until the second century, but it is anticipated in the contrast drawn by New Testament writers between the heavenly glory enjoyed by the resurrected and exalted Jesus and the unglorified human status of his pre-Easter existence. Since early Christians were concerned to emphasize the *continuity* between these two states, it is possible that Matthew regarded "the Son of man," because of its ostensible reference to generic humanity (through its use of *anthrōpos* with the definite article), as an appropriate name for the highly exalted post-Easter figure who nonetheless *remained a human figure*, Jesus of Nazareth.

Whereas "the Son of God" pointed to Jesus' unique relationship to God

90. Waetjen, *The Origin and Destiny of Humanness*, p. 119.
91. Pamment, "The Son of Man in the First Gospel," p. 118.
92. Ibid., p. 126; cf. p. 123, where 16:27f. are briefly referred to.
93. See chapter 2.

(however Matthew conceived that relationship, it was for him clearly *unique*, open to no other human being), "the Son of man" *may* have been taken by him as a way of remembering that Jesus, although uniquely conceived through the agency of God's Spirit (1:18–25), was nonetheless a real man, indeed, "the human being par excellence."[94] Although unambiguous evidence in support of such an understanding is lacking at 8:20, it must be insisted that this hypothesis is just as viable as any other. There is no indication in the context that the phrase connotes Jesus' heavenly glory; no hint of paradox is contained in the narrative. The would-be disciple is invited to share Jesus' human lot.

Narratively, the phrase clearly serves as a self-designation, but it cannot be assumed at this point that it is a "mere self-designation."[95] A very different effect is produced if we substitute "the Son of the carpenter," which would fit this description very well. "The Son of man," as already observed, must have seemed a very strange phrase to Greek readers, and consequently it can be more fairly described as a mysterious self-designation, whose mystery remains undefined at this first appearance.

> **Mt. 9:6** "But that you may know that the Son of man has authority on earth to forgive sins"—he then said to the paralytic—"Rise, take up your bed and go home."

The context in which Matthew has placed this second Son of man saying provides the clearest evidence that the phrase does not for him connote "transcendent, divine being." Whereas the Markan miracle story ends with the crowd glorifying God and declaring, "We never saw anything like this!" (Mk. 2:12), Matthew omits the direct statement and specifies instead the reason for the act of praise: "and they glorified God, *who had given such authority to humans*" (v. 8). We are justified in seeing here Matthew's defense of the Christian practice of pronouncing the forgiveness of sins (cf. 18:18; Jn. 20:23), the authority for which is derived from Jesus.[96] It would, however, be totally inappropriate for Matthew to use the plural *anthrōpois* here if, as alleged, the narrative spoke only of the authority of a heavenly being.[97]

---

94. This possibility is reinforced by the fact that neither docetic nor antidocetic tendencies are perceptible in the First Gospel.
95. Cf. Lindars, *Jesus Son of Man*, p. 117: ". . . there is nothing in the context to suggest that it means to him anything more than a self-reference on Jesus' part."
96. Cf. Beare, *The Gospel according to Matthew*, pp. 223f.
97. Contra Meier, *Vision*, p. 71.

As we saw in the investigation of the Lukan parallel (Lk. 5:24), the phrase "on earth" ought not to be taken as implying that the Son of man normally functions in heaven; the implication of the passage is rather that God's authority has been communicated to one human and through him to those associated with him.

Tödt correctly perceives that "it is not the designation and rights of the *transcendent* Son of man that are claimed in the sayings concerning the activity on earth," but he nonetheless insists that "the Son of man" functions in this pericope as a title connoting Jesus' special authority.[98] That the pericope speaks of this authority is indisputable; that Matthew regards "the Son of man" as peculiarly appropriate here because it *connotes* Jesus' distinctive authority cannot be demonstrated from the context. The response attributed to the narrative audience argues against such an understanding.

Great caution should be exercised by interpreters regarding the christological significance of this passage. Matthew has appreciably emended the blasphemy charge of the Markan opponents, not only by reducing their response to two words, *houtos blasphēmei*, but also by having Jesus judge their response as *immoral* ("Why do you think evil [*ponēra*] in your hearts?" v. 4; cf. Mk. 2:7f.). Matthew regards the charge as frivolous, that is, without basis in the *opponents' theology!*[99]

> **Mt. 10:23** When they persecute you in one town, flee to the next; for truly, I say to you, you will not have completed all the towns of Israel, before the Son of man comes.

This saying occurs only in Matthew. If it is an isolated logion that Matthew derived from oral tradition or a written source, our task is to determine how Matthew understands it in view of the context in which he has placed it.

It is possible, however, that the verse is redactional in whole or in part. Several scholars have argued, in different ways, that v. 23b is a pre-Matthean logion to which Matthew has prefixed an independent saying regarding persecution.[100] It is sometimes suggested that Matthew himself has created v. 23a to facilitate the incorporation of v. 23b.[101] Against these proposals we

---

98. Tödt, *Son of Man*, p. 127, in the comment on Mk. 2:10.
99. Cf. Vermes, *Jesus the Jew*, pp. 68f.
100. Cf. Montefiore, *The Synoptic Gospels*, vol. 2, pp. 149–51, and authors there cited.
101. Klostermann, *Matthäus*, p. 227; G. Barth, "Matthew's Understanding of the Law," p. 100 n. 3.

must observe that v. 23b cannot stand as an isolated logion. At the very least it requires a context of understanding for it to be comprehensible to an audience. That context is the early church's mission to Israel. As W. G. Kümmel and others have pointed out, the verb *telesēte* in v. 23b can properly be taken only with reference to the completion of a task, and we should therefore translate, "You will not bring to an end, finish, the cities of Israel."[102] This negative sentence makes sense only in association, implicit or explicit, with the missionary imperative. For this reason some have proposed that v. 23b was originally more closely related to vv. 5f., where it provided the rationale for the avoidance of Gentiles and Samaritans: "It is not that the gentiles cannot or ought not to be saved, but the time will not be long enough to preach to all, and Israel has the first right to hear."[103] While this is a very attractive proposal, it is better not to resort to conjecture when the verse is perfectly comprehensible as it stands: v. 23b provides the rationale for the command issued in v. 23a.

The first half of the verse does not reflect the motif of eschatological flight in any direct way; it is not a *prediction* concerning the miserable lot of eschatological refugees but a *command*.[104] Moreover, those addressed are commanded to flee to another *city* instead of to "the hills" (cf. 24:16) or to the wilderness (cf. Mk. 1:35). The saying as a whole makes perfectly good sense if we understand it as Matthew's context suggests: persecuted missionaries are urged not to remain in a dangerously hostile situation but to continue their work elsewhere—in another *city* where a significant number of auditors can be found. Thus v. 23a speaks of the urgency of the mission, and v. 23b explains this urgency: the task of bringing the gospel to "the cities of Israel" will not have been completed at the time when "the Son of man comes."[105]

If we can assume the unity of the saying, is it traditional or redactional? On the basis of a careful examination of the vocabulary and syntax, R. H. Gundry concludes that the verse as a whole is a Matthean creation.[106] In response to those who insist that the saying must be pre-Matthean because of its narrowly Judaistic perspective (v. 23b seems to exclude the gentile mission as clearly as do vv. 5f.), Gundry maintains that we should attempt to understand the saying against the background of Matthew's commitment to the gentile mission; Matthew anticipates a worldwide mission to

102. Kümmel, "Eschatological Expectation in the Proclamation of Jesus," p. 42. Cf. his earlier *Promise and Fulfilment*, p. 62.
103. Streeter, *The Four Gospels*, p. 255. Cf. Green, *Matthew*, p. 111.
104. Contra Bammel, "Mt. 10,23."
105. Cf. A. B. Bruce, "The Synoptic Gospels," p. 164.
106. Gundry, *Matthew*, p. 194.

the Gentiles alongside a continuing mission to the Jews.[107] In opposition to the commonly accepted view, Gundry argues that the saying does not stress the imminence of the Parousia; the "you" of this verse must not be taken as limited to the first disciples, and thus the saying is neutral as far as the time of the Parousia is concerned.[108] As it stands, the verse simply states that the mission to Israel will still be incomplete when the Son of man comes, whether that Parousia is soon or greatly delayed.

In support of Gundry it can be argued that v. 23 represents Matthew's *gemara* on the preceding half-verse: "but the one who endures to the end will be saved" (v. 22b). This statement constitutes the closing line of the passage from Mark (13:9–13), which he has extracted from a clearly eschatological setting in the earlier Gospel and has de-eschatologized by placing it in a context concerned with the ongoing mission.[109] Whereas for Mark the persecution belongs to the period of the messianic woes and involves ordinary Christians, for Matthew it concerns missionaries of the gospel and is understood as a natural concomitant of the mission, prompted by Israel's age-old resistance to God's prophets.[110] In view of his adaptation of the Markan passage, Matthew may have felt it necessary to interpret v. 22b. What does it mean for a *missionary* to "endure to the end"? As Gundry tersely comments, "Martyrdom is not to be sought."[111] In the face of persecution a missionary should not assume a martyr's stance but move to another location and begin afresh, as Paul is represented as doing repeatedly in Acts.

Is it conceivable, however, that the Gospel's author penned the rationale for this command (i.e., v. 23b)? Gundry is correct that in itself v. 23b does not exclude the gentile mission, but there is nonetheless an unresolved tension between the assumption of v. 23b that the unsuccessful mission to Israel must be doggedly continued until the Parousia and the perspective of the final editor that the twofold mission of Gal. 2:7–9 must now be replaced by the single mission of Mt. 28:19, "Go, make disciples of all the Gentiles."[112]

If Luz is correct that the author writes for a settled community (and, we would add, for a mixed congregation consisting of both Jews and Gentiles), yet reflects the bitter experience of persecution by Jews in the course

107. Ibid., p. 195.
108. Ibid. This idea is developed more fully by Moore, *The Parousia*, p. 145.
109. Marxsen, *Mark the Evangelist*, pp. 202f.; cf. Hare, *Persecution in Matthew*, pp. 99f.
110. Hare, *Persecution in Matthew*, pp. 137–41, 144, 176.
111. Gundry, *Matthew*, p. 194.
112. Hare, *Persecution in Matthew*, p. 148; also Hare and Harrington, "'Make Disciples of All the Gentiles' (Mt. 28:19)." For a rejoinder to this article, see Meier, "Nations or Gentiles in Mt. 28:19?"

of the mission to Israel, it would seem that for him this mission is over and done with.[113] Why then would he create v. 23? Gundry can quite properly retort, Why would he incorporate this detached logion if it so poorly reflected his own perspective?

Perhaps this saying is best understood by comparing it with 23:34, its nearest parallel. Not only does Matthew attribute this verse directly to Jesus (whereas Luke, probably in dependence on Q, has Jesus quote "the Wisdom of God," 11:49) and amplify the ill-treatment that the messengers will receive, but he also connects this verse to the next with the conjunction *hopōs*, which here, more forcefully than the Lukan *hina*, indicates not result but purpose: "*Therefore* I send you prophets and wise men and scribes . . . some of whom you will flog in your synagogues and persecute from city to city, *in order that* all innocent blood poured out upon the earth . . . may come upon you." The initial "therefore" connects these two verses with the preceding idea that the opponents addressed must "fill up the measure" of their fathers—that is, complete the collective guilt so that God's wrath may be loosed upon them. In this context, then, the unsuccessful, persecuted missionaries fulfill a foreordained role in provoking Israel to complete the full tale of her guilt by rejecting God's ultimate messengers.

If this interpretation correctly perceives Matthew's intention in 23:32–35, then it is possible that he likewise regards 10:23 as primarily negative. In constructing the missionary discourse in chapter 10, he has woven together material from various sources in such a way as to present the mission to Israel in a very negative light. To the Markan motif of passive nonacceptance (Mt. 10:14, from Mk. 6:11) is added the motif of aggressive persecution (vv. 17–22). This redaction surely reflects the failure of the mission. If, then, Matthew creates v. 23 as *gemara* on v. 22 (or vv. 17–22), it would appear that the testimony that the missionaries are to continue to bear to an obdurate Israel is negative in its purpose.[114] Although the conversion of individual Jews is by no means excluded, the *expectation* is that the Jewish communities will continue to reject the message, even if the missionaries persevere in their task "until the Son of man comes." It is possible in this way to concur with Gundry that it is more probable that Matthew created this verse than that he drew it from tradition.

Assuming, then, that the verse is redactional, what is the significance of the allusion to the Son of man? As always in Matthew, it is attributed to Jesus as a self-designation, but here for the first time it is used to refer to his glorious Parousia at the end of the age. It does not, however, constitute

---

113. Luz, *Matthew 1–7*, p. 83; Hare, *Persecution in Matthew*, p. 128.
114. Marxsen, *Mark the Evangelist*, p. 202, regards the "testimony" of Mt. 10:18 as primarily negative in its intent.

proof that Matthew adhered to a "Son of man Christology," i.e., that he articulated the meaning of Jesus by conceiving him *as* the Son of man. The phrase is no more predicative here than in the two preceding instances. It tells no more about the nature and function of Jesus the Christ than the parallel in Paul's eucharistic instruction, "For as often as you eat this bread and drink the cup, you proclaim the Lord's death *until he comes*" (1 Cor. 11:26). The temporal reference is the same as that of "to the end" in Mt. 10:22. That is, the saying, whether Matthean or pre-Matthean, is clearly apocalyptic, but this conclusion by no means requires that "the Son of man" be conceived as an apocalyptic title.[115]

T. W. Manson conjectures that, in view of the parallel between this verse and 16:28, Matthew may have substituted "the Son of man" for "the kingdom of God" here as in the latter saying.[116] If the verse does represent a traditional saying that Matthew has edited, this conjecture is worthy of consideration. The significance of such a substitution will be pondered in connection with 16:28.

Because "the Son of man" is treated by Matthew as self-evidently a self-designation of Jesus, the reference to his "coming" strains the messianic secret, as will also 13:41. This, however, is not due to the use of the name but to the reference to a final coming. As we have seen, the secret is similarly strained by the allusion to Jesus' future role at 7:21f., where "the Son of man" is not used. Matthew was apparently untroubled by such foreshadowings of the solemn disclosure of Jesus' status in Peter's confession.

> **Mt. 11:19** The Son of man came neither eating nor drinking, and they say, "Behold, a glutton and a drunkard, a friend of tax collectors and sinners!"

The authenticity of this fascinating saying will be considered in chapter 8. For the present it is sufficient to recognize that it is almost universally regarded as pre-Matthean. According to the two-document hypothesis it is, like the parallel at Lk. 7:34, drawn from Q.

Because of the close parallel provided by the accompanying statement about John the Baptist, it is clear that "the Son of man *came*" contains no allusion to the incarnation; that is, there is no suggestion that the name designates a transcendent being.[117] The text and its context betray neither

---

115. Contra Dupont, "'Vous n'aurez pas achevé les villes d'Israël avant que le Fils de l'homme ne vienne' (Mat. x.23)," who argues that the verse refers not to the Parousia but to a meeting with Jesus after the apostles' missionary journey.
116. Manson, *The Teaching of Jesus*, pp. 221f.
117. Cf. 21:32.

docetic nor antidocetic tendencies; there is apparently no need for Matthew to insist here or elsewhere in his Gospel that "Jesus Christ has come in the flesh" (1 Jn. 4:2), because no one has challenged the assumption that Jesus was a real human being.

It has nonetheless been argued that, in spite of this passage, "the Son of man" designates for Matthew the incarnate Sophia. Matthew's substitution of "deeds" for "children" in the attached saying, "And Wisdom is justified by her deeds," subsequent to his redactional allusion to "the deeds of the Christ" in 11:2, has been construed as evidence that Matthew equates Jesus and Wisdom.[118]

This is not the place to engage in a full-scale critique of the theory, which has been carefully argued by serious scholars on the basis of a number of texts. Here it must suffice to say that it would appear that too much has been built upon a fragile base. First, the substitution of *ergōn* for *teknōn* by Matthew is not certain. The textual evidence is mixed, and the presence of *teknōn* in many Greek manuscripts, versions, and patristic citations is perhaps not best explained as due to harmonization with Luke, since the process usually went in the other direction.[119] It is possible that the substitution was effected not by Matthew but by an Alexandrian scribe whose theology conceived Jesus as Sophia incarnate. Second, even if the substitution by Matthew is accepted, the equation of Jesus with Sophia is not thereby established. It remains to be demonstrated that "wisdom" is employed by Matthew in the mythical sense; elsewhere in the Gospel the word *sophia* is consistently used in a nonmythical way (12:42; 13:54). One can even argue that if Matthew substituted *ergōn* for *teknōn* in this saying, it was precisely for the purpose of demythologizing *sophia*; for "And Sophia is vindicated by her envoys," he pointedly substitutes "And wisdom is judged by its fruits."

Third, even if the Sophia myth is here preserved, it by no means follows that an equation of Sophia's deeds with Jesus' deeds involves the equation of the two figures, as can be clearly seen from the Fourth Gospel, where the deeds of the Son can be described as the deeds of the Father without collapsing the distinction between the two persons (Jn. 10:32, 37). Fourth, if Matthew conceives Jesus as Wisdom incarnate, how does he understand the relationship between Sophia and the Holy Spirit? Why is blasphemy against Sophia more excusable than blasphemy against the Holy Spirit?

---

118. Cf. Strecker, *Der Weg der Gerechtigkeit*, p. 102; Suggs, *Wisdom*, pp. 56f.
119. Cf. Allen, *Matthew*, p. 120: " . . . *ergōn* may be a late conjectural emendation. There seems to be no trace of it before the fourth century."

(12:32). The most decisive argument against the hypothesis, however, is provided by the absence from this Gospel of incarnational thought.

While Dunn accepts the proposal that Matthew identifies Jesus as Wisdom herself (*sic*), he rightly insists that the First Gospel gives no indication that its author took the dramatic step of "moving from a christology which speaks of Jesus' divinely given *function* to one which speaks of Jesus' metaphysical *status*. . . ."[120] That is, Matthew "seems to think of the *exalted* Jesus as Wisdom and to avoid the implication that Jesus spoke as preexistent Wisdom. . . ."[121] Perhaps all that is meant, Dunn suggests, is that Jesus is "the one through whom God in his wisdom had made his final appeal to [humans] and who, as the exalted one, still provides the medium and the locus for the decisive encounter between God and [humanity]."[122] Given this conclusion, is there any justification for Dunn's acceptance of the Wisdom hypothesis in the first place?

If we are correct in questioning the identification of Jesus with Sophia in 11:19c, there is no further basis in the text or its context for maintaining that "the Son of man" is here employed as the designation of a supernatural being.[123] The term clearly *denotes* a human being who eats and drinks; what it *connotes* to Matthew remains undisclosed.

Mt. 12:8 For the Son of man is lord of the Sabbath.

The pericope in which this verse is set (12:1–8) and the accompanying narrative concerning a Sabbath healing (12:9–14) present the Pharisees as the implacable opponents of Jesus' Sabbath halakah. There may indeed have been such opponents, but we are wisely reminded by Jewish scholars that there was considerable diversity in Sabbath halakah in the period of the Second Temple, and consequently tolerance was the rule.

Phillip Sigal notes that "plucking" (*tolesh*) is not unanimously prohibited by the Mishnah (*Shab.* 10:6), nor is it one of the thirty-nine categories of prohibited work (*Shab.* 7:2).[124] Moreover, the doubtful possibility that the plucking violated the Sabbath had to be considered along with the wide-

---

120. Dunn, *Christology*, pp. 198, 205.
121. Ibid., p. 205.
122. Ibid., pp. 205f.
123. As W. D. Davies demonstrated over forty years ago, there is no evidence in the Similitudes of Enoch of an identification of the Son of man with Wisdom (*Paul and Rabbinic Judaism*, pp. 159f.; cf. also Hamerton-Kelly, *Pre-existence, Wisdom, and the Son of Man*, p. 28, and Colpe, "Ho huios tou anthrōpou," TDNT 8, pp. 411f.).
124. Sigal, *The Halakah of Jesus*, p. 160.

spread tradition that one ought not to fast on the Sabbath.[125] According to Sigal, in this pericope Jesus presents an ironclad case, using the methods of argument that were accepted by the proto-rabbis of his day.[126] Sigal correctly suggests that the Matthean Jesus makes no christological claim in v. 6 ("something greater than the temple is here"). "What is 'greater' is the call to provide for human life, the required response to the love command. The analogy is between two obligations, love of humans and the cult. Jesus is said to tell the Pharisees that if they recognized that it is *hesed* which God requires (v. 7), they would not have held the disciples guilty."[127]

If there is no christological claim in v. 6, is one to be found in v. 8? Sigal finds attractive Bultmann's proposal that in its earliest form v. 8 spoke of humans, not the Son of man.[128] This reading, of course, is excluded for Matthew, who found "the Son of man" in his source (Mk. 2:28). Since it is here as everywhere in Matthew a self-designation, the verse presents Jesus as claiming authority to function as "lord of the Sabbath." This phrase seems to mean that Jesus has the authority to promulgate Sabbath halakah without the necessity of halakic argument. Paradoxically, Matthew has considerably expanded the argument, adding vv. 5–7 to the Markan version. Matthew seems to be at pains to present Jesus as the master halakist and yet far more than a halakist; in virtue of his *status* as the Son of God, he has authority to deliver God's will concerning how Torah is to be interpreted and applied. As W. D. Davies has taught us, Matthew presents Jesus as the ultimate and supreme interpreter of Torah.[129] There is no suggestion, however, that Matthew regards this dominical function as implicit in the term "the Son of man."

> **Mt. 12:32** And whoever says a word against the Son of man will be forgiven; but whoever speaks against the Holy Spirit will not be forgiven, either in this age or in the age to come.

Still more clearly than the statements previously examined, this verse indicates that "the Son of man" does not function for Matthew as a "title of divine majesty." The contrast here drawn is one between the *moral* offense of "speaking evil" concerning human beings (cf. 5:11) and the *religious* crime of speaking irreverently of God. In Matthew's intention

125. Ibid., p. 161.
126. Ibid., pp. 164f.
127. Ibid., p. 163.
128. Bultmann, *History*, pp. 16f.; cf. Sigal, *The Halakah of Jesus*, p. 163 and n. 73.
129. Davies, *Setting*, pp. 107f.

v. 32 gives specific application to the general principle enunciated in v. 31, where "blasphemy" is used in these two very different senses. As Lamar Cope points out, blasphemy against God was generally regarded as unforgivable, and in this context "the Spirit" is obviously a way of speaking about God and his activity. These verses accuse the opponents of blaspheming God by calling the Spirit that empowers Jesus Beelzebul.[130] Reviling Jesus is bad enough (i.e., it is a sin requiring forgiveness), but reviling God is the ultimate sin, which places the sinner beyond forgiveness.

This means, of course, that "the Son of man" here designates the unique human being Jesus of Nazareth, while "the Spirit" designates God's power immanent in Jesus' activity. "The Son of man" cannot intelligibly function in this passage with the connotation "God incarnate" or "Sophia incarnate." Nor is there the slightest suggestion in this context that the one who has been reviled is destined to become a heavenly figure, the eschatological judge.[131] Matthean redaction unmistakably identifies the reviled one as God's Spirit-endowed human servant prophesied by Isaiah (Mt. 12:18–21).[132] Still more improbable is the suggestion that "the Son of man" connotes the hiddenness of the divine figure here reviled.[133] Dalman's judgment is sound: It is impossible that Matthew should intend a distinction between two persons of the Godhead; the distinction is between Jesus as human and the divine Spirit working through him.[134]

> **Mt. 12:40** For as Jonah was three days and three nights in the belly of the whale, so will the Son of man be three days and three nights in the heart of the earth.

A number of scholars have treated this verse as a post-Matthean gloss because of its tension with the surrounding Matthean context and because of its omission by Justin Martyr in a passage where it would have proved very useful to the apologist.[135] As Cope points out, if Jonah's sojourn in the great fish is the exceptive sign, the allusion to his preaching

---

130. Cope, *Matthew*, p. 39.
131. Contra Bonnard, *Matthieu*, p. 182 n. 1.
132. Cope, *Matthew*, pp. 36, 38, correctly emphasizes the importance of the Spirit in vv. 15–32.
133. Hill, *Matthew*, p. 218. Cf. Hamerton-Kelly, *Pre-existence, Wisdom, and the Son of Man*, p. 45: " 'Son of Man' seems therefore to express paradoxically the human humility of the pre-existent Christ." This would be a correct description of the Johannine Son of man (see chapter 4 above) but is not appropriate for Matthew.
134. Dalman, *Words of Jesus*, p. 255.
135. Stendahl, *School*, pp. 132f.

to the Ninevites is rendered superfluous.[136] These arguments deserve serious consideration. Although there is no manuscript support for the hypothesis, there is textual evidence elsewhere for the addition of Son of man sayings (e.g., at Mt. 18:11). Perhaps the strongest evidence against the hypothesis, on the other hand, is the Lukan parallel (11:50), which enigmatically refers to a future functioning of the Son of man as constituting a parallel to Jonah's serving as a sign to the Ninevites. That is, it seems more probable that Mt. 12:40 represents Matthew's explication of the enigmatic Q tradition than that Q lacked anything comparable to Lk. 11:50.[137] Further support for the presence of v. 40 in the original text of the Gospel is found by Gundry at 27:63, where the opponents remember that Jesus predicted his resurrection *after three days* (not "on the third day" as at 10:21, 17:23, and 20:19).[138]

Assuming, then, that the verse is not a gloss, what is its function for Matthew? As the echo at 27:63 indicates, it is a veiled passion prediction, anticipating the more explicit announcements that begin after Peter's confession. Here "the Son of man" designates the human being who can be resurrected because he can also die—that is, genuinely enter into the realm of the dead (poetically described as "the heart of the earth"). The enemies correctly perceive that in speaking of the Son of man, Jesus is speaking of his own destiny (note the use of a first-person verb in 27:63).[139]

Mt. 13:37 He who sows the good seed is the Son of man.

It is generally acknowledged that the interpretation of the parable of the weeds is largely or wholly a Matthean product, but there is considerable dispute about the time of the Son of man's sowing.[140] Many scholars, influenced perhaps by the parable of the sower and its interpretation, regard v. 37 as referring to Jesus' earthly ministry.[141] As Beare points out, however, what is sown is not the gospel, "the word of the kingdom" (13:19), but human beings who are "children of the kingdom" by virtue of their origin.[142] The mythological implications must not be pressed, however. There is no reason to suspect Matthew of a gnostic world view that

136. Cope, *Matthew*, p. 40.
137. Cope's hypothesis seems to require that the glossator had Lk. 11:30 in mind.
138. Gundry, *Matthew*, p. 244.
139. Landes, "Mt. 12:40 as an Interpretation of 'The Sign of Jonah,' " makes the interesting proposal that the point for Matthew is not the passion and implied resurrection of Jesus but his sojourn in Hades. This interpretation does not take 27:63 into account, however.
140. Cf. Jeremias, *Parables*, pp. 81–85.
141. E.g., Tödt, *Son of Man*, p. 72.
142. Beare, *The Gospel according to Matthew*, p. 312.

would ascribe to the Son of man and the devil equal creative powers; he does not really mean to suggest that "the children of the kingdom" and "the children of the evil one" are metaphysically brought into existence by the Son of man and the devil, respectively. His outlook is rather that of ethical dualism. We should therefore assume that "sowing" here means approximately the same as "make disciples of" in 28:19.

Consequently, a number of scholars argue that the time alluded to in 13:37 is that of the post-Easter mission.[143] But perhaps this dispute is unnecessary. It is possible that Matthew does not sharply distinguish Jesus' evangelistic activities before and after Easter. For the evangelist the continuity is real; the same Lord is active now as before his death in drawing women and men into his kingdom.

What is unusual about this verse is not so much its possible challenge to the customary tripartite categorization of the Son of man sayings (earthly activity, anticipated suffering and death, and future coming) but its syntactic uniqueness: only here does "the Son of man" function as a predicate nominative with the copula. This form, however, is required by the allegorical interpretation, as in Gal. 4:24f. In view of Matthew's use here, it is all the more significant that he feels no need at any point in his Gospel to have Jesus identify himself *as* the Son of man in such a sentence. On first impression the phrase appears to function as a title in this declarative sentence, but the form does not require such an inference; "the Son of man" functions here precisely as do the names in Paul's allegory in Galatians 4. It is here—as everywhere in Matthew—Jesus' mysterious way of naming himself. There is no hint that Matthew regards the function of "sowing" as connotatively implied in the phrase.

If Lindars is correct in his proposal that Matthew has substituted "the Son of man" for an original reference to God, as found in the Gospel of Thomas 57, this verse provides additional evidence against the view that Matthew's interest in the term is related primarily to its alleged eschatological connotations.[144] No one has ever proposed that "the late-Jewish conception of the Son of man" included evangelism among his responsibilities! By his use of the term in this context, Matthew demonstrates again that he is not ruled by an apocalyptic understanding of the phrase.[145]

143. Vögtle, "Das christologische und ekklesiologische Anliegen von Mt. 28,18–20," pp. 286–93; Schweizer, "Menschensohn und eschatologischer Mensch im Frühjudentum," p. 100; Kingsbury, *Parables*, p. 99.

144. Lindars, *Jesus Son of Man*, pp. 123f.

145. Cf. M. Müller, *Der Ausdruck "Menschensohn" in den Evangelien*, pp. 113f., who argues that v. 37 refers to the exalted Son of man of 28:18. It is inappropriate to read the term into 28:16, but he rightly suggests that v. 37 alludes to a transcendent function of the resurrected Jesus.

Mt. 13:41 The Son of man will send his angels, and they will gather out of his kingdom all causes of sin and all evildoers. . . .

Here for the first time in Matthew's Gospel, after eight other instances, "the Son of man" is used in a clearly apocalyptic statement (10:23 alludes to the Parousia without providing any apocalyptic detail). This fact alone should caution us against assuming that for Matthew "the Son of man" is an apocalyptic title.

Support for an apocalyptic connotation is, however, found by many in this verse. Tödt, for example, cites 13:41 as evidence that Matthew draws on 1 Enoch, although he cannot demonstrate this with respect to specific passages in the Ethiopic apocalypse.[146] At most he can claim that 13:41 parallels the marked emphasis upon the Son of man's function as judge in 1 Enoch.[147] This is unconvincing, since judgment was attributed to various figures in Jewish literature of the time, including the Messiah (Ps. Sol. 17:21ff.) and Elijah (Lives of the Prophets 21:3).

A more extensive attempt has been made by J. Theisohn to demonstrate that 13:40–43, 49f. incorporates a piece of Jewish tradition that has been influenced by ideas found in the Similitudes of Enoch.[148] Theisohn is careful not to suggest overtly that Matthew is directly dependent on the Similitudes, but he comes very close to making such a claim. In relation to 19:28 and 25:31 he excludes the possibility that Matthew and the Similitudes may be drawing on similar, earlier traditions; in presenting the picture of the Son of man sitting on the throne of his glory, Matthew, he alleges, draws upon no other literature than the Similitudes, although the picture may have reached him in oral rather than in written form.[149] Respecting 13:40–43, he is still more cautious, since it is clear that the Similitudes contains no single passage that brings together the apocalyptic ideas of the Matthean pericope, and moreover the scattered parallels that he considers are by no means exact. Particularly damaging to his hypothesis is the fact that the Enochian Son of man is never described as sending out angels; in the passage upon which Theisohn lays much stress, 1 En. 54:6, the four archangels who throw the hosts of Azazel into the burning oven do so implicitly at the behest of the Lord of Spirits who is mentioned in the next line.[150] Theisohn cites a number of Enochian passages that speak of the

---

146. Tödt, *Son of Man,* p. 92 n. 1, p. 223.
147. Ibid., p. 70 and n. 4.
148. Theisohn, *Der auserwählte Richter,* pp. 183–200.
149. Ibid., pp. 160f.
150. Theisohn (ibid., p. 200) concedes that no parallel to "his angels" is found in the Similitudes.

righteous entering into light or shining, but none of these provides as close a parallel to Mt. 13:43 as does 4 Ezra 7:97, which he excludes from consideration because of its late date.[151]

At the conclusion of his argument concerning the dependence of Mt. 13:40–43 on the Similitudes, Theisohn asks a very significant question: Why did Matthew turn a piece of apocalyptic tradition into a Son of man passage? The question for Theisohn is easily answered: the Son of man is mentioned in the chapter of 1 Enoch following that in which the avenging angels are depicted (i.e., 55:4 and 54:6, respectively), and Matthew's description of the angels as belonging to the Son of man ("his") and sent out by him corresponds with the Matthean tendency to transfer divine epithets to Jesus or the Son of man.[152]

In this context, however, Theisohn does not consider the related, equally critical question: Why does Matthew introduce "the Son of man" at v. 37? It is hardly proper to deal with the appearance of the term in v. 41 in isolation from its previous use in v. 37, where no relationship with the Similitudes can be perceived. Theisohn is correct in arguing that Matthew draws on traditional apocalyptic motifs in 13:37–43, but he fails to demonstrate that any of these are directly connected with the Son of man in 1 Enoch, and therefore his hypothesis regarding the motivation for Matthew's introduction of "the Son of man" fails to convince. All that can be safely inferred is that Matthew wishes to interpret the parable as referring to Jesus' future role, and he finds it appropriate, because of established literary convention, for Jesus to refer to this future role in third-person language employing "the Son of man," as he does when speaking of his present activity and anticipated suffering.

Still to be considered, however, is the possibility that Matthew draws on pre-Christian apocalyptic tradition when speaking here of the Son of man as a heavenly figure who exercises authority over angels (cf. also 16:27 and 24:31). Despite the absence of the idea not only from the Similitudes but also from Daniel 7 and 4 Ezra 13, are we justified in finding here the remnants of a Jewish Son of man conception?[153]

No such hypothesis is required. Matthew's picture of Jesus in v. 41 is fully understandable on the basis of Christian presuppositions without recourse to real or imagined Jewish sources concerning the Son of man.

---

151. Ibid., p. 266 n. 119.
152. Ibid., p. 200; cf. pp. 178, 188.
153. Cf. the proposal of Colpe, "Ho huios tou anthrōpou," TDNT 8, p. 429, that "the oldest stratum of the Synoptic tradition suggests a Jewish Son of Man tradition which provisionally constitutes a fourth source."

First, it must be noted that it is not *Matthew* who reaches back to earlier Jewish apocalyptic ideas as Tödt alleges.[154] Although Matthew further emphasizes the figure's authority by adding the personal pronoun "his," the statement in 13:41, anticipating 24:31, really says no more than the underlying Markan verse (13:27), which attributes to Jesus the authority to dispatch angels. This same authority is evidenced outside the Gospels at Rev. 22:16, where first-person language is used.

Second, a possibly earlier stage is reflected in Mk. 8:38, where the Son of man is depicted as coming "in the glory of his Father with the holy angels." Here the angels serve as his entourage but not specifically as his servants.[155] As commentators have suggested, this idea of an angelic entourage at Jesus' Parousia may have developed on the basis of Zech. 14:5, where it is promised that "the Lord your God will come, and all the holy ones with him."[156] A source nearer in time, however, may be provided by the Qumran War Scroll, where the final eschatological battle is described as involving both angels and men, with God present as the mighty man of war (xii.7–12).[157] It would not have been a great step for early Christians to have taken when they conceived Jesus, their heavenly Messiah, as arriving for judgment with an angelic entourage.

The key to this development is, of course, the resurrection experience and the interpretation of that experience by means of Ps. 110:1.[158] Although it is impossible to ascertain how early this exegetical step was taken and whether prior Jewish messianic use of the psalm encouraged it, it is clear from Rom. 8:34 that Paul could assume without argument that Jesus is seated at the right hand of God.[159] Given this conviction, it was inevitable that the relationship between God's right-hand man and the angels should be explored in Christian speculation. From the polemical assertions of Hebrews 1–2, we infer that unanimity was not everywhere assured, but it was theologically unavoidable that belief in Jesus' superiority to the angels would come to predominate. 1 Pe. 3:22 sounds creedal in its formulation: "Who has gone into heaven, with angels, authorities, and powers subject to him" (cf. also Phil. 2:9–11; Rev. 22:16). Also early, based no doubt in

154. Tödt, *Son of Man,* p. 92.

155. Higgins, *Jesus and the Son of Man,* p. 59, suggests that Lk. 12:8f. represents a still earlier stage, where the Son of man appears as a witness before the angels, i.e., before God.

156. Cf. McNeile, *Matthew,* p. 247. Higgins, *Jesus and the Son of Man,* p. 106 n. 1, refers to "the totally un-Jewish idea of the Son of man accompanied by angels."

157. Black, *The Scrolls and Christian Origins,* pp. 154f., finds a reference to the Messiah in "the king of glory," but this is difficult to confirm.

158. Cf. Perrin, *Modern Pilgrimage,* p. 12f.

159. D. M. Hay, *Glory at the Right Hand,* pp. 23ff., discusses possible pre-Christian uses of Psalm 110.

part on current Jewish apocalyptic conceptions such as we have just seen in the War Scroll, was the conviction that Jesus would come from his exalted location to execute judgment. Even if 2 Thessalonians is not from Paul's hand, there is no need to regard as post-Pauline its expectation that the judgment will occur "when the Lord Jesus is revealed from heaven with his mighty angels in flaming fire" (1:7; cf. also Rev. 19:11ff.; 22:12). This process is fully understandable as a Christian development without inferring that behind 2 Thessalonians lies the postulated Jewish Son of man.

The question whether "the kingdom" here attributed to the Son of man designates the church or the world need not detain us.[160] It is sufficient to observe that those most resolute in relating the Matthean Son of man to the Similitudes do not venture to suggest that this idea derives from that source. The idea, which will recur at 16:28, is adequately explained by the use of "kingdom" at 20:21. For Matthew, as for early Christians generally, Jesus was the ultimate successor of David and hence a king with a kingdom, even though such traditional messianic ideas were found inadequate for the full articulation of Jesus' status.

In terms of Matthew's presentation of the parable and its interpretation, "the Son of man" serves clearly as Jesus' mysterious self-designation. No careful reader of the first century would have mistakenly believed that Jesus was referring to a figure distinct from himself; the one who has referred to his homelessness (8:20) and rejection (11:19) in this indirect way now refers to his glorious, future role using the same language. As far as the *narrative* audience is concerned, v. 41 clearly violates the messianic secret, not because of its use of "the Son of man," but because of its eschatological content. That is, its violation is of the same order as that of 7:21f. and 10:32f., where first-person speech is used. Here as there the secret is not *formally* violated for Matthew because explicitly messianic titles are not used. The fact that 13:41 preempts Peter's confession in 16:16 seems to trouble him as little as the disciples' confession in 14:33.

Mt. 16:13 Who do people say that the Son of man is?

This verse has already been examined at length. There is no need to add further comment at this point, but we will return to it at the end of the chapter.

---

160. Cf. Strecker, *Weg der Gerechtigkeit*, p. 167 n. 7; Tödt, *Son of Man*, p. 71.

Mt. 16:27 For the Son of man will come in the glory of his Father with his angels, and then he will reward each according to what he or she has done.

This verse is generally regarded as Matthew's edited version of Mk. 8:38, on the assumption that he has been following Mark closely throughout this section. Accordingly, Matthew omits Mk. 8:38a, because he has already employed a parallel version at 10:32f., but retains v. 38b because of its reference to the future "coming" of Jesus and, by implication, the judging function he will exercise at that time. As we have seen, Matthew is particularly interested in the judgment motif, and here he makes the allusion more explicit by substituting "and then he will reward each according to his or her behavior" for "will be ashamed of him or her." As in 13:41, he further emphasizes Jesus' future authority by substituting "his" for "holy" in the phrase "with the angels."

E. P. Sanders has recently argued that scholars have here been misled by their dependence on the two-document hypothesis; the Matthean version appears to him to be earlier than the Markan in view of its proximity to 1 Thess. 4:16.[161] This issue need not be decided here. What is of consequence for the present discussion is whether the saying here incorporated by Matthew, either from an earlier source or by redaction, reflects Matthew's concurrence with a pre-Christian conception of a heavenly judge entitled the Son of man.

In his comments on this verse Tödt notes that Matthew emphasizes the Son of man's function as judge through the addition of v. 27b regarding repayment on the basis of behavior. This element, which "does not occur anywhere else in the Synoptic Son of man sayings," is found not only in Ps. 62:13, Prov. 24:12, and Sir. 32:24 but "also, clearly referring to the Son of man, in 1 Enoch."[162] This verse is later cited as evidence that Matthew "reached back independently to apocalyptic concepts which were either present already within the Christian community or drawn by him directly from Jewish sources . . . the elements in the Son of man sayings which are peculiar to him refer repeatedly to 1 Enoch."[163] On a later page he proposes that 16:27 is among those Matthean creations that are "closely related to statements from the book of Enoch"; 16:27 is to be compared with 1 En. 45:3.[164] The scholar must have nodded at this point, for there is nothing in

161. Sanders, *Jesus and Judaism*, pp. 143–45.
162. Tödt, *Son of Man*, p. 86.
163. Ibid., p. 92 and n. 1.
164. Ibid., p. 223.

common between the passages apart from the general idea of judgment. As Theisohn remarks, the specific formulations that characterize the judgment in Mt. 16:27 (i.e., repayment in accordance with practice) is nowhere found in association with the Son of man in the Similitudes.[165] We have already seen that the motif of accompanying angels is absent from those key passages (Dan. 7:13f.; 4 Ezra 13; 1 Enoch 37–71) on which the hypothesis of a pre-Christian Son of man conception has been largely based.[166]

The closest parallels to Mt. 16:27 are provided by Christian literature. Rev. 22:12 presents in first-person language what Matthew, following established convention, attributes to Jesus in third-person speech: "Behold, I am coming soon, bringing my recompense, to repay every one for what he or she has done." In Romans Paul assures his readers that God "will repay each according to his or her works" and that this will be accomplished "on that day when, according to my gospel, God judges humans' hidden acts *through Jesus Christ*" (2:6, 16). Here as everywhere in early Christian eschatological thought, Jesus does not displace God as Judge but acts wholly on God's behalf. In Matthew this idea is presented less clearly through visual imagery: Jesus will come "in the glory of his Father with his angels." Space need not be devoted here to Matthew's understanding of Jesus' filial relationship to God, one of the most frequently recurring themes of the First Gospel. It is sufficient to note that the Enochian Son of man is never identified as God's Son.[167]

Like 10:23, Mt. 16:27 speaks of Jesus' "coming." Tödt stresses the fact that Matthew refers to the Son of man's *coming*, not to his *return*.[168] It is indeed interesting that the gospel writers shrink from attributing to Jesus predictions that refer in the same breath to his going away and his coming again (Jn. 14:3, with its echo in 14:28, stands in glorious isolation; contrast Jn. 21:22f.). This hesitation is difficult to understand in view of their deep conviction regarding the *continuity* between the crucified Jesus and the exalted Lord. We must compare their literary practice, however, with that of Paul and John the Divine; both likewise refer to Jesus' future coming, not to his return. Paul, who is not averse to speaking of his own "coming again" to Corinth (2 Cor. 2:1; 12:21; 13:2), refrains from adding "again" to his statements about Jesus' coming (1 Cor. 4:5; 11:26). The promise "I will

165. Theisohn, *Der auserwählte Richter*, pp. 260f. To Theisohn's observation may be added the following: In 1 En. 62:11 it is not the Son of man (or the Chosen One) but the angels of punishment who repay oppressors for the wrong they have done.
166. See n. 156 above.
167. When the man from the sea of 4 Ezra 13 is identified in the vision's interpretation as "my Son" (13:32, 37, 52), we should regard this as messianic language based on 2 Samuel 7.
168. Tödt, *Son of Man*, p. 93.

come" is a recurring refrain in the letters to seven churches in the Apocalypse (Rev. 2:5, 16, 25; 3:11), perhaps reflecting the liturgical cry to which both Paul and John the Divine bear witness (1 Cor. 16:22; Rev. 22:20).

Clearly, despite the identity of the Crucified and the One who will come in glory, early Christians were also conscious of discontinuity and therefore were inclined to omit "again" when referring to Jesus' glorious arrival. Thus Luke, who can speak of Jesus' return in the thinly veiled allegory of a parable (Lk. 19:15), follows the standard idiom in the ascension narrative: "This Jesus who was taken up from you into heaven will come in the same way as you saw him go into heaven" (Acts 1:11). The "again" is implicit only. It is thus not only Son of man sayings that exhibit the idiom. In Matthew the same phenomenon appears in a statement using third-person language where the subject is not "the Son of man" but "your Lord": "Watch therefore, for you do not know what day your Lord is coming." The Lord in question is unambiguously Jesus; in this statement as in the Son of man sayings, Matthew evinces the common early reluctance to use "again" or "return."

In any event, it is clear that this idiom to which Tödt draws attention does *not* derive from 1 Enoch. In the Similitudes the Son of man is not described as "coming" from heaven to earth for judgment. The idea of such a Parousia is possibly implicit in a few passages (e.g., 45:4; 46:4; 63:11), but the idiom itself is absent, as it is also from Daniel 7 and 4 Ezra 13. It is illegitimate, therefore, to claim support for the alleged Jewish conception of the Son of man from Matthew's sayings about Jesus' future coming. The idiom is adequately explained without recourse to this hypothesis.

> **Mt. 16:28** Amen, I say to you that there are some among those standing here who will by no means taste death until they see the Son of man coming in his kingdom.

All that has just been said about Jesus' coming with reference to v. 27 applies equally to v. 28, where Matthew has transformed a Markan saying about the arrival of the kingdom of God (Mk. 9:1) into a saying about Jesus' eschatological arrival. There is no need to find here an allusion to a pre-Christian conception. As Bultmann laconically comments, "For Matthew this is naturally Jesus."[169]

---

169. Bultmann, *History*, p. 121.

The phrase "in his kingdom" modifies the participle "coming," not "the Son of man."[170] It describes not location but manner.[171] Consequently, it is strictly parallel to "in the glory of his Father" of the preceding verse. That is, *basileia* here connotes not "kingdom" (in the spatial sense) but "royal power," and v. 28 simply repeats the idea of v. 27: it is promised that at least a few (two or three?) of Jesus' contemporaries will still be alive when the events of v. 27 take place.[172]

Is Matthew's redaction of Mk. 9:1 inspired by Dan. 7:13f.? Perhaps (because of the verbs "see" and "come"), but the allusion is by no means clearly made and cannot be pressed.[173] More convincing is the argument that Matthew here anticipates 24:30 (Mk. 13:26) and 26:64 (Mk. 14:62), where the Son of man is seen coming on the clouds of heaven, statements that are undoubtedly allusions to Daniel. On this basis we can say that 16:28 is an indirect allusion to Daniel and that the adverbial phrase "in his kingdom" alludes to the royal power conferred on the "one like a son of man" in Dan. 7:13f.

Even if an indirect dependence upon Daniel is demonstrable, however, such a connection would by no means support the hypothesis of a pre-Christian Son of man conception, as we shall see when we examine 24:30. Here we may simply note that Matthew's use of *basileia* in association with Jesus presents him as a *royal* figure (who also judges, v. 27) rather than as a *judge* endowed with authority to implement verdicts. (In Liv. Pro. 21:3 it is not suggested that Elijah will be a king when he judges Israel.)

Mt. 17:9 Tell no one the vision until the Son of man has been raised from the dead.

On the assumption of Markan priority, Matthew simply takes over from his source this brief statement about the Son of man being raised from the dead. The self-reference is unambiguous; the verse looks

170. Cf. 21:9 and 23:39, where *erchomenos* is similarly modified by an adverbial phrase beginning with *en*.

171. Strecker, *Weg der Gerechtigkeit*, p. 166 n. 7, takes *basileia* spatially (the future home of the righteous).

172. Contra J. A. T. Robinson, *Redating*, p. 24, this verse as redacted by Matthew does not support an early date for the First Gospel. Presumably many of Jesus' younger followers were still alive at the beginning of the war in 66 C.E. The pessimism of this verse must be contrasted with Paul's optimism concerning the imminence of the Parousia in 1 Cor. 15:51, written approximately a decade before the war. Luedemann, *Chronology*, p. 263, places 1 Corinthians in 49; this early dating would weaken the force of my second argument.

173. Gundry's careful eye found no allusion here; it is not treated in his *Use of the Old Testament*.

back to 16:21, where Jesus began to show his disciples that he must be killed and be raised on the third day. (In 16:21, Jesus is not designated the Son of man.)

It is obvious that "the Son of man" here refers to a mortal, one who can really die, not a heavenly figure. Tödt is mistaken in his suggestion that the active verb employed by Mark in the passion predictions, *anistēmi* ("get up," "arise"), emphasizes the "sovereign authority" of the Son of man.[174] Mark uses the same verb when referring to the general resurrection at 12:25. Nor can it be said that Matthew's substitution of *egerthē* for Mark's *anastē* in this verse represents a theological correction. It is possible that Matthew here intends the verb to be taken as a true passive ("be raised"), but in other passages he can employ the passive as a deponent, "rise" (e.g., 8:15; 9:19). Even if Matthew here uses the verb intransitively, he does not imply any special status thereby, since at 27:52 he uses the same verb in the passive with reference to others who get up out of their graves. There is thus nothing in either version of the saying to suggest sovereign authority.

Tödt is also incorrect in his statement about an alleged formal distinction between the passion and Parousia sayings. "In the announcements of suffering Jesus speaks of himself as of the Son of man. The sayings concerning the Parousia, however, either differentiate expressly between Jesus and the Son of man or make Jesus speak of the Son of man as of someone different from himself."[175] *Formally* the two kinds of statement are exactly the same. The distinction lies not in the way "the Son of man" is used but simply and solely in the content of the sayings. If Tödt is to justify his subsequent statement in the same paragraph ("Obviously there are heterogeneous histories of tradition lying behind the two groups of Son of man sayings"), it will have to be on the basis of content, not form. There is certainly nothing in Matthew's use of the sayings to suggest that he would agree with Tödt's proposal. He is able to create new sayings in each of the categories, all conforming to the same basic form. That is, "the Son of man," while serving occasionally as the direct object of a verb or as the object of a preposition, once as a predicate nominative with the copula (13:37), and once in an accusative and infinitive construction (16:13), normally appears as the subject of the verb, and in such cases the verb is always in the third person, so that the identification with Jesus is no more explicit in the suffering sayings than in those which speak of the Parousia.

174. Tödt, *Son of Man*, p. 215.
175. Ibid.

> **Mt. 17:12** But I tell you that Elijah has already come, and they did not know him, but did to him whatever they pleased. So also the Son of man will suffer at their hands.

The relationship of this verse to Mk. 9:12 is not clear, since the two versions are very different, although they share the same context and are both passion sayings. There are three basic proposals. Probably predominant is the view that, despite the drastic changes, Matthew's version is dependent upon Mark. Because of the way that Mk. 9:12b appears to interrupt the flow of thought, however, Bultmann proposed a different understanding: we should regard Mk. 9:12b as a post-Matthean gloss reflecting Mt. 17:12.[176] If this represents a correct conjecture, Mt. 17:12 is probably redactional, constituting (like 26:2) a Matthean addition to the stock of suffering Son of man sayings. A third proposal modifies Bultmann's suggestion by urging that, while Mk. 9:12b probably is a gloss, it should be regarded as pre-Matthean and thus as the source of Mt. 17:12.[177] This third view thus concurs with the first in seeing 17:12 as a traditional saying that Matthew has freely rewritten.

It is not necessary to decide the issue here. It will suffice to observe that, whatever its origin, 17:12 speaks of the suffering of a mortal without betraying any sense of paradox. Although John the Baptist is presented by the passage as in some undefined sense the reincarnation of Elijah (cf. 16:14, where a similar belief is reported concerning Jesus), there is no intimation that "the Son of man" designates a heavenly figure who has become incarnate in Jesus.

> **Mt. 17:22f.** The Son of man is about to be delivered up into the hands of men, and they will kill him, and on the third day he will be raised.

Concerning this passion prediction, nothing need be added to what has just been remarked about 17:9, 12 except the observation that the response of the narrative audience indicates that the hearers perceive that Jesus is speaking about himself: "and they were greatly distressed"; that is, they grieved that *Jesus* must die. This, of course, does not mean that Matthew regarded "the Son of man" as ambiguous in his source. The puzzlement of the disciples in Mk. 9:32 (cf. Lk. 9:45) refers not to the

---

176. Bultmann, *History*, p. 125. He is followed by Perrin, among others (*Modern Pilgrimage*, p. 118).
177. Schmithals, "Die Worte vom leidenden Menschensohn," p. 425.

identity of the sufferer but rather to the announcement that Jesus, now recognized as the Christ, must suffer (cf. Lk. 24:26).

> **Mt. 19:28** Amen, I tell you that you who have followed me, in the regeneration, when the Son of man sits on the throne of his glory, you also will sit on twelve thrones, judging the twelve tribes of Israel.

Respecting the origin of the clause containing "the Son of man," three main possibilities have been considered: (1) the clause was contained in the Q version anterior to Lk. 22:28–30 but was omitted by Luke; (2) the Q version did not contain the clause, and it was added after the bifurcation of Q into Q/Mt. and Q/Lk.; (3) it was added by the author of the First Gospel.[178] Although the first possibility has been pressed by serious scholars, it has not gained wide support, since an omission by Luke appears difficult to justify.[179] The second, while intrinsically more probable, is necessarily conjectural. Both these views urge that Matthew simply took the clause over from his source. Accordingly its presence in 19:28 may tell us little of Matthew's own understanding of the connotation of "the Son of man."

For the purposes of this chapter, therefore, it will be necessary to take most seriously the third view, which appears to be the most probable in any case—namely, that Matthew edited the saying about the Twelve to include the temporal clause, "when the Son of man sits on the throne of his glory." Assuming this to be the case, what does the clause tell us about Matthew's "Son of man Christology"? Does it indicate that he adhered to an Enochian view of the Son of man?

Such a view is apparently espoused by Theisohn. On the basis of a careful study of the phrase "throne of glory," he concludes that the closest parallels to Matthew's use of the phrase all occur in the Similitudes of Enoch, and since this is the earliest writing to suggest that the Son of man will ascend Yahweh's throne, it must be regarded as the source of Matthew's two references to the Son of man sitting on the throne of his

---

178. The first is espoused by Strecker, *Weg der Gerechtigkeit*, p. 109 (cf. p. 125); the second is proposed by Marshall, *Luke*, p. 815. For a listing of scholars subscribing to the third view, see Broer, "Das Ringen der Gemeinde um Israel," p. 151 n. 14, to which should be added Gundry, *Matthew*, p. 392.

179. Kümmel, *Promise*, p. 47 and n. 95, assumes but does not explain Luke's omission.

glory (19:28; 25:31).[180] He concedes that the linguistic expression may not have come to Matthew directly from the Similitudes; Matthew (or his source, if such were the case) could have derived this statement from oral tradition, but he insists nonetheless that the dependency relationship is so clear that one can use it as the basis for dating the Similitudes to the first half of the first century.[181]

That striking parallels to Mt. 19:28 and 25:31 are offered by the Similitudes cannot be denied. Perhaps the most apposite is 1 En. 69:29: "For that Son of man has appeared and has sat on the throne of his glory" (cf. 69:27). In both sets of passages (Matthean and Enochian), the context indicates or implies that judgment is the business at hand. It is not impossible, therefore, that the Matthean motif derives directly or indirectly from the Similitudes (if extant at that time). Several cautionary remarks are in order, however.

1. Although 1 En. 69:29 is a statement about "that Son of man," most of the other parallels in the Similitudes refer to "the Chosen One" rather than to "that Son of man" (45:3; 55:4; 61:8; and 62:3 emended; 62:5 has "that Son of a woman" as the predominant reading). It is obvious that the same figure is meant, but it is not insignificant that the *central* idea is the sitting of a human figure on the throne of glory, not the sitting of *the Son of man* on the throne of glory. Once this is noted, it is possible to find other relevant parallels. Particularly interesting is the statement in the Testament of Abraham, Rescension B, 8:5: "And between the two gates there sat a man upon a throne of great glory." In this passage the man is identified as Adam (v. 12). In the longer rescension (A) at 11:6, the throne is referred to as "the throne of gold," but Adam himself is described as "adorned in such glory" (v. 8). In 12:4f. (Rec. A) a parallel statement is found: "And between the two gates there stood a terrifying throne with the appearance of terrifying crystal, flashing like fire. And upon it sat a wondrous man, bright as the sun, like unto a son of God." This man is then identified as Abel, Adam's son, who is charged with the judgment of all humans (13:1–3).[182] The date of the original testament is uncertain, but the

---

180. Theisohn, *Der auserwählte Richter,* pp. 160f. Tödt, *Son of Man,* appears inconsistent regarding the origin of this verse. On p. 64 he proposes that it is "an early post-Easter prophetic saying" and reasons that it is justifiable to treat it as a Q saying (pp. 65, 91), but on p. 114 he calls it a "late imitative formulation," and on p. 223 he includes it among sayings formed by Matthew that are closely related to statements in 1 Enoch.

181. Theisohn, *Der auserwählte Richter,* p. 253 n. 20; cf. p. 161. But see 4Q161 Comm. Isa. (A) l. 19, which appears to read *ks' kbodh* (J. M. Allegro and A. A. Anderson, *Qumran Cave 4, Discoveries in the Judean Desert,* vol. 5, p. 14).

182. The translation is that of E. P. Sanders, in Charlesworth, *Old Testament Pseudepigrapha,* vol. 1.

beginning of the common era is proposed by several recent commentators.[183] That is to say, unless Theisohn can demonstrate that Matthew's
understanding of the phrase "the Son of man" itself is clearly indebted
to the Similitudes, the conjunction of that phrase with a statement
about sitting on a glorious throne need not indicate dependence on the
Similitudes.

2. Theisohn urges that Matthew's addition of the possessive pronoun
"his" ("upon his glorious throne") does not constitute evidence against a
derivation from the Similitudes, since it can be understood as a further
refinement of the motif, in either Jewish or Christian circles.[184] Once it is
seen that the idea of sitting on a glorious throne was not limited to the
Similitudes, however, the presence of the *autou* must be taken more seriously; that is, it cannot be shown from the two Matthean passages that
Matthew has taken over from the Similitudes the idea of the Son of man
sitting on *the* throne of glory (i.e., God's throne), as Theisohn argues. In
this case the parallel in Sir. 47:11, where "throne of glory" is used with
reference to David, should not be so quickly dismissed by Theisohn, not
because it may have influenced Matthew but because it provides evidence
of the tradition of describing the throne of David's eschatological successor as a "throne of glory."[185]

3. The association of sitting on a glorious throne and judging need not
point in the direction of the Similitudes. Jewish messianism expected the
Messiah to function as a judge. This is attested not only by the Psalms of
Solomon (chap. 17; cf. 4 Ezra 13:31f.) but also by the Qumran commentary
on Isaiah 11.[186] Such a view is, of course, reflected in the New Testament,
as for example at 2 Cor. 5:10, "For we must all appear before the judgment
seat of (the) Christ" (*emprosthen tou bēmatos tou Christou*).

4. It is most unlikely that Matthew had direct knowledge of the Similitudes. The parallels cited by R. H. Charles are too general to be significant, and we have found Theisohn's arguments in favor of Matthew's dependence on the Similitudes for 13:41–43 unpersuasive.[187] The most that can
be said is that the Similitudes and Matthew both make use of common
motifs of Jewish apocalyptic. It is a fascinating coincidence that both
Matthew and the Similitudes identify the leading character in the escha-

183. Sanders (ibid., vol. 1, p. 875) dates the work around 100 C.E., but earlier dates are
proposed by Turner, *The Apocryphal Old Testament*, p. 394., and Delcor, *Le Testament
d'Abraham*, pp. 76f. In any event, it is unlikely that the Testament of Abraham is dependent
on the Similitudes.
184. Theisohn, *Der auserwählte Richter*, p. 160.
185. Ibid., pp. 73, 77.
186. Cf. Dupont-Sommer, *The Essene Writings from Qumran*, p. 275.
187. Charles, *Apocrypha and Pseudepigrapha*, vol. 2, p. 181.

tological drama, the person who is second only to God, by similar names, both of which are roughly translated into English as "the Son of man," but it has remained impossible so far to prove that the Greek and Ethiopic names go back to the same Aramaic or Hebrew form.[188] Indeed, their identity ought not to be assumed, because their linguistic functions are very different. Whereas the Ethiopic phrase serves the narrator as a way of naming his actor, in Matthew the narrator resolutely refuses to use his Greek phrase in this way; it is rigorously reserved for the actor's own use.

5. Even if it were granted that the combination of "the Son of man" and "sitting on the throne of his glory" is so strikingly paralleled in the Similitudes that at least indirect dependency must be assumed, it would not logically follow that Matthew derives his understanding of "the Son of man" from that source. His *Christology* seems not to have been profoundly influenced by the Similitudes. If we were to assume, as Tödt does, that "preexistence" is a central feature of the Enochian Son of man, it must be acknowledged (as Tödt does, at least indirectly) that Matthew betrays no evidence of influence at this point.[189] Moreover, even Matthew's apocalyptic Son of man sayings contain elements foreign to 1 Enoch, such as the references to "his angels" (13:41; 16:27) and to fellow human judges (19:28). Of critical importance, however, is the fact that in Matthew's Gospel the phrase consistently designates not a remote apocalyptic figure but *Jesus*, and does so with reference to his present activity and anticipated sufferings as well as his future glory. Even if it could be demonstrated, therefore, that Matthew borrowed the clause "when the Son of man sits on the throne of his glory" from the Similitudes, it would have to be conceded that *for Matthew* the one who sits on the throne and calls himself the Son of man is a very different figure.

Why, then, does Matthew add the clause? Presumably the earlier version of the saying contained something on the order of Lk. 22:29. That is, any such promise to the Twelve is implicitly contingent upon Jesus' accession to the throne. Matthew chooses to make this more explicit, so that the anticipated judging function of the Twelve may be seen as clearly subordinate to and dependent on the judging activity of the exalted Jesus, an activity in which the First Evangelist is particularly interested, as we have

188. Black, "Aramaic Barnasha and the 'Son of Man,' " p. 202, reiterates the argument that the Ethiopic demonstrative reflects a titular expression in the Greek or Aramaic *Vorlage* of the Similitudes, but he does not respond to M. Casey's challenge: why is the demonstrative not used with "the Elect One," which is clearly titular (*Son of Man*, p. 100)?

189. In chapter 1 I argued that it ought not to be assumed that the author of the Similitudes attributes "preexistence" to the Son of man. Tödt, *Son of Man,* pp. 284ff., attempts to explain why the motif of preexistence is absent from all the Son of man sayings in the Gospels.

seen. The substitution of "throne of glory" for "kingdom" is suggested by the use of "thrones" in the original saying.[190]

Tödt's comment that 19:28 illustrates the fact that Matthew did not "abandon the differentiation between the 'I' of Jesus and his speaking of the Son of man in the third person" is wide of the mark.[191] It is nonsense to insist that the distinction is better preserved in the Parousia sayings than in the earthly sayings, as Tödt proposes.

> Both groups of sayings have in common the fact that the name Son of man is used, but they differ in the way in which it is used. In the one group Jesus speaks of the Son of man as of another, a future being, differentiating between his "I" and the person of the Son of man. In the other group Jesus, expressly identifying the Son of man with himself, speaks of the Son of man as of a being who is active at present.[192]

Matthew would have grave difficulty in comprehending this distinction. In both kinds of sayings the Matthean Jesus uses third-person language to speak of himself, and in both the identification is implicit only; it simply is not true, as Tödt claims, that in the earthly sayings Jesus *expressly* identifies himself with the Son of man. Formally, there is no distinction in Matthew's usage. It is true that Jesus uses both first-person and third-person language with reference to himself in the Matthean version of this saying, but this fact must not be made to carry more weight than it can handle. From *Matthew's* perspective the same is true of the first instance of the phrase at 8:20; it is used there in closely coupled sayings where first-person language is also employed (8:22).

If it is not because of the phrase's associations in Jewish apocalyptic, why does Matthew choose to use it in the clause that refers to Jesus' session on "his throne of glory"? Why not retain the first-person speech of the underlying Q saying (assuming that Lk. 22:28–30 represents the earlier version in this respect)? This is an appropriate question, for which a satisfactory answer may be impossible to provide. If Bultmann is correct that for Matthew "the Son of man" is not an apocalyptic title, we can only surmise that Matthew chooses to use third-person speech here because he regards it as Jesus' preferred means of self-reference in statements pointing to the mystery of his destiny (including suffering as well as future glory). In any event, Matthew's decision to introduce the Son of man clause in this saying does *not* demonstrate that for him the phrase connotes an angelic

---

190. Cf. Lindars, *Jesus Son of Man*, p. 126.
191. Tödt, *Son of Man*, p. 90; cf. p. 65.
192. Ibid., pp. 138f.

being reserved in heaven for manifestation at the last judgment. Throughout his Gospel it denotes the human Jesus, and in this saying more clearly than in any of the other Parousia sayings: here the man who calls himself the Son of man promises his Twelve that they will be associated with him in the coming judgment of Israel.[193]

> **Mt. 20:18f.** Behold, we are going up to Jerusalem, and the Son of man will be delivered up to the chief priests and scribes, and they will condemn him to death, and they will deliver him up to the Gentiles to be mocked and flogged and crucified, and on the third day he will be raised.

Nothing need be added here to what has been said concerning the earlier passion predictions. In all these passages "the Son of man" designates a unique human being who nonetheless shares with other humans the necessity of dying.

> **Mt. 20:28** . . . just as the Son of man has not come to be served but to serve and to give his life as a ransom for many.

Since Matthew takes over Mk. 10:45 unchanged (merely substituting *hōsper* for *kai gar*), no comment is needed. "The Son of man" is used precisely as at 20:18f. Here is added only the thought that the death of the one so designated has soteriological effect.

> **Mt. 24:27** For just as the lightning comes out of the east and shines as far as the west, so will be the Parousia of the Son of man.

At this point we reach Matthew's eschatological discourse, chapters 24–25, where "the Son of man" occurs no fewer than seven times, always in an apocalyptic statement. Because this frequency has encouraged scholars to regard the phrase as constituting an apocalyptic title for Matthew, we must examine these seven instances with care.

Of the seven, only one (24:30b) derives from Mark 13, the "little apocalypse," which serves as the basis for Matthew's longer discourse. Four (24:27, 37, 39, 44) apparently come from Q, and two are probably Matthean interpolations (24:30a; 25:31a).

---

193. Cf. Vögtle, *Kosmos*, p. 160; Strecker, *Weg der Gerechtigkeit*, p. 109; Broer, "Das Ringen der Gemeinde um Israel," p. 162.

The key to Matthew's understanding of the entire discourse is provided by the critical changes he makes in the material taken over from Mark at Mt. 24:3. Whereas in Mark 13:4 the disciples ask Jesus, "Tell us when these things will be and what (will be) the sign when all these things are about to be accomplished," Matthew significantly substitutes: "Tell us when these things will be, and what (will be) the sign of your Parousia and the completion of the age?" In the Markan version the *tauta* ("these things") unites the second half of the verse with the first, and thus relates the whole to the destruction of the temple to which v. 2 refers. By omitting the second *tauta*, Matthew is able to separate the destruction of the temple (now referred to in the first half of the verse only) from the return of Jesus, which will mark the close of the age (*parousias* and *sunteleias*, "completion," are united in a hendiadys by a single article).[194] In the succeeding discourse the destruction of Jerusalem is forgotten; attention is focused rather on Jesus' Parousia, the events or signs leading up to it, and the necessity of preparing oneself spiritually and ethically.

Just as Matthew introduces *parousia* into the Markan question in v. 3, so does he insert it into the Q sayings about the Son of man at vv. 27, 37, 39, 44 (cf. Lk. 17:24, 26, 30; 12:40). It is not easy to discover why Matthew prefers to employ the noun in these passages rather than the verb "come," which he has already used at 10:23 and 16:27f. His use of *parousia* is in any event to be traced back to early Christian practice rather than to the Similitudes, where the "coming" or "arrival" of the Son of man is nowhere mentioned. Paul's use of *parousia* at 1 Cor. 15:23 is unemphasized, as if he is using language with which his readers are very familiar (cf. also 1 Thess. 2:19; 3:13; 4:15; 5:23; 2 Thess. 2:1, 8f.; Jas. 5:7f.; 2 Pe. 1:16; 3:4; 1 Jn. 2:28). Whether the use of the noun with reference to Jesus' return originated in a Semitic or Hellenistic context is a question that need not detain us here.[195] Its use is undoubtedly bound up with other apocalyptic expectations, such as the "coming" of God (Ps. 96:13) or of the day of the Lord (Mal. 4:5), and "the coming age" (*ha 'olam ha ba*; cf. Mt. 12:32; Heb. 6:5). Not to be ignored is the notion of the coming of the Messiah (cf. Jn. 4:25). There is

194. Cf. Marxsen, *Mark the Evangelist*, p. 199; Hare, *Persecution in Matthew*, pp. 163, 177f.
195. Oepke, "Parousia," TDNT 5, p. 561, is manifestly incorrect in his declaration that there are no words for "coming" in Hebrew. In Mal. 3:2 the Qal infinitive of *bo'* functions as a noun with a pronominal suffix; see also 1 Sam. 29:6; Isa. 37:28; Ps. 21:8. In none of the Old Testament instances, however, did the LXX translators choose to render the word with *parousia*; in translation from the MT the latter is found only at Neh. 2:6.

therefore no reason to suggest that Matthew uses *parousia* here because of the presence of "the Son of man" in his source. For him the saying speaks about the eschatological coming of *Jesus*, as he makes unmistakably clear in his redaction of the disciples' question, "Tell us . . . what will be the sign of *your* Parousia" (24:3).

The allusion to lightning in Mt. 24:27 has suggested to some that the saying reflects the alleged pre-Christian Son of man conception because of the symbolic use of lightning in 2 Baruch 53. U. Müller proposes that the messianic and Son of man ideas have "contaminated" each other in the Baruch passage, citing Mt. 24:27 in support.[196] It is to be observed, however, that the lightning functions very differently in Matthew. Whereas in Baruch it is a powerful symbol with theophanous associations, in Matthew it is used in a simile to present a visual image of unexpected, sudden brightness. The simile suggests a supernatural event, but we need not look to a postulated Son of man expectation in Judaism to explain it. The notion of the supernatural empowerment of the Messiah is as old as Isa. 11:4, and the sudden coming of God's judge-delegate is proclaimed in Mal. 3:1–3, a passage treasured by the gospel writers (cf. Mt. 11:10).

Matthew's understanding of "the Son of man" in this verse can be perceived from the setting in which he has placed the Q saying. He has carefully combined this "Behold here, behold there" saying with its Markan parallel, but instead of repeating the "Behold here, behold there," he offers a more specific alternative: "If therefore they say to you, 'Behold, he is in the wilderness,' do not go out; 'Behold, in the inner room,' do not believe (it)." This alteration makes it even clearer than the Lukan formulation (Lk. 17:23f.) that the Son of man whose arrival is referred to is a human being who could (mistakenly) be thought of as hiding in an inner room. And because Matthew has here woven Markan and Q sayings together, it is even clearer than in Luke 17 that the one referred to as the Son of man is the Christ mentioned in v. 23. Thus, regardless of what ultimate origin may be conjectured for the "lightning" saying, in its use by Matthew its expectation focuses not on an angelic figure (with whom he has identified Jesus) but on Jesus himself, whose official title is not "the Son of man" but "the Christ" (v. 5 adds the title, which is not found in the Markan *Vorlage*, 13:6, in the main manuscript tradition).

---

196. U. B. Müller, *Messias und Menschensohn*, p. 139.

Mt. 24:30f. And then the sign of the Son of man will appear in heaven, and then all the tribes of the land will mourn and see the Son of man coming on the clouds of heaven with power and great glory; and he will dispatch his angels with a great trumpet blast, and they will gather together his elect from the four winds, from one corner of heaven to the other.

On the assumption of Markan priority these two verses represent an expanded version of Mk. 13:26f.; after beginning as Mark does with the words "and then" (*kai tote*), Matthew interpolates two clauses before resuming Mark's statement about seeing the Son of man coming. Because the source and meaning of the interpolated clauses are much disputed, it will be best to postpone our examination of them until we have looked at Matthew's appropriation of Mark's verses.

In Matthew's formulation the allusion to Dan. 7:13 conforms more closely to the Septuagint than does Mark's: Matthew has *epi tōn nephelōn tou ouranou* in exact agreement with the Septuagint, where Mark has simply *en nephelais* (Matthew's reading reappears in 26:64, where the Markan parallel has *meta*, in conformity with Theodotion). Nevertheless, Matthew does not drastically reconstruct the allusion to Daniel so as to make it an explicit quotation introduced by a fulfillment formula, as he has done at 13:14.[197] The prepositional phrase with which the Markan verse ends, "with great power and glory," appears to be a midrashic summary of Dan. 7:14.[198] Matthew moves the adjective so that it modifies "glory" more directly (but in this position it may in fact modify both feminine nouns).[199]

It is unlikely that Matthew's substitution of *epi* for Mark's *en* represents a theological *Tendenz*. Dalman regarded the LXX *epi* as reflecting a pre-Masoretic reading, which was modified in order to minimize "the divine manifestation in the one like to a son of man," since "It belongs to God only to move upon the clouds."[200] This view is opposed by Gundry, who properly insists that Dalman exaggerates the distinction between the two Hebrew prepositions.[201] Matthew was surely too much a monotheist to regard the returning Jesus as *a deity*, and, as far as we can tell, he was

197. It is noteworthy that neither Matthew nor any other New Testament writer exploits christologically the mistranslation represented in the LXX text of Dan. 7:13b, "and *as* the Ancient of Days he came, and those who stood by came to him."

198. Cf. Gundry, *Use of the Old Testament*, p. 54.

199. Gundry, *Matthew*, p. 488, suggests that Mark's phrase "with great power" means "with a great army," i.e., the hosts of heaven; Matthew's transposition of the adjective removes this military allusion and lays special emphasis on the heavenly glory of the Son of man.

200. Dalman, *Words of Jesus*, p. 242.

201. Gundry, *Use of the Old Testament*, p. 53 n. 5.

unfamiliar with the sophisticated incarnational Christology of the Fourth Gospel. We must therefore not read more than we should into his adoption of the language of the LXX. The use of clouds as a means of transport does not mark the one called the Son of man as a god or an angel, but simply indicates his origin: he comes from heaven, God's abode, and is thus in some sense God's representative.[202] This conclusion is confirmed by the sequel in v. 31 (based on Mk. 13:27): the one who comes in this fashion will send *his* angels (Matthew adds the possessive pronoun) with a great trumpet blast (also a Matthean addition), and they (Mark: he) "will gather together his elect from the four winds, from one corner of heaven to the other."

The closest parallels to v. 31b, as Gundry points out, are offered by Zech. 2:10 in the LXX ("from the four winds of heaven I will gather you") and Dt. 30:4 LXX, which refers to the scattering of Israel by God and to his subsequent gathering of the dispersed "from a corner of heaven to a corner of heaven."[203] If Gundry is correct, the underlying Markan saying attributes to the Son of man functions that Zechariah and Deuteronomy ascribe to God. This does not mean, however, that the saying regards the Son of man as a "second god." In postbiblical writings it is occasionally suggested that God will gather the dispersed of Israel by means of the Messiah (e.g., Ps. Sol. 17:28; cf. 17:20).[204]

Although Matthew again emphasizes more strongly than Mark the Son of man's authority over the angels by adding "his" (cf. Mt. 16:27), this wording does not really effect any critical change in the statement; in the Markan as in the Matthean version the Son of man possesses delegated responsibility to assign tasks to God's angels. The Matthean addition should by no means be taken as indicating the deity of the Son of man.[205]

The addition of "with a great trumpet blast" gives expression to a common apocalyptic motif, namely, that one or more of the anticipated eschatological events will be signaled by a heavenly shofar. In several passages the trumpet blast is associated with the gathering of Israel's dispersed, most notably in Isa. 27:13.[206] Of special interest is the occurrence of the

202. See above, chapter 1, n. 39.

203. Gundry, *Use of the Old Testament*, p. 55, points out that Matthew's use of the plural *akrōn* agrees with the Peshitta of Dt. 30:4, *Targum Jonathan* and *Targum Onkelos*.

204. J. Klausner, *The Messianic Idea in Israel*, p. 471, cites in further support of this function of the Messiah the *Targum Pseudo-Jonathan* on Dt. 30:4 and Jer. 33:13.

205. Higgins, *Jesus and the Son of Man*, p. 106 n. 1, refers to the fact that in Matthew "the totally un-Jewish idea of the Son of man accompanied by angels" is heightened by alluding to the accompanying angels as the Son of man's. Higgins properly implies that this is a *Christian* development, unrelated to the concept of the Son of man he finds in Jewish apocalyptic.

206. Cf. G. Friedrich, "Salpinx," TDNT 7, pp. 80, 84; Gundry, *Use of the Old Testament*, p. 54.

theme in the tenth benediction of the Shemoneh Esreh: "Sound the great horn for our freedom; raise the ensign to gather our exiles, and gather us from the four corners of the earth. . . . Blessed are thou, O Lord, who gatherest the dispersed of thy people Israel."[207]

The Hebrew of the first line reflects Isa. 27:13 exactly, except for changing the verb to the imperative. What is particularly interesting here is, of course, the collocation of the shofar with the Isaianic motif of raising an ensign. This second line of the benediction echoes two further verses from Isaiah (11:10, 12). The first of these is linked with Isa. 27:13 by the use of the same opening formula, "And in that day."

> And in that day the root of Jesse shall stand
> as an ensign to the peoples.

This verse anticipates and interprets messianically ("the root of Jesse" refers back to the messianic oracle of 11:1ff.) the similar statement of v. 12:

> He will raise an ensign for the nations (goyim)
> and will assemble the outcasts of Israel
> and gather the dispersed of Judah
> from the four corners of the earth.

The number of Isaianic echoes in the tenth benediction is striking. Since the benediction probably formed part of the synagogue liturgy prior to the Christian era, it is reasonable to assume that it was very familiar to Christians of Jewish origin, including the author of the First Gospel.[208] It is not improbable, therefore, that Matthew expanded Mk. 13:26 with this prayer in mind.

On this assumption the Hebrew antecedent for sēmeion ("sign") in Mt. 24:30a is not ot but nes, the word used in Isa. 11:10, 12 and rendered sēmeion by the LXX at 11:12. If Matthew was aware of the Masoretic text for Isa. 11:10, where the Messiah is represented as a nes, or ensign, it is possible that the "ensign of the Son of man" was intended by him as an allusion to this verse, and we should paraphrase v. 30a, "And then the messianic ensign of Isaiah 11 will appear in the sky in the person of him who calls himself the Son of man."

The dispute concerning whether "the sign of the Son of man" is the Son of man himself or a sign (e.g., the cross) that precedes his appearing con-

---

207. Hertz, *The Authorized Daily Prayer Book*, p. 143.
208. Cf. Elbogen, *Der jüdische Gottesdienst in seiner geschichtlichen Entwicklung*, p. 29; Kohler, "The Origin and Composition of the Eighteen Benedictions, with a Translation of the Corresponding Essene Prayers in the Apostolic Constitutions," pp. 393, 400.

tinues unabated.[209] In favor of the former is not only the possible allusion to Isa. 11:10 but also the probability that the next line, also peculiar to Matthew, is an allusion to Zech. 12:10–14, interpreted as predicting a terrified, self-concerned mourning on the part of those responsible for the death of the one being mourned. If this is the case, however, it makes more sense to understand "the sign of the Son of man" as referring to the Crucified himself; it is not the sight of a sign that strikes terror in the hearts of all the tribes of the land but rather the spectacle of the royal victim himself (as in Zech. 12:10; cf. Rev. 1:7).[210]

The combination of Zech. 12:10 and Dan. 7:13 apparently originated in Christian circles at an early date, as evidenced by Rev. 1:7, but the order was not fixed. The sequence represented in the Apocalypse appears more logical. Perhaps Matthew was disinclined to interrupt the flow of Mk. 13:26f. and decided to place the motif of eschatological grief before the Danielic clause, prefacing it with the allusion to the messianic ensign of Isa. 11:10. That no strict separation is intended by Matthew between the appearance of the ensign in v. 30a and the vision of the Son of man coming on the clouds in v. 30c is indicated by the fact that the *tote* has been removed from its location in Mark's text as the temporal specification for the fulfillment of the Danielic prophecy. In any case, there is no justification for arguing, as Tödt does, that Matthew's omission of the allusion to piercing in Zech. 12:10 indicates that he wishes to avoid identifying the Son of man with the Crucified.[211] Matthew's allusion to Zech. 12:10, strained as it is by the negative interpretation of the grief, becomes incredible if the implied reference to the martyr-king is ruled out.

Gundry appears justified in taking the subject of the clause, in conformity with Zechariah, as "all the tribes of the land (of Israel)."[212] Such an understanding anticipates Matthew's harsh presentation of Israel's responsibility for the Messiah's death at 27:25 and conforms with his use of "tribes" in 19:28.

209. Cf. Glasson, "The Ensign of the Son of Man, Mt. xxiv.30," pp. 299f.; K. H. Rengstorf, "Sēmeion," TDNT 7, pp. 236–38; Tödt, *Son of Man,* p. 80; Higgins, *Jesus and the Son of Man,* pp. 109–14.

210. In rabbinic tradition (e.g., *b. Meg.* 3a) this puzzling verse was interpreted in conformity with the Targum, which introduced a reference to Josiah. The allusion in Jn. 19:37 suggests that this verse was already considered a messianic text by pre-Christian Jews. If Higgins, *Jesus and the Son of Man,* p. 113, conjectures correctly that "the sign of the Son of man" replaces an allusion to "piercing" (cf. Rev. 1:7) and thus refers to the cross, Mt. 24:30 becomes a "futuristic passion saying" combining two of the traditional three categories of Son of man sayings!

211. Tödt, *Son of Man,* p. 81.

212. Gundry, *Use of the Old Testament,* p. 234.

Eschatological fear as a response to the judging function of the Son of man is a common motif in the Similitudes (45:3; 46:6; 48:3; 62:3–9), but in none of the passages is this element represented by any verb reminiscent of the *kopsontai* of v. 30b. Since there is no reference to judgment in Zech. 12:10, there is no need to suppose that Matthew's insertion of v. 30b is inspired by the Similitudes and its portrayal of the Son of man.

What, then, is the force of the expanded logion in vv. 30f.? Matthew attributes to Jesus a statement about his future role as glorified Messiah; the Crucified will be seen by his people, the tribes of Israel, as God's ensign when he comes on the clouds in heavenly glory, and with a messianic blast of the trumpet he will dispatch angels to gather his elect (apparently not all of Israel's scattered children) from the four winds in conformity with the hope of the tenth benediction.

In short, Matthew's redaction of these two verses provides no evidence that his apocalyptic thought in general and his understanding of the phrase "the Son of man" in particular were influenced by the Similitudes of Enoch.[213] His additions present common apocalyptic motifs, but their association with the enigmatic phrase does nothing to encourage the view that for Matthew "the Son of man" connotes a preexistent heavenly figure with whom Jesus has been identified following his resurrection.

Mt. 24:37, 39 . . . so will be the Parousia of the Son of man.

With v. 37 Matthew resumes his use of the Q sayings (cf. Lk. 17:23–30) concerning the day of the Son of man, which he began in v. 27. As in the earlier verse he again substitutes "Parousia" for "day" and thus relates these two sayings, like v. 27, back to the disciples' question in v. 3. All three speak of the sudden, unexpected nature of Jesus' glorious return.

It must be noted once more how Matthew in this context is able to express the same sentiment, again attributing third-person language to Jesus but using "your Lord" instead of "the Son of man" at v. 42 (apparently adapting Mk. 13:35, where "the lord of the household" denotes a person in the parable). There is certainly no suggestion that Matthew regards "the Son of man" as more authentic in this respect than "your Lord" because of the former's (alleged) apocalyptic associations.

---

213. Theisohn, *Der auserwählte Richter,* pp. 183, 261, agrees. This conclusion stands, even if we were to agree with Colpe, "Ho huios tou anthrōpou," TDNT 8, p. 437, that Mt. 24:30ab reproduces a tradition older than Mk. 13:26f.

Mt. 24:44 For this reason be prepared, you too, because at an hour you do not consider comes the Son of man.

This fourth saying in the Q series is found in a different context in Luke (12:40). "The day" is not used but rather the verb "come," and consequently Matthew does not here substitute Parousia as in the earlier instances. Nothing new is added by this saying. Like the earlier ones and v. 42, it refers to Jesus' anticipated return in glory and exhorts Christian preparedness.

Mt. 25:31 And when the Son of man comes in his glory and all the angels with him, then he will sit upon the throne of his glory.

The so-called parable of the sheep and goats, so treasured by contemporary Christians because of its emphasis on the importance of helping the poor and needy, is probably one of the most heavily redacted of Jesus' parables. Indeed, on the basis of a careful evaluation of vocabulary and idioms, Gundry maintains that it is largely a Matthean creation, employing various Old Testament texts and dominical tradition.[214] J. A. T. Robinson, while recognizing Matthew's editorial activity, proposes that a genuine dominical parable of separation underlies Matthew's judgment scene; the dialogue proper, he urges, is not only free of editorial traces but contains many parallels in the sayings tradition (e.g., Mk. 9:37; Mt. 10:32f., 40, 42). Thus the dialogue may reflect authentic logia concerning the eschatological consequences of accepting or rejecting Jesus in one's treatment of the needy and outcast.[215]

For many of those who perceive Matthew's hand in the extant text of 25:31–46, v. 31 is included among the redactional elements.[216] If this is granted, there is no need for further comment, because the various apocalyptic motifs represented in v. 31 have already been discussed above in connection with 16:27 and 19:28. It is not possible to ascertain whether the pre-Matthean elements of the parable or poem presented Jesus or God as

214. Gundry, *Matthew*, pp. 511–16. The same conclusion was reached earlier by Cope "Mt. xxv.31–46 'The Sheep and the Goats' Reinterpreted."

215. J. A. T. Robinson, "The 'Parable' of the Sheep and the Goats."

216. To Robinson, Cope, and Gundry should be added (among others) Vielhauer, "Gottesreich und Menschensohn in der Verkündigung Jesu," p. 58; Schweizer, "Der Menschensohn," p. 191; Colpe, "Ho huios tou anthrōpou," TDNT 8, p. 461; Jeremias, *Parables*, p. 206; Tödt, *Son of Man*, p. 73; and Theisohn, *Der auserwählte Richter*, p. 175.

the one who is identified with the needy.[217] If Robinson is correct that we should perceive a relationship between this passage and Mk. 9:37 and Mt. 10:40, 42, the conjecture that the underlying core focused on God rather than Jesus is superfluous. In any event, if Matthew is responsible for creating v. 31 as an introduction to the judgment scene, his intention (in view of his consistent use of "the Son of man" as Jesus' preferred self-designation) is apparently to render it explicit that the judging king is none other than Jesus himself. The third-person idiom of v. 31 is more appropriate than the first-person language of 7:21–23, 10:32f., and 20:23 because the judgment narrative speaks of the king in this fashion.

The consensus concerning the secondary nature of v. 31 is challenged in a stimulating article by David Catchpole.[218] Employing G. Nickelsburg's identification of a "recognition pattern" in 1 Enoch 62, he compares Mt. 25:31–46 with 1 Enoch 62–63 and finds extensive parallels, most significant of which is the idea of recognition: "Both scenes hinge on the idea of recognition . . . correspondingly, both narratives present the equivalence of those who suffer and the one who judges—1 En. 62:11."[219]

Unfortunately, the parallels between the two passages are exaggerated, and Nickelsburg's interpretation of the recognition motif in 1 En. 62:1 is itself open to serious criticism. Italicizing the conditional clause ("Open your eyes and lift up your horns *if you are able* to recognize the Elect One"), he proposes that, since the Elect One is a heavenly figure whom the accused could not have known, "the line must mean that the audience is to recognize in the Elect One, the elect ones whom they persecuted."[220] There is nothing in the verse or its context that suggests the improbable notion that those being judged are being asked to *recognize* those they have injured in the person of the heavenly judge. That Nickelsburg has read far too much into the italicized words is indicated by v. 3, which renders the eschatological recognition unconditional: "And they will see and recognize how he sits on the throne of his glory." Charles's note on "recognition" in v. 1 is still apt: "Recognize him to be what he is—the Messiah."[221] Because of the supposed recognition of the persecuted in v. 1, Catchpole exaggerates the equivalence between those who suffer and the one who judges in

217. Bultmann, *History*, p. 124, conjectures that the story originally presented God as the Judge.

218. Catchpole, "The Poor on Earth and the Son of Man in Heaven: A Reappraisal of Mt. 25:31–46."

219. Ibid., p. 380. "Recognition pattern" appears to be Catchpole's phrase rather than Nickelsburg's, who speaks of "element of recognition."

220. Nickelsburg, *Resurrection*, p. 72.

221. Charles, *The Book of Enoch*, p. 163.

v. 11; the identification between judge and victims here is no stronger than is customary in apocalyptic passages where the God of Israel avenges his people (e.g., Daniel 7). In comparing the two passages, moreover, it is important to note the differences. In 1 Enoch 62–63 no words are attributed to the Chosen One; in Matthew 25 the Son of man speaks extensively and sounds very much like the Matthean Jesus (note especially "my Father," v. 34; cf. 7:21 *et passim*).

Of greater importance to the present study is Catchpole's insistence that the Son of man of Mt. 25:31 is not only pre-Matthean but non-Matthean; whereas Matthew can use "the Son of man" as the earthly Jesus' self-designation, in this pericope the Son of man is an exclusively heavenly figure, as in the Similitudes.[222] It is incontestably true that nothing in v. 31 or the sequel states that the king once walked in Galilee, but the same is true of most statements about Jesus' return in glory (Acts 1:11 is exceptional). What must be contested is Catchpole's claim that the question *pote se eidomen* ("When did we see thee?") indicates that the Son of man is not an earthly figure.[223] The question is truly ambiguous with respect to the possibility of a prior acquaintance; it by no means excludes the possibility that the questioners are represented as genuinely puzzled: "You say that we served (or failed to serve) you, but we have no recollection of encountering you in your distress." If Catchpole is correct in his conclusion (as I think he is), namely, that the Son of man of 25:31–46 is of one mind with the Jesus of the parable of the good Samaritan and of Mk. 9:33–37, 41, "who insists on unrestricted care for the insignificant and needy," there is no basis for his sharp differentiation between the Son of man of this pericope and the *eme* ("me") of Mk. 9:37.[224]

Catchpole has made the most careful attempt to date to demonstrate that Mt. 25:31–46 is imbued with the theological atmosphere of the Similitudes of Enoch. Readers who find his demonstration unconvincing will also be unconvinced by his thesis that the Son of man of v. 31 is non-Matthean as well as pre-Matthean. He seems to espouse the view that the historical Jesus adopted the notion of a never-incarnate Son of man from the Similitudes (or the circles that produced this work) and, naturally, distinguished himself from this figure, since he himself was obviously incarnate. Whether this is a correct perception of Jesus' own thinking must be reserved to a later chapter. At this point it is only necessary to point out

222. Catchpole, "The Poor on Earth," p. 385.
223. Ibid., p. 381.
224. Ibid., p. 392.

that, if there was a pre-Matthean origin for v. 31 (whether or not it went back to Jesus), the *Christians* who transmitted it prior to Matthew must surely have understood it as Matthew himself did—as a statement by Jesus about his own future role. (What it might have meant to Enochian Jews is of no concern to us here.) *At no point in Christian transmission* can v. 31 have referred to "an exclusively heavenly figure" who "has not personally suffered hardship."[225]

That is, *if* the notion of a never-incarnate Son of man was available to Jesus' earliest followers, their appropriation of it as a way of speaking about Jesus constituted a revolutionary transformation of the concept: it could no longer possess its former connotation. If it is argued that pre-Matthean Christians preserved the original connotation by insisting that Jesus and the Son of man were two separate beings until Jesus' resurrection and exaltation, we can only respond: Where is the proof? As has been pointed out repeatedly by previous studies, there is not the slightest evidence in any of the Gospels of the idea that Jesus is destined to *become* the Son of man. Certainly Matthew betrays no awareness of such a view. If such did exist, he is clearly not in sympathy, and one might expect to find polemically-tinged assertions about the "present" and "suffering" Son of man. Such is not the case.

At this point I can see no way of demonstrating the existence of a pre-Matthean, non-Matthean understanding of the Son of man on the basis of Matthew. Of all the Son of man passages in the First Gospel, 25:31–46 holds the greatest promise in this respect, since, like a number of passages in the Similitudes, it depicts a judgment scene conducted by a heavenly figure who is seated on a glorious throne. Even here, however, the parallels do not suggest slavish copying (there are other possible sources of the various motifs), and consequently it is impossible to demonstrate dependency in any convincing way. While others may find the influence of the Similitudes obvious here, I can only conclude: *non demonstratum est.*

> **Mt. 26:2** You know that after two days the Passover occurs, and the Son of man is delivered up to be crucified.

It is not insignificant that Matthew, who has presented "the Son of man" seven times in apocalyptic contexts in chapters 24–25, follows this long eschatological discourse immediately with a saying about the crucifixion of the Son of man. Since v. 2b is not found in Mark (or Luke), it is

225. Ibid., p. 385.

generally agreed that the statement originates with the evangelist.[226] This juxtaposition demonstrates again that for Matthew the Son of man who will sit on the throne of his glory is the man who must first suffer death on a Roman cross. Whatever connotation the phrase held for Matthew, that connotation clearly included the idea of humanity.

> **Mt. 26:24** The Son of man departs as it has been written about him, but woe to that man through whom the Son of man is delivered up.

Since Matthew did not use Mk. 9:12 at 17:12 but a different (or greatly reformulated) saying, this is the first instance in his Gospel of a saying that links the suffering of the Son of man with scriptural prediction. Here the idea is taken over without alteration from Mk. 14:21. In view of Matthew's omission of the earlier Markan reference to the fulfillment of scripture, it is significant that there is no omission here.

The statement is as vague as the parallel in 1 Cor. 15:3 ("Christ died for our sins in accordance with the Scriptures"), and it is fruitless to speculate on what texts Matthew would have adduced if questioned, but surely Daniel 7 would not have been among them. There is no suggestion in that chapter that the one like a son of man must suffer and die.[227] Matthew's inclusion of this saying indicates again that for him "the Son of man" does not mean "that nonhuman Son of man about whom Daniel prophesied."

There may be an intentional play on words in the repetition of "the Son of man" in the second half of the verse ("but woe to that *man* through whom the Son of *man* is delivered up"), but there is no way of determining whether this repetition is meant to point to similarity or contrast, or, if the latter, what the nature of the contrast is. The contrast, if intended, is more likely to be ethical than metaphysical.

> **Mt. 26:45b** Behold, the hour has arrived, and the Son of man is delivered up into sinners' hands.

This final "suffering" saying, taken over with only minor alteration from Mk. 14:41, is of particular interest because it is followed immediately by a saying employing the participle of the same verb (*paradidōmi*,

---

226. Cf. Senior, *Passion Narrative*, p. 21; Tödt, *Son of Man*, p. 149.

227. Contra Caragounis, *Son of Man*, p. 200f., it is incorrect to propose that Jesus, in assuming the role of the Son of man of Daniel 7, applied to himself ideas relating to the suffering of the saints. It is nowhere suggested that the saints as a group suffer martyrdom, nor is the death of any of them explicitly mentioned.

"deliver up," "give over") and attributing first-person language to Jesus: "Get up, let us go; behold, the one who delivers *me* up has arrived." This identification is, of course, superfluous and hardly to be noticed by the readers, because it has been obvious since the very first instance of "the Son of man" at 8:20 that the Matthean Jesus refers to no one but himself when using the phrase.[228]

> **Mt. 26:64** You have said so; but I say to you, hereafter you will see the Son of man sitting at the right hand of the Power and "coming on the clouds of heaven."

This verse has already been examined, and its use of "the Son of man" was found to be mute concerning the significance of Jesus' person and work. The allusion to Daniel is unmistakable, and we must assume that Matthew regards it as a messianic proof text. His employment of the text does not, however, disclose his understanding of the connotation of "the Son of man." As we have seen in chapter 1, rabbinic allusions to the same text do not indicate a belief in a divine Messiah (or a preexistent angelic judge); it was possible to take the verse as referring to a supernaturally endowed human Messiah.

Matthew does not reveal to his readers what precisely in Jesus' response is to be regarded as constituting blasphemy in the eyes of the narrative opponents, but we can safely exclude Jesus' application to himself of the name "the Son of man." The Matthean Jesus' use of the self-designation has provoked no narrative response at any of its previous appearances, and there is no *literary* basis for the proposal that the term bears a different connotation here.[229] No secret meaning is disclosed. The angry response of the narrative audience is provoked not by the familiar term but by the statement in which it occurs. Here as elsewhere in the First Gospel, the self-designation points to the mystery of Jesus' destiny without explicating it.

---

228. It is most unlikely that it would have occurred to Matthew's readers to ponder whether "the Son of man" in 8:20 was intended by Jesus in a corporate or in a singular sense. Even if we are correct in seeing a corporate symbol for Israel in the "one like a son of man" of Dan. 7:13f., the Greek phrase *ho huios tou anthrōpou*, whatever its relationship to the Danielic vision, would suggest an individual to the Greek reader. In view of the context of 8:20, therefore, it would be natural for the reader to infer that Jesus is using this strange phrase as a name for himself.

229. The Jonah saying (12:40) is "remembered" by the narrative opponents at 27:63 without any quickened awareness of the blasphemy it is alleged to have contained; for them the Jonah saying is the word not of a blasphemer but of a deceiver (cf. 27:64).

Conclusion

What does the Son of man mean to Matthew? It *denotes* Jesus, a human being whose supernatural conception through the agency of the Holy Spirit marks him as unique, who is acknowledged by God as God's Son, yet who must suffer and die before being raised to a position at God's right hand, from which he will come as God's judge-delegate at the completion of the age. It cannot be demonstrated from Matthew's use, however, that the phrase *connotes* any of this. To Matthew it may possibly mean "the Human Being par excellence," but, while such a meaning is *possible* in every instance, there is no way to demonstrate its probability. The most that can be claimed is that this hypothesis is as valid as any other yet proposed, that is, that there is no literary basis for its invalidation.

Two proposed connotations can be confidently eliminated. First, the phrase cannot be taken as synonymous with "Christ" and "Messiah." It clearly is not heard as such by any of the narrative audiences, and there is not the slightest hint from the narrator that the phrase possesses this as a secret or ignored meaning. Second, it cannot mean "never-incarnate heavenly judge," because of its application to the mortal Jesus. Despite its frequent appearances in apocalyptic contexts, it does not function as an apocalyptic title.

Because the term never has any narrative effect, we should probably conclude that for Matthew it is not a revelatory expression. It communicates nothing of importance regarding Jesus' nature, functions, and destiny. It may well be that for Matthew the term is a name whose function as Jesus' preferred self-designation is remembered but whose origin is forgotten, just as Mark remembers that Zebedee's sons were nicknamed "Sons of Thunder" (Mk. 3:17) but has forgotten (or at least finds insignificant) the original reason for this naming.

We can be sure that for Matthew the name is not trivial. He never uses it as the subject of a verb of speaking, for example ("You have heard it said . . . but the Son of man says to you . . .").[230] It is found primarily in passages where Jesus speaks of his vocation and destiny.[231] It is more than a casual self-reference; in Matthew's use it is an elevated term, pointing to

---

230. Cf. Leivestad, "Der Apokalyptische Menschensohn ein theologisches Phantom," p. 100; his comment concerns the Son of man sayings in general, not specifically those found in Matthew.

231. Cf. ibid., p. 99. Mt. 12:32 and 16:13 appear to be exceptions to the rule, but it can be argued that these verses occur in passages where Jesus' vocation and destiny are under consideration.

the mystery of Jesus' destiny without "containing" that destiny as its connotation.

If the First Gospel was known to Ignatius, as has sometimes been maintained, we can readily understand why he was able to employ *huios anthrōpou* as a way of speaking about Jesus' humanity.[232] Not once does Matthew use the phrase in a way that would preclude such an understanding. Even in those sayings that anticipate Jesus' return in resplendent glory, "the Son of man" designates the man Jesus; the identity of the Crucified and the Exalted is as important to Matthew as it is to Luke (". . . because he has fixed a day on which he will judge the world in righteousness *by a man* [*en andri*] whom he has appointed, and of this he has given assurance to all by *raising him from the dead,*" Acts 17:31).

Bultmann was correct; if the term originally connoted a heavenly figure, this meaning is unknown to Matthew.[233] If evidence for such a use by Jesus or his followers is to be found, it must be at an earlier stage of the tradition. Perhaps Mark will provide the necessary clues.

232. Ignatius, Eph. 20:2. See chapter 2.
233. See n. 1 above.

6 | MARK

The phrase "the Son of man" occurs fourteen times in the Gospel according to Mark. Only three times does the expression appear in a saying referring to Jesus' future role (8:38; 13:26; 14:62). It is found predominantly in sayings that speak of his earthly activity or anticipated suffering, death, and resurrection. As a result, the unsophisticated reader is led to assume that "the Son of man," whatever its meaning, is a name for the *earthly* Jesus and thus *also* applicable to him with reference to his future role. It would not occur to such a reader to reverse this priority and suppose that the name properly refers to the heavenly Lord and only paradoxically applies to the earthly Jesus.

It is entirely possible that the unsophisticated reader's perception is correct. Scholarly support for such a view was provided by Bultmann, who maintained that the passion predictions (8:31; 9:31; 10:33f.) and the related sayings at 9:9 and 14:21, 41 (and 9:12, if not a post-Markan gloss) were all products of the Hellenistic church, "in which the title 'Son of man' was no longer understood in its original sense."[1] To Bultmann it was clear that Mark, like the later evangelists Matthew and Luke, did not distinguish between Jesus and the Son of man; like the Hellenistic church, which created the passion sayings, Mark was no longer aware of (or at least no longer interested in) the "original sense" of the phrase as an apocalyptic title designating a transcendent, angelic being.[2]

Further support for this assessment of Mark can be found in the appropriation of this earlier Gospel by Matthew and Luke. If we have been correct in the conclusions drawn in chapters 3 and 5—namely, that neither Luke nor Matthew understood "the Son of man" as an apocalyptic title—

---

1. Bultmann, *Theology*, vol. 1, p. 30; cf. his *History*, p. 152.
2. Bultmann, *Theology*, vol. 1, p. 29.

then they likely read Mark just as our unsophisticated modern reader does. Nothing they found in Mark inclined them to the view that they ought to reserve "the Son of man" for apocalyptic settings. We can assume that they saw themselves as continuing Mark's usage. From this perspective it can even be argued that the burden of proof rests on any who would propose a radical disjunction between Mark's understanding of the phrase and that of his two successors. Since this last suggestion is not likely to obtain much sympathy among those convinced that "the Son of man" served earliest Christianity as an apocalyptic title, the question of the burden of proof must be disregarded. Ignoring the subsequent history of the Son of man tradition, we must focus here on the immediate question: What does the phrase mean to Mark?

Four possibilities must be kept in mind: (1) the tradition before Mark regarded "the Son of man" as an apocalyptic title, and he is fully aware of this meaning, even though he uses the term primarily in nonapocalyptic contexts; (2) as Bultmann proposed, an earlier apocalyptic tradition has been forgotten, and for Mark the phrase possesses some other meaning; (3) the phrase did *not* function as an apocalyptic title in the pre-Markan tradition but has been apocalypticized by him as a result of his appropriation of Dan. 7:13f. (i.e., he has "Danielized" the Son of man tradition); (4) given the statistics of Mark's usage, the phrase served neither Mark nor the pre-Markan tradition as a "title of majesty" connoting Jesus' apocalyptic glory.

How shall the competing claims of these four postulated situations be adjudicated? All are theoretically conceivable, but which is historically the most probable? The first two will, of course, appear more probable to scholars who are convinced that earliest Christianity appropriated a Jewish myth about a transcendent Son of man and applied it to Jesus in response to the resurrection. Since the method adopted for this study cannot treat such a thesis as already demonstrated, however, it cannot be assumed in our examination of Mark. The various possibilities must be assessed exclusively on the basis of Mark's redaction and/or creation of the Son of man material.

Several questions must thus be considered with respect to each of the Son of man passages in Mark. How does the statement relate to Mark's composition as a whole? Is it a Markan creation, or does he derive it from tradition? Is there evidence that he has significantly altered traditional material? These questions are more easily asked than answered. Even if the answers must remain very tentative, they must be ventured, if the issue of Mark's understanding of the phrase is to be resolved. Despite its hazards, the seriatim approach will again be adopted, since it appears least likely to prejudice the investigation.

Mk. 2:10 But in order that you may know that the Son of man has authority to forgive sins on earth . . .

Although William Wrede's portrayal of the motif of the messianic secret has been subjected to rigorous criticism, a scholarly consensus has emerged around the modified proposal that the motif is located primarily at the redactional level. The fact that Jesus is the Messiah, although revealed to the readers in the Gospel's opening line (1:1) and at the baptism (1:11), remains hidden from the disciples until Peter's confession and is publicly disclosed only in the trial scene.[3] Scholars who regard "the Son of man" as a messianic title of some sort are thus puzzled by its appearance at 2:10. Although the phrase clearly functions in the context as a self-designation (the narrative makes no sense if the appellation is taken as referring to someone else), the messianic secret is betrayed if Jesus is here represented as divulging that he is the Son of man of apocalyptic expectation.

Various attempts have thus been made to explain Mark's apparent violation of his own rule. One of the most popular is the proposal that v. 10 does not belong to the narrative but is a parenthetical remark directed to the reader. The inadequacies of this hypothesis have already been discussed in chapter 3 in relation to the Lukan parallel (Lk. 5:24). As critics have pointed out, the Markan anacoluthon is not remedied by placing v. 10 in parentheses; indeed, it is aggravated. Moreover, neither Matthew nor Luke found Mark's language so intolerable as to demand editorial revision.[4] Morna Hooker points to a parallel elliptical construction with *hina* at Mk. 14:49, thereby demonstrating that Mark is not averse to ellipsis in narrative.[5]

Others have argued that Mark only imperfectly applies his theory of the messianic secret to the material he received from the tradition. It is suggested that Mark found the material in 2:1—3:6 as a collected body and incorporated it at an early point in his narrative framework without taking serious notice of the way that 2:10, 28 violated his theory.[6] In view of the careful way he refused to allow unambiguous titles to identify Jesus before

3. Wrede's *Messianic Secret* has been subjected to a thorough reassessment by Räisänen, *Das "Messiasgeheimnis" im Markusevangelium*. An excellent review of the current state of the question is provided by Tuckett, *The Messianic Secret*.
4. This fact is noted by Hooker, *The Son of Man in Mark*, p. 84.
5. Ibid.
6. Cf. Tödt, *Son of Man*, p. 132.

Peter's confession, however, the carelessness is to be attributed rather to Mark's modern interpreters. It is inconceivable that he would have allowed "the Christ" or "the Son of God" to stand here, had he found either in the tradition. That he permitted Jesus to name himself "the Son of man" in the presence of the crowd and his opponents is the clearest evidence that Mark did *not* regard this appellation as a recognized messianic title. Whereas the application to Jesus of one of these other titles by demons (3:11) or Peter (8:29) or the high priest (14:61) provokes a narrative response, neither here nor elsewhere in Mark is there any reaction to Jesus' use of "the Son of man" as a self-designation.[7]

The third proposal, consequently, is that the phrase is regarded by Mark as ambiguous. While Mark and his readers know that it is a messianic title, this knowledge is not available to the narrative audience. One of the most ardent champions of this view is Walter Schmithals.

> In fact, the term "Son of man" is in and of itself a concealing expression. It *can* be understood as a messianic title of majesty, but it *can* also mean simply "human." . . . For the contemporary, who knows nothing about the secret of Jesus' person, can only (mis)understand 2:10 and 2:28 as suggesting that Jesus is speaking (in the third person!) *about humans in general.*[8]

Unfortunately, this proposal fails to take seriously the peculiarities of the Greek phrase. Neither Mark nor any of his Greek readers would have perceived such an ambiguity in *ho huios tou anthrōpou*. Although the anarthrous *huios anthrōpou* could be used generically (and *not* as a title), the form with articles could by no means be understood as referring to "humans in general" or "any man whatsoever."[9] It is no more generic in its formulation than the parallel expression *ho huios tou theou*.

More defensible is the proposal that "the Son of man" functions here as a *secret* title; for the narrative audience the term is opaque, conveying no meaning whatsoever, but for Mark and his readers it connotes Jesus' messianic majesty. But where is the evidence in support for this hypothesis to be found? Wrede quite correctly comments: "I would not know what in [Mark's] gospel is indicative of this view."[10] At no point does Mark disclose

---

7. Cf. Hooker, *The Son of Man in Mark*, pp. 92, 177.

8. Schmithals, "Die Worte vom leidenden Menschensohn," p. 432: "In der Tat ist der Begriff 'Menschensohn' selbst und als solcher ein verhüllender Ausdruck. Er *kann* als messianischer Hoheitstitel verstanden werden, *kann* aber auch einfach 'Mensch' bedeuten. . . . Denn der Zeitgenosse, der vom Geheimnis der Person Jesu nichts weiss, kann 2,10 und 2,28 nur so (miss)verstehen, dass Jesus (in dritter Person!) *vom Menschen überhaupt* spricht." The translations of this and subsequent quotations of Schmithals are my own.

9. Schmithals, *Das Evangelium nach Markus*, vol. 1, p. 153.

10. Wrede, *Messianic Secret*, p. 20.

the hitherto secret meaning of the phrase—neither at 8:31, nor at 14:62 (see below).

It has been alleged that Mark must have regarded "the Son of man" as an exalted title because of the adverbial phrase "upon the earth" that accompanies its first appearance in his Gospel; these words must imply that the Son of man normally functions in heaven.[11] Since nowhere in Jewish apocalyptic literature is it suggested that the Son of man will forgive sins in heaven, the inference is erroneous, as we have seen in chapter 3. Whatever its origin, v. 10 functions in its present context as a response to v. 7, where Jesus' opponents ask, "Who can forgive sins except one, God?" The Markan Jesus challenges this assumption by demonstrating through a spectacular miracle that God has conferred on him the authority to declare forgiveness. In this respect 2:1–12 constitutes a parallel to 1:21–28, where Jesus' authority as a God-authorized teacher is confirmed by an exorcism.[12]

There is no suggestion in the Markan pericope that the authority of a transcendent, eschatological figure has been "read back" into the life of the earthly Jesus.[13] The Christian readers of the Gospel already know the end of the story; they know that Jesus, the Son of God, has been exalted through resurrection to the right hand of God. They know that the Jesus about whose life they are reading is destined to appear as the glorious *Kyrios*. This does not mean that they regard him as invested with his future glory during his earthly life. They are consequently not disposed to regard the self-designation "the Son of man" in v. 10 as an allusion to Jesus' transcendent status. As Christopher Tuckett points out, if Jesus is to be represented as appealing to the accepted authority of an authoritative figure, the saying should be reversed: "But that you may know that I am the Son of man. . . ." The narrative emphasizes that what justifies Jesus' claim to forgive is not his application to himself of the name "the Son of man" but his demonstration of the (God-given) power to heal.[14] Indeed, as far as the narrative itself is concerned, nothing is changed if we substitute first-person language ("But that you may know that I have authority to

11. E.g., Thompson, "The Son of Man—Some Further Considerations," p. 205; Hamerton-Kelly, *Pre-existence, Wisdom, and the Son of Man*, p. 62. For a response to the latter, cf. Dunn, *Christology*, p. 88.

12. Mark's readers may have understood *epi tēs gēs* as referring to Jesus' earthly life as contrasted with his current activity as exalted *Kyrios*. Such an understanding, however, would depend not on the appearance in the saying of "the Son of man" but rather on their faith in Jesus as resurrected Son of God. Cf. Hooker, *The Son of Man in Mark*, p. 90.

13. This point is correctly emphasized by Tödt, *Son of Man*, p. 127. For a different opinion, cf. Kertelge, "Die Vollmacht des Menschensohnes zur Sündenvergebung (Mk 2,10)," pp. 206, 211.

14. Tuckett, "The Present Son of Man," p. 62.

forgive sins on earth . . ."), since the response of the narrative audience pays no attention to Jesus' self-designation.

Before we can address the question of what "the Son of man" here means to Mark, we must ask whether its use in this instance is redactional or traditional, and, if the latter, whether Mark derived it from Greek or Aramaic tradition.

One of the earliest proponents of the view that v. 10 is redactional was Emil Wendling. In his 1908 monograph, *Die Entstehung des Marcus-Evangeliums,* he argued that all Son of man sayings in the Gospel derive from the final redactor. Concerning 2:10 he proposed that the pre-Markan narrative demonstrated Jesus' authority to forgive by means of a healing. The redactor, he urged, wishes to go further; he wants to respond to the charge of blasphemy by suggesting that Jesus has divine authority because he is the Messiah, but his claim is presented through the veiled expression "the Son of man."[15] Partly in dependence upon Wendling, Schmithals has recently presented a similar argument: 2:10 is redactional and is introduced by Mark as a veiled messianic title.[16]

The same position was reached independently by Norman Perrin, who was convinced that 2:10 represents Mark's own creative use of the phrase as a means of presenting his own theological emphasis on the authority of Jesus: "Mark intends both to stress the authority of Jesus and to claim that he exercised that authority as Son of Man. This is the first element of his christology."[17] According to Perrin, Mark was not the first to employ "the Son of man" with reference to the earthly activity of Jesus, but he was the first to associate it explicitly with authority; Mark uses it "to give content to the idea of Jesus as the Son of God."[18] It was a natural title for Mark to use, "because it was comparatively unused in the tradition before him and was not a confessional title," and consequently "there was no weight of traditional use to predetermine the understanding of the audience."[19]

Unfortunately, Perrin is vague about what Mark intended "the Son of man" to convey to his readers. As far as I can discover, Perrin did not concern himself with the relationship between the messianic secret in Mark and the appearance of "the Son of man" at 2:10, 28. He proposes that the term is useful to Mark because it "lends itself to the necessary combination of theological motifs," namely, "earthly authority, the necessity of suffer-

---

15. Wendling, *Die Entstehung des Marcus-Evangeliums*, pp. 209f.
16. Schmithals, "Die Worte vom leidenden Menschensohn," p. 432.
17. Perrin, *Modern Pilgrimage*, p. 89.
18. Ibid., p. 78; cf. p. 121. A similar opinion is expressed by Achtemeier, " 'He Taught Them Many Things': Reflections on Marcan Christology," pp. 471f., 481.
19. Perrin, *Modern Pilgrimage*, p. 82.

ing, apocalyptic authority and soteriological significance."[20] Does Perrin mean to suggest that "the Son of man" encompasses all this as its content? It would appear that Perrin is guilty of the fallacy of blurring the subject-predicate distinction. The statement "The Son of man must suffer . . ." by no means implies that suffering belongs to the definition of the subject. The most that can be inferred is that the one designated by the phrase "the Son of man" must be conceived as a being capable of suffering.

The varied and interesting arguments presented by Wendling, Schmithals, and Perrin cannot be reviewed here in extenso; we must limit ourselves to the observation that they fall short of demonstration. We ought therefore to remain with the consensus that regards v. 10 as derived from tradition. Consideration of its function at the pre-Markan stage must be delayed until the next chapter.

Did Mark find the statement in Greek, or was he personally responsible for translating it from Aramaic? The presence of Aramaic words in Greek transliteration at 5:41, 7:34, and 14:36 naturally suggests the possibility that Mark was bilingual and that he may have been responsible for rendering Aramaic source material into Greek. This conclusion, however, is by no means certain; it is entirely possible that Aramaic words such as the ones that appear in these verses were transmitted in the oral tradition of the Greek-speaking church (cf. Paul's use of *marana tha* at 1 Cor. 16:22).[21] The fact that *ephphatha* (7:34) reproduces only imperfectly the underlying Aramaic imperative *ethpathach* does not increase one's confidence in Mark's Aramaic competence.[22] *Boanērges* (3:17) is likewise hardly what one would expect as a transliteration of *bene regesh*.[23] It will be best, therefore, to assume with Lindars that 2:10 was received by Mark in Greek and that, because the phrase contained the customary articles, he naturally regarded it as Jesus' exclusive self-designation, not a generic reference.[24]

Three of the scholars who have devoted special attention to Mark's use of "the Son of man"—Tödt, Hooker, and Perrin—concur in the view that for Mark the phrase connotes authority. "What is conveyed by it is Jesus' *exousia*," writes Tödt, for example.[25] It is obvious that Mk. 2:10 speaks of

---

20. Ibid., p. 83.
21. Farmer, *The Synoptic Problem*, p. 172, points out that foreign words were sometimes introduced into Hellenistic healing stories.
22. Cf. Gould, *Mark*, p. 139 n. 1.
23. Ibid., p. 57. In this case one might postulate that the original had been corrupted in oral transmission.
24. Lindars, *Jesus Son of Man*, p. 102.
25. Tödt, *Son of Man*, p. 127; cf. Hooker, *The Son of Man in Mark*, p. 179; Perrin, *Modern Pilgrimage*, p. 89.

the authority of Jesus. It is *not* self-evident that the self-designation connotes authority for Mark to any greater extent than the name "Jesus."
Perrin is absolutely correct in insisting that Mark has a special interest in
attributing *exousia* to Jesus, but, as Perrin himself would concede, there is
no necessary connection between this motif and "the Son of man."[26] The
first (and therefore critical) instance of *exousia* occurs at 1:27, where the
audience in the Capernaum synagogue express amazement at the authority of Jesus' teaching; there is no occasion in this passage to use "the Son of
man." The *exousia* here as everywhere is ascribed by Mark to *Jesus*, who is
proclaimed by this Gospel as the Son of God. It is premature, therefore, on
the basis of the use of *exousia* in 2:10 to refer to "the authority of the Son
of man," as if the text identified Jesus *as* the Son of man ("I am the Son of
man") and ascribed to Jesus the authority normally attributed to the figure
so named. Misleading, therefore, is Perrin's suggestion that "Mark intends
both to stress the authority of Jesus and to claim that he exercised that
authority *as Son of Man*."[27] Since Mark does not present Jesus as the Son
of man but rather as the Son of God, the proposal cannot be substantiated.

All that can be asserted with certainty regarding this first instance of the
phrase at 2:10 is that Jesus is represented as publicly referring to himself as
the Son of man, using third-person language, and that this usage attracts
no narrative reaction. The connotation of the phrase cannot be read from
the predicate; at most one can argue that "the Son of man" cannot be
regarded as an inappropriate designation for a human being who claims
the conferred authority to forgive sins. That is, we may postulate that the
phrase connotes an eschatological redeemer figure or that it bears no
conceptual connotation at all, but the context of this instance does not
support the superiority of the former over the latter.

Mk. 2:28 Therefore the Son of man is lord also of the Sabbath.

Verse 28 cannot be understood independently of v. 27. That is,
v. 27 cannot be treated as a post-Markan interpolation (even if Mark is
treated from a Griesbachian perspective), and consequently the function
of v. 28 in Mark's narrative can be comprehended only by taking seriously
its relationship to the preceding logion.

One of the most compelling treatments of the pericope is that of Ernst
Haenchen, who argues convincingly that this is not an "ideal scene"

26. Perrin, *Modern Pilgrimage*, pp. 74, 80, 89.
27. Ibid., p. 89 (my italics). This position is reiterated in Perrin's "The Hign Priest's Question and Jesus' Answer (Mark 14:61–62)," p. 90.

created by the early church in defense of its own freedom from Sabbath observance (as proposed by Bultmann), but rather a genuine reminiscence from the ministry of Jesus.[28] In response to sabbatarian critics Jesus enunciated the halakic principle: "The Sabbath was made (by God) for humans, not humans for the Sabbath."

It is by no means suggested by this logion that those who transmitted the story believed that Jesus had abolished the Sabbath law.[29] None of the Sabbath stories in any of the Gospels makes so radical a claim; indeed, they all demonstrate the opposite. The point of each story is that Jesus *interpreted* the law in a way that was unacceptable to more rigorous sabbatarians. There is not the slightest hint that Jesus instructed his followers that it was permissible to follow their normal vocations on the seventh day. What he did teach was that human need should be given precedence over Sabbath observance. As Phillip Sigal and others have argued, there was nothing "un-Jewish" in this approach, even if it made Jesus anathema with some of his contemporaries.[30]

What, then, is the function of v. 28? Haenchen proposes that the pre-Markan community that transmitted the pericope found v. 27 too bold, because it appeared to grant ordinary humans the right to dispense with Sabbath observance whenever they wished. They felt it necessary to circumscribe this freedom by reference to Jesus' teaching authority; as his followers, they were bound to observe the Sabbath as he himself had taught. This limitation was given expression in the Son of man saying that the pre-Markan tradition created as a commentary on v. 27.[31]

If this is a correct reconstruction of the history of the tradition, we are curious to know what prompted the pre-Markan originator of v. 28 to couch it in terms of the Son of man; consideration of this issue, however, belongs in the next chapter. What concerns us here is Mark's appropriation of the logion. It is perhaps impossible to determine with certainty whether Mark's church was a Torah-free gentile congregation in Rome (as is usually assumed) or a Jewish-Christian community in Galilee (as Willi Marxsen has proposed).[32] If this question could be answered, we might know whether the pericope had direct or only indirect relevance for the intended readers, that is, whether it governed their Sabbath observance or was employed

28. Haenchen, *Weg Jesu*, pp. 121f.; cf. Bultmann, *History*, p. 16.
29. It is misleading, therefore, when Merkel, "The Opposition between Jesus and Judaism," p. 139, proposes that Jesus attacked the Sabbath law as such rather than contemporary interpretations of Sabbath requirements.
30. Sigal, *The Halakah of Jesus*, pp. 119–53.
31. Haenchen, *Weg Jesu*, p. 121.
32. Marxsen, *Mark the Evangelist*, pp. 84, 114n.

analogically to remind them that Jesus' teachings must guide them in their moral choices. In either case, however, "the Son of man" serves to designate Jesus as the community's God-authorized teacher. This does *not* mean that "the Son of man" *connotes* teacher for Mark. We can properly infer that Mark regarded the designation as *not inappropriate* for a teacher. Since there is nothing in the context to suggest that the evangelist viewed this as a paradoxical use of the phrase, we must assume that for him, as for Matthew, Luke, and John, it is the designation of a human being, not of an angelic or supra-angelic being whose domicile is heaven.

Since Jesus' authority as the church's teacher is presumably associated by Mark with his status as the Son of God (it is not attributed to his superior competence in halakic exegesis), we must consider the possibility that the phrase here serves as a synonym for "the Messiah" (as numerous commentators have proposed). For this to be the case, however, we must further assume that for Mark it is a secret title; its public use again provokes no narrative response.

> **Mk. 8:31** And he began to teach them that it was necessary for the Son of man to suffer many things and be rejected by the elders and the chief priests and the scribes and be killed, and after three days to be resurrected.

There seems to be a consensus that at least one of the three passion predictions (8:31; 9:31; 10:33f.) is basically pre-Markan, but scholars are divided concerning whether 8:31 or 9:31 more closely represents the pre-Markan version. It is generally agreed that 10:33f. is a Markan creation in which the earlier formulation has been greatly expanded.

This consensus has been challenged by some who argue that the author of the Second Gospel is himself responsible for all three passion predictions. Schmithals, for example, maintains that, since the framework of the three passion predictions is redactional, it is probable that Mark created all three.[33] The same conclusion was reached independently by Perrin.[34] In response to Schmithals and Perrin it must be insisted that with respect to the first of these predictions, *either* the entire pericope is redactional as Catchpole has argued, *or* something like 8:31 existed in the pre-Markan version of the narrative.[35] That is, v. 31 cannot be regarded as a secondary

33. Schmithals, "Die Worte vom leidenden Menschensohn," p. 420.
34. Perrin, *Modern Pilgrimage*, p. 120.
35. Catchpole, "The 'Triumphal' Entry," pp. 326–28. Schweizer, "Der Menschensohn," p. 195, is right in insisting that the Satan passage cannot be attributed to the early church and that it makes no sense without some kind of passion prediction.

intrusion in a pericope consisting of Peter's confession and Jesus' rejection of that confession by means of the Satan logion of v. 33.

Erich Dinkler, who postulates this earlier form, has not proposed a credible *Sitz im Leben* for the transmission of such a narrative. We know of no group in the early church that vehemently denied the messiahship of Jesus and could thus be credited with creating or transmitting the narrative in this form.[36] Moreover, the *titulus* on the cross (Mk. 15:26) renders improbable a *Sitz im Leben Jesu*; it is unlikely that the political charges against Jesus would have been formulated precisely in this way had he so emphatically denied the suggestion of his supporters that he was the Messiah.[37] We should therefore regard the Satan word of v. 33 as a response to Peter's rejection of an announcement by Jesus that he, the Messiah, must suffer.[38] This, of course, does not mean that the pre-Markan pericope (if such existed) must have expressed this statement in third-person language employing "the Son of man." It is conceivable, as Jeremias and Colpe have argued, that an earlier form of the passion predictions attributed first-person language to Jesus.[39]

Let us, then, suppose for the moment that those scholars are correct who say that Mark himself is responsible for introducing "the Son of man" at v. 31, either as an addition to an earlier passion saying or as part of a verse or pericope for which he is entirely accountable. What can he have meant the phrase to communicate to his readers? Several possibilities must be considered.

First, he may have intended "the Son of man" to be understood as a synonym for "the Christ" of v. 29.[40] As we saw in relationship to 2:10, 28, however, this would require that the phrase be treated by Mark in its two prior instances as a secret messianic title, whose meaning must be disclosed at a subsequent point in the narrative. If there is no subsequent disclosure, the hypothesis of secrecy must be discarded as undemonstrable and thus superfluous. There is nothing in the present pericope to suggest such a disclosure. Scholars have been misled into supposing that it is narratively presented as a synonym for "the Christ" by the fact that the

---

36. Dinkler, "Petrusbekenntnis und Satanswort."

37. The historicity of the *titulus* is strongly affirmed by Winter, *On the Trial of Jesus*, pp. 153–56. Bammel, "The *Titulus*," regards the *titulus* as historical but ambiguous evidence regarding the actual charge. Catchpole, "The 'Triumphal' Entry," pp. 328–30, regards the *titulus* as a Christian invention.

38. In addition to the article by Schweizer cited in n. 35, see his "The Son of Man," p. 120.

39. Jeremias, "Die älteste Schicht," p. 160; Colpe, "Ho huios tou anthrōpou," TDNT 8, p. 444.

40. So Dinkler, "Petrusbekenntnis und Satanswort," p. 139.

denotation of the two terms is the same. The hypothesis of disclosure is easily disproved by substituting "the Son of the carpenter" for "the Son of man." In this case no scholar would venture to suggest that "the Son of the carpenter" is *synonymous* with "the Christ," even though the linguistic function of the substituted phrase is exactly the same as that of the original. All that can be established from the common denotation of "the Christ" and "the Son of man" is that the connotations overlap to the extent that both terms can appropriately designate the same entity (in this case, a male human being). Moreover, since Mark never employs "the Son of man" confessionally, or, as Jack Kingsbury would express it, in "predicative" fashion, there is no reason to assume that he regards the two appellations as interchangeable.[41]

Also popular is the thesis that Mark uses "the Son of man" to qualify or explicate "the Christ." Perrin, for example, urges that the phrase is used here and elsewhere in Mark to "correct" a faulty Christology.[42] It is indisputable that Mark's organization of the second half of his Gospel is governed by the passion predictions and the disciples' misunderstanding of their significance. Peter's rebuke of Jesus and Jesus' response are sufficient in themselves to demonstrate that Mark espouses the view that the Christ must suffer. It is also true that the passion predictions all employ third-person language and "the Son of man." It does not logically follow, however, that for Mark "the Son of man" is a more "correct" christological title than "the Christ" or "the Son of God."

This point has been effectively demonstrated by Kingsbury, and we need only summarize his argument. Peter's use of "Christ" in 8:29 is "correct" but "insufficient"; it identifies Jesus' royal status but does not take account of his passion.[43] It is insufficient even as an identification term, because of its vagueness; its connotation is clarified by the parallel but more adequate term "the Son of God," whose importance is highlighted by the fact that twice in the narrative God himself declares that Jesus is his Son (1:11; 9:7).[44] In this way Mark indicates that the "normative" title for "explaining who Jesus is" is not one that Mark chooses as author, nor even one that Jesus applies to himself ("the Son of man") but the one employed by God.[45] Thus 8:31 predicts the destiny that awaits the one whom Peter has identified as the Christ and whom God has called "my Son"; it does

41. Kingsbury, *The Christology of Mark's Gospel*, pp. 162f.
42. Perrin, *Modern Pilgrimage*, p. 78.
43. Kingsbury, *The Christology of Mark's Gospel*, p. 97.
44. Ibid., p. 98.
45. Ibid., p. 158.

not teach that Christians ought to refer to this person as "the Son of man" if they wish to exhibit a correct Christology. The emphasis lies not on the name but on the sufferings that the one so named must experience. Donald Juel's remark is apt: the point of this first passion prediction "would be just as clear if nothing more were known about the title 'Son of man' than that it was an enigmatic self-designation of Jesus. The content of the saying, not the title, is decisive."[46]

Critics will ask, If "the Son of man" serves here neither as a synonym for "the Christ" of v. 29 nor as a more adequate christological title, why does Mark choose it? In response, it must be insisted that its use here, if redactional, indicates only two things: first, that Mark is familiar with the idiom attributed to Jesus by the tradition, according to which Jesus frequently referred to his vocation and destiny in "elevated language" employing "the Son of man" in the place of first-person speech; second, that he regards it as appropriate for Jesus to speak of his forthcoming death in this way. We cannot assume that Mark thinks he knows its "original" meaning and regards it as particularly appropriate for this context; he may well view it as a mysterious term whose origin is unknown.[47] We can deduce only that he does *not* think that it "correctly" connotes an angelic being who by nature is incapable of experiencing death. This we learn from the immediate context, where Peter's rebuke responds not to the fantastic paradox of the incarnation of a heavenly being but to the lesser paradox that the Christ of Jewish expectation must suffer ignominy and death prior to vindication. Peter's response assumes that "the Son of man" of v. 31 is self-evidently and unambiguously a self-designation *and that it provides no further information about who Jesus is*. This is confirmed by the sequel in v. 34, which attributes first-person speech to Jesus in a saying that implies his crucifixion.

If, on the other hand, the consensus is justified that regards v. 31 as traditional, either in its present form or perhaps in a form closer to that of 9:31, what does Mark intend to communicate by the impersonal verb of necessity, *dei*, "*it is necessary* that the Son of man suffer many things"? Tödt is surely justified in his judgment that allusion is here made not to the apocalyptic necessity of Dan. 2:28 LXX but to scriptural necessity.[48] Because of the prominence of *apodokimasthēnai* ("to be rejected"), we should

---

46. Juel, *Messiah and Temple*, p. 90.
47. In his discussion of this passage, Luz, "The Secrecy Motif and the Marcan Christology," p. 95 n. 67, pertinently asks with respect to Mark's use of the term, "Did he still understand it at all?"
48. Tödt, *Son of Man*, pp. 167f.

probably (with Tödt) see here rather an allusion to Ps. 118:22. There is certainly no evidence in 8:31 that Mark has Daniel 7 in mind by attributing the implied sufferings of "the saints of the Most High" to their representative, the "one like a son of man"; linguistic echoes of the Danielic passage are not to be found. Hooker argues that the Son of man of Daniel 7 "suffers" when his rightful position and God's authority are denied— a situation she finds depicted in that chapter.[49] This suggestion is ingenious, but it requires that we read a great deal into Daniel 7 that is not explicit. Moreover, the point of the Markan passage is not to urge that Christ suffers psychologically when his rightful authority is denied but rather to prepare Christians for physical suffering and possible martyrdom by pointing to the Christ who suffered not only rejection but also a violent death. Respecting other passages of Scripture that may here be implied, it is impossible to be specific, but we should assume that they belong to the same collection alluded to in the pre-Pauline kerygma, "Christ died for our sins in accordance with the Scriptures" (1 Cor. 15:3). In any event, the passage as a whole makes it clear that for Mark it is the Christ who suffers in accordance with scriptural necessity, not some other figure named "the Son of man."

In opposition to Tödt and Hooker, it must be urged that v. 31 is not a statement about Jesus' authority or, to use their language, the authority of the Son of man.[50] Every statement the evangelist makes about Jesus *implies* his authority as God's Son. It simply cannot be demonstrated that the Son of man statements regarding Jesus' betrayal, suffering, death, and resurrection imply this authority more emphatically than, say, 8:34, in which first-person language is used. Moreover, even where authority is explicitly mentioned in a statement employing "the Son of man" (2:10), it cannot logically be inferred that the authority in question belongs to the connotation of the term. The predicate clearly says something about the subject but is not logically included in the subject as its "content."

If Mark, then, received v. 31 (including "the Son of man") from the tradition, he understood the term to function as the peculiar self-designation preferred by Jesus in solemn statements about his vocation and destiny, and he treated it as having no narrative effect. The response he attributes to Peter (whether traditonal or redactional) ignores the term as if it had no connotative force. This, of course, is precisely what we found at 2:10 and 28.

---

49. Hooker, *The Son of Man in Mark*, pp. 108f.
50. Tödt, *Son of Man*, p. 178; Hooker, *The Son of Man in Mark*, pp. 108f.

> **Mk. 8:38** For whoever is ashamed of me and my words in this adulterous and sinful generation, of that person will the Son of man also be ashamed when he comes in the glory of his Father with the holy angels.

One of the most striking features of this logion is its apparent differentiation between Jesus and the Son of man. This feature caused Bultmann to argue for its authenticity, on the grounds that the early church, which quickly came to identify Jesus with the Son of man, could scarcely have created a saying that in effect denies this identification.[51] What Bultmann failed to take seriously is the fact that *all* the Son of man sayings, by virtue of the third-person language they employ, appear to distinguish between Jesus (the speaker) and the figure so named, and yet *all* of them in their present contexts in the Gospels imply the identification. For example, even if it could be demonstrated beyond doubt that Mk. 13:26 derives from a pre-Christian Jewish apocalyptic pamphlet, its placement in the Gospel of Mark is inconceivable apart from the implied identification of Jesus with the one there referred to as the Son of man. The statement would otherwise be unusable for Christian proclamation.

Consequently, it is possible that the saying derives either from pre-Markan tradition or from Mark himself. Schmithals maintains that 8:38 and 13:26 are the only two pre-Markan Son of man sayings in the Gospel. Why? Because he regards "the Son of man" as an apocalyptic title, and thus these two sayings represent the "correct" pre-Markan use. Since the backward method employed in our study disallows this presupposition, pending a final determination, it must be insisted that the possibility of Markan creativity here cannot be ruled out ex hypothesi. If, as Schmithals argues, Mark was capable of creating all the passion predictions, where "the Son of man" occurs in statements regarding Jesus' human suffering and subsequent vindication by resurrection, there was certainly nothing to prevent him from creating a saying concerning Jesus' future destiny as eschatological witness or judge. That is, if Mark regarded "the Son of man" as an appropriate self-designation for "earthly" and "suffering" sayings of Jesus, he could naturally extend that usage to "future" sayings without being aware of the term's use in Jewish apocalyptic (if that were the case). Nothing requires us to believe that *Mark* regarded 8:38 as constituting a more authentic or correct employment of the term than is found in the prior instances in his Gospel.

---

51. Bultmann, *History*, pp. 151f.

The same conclusion holds if, following Jeremias's lead, we were to propose that "the Son of man" has here been added by Mark to a saying that originally used first-person language in both halves, as in Mt. 10:32f.[52] In view of Mark's abundant use of the phrase in passion sayings, his postulated addition of it to 8:38 could by no means be taken to demonstrate that he was aware of its "correct" apocalyptic meaning.

Because of the Q parallel at Lk. 12:8f., however, it is generally agreed that Mk. 8:38, including "the Son of man," derives from pre-Markan tradition.[53] Possibly redactional are the phrases "and my words" and "his Father."[54] Unless we subscribe to Schmithals's improbable hypothesis that Mark derived the logion from a *non*-Christian collection of Jesus' sayings, we must infer that Mark's source assumed that "the Son of man" was a name for Jesus, whose return in glory was fervently anticipated (cf. 1 Thess. 4:15f.).[55] Whether that source also attributed an apocalyptic connotation to the phrase is a question that must be deferred to the next chapter. All that need be said here is that Mark may not have been aware of such a connotation, in view of the preponderance of "suffering" sayings in his Gospel.

Tödt, who firmly maintains that the "suffering" and "future" sayings were strictly separated in the pre-Markan tradition, acknowledges that in this passage Mark has brought them into relationship, that is, that v. 38 follows shortly upon v. 31.[56] He insists, however, that the relationship here established is not christological but soteriological; "there is no direct connection of the Son of man's state of humility with his state of glory," but the two sayings are "connected by way of the disciples' following."[57] This represents a correct perception of the way Mark presents his material, but it constitutes an unjustified evasion of the connotative question. Apparently Tödt cannot believe that Mark would understand "the Son of man" to function in the same way in these two very different sayings. This appears to be Tödt's problem, not Mark's. The evangelist uses the phrase in sayings that imply Jesus' mortal nature as well as in logia concerning his destined heavenly glory without perceiving that one use is more appropriate than the other.

52. Jeremias, "Die älteste Schicht," pp. 159–61, 170.
53. Cf. Donahue, *Are You the Christ?* p. 167.
54. Cf. Horstmann, *Studien zur markinischen Christologie*, pp. 53f.; Donahue, *Are You the Christ?* p. 163; Lindars, *Jesus Son of Man*, p. 114. Pace Lindars, the allusion to Dan. 7:13f. is not "clear" (p. 107).
55. Schmithals, "Die Worte vom leidenden Menschensohn," p. 442.
56. Tödt, *Son of Man*, pp. 144–46.
57. Ibid., p. 146.

Does 8:38 violate the messianic secret? If the "crowd" of v. 34 is intended by Mark to include nonbelievers, it follows that the secret is prematurely divulged, since the one who publicly identified himself as the Son of man in 2:10, 28 here speaks in the same indirect way of his future glory.[58] Although *we* see the third-person language as ambiguous, so that the narrative audience can be understood as failing to perceive that Jesus is referring to his own future role, it must not be assumed that Mark was conscious of the possible ambiguity. He makes no effort to remove the ambiguity in any of the fourteen instances of the phrase and thereby reveals that for him the term is unambiguously a self-designation of Jesus. It is possible, however, that Mark employs "the crowd" in a special way at this point, not to introduce a hostile or neutral audience but rather to expand the band of disciples to include rank-and-file members of the church.[59] In any event, the secret is violated not by the use of "the Son of man" but by the reference to Jesus' coming in glory as God's exalted Son.

> **Mk. 9:9** And as they were coming down from the mountain, he charged them that they should report to no one what they had seen until the Son of man had risen from the dead.

It is possible that this verse, perhaps in slightly different form, was transmitted in conjunction with the transfiguration narrative in the pre-Markan tradition, where it served to explain the narrative's late appearance among the stories of Jesus.[60] More probably, however, it is redactional, exhibiting Mark's secrecy theme and providing (with its complement, v. 10) a transition to the Elijah material in vv. 11–13.[61]

J. Wellhausen observes how casually the allusion to Jesus' resurrection from the dead is introduced, as if it were a well-known matter.[62] Mark here assumes 8:31, where the resurrection is predicted for the first time. If the disciples are forgetful and therefore nonplussed in v. 10, this response is probably to be attributed to Mark's theme of the blindness of the disciples.[63]

As the sequel to 8:31, this verse likewise speaks of Jesus' destiny in the customary, indirect language employing "the Son of man." Here also the phrase clearly denotes a mortal, whose death places him in the shadowy

---

58. Cf. Wrede, *Messianic Secret*, p. 67.
59. Cf. Haenchen, *Weg Jesu*, p. 296.
60. Ibid., p. 312.
61. Perrin, *Modern Pilgrimage*, p. 116.
62. Wellhausen, *Das Evangelium Marci*, p. 70.
63. Cf. Tyson, "The Blindness of the Disciples in Mark."

world of the dead, from which he can be removed only by an act of God. It is true that Mark does not make this theological conviction explicit; in the three passion predictions, as here, he prefers to use the intransitive verb "rise" instead of *egeirō* in the active with God as subject (contrast Acts 3:15, "whom God raised from the dead"), and even when he later employs *egeirō* in the passive, there is the possibility of a deponent use (12:26; 14:28; 16:6) rather than a "divine passive." Nevertheless, it cannot be inferred that Mark wishes to suggest that Jesus arose by his own power (i.e., in virtue of his divine nature). Mark uses the same two verbs in the same way when speaking of the general resurrection of ordinary mortals in 12:25f.

It is to be noted, as Wellhausen also remarks, that the response of the disciples in v. 10 ignores "the Son of man."[64] That is, Mark here as everywhere assumes that "the Son of man" is perceived by all narrative audiences as Jesus' self-designation and consequently does not contribute to the puzzlement of the disciples.

> **Mk. 9:12** Elijah does indeed come first to restore everything; and yet how does it stand written concerning the Son of man, that he should suffer many things and be rejected?

Very attractive at first sight is Bultmann's proposal that this question concerning the Son of man is a post-Markan interpolation based on Mt. 17:12.[65] Since interpolation is rightly regarded as a hypothesis of last resort, however, it is incumbent upon us to try to understand the difficult passage as it stands.

One of the most fruitful discussions is that of Haenchen, who proposes that Mark has here conjoined two radically different Christian responses to the objection raised by Jewish opponents that Elijah must come first (i.e., before the arrival of the kingdom of God of 9:1). The first of these *questions* the premise: "Elijah comes first and *restores all things*." Such a belief must be false, because it renders superfluous the suffering and rejection of Jesus. Since the suffering of Jesus is divinely established in the Scriptures, the role attributed to Elijah has been misconstrued. The second response *affirms* the premise by spiritualizing it and treating it as fulfilled in the life and death of John the Baptist.[66]

---

64. Wellhausen, *Das Evangelium Marci*, p. 70.
65. Bultmann, *History*, p. 125 n. 1. Strecker, "Die Leidens- und Auferstehungsvoraussagen im Markusevangelium," p. 29 n. 32, agrees that it is an interpolation but maintains that it is pre-Matthean rather than a gloss based on Mt. 17:12; he is followed by Schmithals, "Die Worte vom leidenden Menschensohn," p. 425.
66. Haenchen, *Weg Jesu*, p. 313, building in part on Wellhausen, *Das Evangelium Marci*, pp. 70f. Cf. W. C. Robinson, "The Quest for Wrede's Secret Messiah," pp. 111f., and Tödt, *Son of Man*, pp. 168f., 196.

Haenchen assumes that the contradiction between verses 12 and 13 is due to Markan juxtaposition of divergent traditions and thus infers that v. 12b is pre-Markan. Even if we were to argue that v. 12b is a Markan creation, however, the import would be the same. Whatever its origin, the question assumes that "the Son of man" is an appropriate self-designation for the Jesus of the passion kerygma, whose sufferings and rejection are foretold in the Scriptures. As in 8:31, the idea of rejection, while conveyed by a different Greek verb, suggests an allusion to Ps. 118:22.[67] Since this psalm refers explicitly neither to the Messiah nor to the Son of man, there is no reason to regard Mk. 9:12 as employing "the Son of man" as a synonym for "the Messiah." For Mark and his readers both terms *denote* Jesus; it cannot logically be inferred from this conclusion that their *connotations* have coalesced.

> **Mk. 9:31** The Son of man is delivered up into the hands of men, and they will kill him, and, having been killed, after three days he will rise.

The question whether 9:31 is traditional or redactional is the subject of ongoing debate. Whereas Tödt, with support from Schlatter, argues that its idioms reflect the Palestinian rather than the Hellenistic milieu, Strecker is convinced that these can be accounted for on the basis of the Septuagint and the passion narrative.[68]

It appears that there can be no final resolution of this issue, but further consideration of its implications must be deferred to the next chapter. For the moment it is sufficient to note that in terms of narrative structure this logion is closely allied by Mark with 8:31 and 10:33f. and must therefore be interpreted in the same way. "The Son of man" here again denotes a mortal who must die before he can experience resurrection life.

> **Mk. 10:33f.** See, we are going up to Jerusalem, and the Son of man will be delivered up to the chief priests and the scribes, and they will condemn him to death and deliver him up to the Gentiles, and they will mock him and spit at him, flog and kill him, and after three days he will rise.

The third passion prediction is so circumstantial in its anticipation of the Markan passion narrative that it is difficult to believe that it ever

---

67. Tödt, *Son of Man*, p. 196.
68. Ibid., p. 160, cites Schlatter, *Matthäus*, pp. 537f. For Strecker's view, see article cited in n. 65 above, p. 30.

circulated independently. Strecker is fully justified in regarding it as a sketch of the "six stations of the passion."[69] Tödt's proposal that it must be pre-Markan because of its antigentile bias is unconvincing; even the pro-gentile Acts does not attempt to deny the complicity of the Gentiles in the death of the Christ (4:25–28).[70]

Because this extended saying simply expands upon the theme of the first two passion predictions, it adds nothing to our understanding of Mark's use of "the Son of man."

> **Mk. 10:45** For the Son of man came not to be served but to serve, and to give his life as a ransom for many.

There appears to be a consensus in favor of attributing this saying in its entirety to pre-Markan tradition. In view of its crucial importance as the climax of the central section of the Gospel, which begins with Peter's confession and is organized in relationship to the three passion predictions, it is certainly not impossible that Mark has created this saying or has reformulated it on the basis of a much simpler saying such as we find in Lk. 22:27.[71] Since the case for a redactional origin is not particularly strong, however, it will here be presupposed that the saying is traditional. An investigation of its tradition history must be deferred to a later chapter.

Mark's understanding of the verse may be detected from its location and from parallel statements in his Gospel. Its placement as the climactic ele-ment in the central section (8:27—10:45) indicates that it is the ultimate assertion about the suffering Christ. For this reason we must discount Strecker's suggestion that v. 45 is incorporated by Mark simply to provide an ethical illustration, i.e., that Mark is not interested in the atonement idea.[72] Such an interpretation renders v. 45 anticlimactic after three great passion predictions. More satisfactory is the view that regards the third narrative regarding the disciples' misunderstanding of the passion announcements as providing the occasion for a fuller revelation of the meaning of the passion, in anticipation of the cup word of 14:24.

The antithetical formulation of the saying (which contrasts with the simple form found at Lk. 19:10, "For the Son of man came to seek and to save the lost") suggests the possibility of polemic (cf. Mt. 5:17; 10:34). Does Mark perceive a polemical intention in the saying? It appears to constitute an

---

69. Strecker, "Die Leidens- und Auferstehungsvoraussagen," p. 31.
70. Tödt, *Son of Man*, p. 202.
71. As proposed, for example, by Perrin, *Modern Pilgrimage*, pp. 91f.
72. Strecker, "Die Leidens- und Auferstehungsvoraussagen," p. 36.

important weapon in Mark's battle against Christians who are intoxicated by their anticipated participation in the glory of King Jesus and whose theology is uninterested in his passion.[73] These glory-hungry Christians are narratively symbolized by James and John, who desire power and influence in Jesus' kingdom (10:37; cf. v. 42). Mark employs v. 45 to castigate such a view of discipleship.

It is probable, therefore, that for Mark v. 45 is a strong statement concerning the earthly destiny of the anointed king who was confessed by Peter at the beginning of the section, whose glorious rule is anticipated by James and John in this climactic pericope. It is normal for kings to be served, but this one came rather to serve, and his ultimate act of service was the giving of his life as a ransom for many.

The paradox is clear at this level, but we must explore it further. Does Mark intend the reader to perceive here the still greater paradox that the heavenly Son of man of Jewish apocalyptic became incarnate in Jesus the servant? Although "came" might be taken as alluding to Dan. 7:13 (". . . and behold, with the clouds of heaven there *came* one like a son of man . . ."), it is clear that there is no thought of either earthly Parousia or incarnation in that verse, which speaks rather of an audience with the Ancient of Days. Nor is there any indication in Mark's use of "came" elsewhere that he has incarnation in mind (cf. 2:17). Since Matthew and Luke use the same verb to speak of John the Baptist's ministry (Mt. 11:18; 21:32; Lk. 7:33), it will require other evidence of incarnational thought in Mark's Gospel to convince us that "came" is here to be understood as "came from heaven."[74]

Is there nonetheless an allusion in this verse to the royal figure of Dan. 7:14, whom "all peoples, nations, and languages will *serve*"? This is improbable, since neither rescension of the Greek Daniel employs *diakoneō*, the verb for "serve" used by Mark. It is promised in Dan. 7:14 that the entire human population will "serve" the one like a son of man in the sense of offering him homage, that is, acknowledging his sovereign authority. Mark's *diakoneō* implies a very different kind of service. Although it can be used in a more general sense in the New Testament (e.g., 2 Cor. 8:19f.), it most often means "provide a personal service," especially "serve food or drink." Mark uses it of the service provided by angels to the famished Jesus at the conclusion of his fast (1:13), by Peter's mother-in-law (1:31), and by the women who followed Jesus from Galilee (15:41). It thus

---

73. Cf. Achtemeier, *Mark*, esp. pp. 105–13.

74. The incarnational interpretation, urged by Hamerton-Kelly, *Pre-existence, Wisdom, and the Son of Man*, p. 64, is rejected by Dunn, *Christology*, p. 89.

functions here to point not to the passive service offered to a king by his most distant subject (as in Dan. 7:14) but to the concrete and practical service provided to any master by his hired servants or slaves (as in the parable of the farmer's servant in Lk. 17:7–10). An investigation of the tradition-historical relationship between Mk. 10:45 and Lk. 22:27 must be deferred to a later page, but there is every reason to believe that both passages use *diakoneō* with reference to a very concrete act of service. The proposal that the Markan as well as the Lukan version must be seen as deriving from the complex of traditions associated with the last supper must consequently be taken very seriously.[75]

It must be concluded, therefore, that this verse contributes nothing additional to our understanding of Mark's use of "the Son of man." If we knew on other grounds that the term connoted "Messiah" or "heavenly judge," its paradoxical use here would be striking indeed, but that is precisely what we do not know. All that can be certainly inferred is that, as in the other passion sayings, the phrase is regarded by Mark as an appropriate designation for the one who must die.

> **Mk. 13:26** And then they will see the Son of man coming in clouds with great power and glory.

Careful examination of Mark's apocalyptic discourse reveals considerable redactional activity on the part of the evangelist. Relevant at this point is the question whether that activity extends to the Son of man saying itself. If it is permissible to argue that Mark has created one or more of the passion sayings on the basis of an earlier model, it is certainly possible that he has similarly created a "future" saying on the basis of 8:38 and/or 14:62. Donahue appears to suggest this when he proposes that this verse is dependent on 14:62.[76]

Whether or not Mark has created the extant form of the saying, it is exceedingly unlikely that he was the first to reinterpret Dan. 7:13f. as a prediction of the glorious return of Jesus. There is general agreement that Rev. 1:7 alludes to Dan. 7:13, and nothing intimates that the author is dependent on Mark. It is very important, consequently, to observe that the exegetical tradition to which Rev. 1:7 (and possibly Mk. 13:26) witnesses

---

75. Cf. Wellhausen, *Das Evangelium Marci*, pp. 84f.
76. Donahue, *Are You the Christ?* p. 169.

applies Dan. 7:13 to the *Crucified*, as is demonstrated not only by the conjoined allusion to Zech. 12:10 but also by the fact that the implied subject is "the one who loves us and who loosed us from our sins by his blood" (Rev. 1:5). Since there is no evidence whatsoever of a pre-Christian Jewish exegesis of Dan. 7:13f. that radically reinterpreted the passage so as to make it predict the coming *to earth* (instead of to the Ancient of Days) of a heavenly Messiah or eschatological judge, we need not postulate such a source for Mk. 13:26 and may relate it instead to a *Christian* exegetical tradition that was concerned to find scriptural support for the conviction that the resurrected and exalted Crucified would soon return in glory as messianic king.[77]

It may be objected that the use of "the Son of man" in Mk. 13:26 characterizes the saying as different in kind from the prediction of Rev. 1:7; whereas the latter concerns Jesus, the former speaks of *the Son of man*, an apocalyptic figure with whom Jesus has been identified. But this distinction cannot be demonstrated on the basis of *Mark*! The Second Evangelist uses "the Son of man" far more frequently in passion sayings than in apocalyptic logia. Since he so emphatically employs the term as the self-designation of the mortal Son of God, and in so doing makes no explicit reference to the alleged paradox, he provides no direct evidence for the hypothesis that at an earlier stage "the Son of man" was correctly perceived as an apocalyptic title. This may have been the case, but it cannot be proved from Mk. 13:26. Whether this verse is a Markan creation, a traditional saying, or a pre-Markan saying that Mark has reformulated, in its Markan context, surrounded as it is by sayings in which Jesus speaks of his death using "the Son of man" as a self-designation, it cannot be taken as connoting a never-mortal being. Either Mark is unaware of the alleged earlier connotation, or he has deliberately reinterpreted the phrase. Since he provides no polemical hints of the latter, the former is to be preferred.

D. Juel correctly observes that in 13:21-27 the contrast that is posed to the "false Christs" of v. 22 is not the Son of man but the true Christ: "The Son of man saying does not provide new information about Jesus' identity; its function is to point the reader to the final, public vindication of Jesus and of the faith of those who confess him to be the true Christ."[78]

---

77. Neither 4 Ezra nor the Similitudes of Enoch employs Dan. 7:13 in order to portray the coming from heaven to earth of a manlike figure.
78. Juel, *Messiah and Temple*, p. 92.

Mk. 14:21 For the Son of man goes as it has been written
about him, but woe to that man through whom the Son of man
is delivered up; it would be better for that man if he had not
been born.

No attempt will be made here to resolve the issue of whether or
not this verse is a product of the evangelist's hand.[79] It is sufficient to note
that there is ample reason to believe that the application of the verb
paradidōmi to Judas Iscariot in John (6:65, 71; 12:4, etc.) is independent
of Mark and thus evidence in favor of attributing a statement such as
Mk. 14:21 to pre-Markan tradition (cf. also 1 Cor. 11:23). This argument,
however, by no means proves that the pre-Markan logion (if such there
was) employed "the Son of man." Indeed, the first half of the verse constitutes a parallel of sorts with Lk. 13:33, according to which Jesus "goes"
in accordance with his predetermined destiny, and in which first-person
language is found. It is thus not impossible that Mark has here introduced
"the Son of man" in conformity with his conviction that this self-designation
is particularly appropriate in sayings concerning the passion of Jesus. If, on
the other hand, he takes this logion from the tradition without alteration,
the function of "the Son of man" remains the same.

Mk. 14:41 The hour has come; see, the Son of man is being
delivered up into the hands of sinners.

What has just been said respecting 14:21 applies equally to v. 41.
Whether the verse is regarded as traditional or redactional, "the Son of
man" functions as the self-designation of Jesus, who must be delivered up
to death at the hands of sinners before he is exalted to the right hand of
God. Tödt's effort to find the idea of sovereign authority implied here in
"the Son of man" (because "all initiative lies with Jesus") comes to grief
in the observation that the same kind of foreknowledge and initiative
is attributed to Jesus quite apart from the use of "the Son of man"
(cf. 11:1–6).[80]

79. Cf. Schmithals, "Die Worte vom leidenden Menschensohn," p. 427; Perrin, *Modern
Pilgrimage*, p. 132.
80. Tödt, *Son of Man*, p. 200.

Mk. 14:62 I am, and you will see the Son of man seated at the right hand of the Power and coming with the clouds of heaven.

We come finally to the last and climactic instance of "the Son of man" in Mark. It has proved particularly fascinating to scholars because of its occurrence in close proximity to "the Christ" and "the Son of the Blessed" (v. 61). Because of this apparent concatenation of titles, some have proposed that Mark is here "assimilating" the titles, or "qualifying" or "correcting" the first two by introducing "the Son of man," understood as a more adequate title.[81]

Schmithals goes even further, proclaiming that this verse constitutes the key to all the Son of man sayings in Mark, since it unveils for the narrative audience the true meaning of the phrase: "Wherever he had spoken of the Son of man, Jesus had thus spoken of himself as the Messiah and Son of God. . . ."[82] This conclusion, of course, presumes Schmithals's understanding that *Mark* regarded the phrase as genuinely ambiguous, capable of being construed by the narrative audience as a generic reference to male humans.[83] The weakness of this proposal has been discussed above in connection with Mk. 2:10. At that point it was intimated that Schmithals's argument would be more defensible were he to propose that at 2:10 "the Son of man" is a secret title whose connotation is familiar to Christian readers but unknown to the narrative audience, to whom the phrase communicates no meaning. Can it be maintained that this secret meaning is finally disclosed at 14:62?

The answer is most certainly no, at least as Schmithals presents the argument. It simply is not the case *for Mark* that in this passage Jesus reveals "the identity of his person, as encountered in the christological confession of the community, with the Son of man of his teaching."[84] For Mark and his readers—and the narrative audiences of the Gospel—"the Son of man" has always denoted Jesus without ambiguity. It is by no means true that this last instance identifies Jesus as the Son of man. This identification has been assumed since the first instance.

---

81. Cf. Catchpole, "The Problem of the Historicity of the Sanhedrin Trial," p. 65; Petersen, *Literary Criticism for New Testament Critics*, p. 75; Perrin, *Modern Pilgrimage*, pp. 92, 121; Donahue, *Are You the Christ?* p. 184.

82. Schmithals, "Die Worte vom leidenden Menschensohn," p. 435: "Wo immer er vom Menschensohn sprach, hatte Jesus also von sich selbst als von dem Messias und Gottessohn gesprochen. . . ."

83. Ibid., p. 432.

84. Ibid., p. 435: "die . . . Identität seiner Person, wie er im christologischer Bekenntnis der Gemeinde begegnet, mit dem Menschensohn seiner Lehre." (emphasized in the original).

Does Mark's use of the phrase here nonetheless reveal its proper connotation, that of a never-incarnate heavenly figure? This might be a legitimate inference if Mark contained only apocalyptic sayings. Since this is
not the case, such a conclusion is indefensible. This saying provides us not
with the correct understanding of the phrase but simply with *additional
information* concerning the one so designated. After speaking of his vocation and destiny in a variety of ways by employing "the Son of man" and
third-person language, Jesus now announces that his judges will see him
seated at the right hand of God in fulfillment of the prophecy of Ps. 110:1,
and coming with the clouds of heaven as prophesied in Dan. 7:13.

As was pointed out above in connection with 8:31, it cannot be inferred
from the common denotation that "the Son of man" must be construed as
connotatively synonymous with "the Christ, the Son of the Blessed." Nor
can it be demonstrated that "the Son of man" is here regarded by Mark as
a more "correct" christological title.[85] In his response "I am" to the high
priest's question, the Markan Jesus certifies the correctness of the titles
proposed by the questioner.[86] The remainder of v. 62, conjoined to this
asseveration by a simple "and," does nothing to negate this identification
but simply adds further information concerning the vindication of the one
who is properly designated "the Christ, the Son of the Blessed."[87]

Since the self-designation was employed in the presence of the opponents at 2:10, 28, it is obvious that as far as Mark is concerned, the charge
of blasphemy of vv. 63f. is not provoked by Jesus' use of the phrase.[88] As in
all the earlier passages, its use here is without narrative effect. In the
following paragraphs Jesus is mocked not because he claimed to be the
Son of man but because of his royal pretensions (15:18, 32).

Nor can it be maintained that Mark's understanding of "the Son of
man" is here finally defined by means of the allusion to Dan. 7:13. We
have already noted in connection with 13:26 that Mark was probably not
the first to cite Dan. 7:13 as a proof text regarding the Parousia of Jesus. It
is natural to assume that he regarded this text as particularly apposite
because he saw a relationship between Jesus' self-designation and Daniel's
reference to "one like a son of man."

85. Contra Donahue, *Are You the Christ?* p. 184.
86. Kingsbury, *The Christology of Mark's Gospel*, p. 162; Juel, *Messiah and Temple*, pp.
84f., 93.
87. Juel, *Messiah and Temple*, p. 93, contra Donahue, *Are You the Christ?* p. 95, who
maintains that "the Son of man title in 14:62 serves . . . to give content and meaning to the
other titles. . . ."
88. According to Linton, "The Trial of Jesus and the Interpretation of Psalm CX," p. 259,
the charge of blasphemy is a response to Jesus' appropriation of Psalm 110. Cf. Juel, *Messiah
and Temple*, p. 104.

This does not mean, however, that Mark, in taking over the tradition that applied Dan. 7:13 to Jesus' Parousia, assumed that all of Jesus' uses of the self-designation were grounded in the Danielic prophecy. Nothing in 14:62 *explicitly* encourages such an understanding. If the verse is to be taken as *implicitly* suggesting this, we must note that the implication would have been clearer had Mark not interposed the allusion to Ps. 110:1 between "the Son of man" and the Danielic language. Moreover, an important corollary of postulating such an implication must be recognized. If the Markan Jesus is to be perceived in 14:62 as saying in effect, "Whenever I have called myself 'the Son of man,' I meant to identify myself as the 'one like a son of man' of Daniel who is to come on the clouds of heaven,'" it is clear that Mark perceived the Danielic figure in terms very different from those espoused by many of his modern interpreters. Since Mark employs "the Son of man" predominantly in passion sayings, it would follow that for the Second Evangelist the figure of Dan. 7:13 is *a human being* whose death has been vindicated by resurrection and exaltation.[89] That is, the postulated implication of 14:62 cannot logically be construed as providing evidence of a pre-Christian Jewish conception of a supernatural, never-incarnate being known by the title "the Son of man."

There is, however, little in favor of the supposed implication. The allusion to Daniel is unemphasized. If Mark had really intended his readers to regard Dan. 7:13 as the key to all the Son of man sayings in the Gospel, he would surely have attempted to make this suggestion more explicit. Most ancient readers, like unsophisticated readers of today, would undoubtedly have missed Schmithals's "key" when reading the extant text. From the New Testament as a whole and from other early Christian literature (e.g., the Didache), we learn that, while the Parousia of Jesus was an important constituent of faith, Dan. 7:13 was not commonly employed in its support.[90] Indeed, it is not improbable that many of Mark's first readers (like their modern counterparts), while recognizing the allusion to Ps. 110:1 because of that psalm's great importance, may have failed to notice that "coming with the clouds of heaven" constitutes an allusion to Daniel. Such a phrase may have quickly detached itself from its source and have become, as far as Christian consciousness was concerned, simply a stereotypical way of referring to Jesus' Parousia. I am not proposing that Mark himself was unaware of the source of his phrase, but only that it was apparently not of

89. See the discussion of 13:26 above.
90. Cf. Seitz, "The Future Coming of the Son of Man: Three Midrashic Formulations in the Gospel of Mark," p. 488.

great importance to him that his readers be conscious of that source. While the validity of this proposal cannot be demonstrated, it is surely as defensible as the opposing view.

Is Mark himself responsible for creating the high priest's question and Jesus' response? This view has been proposed recently by Lindars, partly in dependence on Wellhausen.[91] Ernest Best, on the other hand, argues that 14:62 "is too closely interwoven into its incident for it to have been added" by Mark.[92] Is the whole scene, then, a Markan creation? Such a possibility has been argued by Donahue, who presents linguistic evidence for his view that Mark has combined the tradition that Jesus was led away to his condemnation and death with several Old Testament allusions that he has historicized, thereby creating a formal trial.[93] Into this carefully constructed scene is introduced the high priest's question and Jesus' answer, both of which are Mark's creations.[94]

There is nothing intrinsically improbable in this proposal. Because of the nature of the evidence, however, a firm demonstration seems to be out of the question. Consequently, the next chapter must reckon with the possibility that Mark is transmitting traditional material in 14:62f.[95] This does not affect the way Mark employs the material in the context of the trial. Here as everywhere in the Second Gospel, "the Son of man" functions as Jesus' self-designation and is recognized as such by the narrative audience, and yet its use attracts no negative response from his judges. This state of affairs suggests that Mark did not regard "the Son of man" as part of the agenda of the dispute separating Jews and Christians. For him the self-designation was apparently innocuous, either because it possessed no recognizable meaning or because its meaning was perceived as no more controversial than a phrase such as "the Son of the carpenter."

Conclusion

Over against most recent interpreters of Mark, Kingsbury is fully justified in his conclusion that the Second Evangelist does not employ this "title" as a means of telling who Jesus is.[96] It is a mistake, therefore, to

91. Lindars, *Jesus Son of Man*, p. 111; cf. Wellhausen, *Das Evangelium Marci*, pp. 14f., who regards the interpolation as pre-Markan.
92. Best, *The Temptation and the Passion*, p. 163.
93. Donahue, *Are You the Christ?* pp. 101f., 237.
94. Ibid., pp. 162–87.
95. Vielhauer, "Erwägungen zur Christologie des Markusevangeliums," p. 159, urges that the logion is post-Easter but pre-Markan.
96. Kingsbury, *The Christology of Mark's Gospel*, pp. 162f.

attribute to Mark a "Son of man Christology." We might just as well speak of a "Jesus Christology," because, whether traditional or redactional, all instances of "the Son of man" in Mark occur in statements that Jesus makes about himself. If we rephrase them, substituting "Jesus" for "the Son of man" in each case, we would have a good summary of the Markan view of Jesus' self-understanding, without being distracted by the self-designation itself. That is, it is the *statements* that are significant to Mark, not the appearance therein of "the Son of man." Nonetheless, Kingsbury is right in insisting that for the evangelist and his community, it is *God's* Christology that is paramount. The one who calls himself "the Son of man" is identified for faith by God's own voice as the Son of God.

With respect to the four possibilities contemplated at the beginning of this chapter, we must conclude that Mark has neither "Danielized" an earlier nonapocalyptic tradition nor betrayed any awareness of a prior stage in which "the Son of man" was perceived exclusively in apocalyptic terms. This leaves us with two possibilities: either Bultmann is correct that the earlier apocalyptic conception has (remarkably) been forgotten by the Hellenistic churches known to Mark, or Mark's usage should be taken as evidence that the phrase was never so conceived in the pre-Markan tradition. To this issue we must now turn.

7 | THE PREGOSPEL TRADITION

Our study of the four canonical Gospels is now complete. With respect to each it has been shown that resort to the hypothesis of an apocalyptic myth concerning an angelic judge entitled "the Son of man" is superfluous. None of the evangelists betrays any awareness of the alleged myth. If such a conception does in fact underlie the gospel material in which the phrase is used, the evidence must be sought further back in the tradition, and a reasonable explanation must be offered for the remarkable fact that this original meaning was so quickly forgotten.

Two assumptions must be made explicit before this study of the pregospel material is begun. First, it is here presupposed, in concurrence with the scholarly consensus, that there was a pregospel use of the phrase. That is, W. Schmithals' opinion that "the Son of man" was not to be found in Christian material prior to Mark is hereby rejected.[1] Nor is Matthew, if we were to accept the Griesbach hypothesis, a likely candidate for the honor of having introduced the term to the Christian community. The diversity of the uses of the phrase in each of the Gospels suggests that none of the evangelists can be credited with inaugurating the tradition.

Second, it will be assumed that the evangelists were capable of both adding and deleting the phrase in their redaction of received material. That is, the question concerning whether Luke added or Matthew deleted at Lk. 6:22 and 12:8 (Mt. 5:11 and 10:32) will not be resolved on the basis of a rule, contra Jeremias, who argues that sayings couched in first-person language regularly antedate parallels containing "the Son of man."[2]

Conversely, it will not be assumed at this stage of the argument that any of the Son of man sayings derive from Jesus. That question, to be

---

1. Schmithals, "Die Worte vom leidenden Menschensohn," pp. 443f.
2. Jeremias, "Die älteste Schicht," p. 169; reiterated in his *New Testament Theology*, pp. 262f.

addressed in the next chapter, must await the conclusions to which this chapter will bring us. Nor will it be here presupposed without argument that the sayings derive from Aramaic-speaking Christians. That issue involves important linguistic considerations still to be addressed.

Consequently this chapter comprises two major sections, treating the Greek and Aramaic traditions respectively.

The Greek Tradition

The Q Material

It is generally agreed that Greek sources underlie our canonical Gospels, but there is no consensus concerning the nature and extent of those sources. Especially vulnerable to attack is the hypothetical sayings source referred to by the siglum Q. Although significant efforts have recently been made to rehabilitate the Q hypothesis, its conjectural nature is such that even its supporters are for the most part ready to admit that it is impossible to obtain any consensus regarding its compass (did it contain narratives, such as the temptation story?) and the form in which it was available to Matthew and Luke (did the collection bifurcate at an earlier stage and each version continue to expand as oral traditions were subsequently added?).[3] Despairing of firm source-critical results, some are content to speak simply of "the Q tradition," meaning thereby not a unified document but merely the conglomerate of traditions shared by Matthew and Luke but absent from Mark, traditions that may have been received by the evangelists partly in oral and partly in one or more written tracts.[4]

Since the investigation of the Son of man tradition becomes more and more hypothetical as soon as we leave the firm ground of the canonical Gospels, it will be unwise to depend too heavily on the postulated Q for our understanding of the pregospel use of the phrase. It would be inappropriate to dismiss the Q hypothesis at this stage, however, for the simple reason that it has become commonplace to speak of "the Son of man Christology of Q."[5] This phrase is widely understood to mean: "The community in which the Q document originated confessed its faith in Jesus as the Son of man of Jewish apocalyptic." Assuming, then, the legitimacy of the Q hypothesis, what justification is there for this common opinion?

---

3. The latter was forcefully argued by J. P. Brown, "The Form of 'Q' Known to Matthew."

4. For a helpful survey of contemporary opinions on the issue, see Vassiliadis, "The Nature and Extent of the Q-Document."

5. E.g., Tödt, *Son of Man*, pp. 235, 265, 269; Hoffmann, *Studien zur Theologie der Logienquelle*, p. 82 and elsewhere.

Does the use of "the Son of man" in the reconstructed document support such a view?

A few methodological observations are in order. Supporters of the Q hypothesis assume that the document was used without radical correction by the mainline Gospels of Matthew and Luke. This assumption strongly suggests that Q was not the product of an isolated, esoteric Christian group, of which Paul would have been totally unaware. There is no reason to suppose, therefore, that its Christology was markedly different from that of the broad Christian stream (including Paul and all other New Testament writers) that confessed faith in Jesus as Christ and Lord. Diversity in the early church is not to be ignored; we must resist the temptation to homogenize first-century Christian thought by artificial harmonization. Such diversity is to be established, however, on the basis of unequivocal statements, not by the *argumentio e silentio*.

It is methodologically unsound to argue that the Q community did *not* confess Jesus as Lord and Christ simply because the sayings material shared by Matthew and Luke contain no confessional statements employing these terms. In view of the form and function of the nonnarratival material attributed to Jesus in the hypothetical Q, we ought not to expect to find a confessional statement comparable to Mk. 8:29.[6] For the same reason we ought not to expect to find a confessional statement indicating that the Q community expressed its faith by saying "Jesus is the Son of man." The argument from silence can rule out this last as little as any other. On the other hand, since we possess no positive evidence from elsewhere in the Gospels and other early Christian literature that such a confession was ever employed by any Christian anywhere, we cannot *assume* without careful argumentation that the Q community employed this confession, whereas we are justified in presupposing for that community the common Christian confession in Jesus as Christ and Lord.

With these methodological observations in mind, let us turn to the argumentation developed by Tödt in support of his conclusion that the Q community adhered to a Son of man Christology. Following Bultmann, Tödt begins with the assumption that there was a pre-Christian Jewish myth in which a transcendent figure entitled "the Son of man" was portrayed as functioning as judge on God's behalf at the last judgment. This myth he finds reflected directly or indirectly in the Synoptic sayings that speak of

---

6. It is similarly fallacious to argue that the *absence* from Q of passion sayings constitutes *positive* evidence that they represent a later development (see Tödt, *Son of Man*, pp. 17, 144). If the compilers of the sayings source included no passion narrative, they had no motive for including these sayings, whose function it is to anticipate the death and resurrection of Jesus.

the Son of man coming in the future. He readily admits that most of these sayings contain no reference to the *specific* elements of the myth. Indeed, concerning the "authentic sayings of Jesus" (Mt. 24:27 par.; 24:37, 39 par.; Lk. 17:30; 11:30; Mt. 24:44 par.; Lk. 12:8 par.), he writes: "There is no apocalyptic description whatsoever of the figure or the activity of the Son of man. He is spoken of as someone who is well known."[7] The absence of specific features poses no problem to Tödt, because of his original starting point: "The intimate connection of the synoptic presentation of the Son of man with that of Jewish apocalyptic literature can no longer be seriously contested."[8] He therefore finds no reason to question the authenticity of most of the sayings about the future coming of the Son of man that can be attributed to Q.[9] In these the historical Jesus points away from himself to the well-known apocalyptic figure.[10]

This step makes it simple for Tödt to treat Q's sayings about the earthly activity of the Son of man as inauthentic: since Jesus spoke of another as Son of man in the future sayings, he can hardly be credited with speaking of himself as the Son of man in another group of sayings.[11] His attempt to buttress this deduction with an observation of a formal kind is misguided; it simply is not the case, as he alleges, that the first group formally preserves the distinction between the "I" of Jesus and the Son of man whereas the second does not.[12] In formal terms there is no difference between the two groups; both refer to the Son of man in third-person language, and in none is there an explicit identification between the speaker (Jesus) and the Son of man.

Tödt tries valiantly to explain how it was possible for sayings about the "earthly" Son of man to emerge and be treasured by the Q community, whose Christology was focused on the apocalyptic Son of man. He correctly observes that in none of Q's "earthly" sayings is there the slightest trace of an attempt to portray the Galilean Jesus with the transcendent features of the apocalyptic figure.[13] There is no suggestion in them of the idea that the earthly Son of man is the incarnation of a preexistent heavenly being.[14] The same name, he explains, can be applied by the Q community to the

7. Tödt, *Son of Man*, p. 224.
8. Ibid., p. 22.
9. Tödt also attributes to Q Mt. 10:23 and 19:28 but regards these as secondary (see *Son of Man*, pp. 65, 270).
10. Ibid., p. 124.
11. Ibid.
12. This fallacy was clearly identified by Vielhauer, "Jesus und der Menschensohn," p. 145.
13. Tödt, *Son of Man*, pp. 116, 273.
14. Ibid., pp. 66, 220.

earthly Jesus and to the transcendent Jesus whose Parousia is awaited, because (1) it ascribes a unique sovereignty to Jesus (i.e., his peculiar *exousia*), and (2) "In the attitude towards this person an eternal decision takes place in the realm of history."[15] His preferred way of speaking of this second element employs the phrase "soteriological correlation," by which he means that the fellowship bestowed by Jesus on his followers is to be guaranteed by the Son of man.[16]

Despite the theological sophistication of Tödt's argumentation in this section of his book, one is troubled by the ease with which he assumes that it would have been a simple matter for the alleged apocalyptic title "the Son of man" to be transferred to the earthly Jesus once the resurrected Jesus had been identified with the heavenly figure. Although the earliest Christians identified Jesus as the coming Messiah, the tradents of the gospel narratives were very circumspect in their use of "the Christ." In the pre-Markan controversy narratives and miracle catenae, we never read the statement, "And the Christ said. . . ." That is, a popular confessional use of this title did *not* encourage a facile transfer to the earthly Jesus. This should caution us against assuming with Tödt that the best explanation for the earthly Son of man sayings is such a transfer.

Before continuing, we must note several less sophisticated attempts to explain the secondary appearance of these earthly sayings in the Q tradition. Bultmann's explanation was a very simple one: in each case the appearance of the Greek phrase *ho huios tou anthrōpou* was due to the mistranslation of a generic expression in the underlying Aramaic saying.[17] Our investigation of the difficulties inherent in the theory of mistranslation must be deferred to the second half of this chapter. Here we need only note that for Bultmann the Greek-speaking Christians who served as tradents of these mistranslated sayings did not themselves believe that they were applying a celestial title to the earthly Jesus; like the later evangelists, these Hellenistic Christians were no longer aware of the original meaning of the Aramaic title employed in the authentic sayings.[18]

The same conclusion is reached via a different route by scholars who argue that the earthly sayings in the Q tradition were created (rather than

15. Ibid., p. 140. Jesus' *exousia* is discussed on p. 124.
16. Ibid., p. 229.
17. Bultmann, *Theology*, vol. 1, p. 30. Tödt's rejection (*Son of Man*, p. 114) of Bultmann's proposal seems to be unrelated to any misgiving of a linguistic sort; he appears unaware of the seriousness of the linguistic problem. Lietzmann's epochal study, *Der Menschensohn*, is listed in Tödt's bibliography but, as far as I can determine, is never mentioned in the notes. Paul Fiebig's work does not appear in the bibliography.
18. Bultmann, *Theology*.

mistranslated) by Hellenistic Christians. In this group are included not
only S. Schulz, who accepts Bultmann's position regarding the priority of
the future sayings, but also H. Teeple and W. Walker, who, in very different ways, argue that the entire Son of man tradition originated with Greek-
speaking Christians.[19] For Walker there is no need to explain how early
Christians could apply a celestial title to the earthly Jesus, because they
did not do so; for these Hellenistic Christians the term was a way of
interpreting the meaning of Jesus' life, death, resurrection, and future
coming by relating him exegetically to the figure of Dan. 7:13f.

For all those scholars of varying persuasions who concur in ascribing to
the Q community a Son of man Christology (whether at the earliest stage
of this community's existence only or also at the stage of the final redaction of Q), the existence of the earthly Son of man sayings is a critical
factor—or should be considered such. If the alleged myth of the Son of
man was known to the Q community, and if its members were united by
the shared confession "Jesus is the Son of man," then it is not readily
comprehensible how they transferred this exalted title to the earthly Jesus
without attributing to him any of the traditional features associated there-
with (Tödt) or so quickly forgot its original meaning that they could treat
it as a mysterious self-designation that could be used by Jesus of his earthly
life as appropriately as of his future coming (Bultmann). That is, the existence of the earthly sayings in the hypothetical document must be counted
as valid evidence *against* the alleged Son of man Christology. The proposal
that an apocalyptic title was so quickly demoted to a simple self-designation
devoid of apocalyptic coloration must be deemed very improbable.

Critics will retort: While the so-called demotion may appear improbable, it is nonetheless more readily comprehensible than the supposition
that early Christians created first the earthly Son of man sayings and only
subsequently apocalypticized the self-designation. Our response must be
to raise the critical question, Why should any early Christian have created
this strange idiom whereby Jesus speaks of himself as the Son of man,
whether in future or present terms? Supposing we accept Käsemann's
argument that Lk. 12:8f. is the product of a post-Easter prophet, we must
still explain why such a prophet chose to ascribe this strange third-person
language to Jesus instead of the much more natural first-person speech
attributed to the risen Christ by the prophet John in the Apocalypse (Rev.
1:17f. etc.)—*unless he had before him, as a model, sayings in which Jesus*

19. Schulz, *Q: Die Spruchquelle der Evangelisten*, p. 70; Teeple, "The Origin of the Son of
Man Christology"; Walker, "The Son of Man: Some Recent Developments," p. 602.

referred to himself in this way.[20] We will deal with this question more extensively in the next chapter. Here it will suffice to note that, if models are not provided by authentic logia, it is not any less difficult to postulate the creation of earthly sayings than of future ones; either group could have provided models for the other, because their one shared characteristic is that Jesus is represented as using *ho huios tou anthrōpou* as a self-designation.

Two other attempts to support the priority of the apocalyptic sayings in Q deserve serious consideration.

The argument from order. It has been proposed that, when the structure of the Q document is examined, the Son of man sayings appear precisely at critical junctures. U. Luz, for example, argues in his commentary on Matthew that the judgment motif so pervasive in Q is intimately related to the figure of the Son of man at the beginnings and/or endings of the major blocks of material.[21] That the judgment theme is prominent in the material shared by Matthew and Luke is universally acknowledged. It is not the case, however, that the judgment warnings are regularly related to the Son of man.

The programmatic discourse with which, according to many, the original Q collection opened (the pre-Lukan version of Lk. 6:20–49) does indeed conclude with a stern warning regarding judgment, but the tradents and redactors of the collection found no need to mention the Son of man at this significant juncture (Lk. 6:46–49; cf. Mt. 7:21–28). Even if it could be demonstrated that Matthew better preserves the Q tradition in allowing Jesus here to refer to his function as eschatological judge, it must not be regarded as a simple oversight that the name "the Son of man" does not appear.[22] Had the Q community focused its theological energy on the proclamation of the judgment theme in terms of Jesus' future function as the judging Son of man, that christologically loaded term ought to have appeared here in the frontispiece of the entire sayings collection. Its

20. Käsemann, "Sätze heiligen Rechtes im Neuen Testament," pp. 256f., and *New Testament Questions of Today*, pp. 70f. In this brief treatment Käsemann does not consider why it would occur to an early Christian prophet to create a "sentence of holy law" in which Jesus speaks of his own future role in third-person terms using "the Son of man."

21. Luz, *Matthew 1—7*, p. 74. Luz may here be dependent on the work of Schürmann, "Beobachtungen zum Menschensohn-Titel in der Redequelle."

22. Luz, *Matthäus*, p. 405 n. 39, comments: "Der Weltrichter, der als *Kurios* angesprochen wird, ist der Menschensohn, von dessen Parusie 24,29–44 spricht. . . ." (See *Matthew 1—7*, p. 444 n. 39.)

absence casts serious doubt upon the hypothesis of "Q's Son of man Christology."

Further confirmation of this doubt is provided by the fact that when the phrase "the Son of man" makes its first appearance in the postulated Q document, it is as a simple self-designation of the earthly Jesus. This is true whether one treats the appearance of the phrase in Luke's version of the beatitude for the persecuted as deriving from Q, or regards the first instance as occurring in the twin sayings about John and Jesus (Lk. 7:33f.; Mt. 11:18f.) rather than in the saying about homelessness (Mt. 8:20; Lk. 9:58). In all three cases it is clearly to the earthly Jesus that the phrase refers, and always without any "halo effect"; Tödt is absolutely correct in insisting that the application of the term to the earthly Jesus carries with it none of the transcendental features that are normally thought to be associated with the apocalyptic Son of man.[23]

Since the first three instances of the phrase in Luke's presentation of the Q material all refer unambiguously to the earthly Jesus, one must be slow to assign an apocalyptic reference to the fourth (11:30). Lührmann has argued that the Jonah saying must refer to the eschatological judgment, in view of the literary function of the verse: it connects the apothegm concerning the demand for a sign with the twofold threat against "this generation."[24] This analysis is far from certain. If, as Lührmann urges, v. 30 serves as a redactional introduction to vv. 31f. (as well as a redactional conclusion to v. 29), the specific allusion to the Ninevites of v. 32 in v. 30 must not be dismissed as insignificant; v. 30 speaks of the Son of man as a sign that ought to provoke repentance on the part of "this generation," just as Jonah prompted the repentance of the Ninevites. It can no longer be determined whether the intention of the redactor was to point to the death and resurrection of Jesus as Matthew supposes (12:40), or to Jesus' prophetic ministry, which, considered from the point of view of the narrative, could be referred to by a future tense (*estai*).[25]

In support of Matthew's interpretation is the fact that the First Evangelist does indeed present an eschatological saying about "the sign of the Son

23. Tödt, *Son of Man,* pp. 123, 230.
24. Lührmann, *Die Redaktion der Logienquelle,* pp. 40f. Lührmann maintains that the parallel is between the appearance of Jonah in Nineveh and the eschatological Parousia of the Son of man; in both cases the appearance signifies judgment. This is dubious. In popular thought Jonah represented not judgment (since this was averted) but the availability of God's grace to repentant Gentiles. See Liv. Pro. 10:3, "So shall I remove my reproach, for I spoke falsely in prophesying against the great city of Nineveh" (Hare, "Lives of the Prophets," p. 392).
25. The former is argued by Edwards, *The Sign of Jonah,* p. 56; the latter, by Schweizer, "Der Menschensohn," p. 200.

of man" (24:30) and, as is well known, is particularly interested in eschatological judgment. It is difficult to believe that Matthew would have altered the Q saying so as to make it refer to the resurrection if it clearly presented the apocalyptic Son of man as an imminent sign of judgment upon "this generation." Moreover, it appears unlikely that an apocalyptic community would employ the word "sign" with respect to the Parousia of the eschatological judge.[26] Although the reference of Lk. 11:30 in its pre-Lukan setting must remain ambiguous, the balance of probability inclines toward a noneschatological interpretation.

As in Luke, so also in Matthew, the first four instances of the Q Son of man sayings are nonapocalyptic: 8:20, 11:19, 12:32, and 12:40. Of these the third, concerning forgiveness of one who speaks a word against the Son of man (the sixth in Luke's presentation of Q, 12:10) is as unmistakably an earthly saying as the others; it is inconceivable that the community would either transmit or create a saying regarding the availability of forgiveness to one blaspheming the eschatological judge.[27]

It is to be observed, therefore, that *the location of the Son of man sayings in the hypothetical Q argues against rather than in favor of the alleged Son of man Christology.* Whether the original order of Q is preserved better by Matthew or by Luke, the first four instances of "the Son of man" refer to the earthly Jesus rather than to an angelic figure with whom the community had identified Jesus. Is it reasonable to suppose that the redactor or redactors of the collection would have been content to defer allusions to the central article of the faith of the Q community ("Jesus is the coming Son of man") to so late a point when in fact the presence of the judgment motif encouraged such allusions at a number of earlier locations (i.e., not only at Lk. 6:46–49 but also 7:31–35; 10:10–14; 11:29–32, 37–52)?

The argument based on Lk. 12:8f. Critical to Tödt's reconstruction of the history of the Son of man tradition in general and of the Son of man Christology of Q in particular is his interpretation of the fifth saying in Luke's presentation, Lk. 12:8f. We have already seen in chapter 1 how important this logion was to Bultmann's understanding of the Son of man as a figure distinct from Jesus. Tödt follows Bultmann in regarding this as an authentic saying in which Jesus promised that the eschatological fellowship into which he had summoned his disciples would be confirmed at the last judgment by the apocalyptic judge, the heavenly Son of man;

---

26. See the discussion of Mt. 24:30 above, in chapter 5.
27. Correctly perceived by Tödt, *Son of Man,* p. 119.

only after Easter did the disciples come to believe that the one who would confirm the fellowship was the one who had first established it and were thus led to identify Jesus with the Son of man.[28] Plausible at first sight, this proposal is problematic at two points.

First, the argument in favor of the authenticity of the saying is wrongly conceived; it simply is not the case that the saying distinguishes between Jesus and the Son of man so sharply that it cannot have been created by the post-Easter community that identified the two. In formal terms *all* the Son of man sayings make this distinction, because the speaker (Jesus) refers to the Son of man in third-person terms, and on Tödt's analysis many of these were created by the early church. It is entirely possible, therefore, that this logion is also secondary, as Käsemann, Vielhauer, and others have urged.[29] In this case the saying will have alluded from the instant of its creation to a future function of *Jesus*, since it would not otherwise have been created by an early believer.

Second, the proposal is vitiated by the unproved assumption that the clause containing "the Son of man" alludes to the Enochian figure. This assumption has been challenged by E. Schweizer, who has proposed that the language of confessing and denying refers more appropriately to the function of a witness than to that of a judge at the last judgment.[30] The implications of Schweizer's observation deserve elaboration. The saying speaks of direct reciprocity; the witness who confesses or denies must be the same as the one who was confessed or denied. The form of this state-ment must not be confused with that of ordinary eschatological warnings, including those identified by Käsemann as "sentences of holy law" or "the eschatological *jus talionis*."[31] It does not coordinate good and bad behavior with future reward and punishment respectively (as, e.g., at Mt. 5:7; 6:14f.). It is not to be understood as saying, "As you treat me, so also will the eschatological judge treat you." Nor does it mean: "If you acknowledge me (under the duress of persecution), the ultimate judge will acknowledge you," because this ignores the fact that the verbs "confess" and "deny" point not simply to acts that will be judged good or bad by the heavenly judge but rather to a *relationship*, as Tödt correctly emphasizes.[32]

The saying promises that those who publicly acknowledge that they are Jesus' disciples will be acknowledged as disciples *by Jesus himself* at the last

28. Tödt, *Son of Man*, pp. 56f.
29. See notes 12, 20 above.
30. Schweizer, "Der Menschensohn," p. 188, and "The Son of Man," p. 120.
31. See n. 20 above.
32. Tödt, *Son of Man*, p. 57.

judgment (cf. 2 Tim. 2:12; Rev. 3:5). This does not mean that the one who identifies his authentic disciples "before the angels of God" (possibly a euphemism for "before God") cannot at the same time be serving as judge on God's behalf. There is thus no basis for the suggestion that this saying "demotes" Jesus to the role of an ordinary witness.[33] If we are correct in assuming that whatever Christian community created and/or transmitted this logion must also have honored the risen Jesus as the Christ, the eschatological king, we can also assume that it revered him as judge, since judging was considered one of a king's prerogatives (cf. Ps. Sol. 17:26; 2 Cor. 5:10). In this saying, however, the king is represented as passing verdict not on the morality of deeds performed by his subjects but rather on the allegiance of his followers. Taken in this way, the logion remains an apocalyptic saying, but the judge is no longer to be seen as the shadowy figure of the Similitudes of Enoch but as Jesus himself, to whom an eschatological role is attributed. Thus, while it is proper to call this a "future" saying, it is also closely related to the "earthly" sayings because it is the human Jesus, translated to a heavenly sphere, whose judgment of his followers is anticipated.

The remaining Son of man sayings attributable to Q require no extensive examination. All four are future in orientation; they speak either of the expected coming of the Son of man (Lk. 12:40 // Mt. 24:44) or of the day or days of the Son of man (Lk. 17:24, 26, 30; cf. Mt. 24:27, 37, 39). As we have already seen when studying these sayings in their Lukan and Matthean contexts, they are fully comprehensible in terms of the church's expectation of Jesus' return in glory. Exegetical resort to the Similitudes of Enoch is totally unwarranted, since that source says nothing about the Son of man's coming, his day(s), or his being revealed.[34]

Supporters of Tödt will undoubtedly respond: "It is entirely possible that the Jewish apocalyptic tradition with which the Q community was familiar differed significantly from that represented in 1 Enoch; the figure of the Son of man may have been painted with very different brush strokes in the two streams of tradition. Awareness of the tradition in some form or other is sufficiently evidenced by the fact that in these four authentic sayings preserved by Q, Jesus points away from himself to a heavenly

33. Schweizer, "Der Menschensohn," pp. 193f., cites as a parallel the Jewish motif of the exaltation of the persecuted righteous individual to the role of heavenly witness against the wicked.

34. The "revealing" of the Son of man to which 1 En. 48:7 and 62:7 witness is preeschatological, as explained in 69:26: his name (i.e., the reality of his future role) has been revealed to the elect. The eschatological appearance of the Son of man in 69:29 occurs apparently in heaven; there is no indication that he comes to earth to establish his throne in Jerusalem.

figure bearing the title 'the Son of man.' " But this argument is assumed rather than demonstrated by Tödt! It remains to be proved (1) that they are authentic, and (2) that in them Jesus speaks of a well-known figure distinguishable from himself. It should be observed that none of the so-called authentic logia is formulated in such a way that would suggest that Jesus announced the imminent coming of the Son of man to *nondisciples*; in each, "your Lord" could be substituted without changing the force of the saying. There is no "missionary" use of the term (e.g., "Repent, for the Son of man is coming!"). Since in Tödt's presentation (1) is clearly dependent on (2)—that is, the future sayings are assumed to be authentic precisely because in them Jesus points away from himself to another figure—there is here a serious begging of the question.

In the entire corpus of gospel Son of man sayings, the one consistent feature of the idiom is that it serves (with the possible exception of Lk. 24:7) as a self-designation of the speaker, regardless of whether the content refers to present or future activity on the part of the one so designated. The hypothesis that at the earliest stage of the tradition, the stage represented by authentic logia, the name was used by Jesus to point away from himself to an apocalyptic figure must be supported by the presence of specific features derived from Jewish apocalyptic literature, but such evidence is totally lacking in these four sayings! Without such evidence in favor of *discontinuity* between the earliest post-Easter use and the usage evidenced in the reconstructed Q, it is methodologically sounder to assume *continuity*—that is, to assume that the earliest sayings employed the term precisely as the tradition uniformly implies, as Jesus' self-designation. The apocalyptic sayings attributable to Q, whether authentic or inauthentic, are thus to be taken as evidence of a literary tradition (whatever its origin) according to which Jesus spoke of himself in third-person terms, employing "the Son of man" as a name for himself.

The existence of the postulated "Son of man Christology" in some Christian group influenced by a no-longer-extant apocalyptic tradition different from and earlier than that represented by the Similitudes of Enoch cannot be categorically denied, but it must be insisted that the occurrence of these four sayings in the hypothetical Q provides no dependable evidence in support of the conjecture. All four sayings are fully intelligible as allusions to the well-known Christian belief that the risen Jesus would return as Lord and Christ, allusions that are couched in a firmly established literary form employed for Jesus' statements about himself.

The same conclusion holds if we abandon the Q hypothesis and speak simply of the traditions, oral or written, common to Matthew and Luke. In this case we can infer nothing from the location of the sayings in a source, and we will not be able to assume that the "earthly" and "future" logia were treasured by the same group. The four future sayings shared by Matthew and Luke are, however, so colorless that they provide no reason to conjecture the existence of a group that transmitted these only and refused to receive earthly sayings.

The Pre-Markan Material

When we attempt to go behind Mark to the material from which he drew, there is nothing like the Q-hypothesis to help or hinder us. Achtemeier's thesis concerning pre-Markan miracle catenae is of no assistance here, since "the Son of man" does not occur therein.[35] Consequently we cannot infer anything from an alleged ordering of the pre-Markan Son of man sayings and can say nothing about the way in which sayings of different types cohere in his source(s). At most it can be argued that 2:1—3:6 constitutes a pre-Markan complex of controversy narratives in which "the Son of man" occurs twice, in each instance in a statement regarding Jesus' earthly authority (2:10, 28).[36]

It is possible, of course, that Mark himself is responsible for the Son of man statement in each case. In chapter 6 we have noted the clumsy construction in 2:10, the parallel anacoluthon in 14:49, and M. Hooker's observation that Mark is apparently not averse to ellipsis. Something like v. 10 is, however, required by the structure of the narrative, and we have no reason to suspect that Mark was motivated to substitute a Son of man statement for an earlier version employing first-person language. Similarly, while it is not impossible that the final redactor added the Sabbath saying as a commentary on and limitation of the halakic principle enunciated in v. 27, the arguments in favor of this proposal are not impressive. We will therefore proceed on the assumption that both statements derive from Mark's controversy source.

What is the function of the Son of man statements in such a source? Assuming for the moment that neither is authentic and that perhaps neither originated in the Aramaic-speaking church, what could have prompted the Greek-speaking tradents to formulate the controversy narratives in this way? Their general intention can be inferred from the two narratives considered as wholes: the first displays Jesus' authority to pronounce the forgiveness of sins by recounting a miracle; the second restricts the scope

35. Achtemeier, "Toward the Isolation of Pre-Markan Miracle Catenae," and "The Origin and Function of the Pre-Markan Miracle Catenae."
36. Tödt, *Son of Man*, pp. 126–32.

of v. 27 by proclaiming that Jesus is the authoritative teacher. In each case the Son of man statement would have fulfilled its function just as well had it been couched in first-person language.

Two explanations for the choice of third-person speech deserve consideration. According to Tödt and others, "the Son of man" was employed by these tradents as a title of majesty connoting the special authority of the earthly Jesus, who was destined to return *as* the Son of man. While this thesis is not impossible, nothing in the texts favors it; there is nothing in the collection of controversy narratives taken as a whole that suggests that Jesus is presented as saying in effect, "I am the one who is destined to come on the clouds of heaven as apocalyptic judge, and I hereby display my future authority by forgiving sins and defining Sabbath observance." While both logia are concerned with Jesus' authority, neither defines the source or basis of that authority for the narrative audience. This conclusion can be tested by supposing that the Hellenistic tradents had employed "the Christ" in v. 10: "But in order that you may know that the Christ has authority to forgive sins on earth. . . ." In such a case the statement would indeed function in the narrative as a public confession of royal authority, and we should be hard-pressed to explain why the narrative audience in v. 12 takes no account of it. No, at the pre-Markan level of 2:10, as at the level of the three Synoptic Gospels, "the Son of man" is attributed to Jesus as a self-designation without any clear content.

The second explanation builds on this insight. It would appear that "the Son of man" is employed in these controversy narratives not because of its connotative force but rather because of its denotative function. It is a linguistic tool by means of which a grandiose claim can be attributed to Jesus without making him appear excessively arrogant, as is the case when 2:28 is formulated in first-person speech, "So *I* am lord also of the Sabbath." The meaning is the same, but the claim is more modestly expressed.

Does this mean that the tradents responsible for the collection of controversy narratives were unaware of the apocalyptic Christian tradition that produced and/or transmitted Mk. 8:38, 13:26, and 14:62? As we have already seen, this hypothesis was proposed by Bultmann, who insisted that the Hellenistic Christians who created the earthly and suffering sayings no longer understood the title's original function.[37] Certainly nothing in Mk. 2:1—3:6 contradicts Bultmann's proposal. We must see if it applies equally to other pre-Markan sayings.

---

37. Bultmann, *Theology*, vol. 1, p. 30.

Respecting the Markan passion sayings, there is no consensus regarding which are traditional and which redactional. While Schmithals argues that all are redactional, his opinion does not seem to be widely shared. Because of the structural importance of the three leading passion predictions (8:31; 9:31; 10:33f.), there is a widespread suspicion that one or more of these must be attributed to the author. This suspicion attaches most strongly to the third because of its circumstantial reflection of the passion narrative, but there is little agreement regarding whether 8:31 or 9:31 better represents a pre-Markan tradition.[38]

Little is to be gained here by a detailed review of the arguments and counterarguments concerning the origin of each of the various Markan passion sayings (those just cited, plus 10:45; 14:21, 41). A mediating position will be adopted: it will be assumed that, while some of these are probably redactional, Mark derived his model for speaking of Jesus' passion in this way from earlier tradition. For our purposes it is immaterial which of the sayings corresponds most closely to the model Mark followed. All the sayings equally reflect the tradition (authentic or inauthentic) that Jesus spoke to his disciples about his impending passion in third-person statements employing "the Son of man." With the exception of 10:45, where the soteriological phrase ("and to give his life as a ransom for many") may or may not be redactional, these sayings do not reflect a specific understanding of Jesus' death; they could have been created or transmitted by the Ebionite stream of Jewish Christianity that declined to regard Jesus' death as an atoning sacrifice.[39] That is, the import of the sayings is christological (and apologetic) rather than soteriological. Their function is to show that Jesus was not caught by his fate unawares and that he manifested conformity with God's will by announcing to his own that his death was required by scriptural necessity.[40] What, then, is the function of "the Son of man" in the passion sayings?

As Tödt rightly observes, none of the transcendent features normally associated with the apocalyptic Son of man are reflected in this group.[41] None of them, not even 10:45, presents the shocking paradox that one normally domiciled in heaven must experience a painful human death. All imply that the speaker who employs this unusual way of referring to him-

---

38. For Schmithals, see n. 1 above. The priority of 9:31 is argued by Jeremias, *New Testament Theology*, p. 281, but rejected by Strecker, "The Passion- and Resurrection Predictions in Mark's Gospel," p. 434.

39. Cf. Schoeps, *Jewish Christianity*, pp. 62, 83.

40. See Tödt, *Son of Man*, p. 201.

41. E.g., ibid., pp. 178, 216.

self is a mortal who is fully liable to human pain and death. Nothing in the texts themselves suggests that the figure so designated is a royal personage possessing special authority in virtue of his office. If we were, in imitation of the Ebionites, to substitute the phrase "the True Prophet," the force of the passion sayings would not be altered; they would not tell us anything about the connotation of the substituted self-designation except to indicate that the True Prophet must be someone who is mortal and who knows his fate in advance. Indeed, to the extent that foreknowledge is presented in the New Testament as a whole as a prophetic gift, Tödt is unjustified in proposing that these sayings imply an authority specific to the Son of man.[42] How different is this "authority" from that attributed to Paul in Acts 20:23, where the apostle announces his future imprisonment and sufferings?

If *ho huios tou anthrōpou* connotes neither the heavenly judge of Jewish apocalyptic nor a special authority, why is it used in these passion sayings? Assuming for the moment (with Bultmann and Tödt) that none is authentic and (with Bultmann) that they all derive from Greek-speaking Christians, we can only infer—again, with Bultmann—that the creators were uniformly unaware of the apocalyptic meaning that has been postulated for the phrase. There is not the slightest hint that the creators were conscious of using "the Son of man" in a new and controversial way. All the sayings assume that it is appropriate and natural for Jesus to speak of his suffering in this indirect fashion. In the absence of a better hypothesis, we must infer that Christians who created such sayings for the purpose outlined above did so on the assumption that this strange idiom would be accepted as "authentic" by their contemporaries because it was already well established in the tradition of Jesus' sayings.

Can we infer anything about the saying that served as a model for the passion sayings? It is possible, of course, that one or more of the Markan passion sayings was created or transmitted in Aramaic by Palestinian Christians and, when translated into Greek, became a model or models for the production of similar sayings by Hellenistic Christians.[43] This proposal will be considered in the second half of this chapter. In the meantime it can be asserted that any earlier sayings that functioned as models for the creators of the passion sayings cannot have employed the phrase in a discernibly

42. Ibid., p. 220.
43. Tödt (ibid., p. 214) proposes that the ultimate source of the Markan passion sayings was "an earlier, partly Palestinian, stratum of tradition." He finds an Aramaic play on words in 9:31 but stops short of saying that this logion as a whole was transmitted in Aramaic (see p. 178).

different way. That is, if we are to postulate (with Bultmann) that the earthly or suffering sayings were created by Hellenistic Christians on the basis of earlier future sayings that had been translated from Aramaic into Greek, we would then have to infer that these latter were perceived by their imitators as using "the Son of man" *in a nonapocalyptic way.* Such future sayings must have been perceived as presenting a strange idiom whereby Jesus referred to his future destiny in an indirect and mysterious fashion, possibly for reasons of modesty or reserve.

This brings us to a consideration of the possible antecedents of Mark's three future sayings (8:38; 13:26; 14:62). We will begin with 8:38, since it seems to have the best claim to a pre-Markan origin, in view of the fact that Matthew and Luke apparently draw on a divergent version of the same saying (Lk. 12:8f.; Mt. 10:32f.). We will not ask which version better represents a possible Aramaic antecedent. At this point it is sufficient to note that Mark's "be ashamed of" clearly implies the same kind of reciprocity that was discovered above in the use of "confess" and "deny" in the alternate version. In formal terms only does the logion distinguish between the speaker and the Son of man; its content identifies them.[44]

Concerning the second of Mark's future sayings (13:26), it was noted in the last chapter that the evangelist himself may have been responsible for its creation. In any event, it does not have the appearance of a floating saying that was loosely incorporated into its present context; it serves as the climax of the passage regarding false Christs by promising that the true Christ will appear with unmistakable apocalyptic glory.[45] Consequently, whether created by Mark himself or by a pre-Markan apocalyptist (assuming for the moment, with Tödt, that it is inauthentic), the saying speaks of the apocalyptic arrival of Jesus as the Christ.[46] That the creator of the saying was originally inspired by a Jewish myth about a heavenly Son of man cannot be disproved, but nothing in the text or context requires such a derivation. As we have seen, the apocalyptic prophet responsible for the Revelation of John interpreted Dan. 7:13f. as a prophecy concerning the Crucified, and there is no need to posit radical discontinuity between Mark (or Mark's source) and John of Patmos in this instance.

---

44. Schniewind, *Das Evangelium nach Markus*, p. 120, points out that, if the Son of man is ashamed of one who denies Jesus, it is presupposed that he knows this human being as one of his own. That is, it is not an utterly transcendent figure who will be ashamed of Jesus' disloyal disciples but Jesus himself.

45. Cf. Juel, *Messiah and Temple*, p. 92. See the studies by Teeple and Walker referred to in n. 19 above.

46. Tödt, *Son of Man*, p. 35.

While the third future saying (14:62) may well be the product of Markan redaction, we must here consider the possibility that the evangelist received it as part of a pre-Markan passion narrative. This verse is by no means to be seen as an independent logion; even more clearly than was the case respecting 13:26, this saying belongs with its context, namely, the narrative concerning the trial of Jesus before the high priest's council (14:53, 55–65). In this context the statement clearly says something about *Jesus* being seated in the future at the right hand of God and coming with the clouds of heaven. It did not occur to the pre-Markan creator (if such there were) to have Jesus declare to the high priest, "I am the Son of man." Here as everywhere in the gospel tradition, the phrase serves not a declarative but a denotative function. Consequently this verse cannot be taken as evidence that the phrase originally designated a heavenly figure distinct from Jesus.

We can thus conclude that any of the three future sayings, if pre-Markan, could have served as a model for the earthly and suffering sayings; none of them speaks of a never-incarnate heavenly being. In each case "the Son of man" serves recognizably as Jesus' self-designation.

For this reason it is impossible to establish any priority among the three groups of sayings at the Greek stage. Since all the sayings function as statements of Jesus about his vocation and destiny, it is just as possible that future sayings were modeled on suffering sayings as the other way around.

Sayings from Matthew's and Luke's Special Sources

There is no need to prolong this discussion with a detailed examination of sayings peculiar to Matthew or Luke. Each of these has been studied in the relevant chapter, and in no instance was it concluded that one of these pointed to an earlier perspective. In most cases reason was found to suspect redactional creativity.

We conclude the first half of this chapter with the observation that Bultmann's proposal regarding the Hellenistic Christians who transmitted earlier sayings and created new ones modeled on them seems to be well founded: they were unaware of what Bultmann considered the original apocalyptic connotation of the phrase. Although its content was not clear to them (did they wonder whether it meant "The Man Who Excels All Others"?), its linguistic function was firmly established, and they were thus able to produce new sayings that were accepted as "authentic" by their contemporaries.

The Aramaic Tradition

What requires us to infer that at least some of the Son of man sayings were treasured in Aramaic by Palestinian Christians? For some scholars this is not a necessary inference. Lietzmann and his followers assert that the entire Son of man tradition originated with Greek-speaking Christians.[47] In this view, the creator of the first Son of man saying either borrowed the phrase from a non-Christian Greek source or coined it.

Let us briefly pursue the first possibility. The postulated source was presumably Jewish, since none of the gospel Son of man sayings reflect any of the features peculiar to the later pagan Gnosticism. The nature of the source is conjectural, since the Greek phrase never occurs in the expansive literature of Hellenistic Judaism. Can we assume that this source was in some sense a precursor of the Ethiopic Similitudes of Enoch (of which no trace has been left in Greek translation)? In this case our Christian innovator, like the author of the Similitudes, would be involved in introducing to his or her religious community a new name for a known figure. Just as the Enochian writer indicates in 1 Enoch 46 that "this Son of man" is an appropriate way of speaking about the Elect One, so the Christian writer would have to establish the identity of Jesus and *ho huios tou anthrōpou*. But none of the extant Son of man sayings do this; all *presuppose* the identification! This is astonishing, especially in view of the fact that both the Revelation of John and the Fourth Gospel exhibit the genre of "I" sayings that could have provided the model for such a self-disclosure statement.

Moreover, even if we were to postulate further that such a statement was promulgated and has been lost, this assumption does not help us to understand why those who accepted it failed to produce any apocalyptic sayings employing first-person language (e.g., "I the Son of man will come on the clouds of heaven"), to say nothing about the remarkable absence of confessional statements concerning Jesus as the Son of man. Must we hypothesize that these Greek-speaking Christians were unable to convince Paul and other New Testament authors of the validity of their christological claim? The thesis that the originator of the Son of man tradition borrowed the title from a Greek-speaking Jewish sect must thus be regarded as too conjectural for serious consideration.

We turn, therefore, to the second possibility. This is not ruled out by the common assumption that *ho huios tou anthrōpou* is barbaric Greek and

47. Lietzmann, *Der Menschensohn*, p. 92. See the studies by Teeple and Walker referred to in n. 19 above.

could not have originated in that language, because the assumption is erroneous.[48] Although it could be considered a sign of a more elevated Greek style to enclose the genitive phrase between the main noun and its article (cf. *ho tou theou anthrōpos* in 2 Tim. 3:17), the form that places the genitive phrase after the noun it modifies was common in profane Greek, and many models were available in the Christian tradition (e.g., *ho huios tou theou, ho logos tou theou*). More problematic is the coiner's intention.

What did the postulated innovator wish to say when he or she dubbed Jesus "the Son of the Man" or "the Son of humanity"? We could suspect an allusion to Adam in the first alternative. The second suggests the possibility that Jesus was being presented as "the human being par excellence." Both are attractive at first sight, but neither is supported by the extant texts.[49] Moreover, we are stuck with the same problems that were addressed above in connection with the hypothesis of borrowing from a Jewish apocalyptic source: we must explain why this new name for Jesus was never used of him by others and, when attributed to Jesus, was always employed with third-person language.

An important variant of this second proposal is more sophisticated and deserves careful consideration. N. Perrin and others hypothesize that the entire Son of man tradition has its origins in Christian exegesis of Dan. 7:13f.[50] Again we must ask what this means. We are familiar with the habit of first-century Jews and Christians of interpreting texts from the Scriptures as being "fulfilled" in contemporary phenomena. The Qumran exegetes make frequent use of the word *pesher* as a linguistic tool for moving from text to application. There is nothing quite like this in the New Testament. The closest parallel, perhaps, is the formula found so frequently in Matthew, "All this took place to fulfill what the Lord had spoken through the prophet" (1:22; the formula varies in details in subsequent uses), where the prophetic text follows the application rather than preceding it as in the Habakkuk Commentary at Qumran. It is clear that no New Testament

48. The phrase constituted a barbarism only in the more limited sense that it was not extant in contemporary Greek. The point here being made is that neologisms were linguistically just as possible in Christian Greek as in profane Greek.

49. The former might occur to a reader of the Septuagint of Gen. 2:7, 15, 18, where Adam is referred to as *ho anthrōpos*; see Cortis and Gatti, "The Son of Man or the Son of Adam," p. 470. Fitzmyer, "The New Testament Title 'Son of Man' Philologically Considered," p. 145, finds no evidence that the New Testament authors perceived such a meaning in *ho huios tou anthrōpou*.

50. See especially Perrin, *Modern Pilgrimage*, pp. 10–18, and *Rediscovering the Teaching of Jesus*, pp. 164–99. As far as I can determine, Perrin does not make clear whether he believes the development of the "title" *ho huios tou anthrōpou* as a result of this exegesis occurred first at the Greek stage or was simply the translation of a phrase created by Aramaic-speaking Christians. Perrin pays very little attention to the linguistic problem.

passage presents the Danielic text in either the Qumran or the Matthean form—certainly not Mk. 13:26 and 14:62—and therefore it is inappropriate for Perrin to speak of a *pesher* interpretation of the text.[51] Far more common in the New Testament than "fulfillment" texts are allusive quotations, among which Mk. 13:26 and 14:62 are surely to be included. An excellent example of the allusive use of Dan. 7:13f. is provided by Rev. 1:7, "Behold, he is coming with the clouds." The accompanying allusion to the pierced one of Zech. 12:10 makes it clear that Jesus the Crucified is here being presented as the one who at some unspecified time in the future will fulfill the prophecy of Daniel. John of Patmos thus witnesses to an early Christian appropriation of Dan. 7:13f. as a way of speaking about Jesus' anticipated return in glory.

Perrin seems to presuppose that the originator of the exegetical tradition represented by Mk. 13:26 and 14:62 went a step further: he or she coined a new name for Jesus on the basis of the Danielic text.[52] If we assume, as Walker does and Perrin seems to, that this happened at the Greek rather than at the Aramaic stage, we must ask what impelled this creative Christian to move from the Septuagint phrase *hōs huios anthrōpou* to *ho huios tou anthrōpou*. The Septuagint phrase is very bland, indicating merely that the figure so described had a human rather than a bestial appearance. If our postulated originator wished to create a new name for Jesus that would identify him as the figure of Dan. 7:13f., why did he or she focus attention on this phrase rather than on the verb or adverbial phrase? A clearer reminiscence of the Danielic text would have been provided had the newly coined name been *ho meta tōn nephelōn erchomenos* ("He who comes with the clouds") or something similar. Alternatively, as C. F. D. Moule has proposed for an earlier stage of the tradition, the coiner could have used a demonstrative pronoun as a means of making clearer the intended allusion to Daniel, *ekeinos ho huios tou anthrōpou* ("that Son of man"), or possibly even *ho hōs huios anthrōpou* ("the one 'like a son of man' ").[53]

51. For helpful comments on the use of *pesher* at Qumran, see Wacholder, *The Dawn of Qumran*, pp. 89ff.

52. While not clearly stated, this view seems to be implied in Perrin's assertions: "First, there was the ascension use of Dan. 7:13 in a tradition already using Ps. 110:1. This tradition establishes *the concept* of Jesus at the right hand of God *as Son of Man*" (*Rediscovering the Teaching of Jesus*, p. 184 [my italics]).

53. Moule proposes that *ho huios tou anthrōpou* is a literal translation of an Aramaic phrase created by Jesus to serve as an allusion to Dan. 7:13. In "Neglected Features," p. 421, he suggests that the form may have been *brh dgbr*; later, in *The Origin of Christology*, p. 15, Moule is content to speak in more general terms: "I cannot believe that it was impossible to find a phrase in Aramaic that would unequivocally mean 'that Son of Man' or '*the* Son of man.' "

Lietzmann was aware of the linguistic problem and made a reasonable suggestion. While *bar nash*, he argued, had a very unimpressive sound as an everyday expression in Aramaic, *huios anthrōpou* must have sounded quite foreign and unusual to Greek ears, and thus there was a real possibility that it would be taken as the designation of an individual. As soon as Dan. 7:13 was interpreted messianically, the unusual phrase would be taken as an epithet for the Messiah. Lietzmann was confident that, once this move had been made, it would have been no great step for Greek-speaking Christians to add the articles and thereby create a title.[54] While this may indeed explain how *huios anthrōpou* became a divine epithet in later pagan Gnosticism, it seems a very unlikely explanation for Christians (or Hellenistic Jews, as Lietzmann proposed) who were steeped in the Septuagint, where *huios anthrōpou* appears so frequently without any messianic associations.[55] And one wishes that Lietzmann had provided linguistic evidence in support of his contention that the addition of the articles posed no big step. If *huios anthrōpou* was perceived as a name, there was no need to add the articles to make it definite. The anarthrous form functioned effectively as the designation of an individual aeon in gnostic writings, as we have seen in chapter 2.

Still another variant of this proposal must be mentioned. Is it possible that the postulated Greek-speaking Christian who coined the phrase was confronted by sayings attributed to Jesus in which the speaker referred to himself indirectly using the anarthrous *huios anthrōpou* ("a son of man must suffer," "a son of man has authority to forgive sins") and, inspired by Daniel's prophecy, created a title out of the indefinite phrase?[56] Unfortunately, this variant of the proposal is attended not only by all the problems inherent in those already examined but also by an additional one. We must now explain why all the postulated sayings employing *huios anthrōpou* were either suppressed or altered through the substitution of the full title *by a Greek-speaking church that found the title of no value whatsoever for liturgy and confession.*

In view of the difficulties thus confronted when postulating an origin among Greek-speaking believers, we are justified in accepting the consen-

---

54. Lietzmann, *Der Menschensohn,* pp. 91f.; Lietzmann, however, believed that the phrase was coined by Greek-speaking pre-Christian Jews, probably at Alexandria (see pp. 92f.).

55. Grässer, "Beobachtungen zum Menschensohn in Hebr 2,6," points out that the classic instance in Ps. 8:6 was not taken messianically by the rabbis, and the same seems to be the case in Heb. 2:5–9.

56. This explanation is proposed by Lindars, *Jesus Son of Man,* pp. 85, 95.

sus of scholarly opinion that regards *ho huios tou anthrōpou* as the Greek translation of an underlying Aramaic phrase.[57]

We have reached a critical point in the study. Whatever conclusions are reached in the final chapter concerning Jesus' use or nonuse of the phrase will depend on inferences drawn in this section. And inferences are all that can be presented, since we possess none of the Son of man sayings in its original Aramaic form. Of crucial importance is the determination of the probable form and function of the Aramaic phrase. In terms of *function* six different possibilities have been suggested.

1. It was a well-known apocalyptic title.
2. It was easily perceived as a title, even by those who may have been ignorant of its meaning.
3. It was genuinely ambiguous, so that hearers/readers would not be immediately certain whether it was titular or nontitular.
4. It was a special idiom that was used only for general statements in which a speaker could refer to himself indirectly but not exclusively.
5. It was an everyday expression meaning "a man," or "someone."
6. It was an easily recognizable circumlocution for "I."

All six of these options have been proposed. Indeed, all have been defended on the basis of the same postulated Aramaic form, *bar enasha*, but other forms have also been hypothesized: *bar nash*, *bareh de-enasha*, the Hebrew *ben adam*, and its Aramaized version *bar adam*.

On what basis can a sound inference be drawn concerning whether the perceived function of the phrase (whatever its form) was titular or nontitular? Those who argue that the phrase functioned as a title draw their strongest support from the fact that the Greek translation, *ho huios tou anthrōpou*, appears to have both the form and the function of a title in the gospel tradition. It is then further inferred that the phrase, in view of its frequency, was not an "informal title" comparable to the parallel construction "the son of perdition" (Jn. 17:12) but one with significant apocalyptic content derived from a tradition similar to that evidenced in the Similitudes of Enoch. Once this second inference has been made, it follows logically that the earliest use of the phrase in the Christian tradition occurred in the future or apocalyptic sayings, which then served as models for the later creation of nonapocalyptic sayings by believers who were no longer aware of the pre-Christian apocalyptic use. Alternatively, it is argued that the

---

57. The improbability of a Hebrew antecedent is considered below (see the discussion of *ben ha-adam*).

title as such did not occur in pre-Christian Judaism but was created (whether by Jesus or by an early follower) as a way of referring to an important messianic proof text, Dan. 7:13f. The earliest sayings, then, are those that most clearly reflect the influence of the Danielic text.

Those, on the other hand, who hypothesize a nontitular function for the phrase place a heavy emphasis on extant Aramaic sources. They argue that, despite the alleged evidence of the Ethiopic Enoch, there is no instance in the Aramaic documents at Qumran, the early Palestinian Targums, or in the later rabbinic literature of *bar enasha* or any variant thereof occurring as a title. While the argument from silence cannot absolutely exclude the possibility that some variant was employed by Palestinian Christians as a title, its absence from the earliest confessions renders such an assumption very improbable. It is then inferred that the earliest sayings are those in which the phrase manifestly serves not as a title but as an idiomatic self-reference. Later Christians, misunderstanding the idiom, created apocalyptic sayings, under the impression that the phrase alluded to the figure of Daniel 7.

The two arguments are presented with great sophistication and in many variations by their respective proponents. In each there is obviously a close relationship between the function hypothesized (titular or nontitular) and the selection of earliest sayings. An impasse seems to have been reached in current scholarship. Those interested in the question affirm their support of one or the other of the two arguments but seem to have little success in demonstrating the untenability of the alternative.

Given this state of affairs, the soundest procedure would seem to be to ignore temporarily the question of the form and function of the underlying Aramaic phrase and to ask instead: Assuming for the moment that no Son of man saying is authentic, did apocalyptic sayings provide models for the later development of nonapocalyptic logia, or was the reverse true? (This way of putting the question does not preclude later consideration of the possibility that Jesus was the originator of the earliest sayings of either or both types.)

The first step in seeking an answer to this question is to establish whether the Aramaic tradition contained both kinds of sayings. It is possible, after all, that sayings about the earthly activity of the Son of man were created only after apocalyptic sayings were translated into Greek, or vice versa.

Did the Aramaic Tradition Include
Apocalyptic Sayings?

That Aramaic-speaking Christians awaited Jesus' return in glory is incontestably witnessed by the invocation *marana tha* (1 Cor. 16:22). Did they also give expression to this hope in sayings placed in Jesus' mouth in which the Master referred to his future coming in indirect language employing "the Son of man"? This development has generally been assumed, but the currency of the hypothesis that the entire corpus of Son of man sayings began with a few statements in which Jesus alluded to his earthly activity and suffering ("A son of man must suffer . . ."; "a son of man has nowhere to lay his head") requires that the assumption be justified. Lietzmann, as we have seen, maintained that all the apocalyptic Son of man sayings emerged at the Greek stage of the tradition.[58] More recently Lindars has suggested that, if Jesus had already been identified with the figure of Daniel 7 at the Aramaic stage, the titular expression *ho huios tou anthrōpou* may have been deliberately coined by the bilingual translators in order to give expression to this identification.[59]

There is virtual certainty that Jesus' future coming was indeed interpreted in terms of the Danielic prophecy by Aramaic-speaking Christians (Rev. 1:7).[60] There is thus no cause for denying the possibility that these Christians treasured sayings attributed to Jesus in which he spoke of his fulfillment of the prophecy. Lindars's inference that the future Son of man sayings originated at the Greek stage is a corollary of his hypothesis that the underlying phrase (*bar nasha*) constituted an idiom whereby a speaker "refers to a class of persons, with whom he identifies himself"; since in these apocalyptic sayings "the Son of man" refers exclusively to Jesus, they cannot have appeared in Aramaic.[61] Since the method we are following temporarily ignores the question about the form and function of the Aramaic expression, however, we are not permitted to draw such an inference. The decision must be made on the basis of the content and language of the sayings apart from their use of "the Son of man."

Did Lk. 12:8f. circulate in Aramaic? An affirmative response is supported not only by the fact that the existence of an independent version in Mk. 8:38 points to an early date but also by the presence of an Aramaism in the prepositional phrases (*en emoi, en autō*) after *homologeō*, a verb followed in normal Greek by the accusative (cf. 1 Jn. 2:23).[62] While this logion is not apocalyptic in the sense of referring to Jesus' future coming,

---

58. See n. 47.
59. Lindars, *Jesus Son of Man*, p. 26. Cf. p. 85: "As the use of *bar enasha* is incorrect for an exclusive self-reference, it is probable that those sayings in which the Son of man functions in this way have been developed only after the transference of the sayings into Greek."
60. There is little reason to question the common view that the Apocalypse is the product of a Jewish Christian whose mother tongue was Aramaic.
61. Lindars, *Jesus Son of Man*, pp. 24, 59.
62. Bauer, *A Greek-English Lexicon*, p. 571. Cf. Boring, *Sayings of the Risen Jesus*, p. 165 n. 85.

it does suggest that Aramaic-speaking Christians considered it appropriate for Jesus to speak of his future role in heaven by means of "the Son of man." It is probable, therefore, that the Aramaic church treasured other future sayings. Among these is to be included Lk. 17:24 // Mt. 24:27, since the peculiar phrase *ek tēs hypo ton ouranon* is apparently a Semitism related to the Hebrew expression *mitahath ha-shamayim* (Ex. 17:14; Dt. 25:19), which was closely imitated in the Aramaic of *Targum Neofiti*.[63] Zahn helpfully suggests that in the Lukan *Vorlage* the expression was doubled on the analogy of phrases such as "from land to land" and "from sea to sea."[64]

Did the Aramaic Tradition Include
Nonapocalyptic Sayings?

Scholars who maintain that "the Son of man" made its initial appearance in the Aramaic tradition as an apocalyptic title are inclined to suggest that earthly sayings did not emerge until the Greek stage.[65]

Did Mt. 11:18f. // Lk. 7:33f. circulate in Aramaic? Let us begin with the consensus that this double logion belonged to the pregospel tradition. It has been argued that it is secondary, having been created as a "commentary word" to be attached to the parable about the children in the marketplace.[66] Was it added to the Greek form of the parable, or was it present in the Aramaic tradition?

There is no reason to discount M. Black's suggestion that the pleonastic *anthrōpos* ("Look, a man, a glutton . . .") represents a Semitism, most probably an Aramaism.[67] Moreover, contempt for Jewish tax collectors seems to have been more characteristic of Palestine than the Diaspora. Nothing in the form or content of the double saying excludes an origin in Aramaic. Later we must consider the possibility that the double saying is in fact an authentic utterance of Jesus. At that point we will weigh the proposal of A. J. B. Higgins that, while the saying originally derived from Jesus, it has been altered from a first-person to a third-person form employing "the Son of man" by a tradent who was possibly Greek.[68] It is obviously impossible to disprove such a proposal. It is entirely conceivable that "I" sayings have been turned into Son of man sayings (Lk. 6:22?), just

63. Diez Macho, *Neophyti 1*, vol. 2, p. 115; vol. 5, p. 211.
64. Zahn, *Das Evangelium des Lucas*, p. 602 n. 47.
65. See above, n. 47.
66. See Lührmann, *Die Redaktion der Logienquelle,* p. 29, and literature there cited.
67. Black, *An Aramaic Approach to the Gospels and Acts*, pp. 106f.
68. Higgins, *Jesus and the Son of Man*, p. 122.

as Son of man sayings seem to have been changed into "I" logia (Mt. 10:32f.). Methodologically, however, it is inappropriate at this stage to delete "the Son of man" from this logion in order to avoid the difficulty it presents for a particular theory regarding the form and function of the Aramaic phrase.

If the logion was created not by Jesus but by an Aramaic-speaking Christian who wished to provide the parable with an interpretive conclusion, what was its intention? The originator, it could be inferred, understood the parable as offering consolation to Jewish Christians involved in the unfruitful mission to Israel. The parable demonstrated that, regardless of whether God's messengers brought good news or bad to Israel, the response was rejection. The double saying was created to make this more explicit; John the Baptist, it was explained, had fasted from ordinary food and drink in order to call Israel to repentance, but God's people had refused to join him in fasting. Jesus celebrated the impending arrival of the joy of God's kingdom, but his people would not rejoice with him. If this was his understanding, what would have prompted the postulated originator of this commentary word to have Jesus refer to his ministry by using "the Son of man" and a third-person verb? We must presuppose that this unusual idiom was attributed to Jesus because of earlier sayings containing it. That is, it appears unlikely that this saying, if secondary, was the earliest of all the Son of man sayings and thus the model for all subsequent ones. Those who maintain that the entire Son of man tradition is secondary usually argue that the originator of the earliest saying either borrowed the appellation from Jewish apocalyptic or created it as an allusion to Dan. 7:13f. Since this saying reflects neither the Danielic passage nor apocalyptic ideas, there seems to be no reason to assign it such a primacy.

What kind of a model, then, was the alleged creator following? It is possible that this was a relatively late saying and that the tradition already contained a variety of sayings in which Jesus was represented as speaking both of his future glory and of his earthly activity by means of the idiom. Let us suppose, however, that the tradition possessed at this point apocalyptic sayings only and that the double logion attached to the parable about the children constituted the very first nonapocalyptic saying employing "the Son of man." Our postulated commentator had no models to follow except apocalyptic sayings, such as the one that compares the coming of the Son of man to a flash of lightning (Mt. 24:27 // Lk. 17:24). This logion was taken in the Christian community to be a statement made by Jesus about his own future coming in glory. The commentator must have assumed that it was permissible (i.e., that it would be acceptable to the church) to follow this model by having Jesus speak about his earthly activity in the same indirect way. What would make this assumption possible? The commentator must have taken for granted that the lightning saying and others about the anticipated Parousia had been *created* by Jesus and not *borrowed* from Jewish apocalyptic. Nothing in the tradition would encourage one to suppose that Jesus had appropriated for himself the title of a heavenly figure; no saying *identifies* Jesus as the Son of man.[69]

We can test this chain of inferences by a substitution. Let us suppose that Jewish apocalyptic (or Jesus himself!) had prophesied that the archangel Michael would appear to deliver God's people (cf. Dan. 12:1) and that his coming would be like lightning. Suppose, further, that the resurrection experience convinced the disciples that Jesus himself would return *as* Michael. The original Michael saying could then serve as a model for the production of new sayings about Jesus' anticipated angelic role. Is it conceivable, however, that any Palestinian Aramaic-speaking Christian would become so inattentive to the significance of Michael in Jewish tradition that he or she would create a saying in which Jesus compared himself to John the Baptist by declaring, "Michael has come eating and drinking, and they say, 'Look, a glutton and a drunkard!' "? Would other Jewish Christians accept this comment on the parable as "authentic" in any sense? This is an inconceivable state of affairs, even if we were to push the creation of the simulated "earthly Michael saying" to a point four decades after the death of Jesus—which is as late a date as can be assigned to the Aramaic antecedent of Mt. 11:19.

It follows, therefore, that if even one "earthly" or "suffering" Son of man saying was created (or transmitted) by a member of the Aramaic-speaking church of Judea or Galilee, we must disabuse ourselves of the notion that the believers cherished the apocalyptic sayings as evidence that Jesus identified himself with the heavenly Son of man of Jewish apocalyptic. Even if we hypothesize the existence of an esoteric sect that proclaimed the imminent arrival of Enoch as the heavenly judge, the presence of nonapocalyptic sayings in the Aramaic Jesus-tradition constitutes sufficient proof that Christians were either unaware of the Enoch sect or regarded its foolish ideas as totally irrelevant for a proper understanding of Jesus.

This being the case, there is no longer any need to presuppose that apocalyptic sayings provided the models for the creators of nonapocalyptic

---

69. Even if the commentator were aware that some sayings, perhaps Lk. 12:8f. as Käsemann proposes (see n. 20 above), had been revealed by the resurrected Jesus to a Christian prophet, he or she would still assume that the original model for such new revelations had been provided by the earthly Jesus.

ones. If the Aramaic-speaking believers did not regard their version of the phrase "the Son of man" as a borrowed apocalyptic title, it is just as possible that apocalyptic sayings were modeled on nonapocalyptic ones. Moreover, since both kinds of sayings were treasured in the Aramaic tradition, there is no basis for arguing that one of these two groups preceded the other as a group, unless we can demonstrate that authentic logia are to be found only in one of the groups.

While this issue will be treated in greater detail in the next chapter, it is appropriate to observe here that, if the pre-Easter tradition contained a few apocalyptic sayings and no nonapocalyptic ones (as Bultmann argued), this limitation apparently had no influence on the understanding of the phrase. The hospitable reception of newly coined nonapocalyptic sayings would indicate that the Palestinian Christian community had not inferred from the alleged limitation that Jesus intended to refer to himself by the phrase "the Son of man" only when speaking of his apocalyptic role.

Was the Underlying Phrase Titular or Nontitular?

We are now in a better position to respond to the other possibilities raised above concerning the function of the underlying Aramaic phrase. Consideration of its form will accompany this step.

Of the six possibilities listed, the first can now be discarded. The inclusion of earthly sayings such as Mt. 11:19 // Lk. 7:34 demonstrates that Aramaic-speaking Christians did not regard the phrase as the title of a heavenly being. Did they, however, regard it as a freshly coined title that Jesus had created for himself? This second proposal cannot be immediately dismissed, since Aramaic-speaking Christians chose to translate the phrase into Greek as *ho huios tou anthrōpou*, which has the appearance of a title.

On the assumption that the Greek articles represent an accurate translation, three retroversions have been proposed.

1. *Ben ha-adam.* The phrase *ben adam*, "son of (a) man," occurs frequently in the Hebrew Scriptures, most often in Ezekiel as the appellative with which God addresses the prophet (e.g., Ezek. 2:1; cf. Dan. 8:17). It never occurs in Hebrew literature with the article except in one instance in the Qumran material, where the article has been added above the line in a generic use of the term.[70] A number of scholars have conjectured,

---

70. 1QS xi.20. Vermes, "The Use of *bar nash/bar nasha* in Jewish Aramaic," p. 327, proposes that the unusual Hebrew phrase is an Aramaism.

however, that Jesus called himself either *Ben ha-adam* or *Bar ha-adam*, or perhaps simply *Bar-adam* (as Ezekiel is addressed by God in the Targums).

A thorough review of this fascinating proposal in its diverse variations would take us too far afield. It must here suffice to say that the texts themselves provide no support for the conjecture. Had Aramaic Christians believed that Jesus intended to call himself "the Son of Adam," they would never have translated *adam* as *anthrōpos* but would have transliterated the Hebrew name, as Paul and other New Testament writers do (cf. Rom. 5:14; Lk. 3:38; Jude 14). Moreover, one would expect that the Son of man sayings would include some clear indications of the Adam typology. Paul's treatment of the second-Adam motif is unrelated to the Son of man tradition, as Vögtle correctly observes.[71] Despite the attractiveness of the proposal in terms of its usefulness for Christology, it must be rejected as implausible.

2. *Bereh de-enasha.* Syriac translators of the Gospels, when rendering *ho huios tou anthrōpou*, employed not the everyday expression *barnasha* or *bar enasha* (which they used for the simple *anthrōpos*) but a neologism, *bareh de-nasha* (with minor variants).[72] Although we have no evidence that such a title was extant in first-century Palestinian Aramaic, there is no a priori reason why Jesus or one of his followers could not have coined the phrase.[73] This hypothesis provides the easiest explanation for the presence of the articles in the Greek translation.

How would Aramaic-speaking Christians have understood this neologism? Since their tradition apparently contained no saying attributed to Jesus in which he explained its meaning, they were obliged (as we are) to infer its linguistic function from the various uses made of it. Its denotation would be clear; in all the sayings the phrase is used by the speaker, Jesus, as a way of referring to himself. What impression would they receive concerning its connotation? They might regard it as a mysterious title, but in this case we should expect to find some evidence of midrashic or targumic attempts to unravel its meaning. It could be hypothesized that Mk. 13:26 and 14:62 represent such attempts. The similarity between *bareh de-enasha*

71. Vögtle, " 'Der Menschensohn' und die paulinische Christologie." Fitzmyer, *A Wandering Aramean*, pp. 144f., regards it as wholly improbable that *ho huios tou anthrōpou* was understood by the New Testament writers as meaning "Son of Adam."

72. See the discussion by Dalman, *Die Worte Jesu*, p. 196; Zahn, *Das Evangelium des Matthäus*, pp. 359f. n. 25.

73. Pace Lietzmann, *Der Menschensohn*, p. 85, who with youthful brashness insisted: "Jesus hat sich selbst nie den Titel 'Menschensohn' beigelegt, weil derselbe im Aramäischen nicht existiert und aus sprachlichen Gründen nicht existieren kann" (the whole statement is emphasized in the original).

and *kebar enash* in Dan. 7:13 renders it probable that Christians would relate the mysterious title and the Danielic prophecy. If either of these Markan verses was created by an Aramaic-speaking Christian, what would this tell us of the Palestinian understanding of *bareh de-enasha*? We could infer the following belief: "Jesus, when he referred to himself as *bareh de-enasha*, was indicating that he would one day, after his death and resurrection, be *the human being* who would fulfill the prophecy of Daniel." That is, if *bareh de-enasha* had been taken by Aramaic-speaking Christians as a *title* coined by Jesus in order to refer to his significance in God's plan, they would have understood it as the designation of a *human* figure, as their transmission of the earthly sayings testifies.

Unfortunately, we cannot be certain that either of the Markan sayings alluding to Dan. 7:13 circulated in Aramaic, and the small amount of attention paid to the Danielic passage in the rest of the New Testament does little to encourage the view that a mysterious title was rendered meaningful by reference to Daniel. Even Rev. 1:7, where an allusion to the prophecy is incontestable, gives no evidence of the postulated title. It must be inferred, therefore, that if a complex phrase such as *bareh de-enasha* constituted the Aramaic antecedent of *ho huios tou anthrōpou*, it was not perceived by the tradents as a mysterious title connoting "the figure prophesied by Daniel." As far as we can gather from the transmitted sayings, the Aramaic-speaking Christians made little effort to interpret the phrase. The very fact that the phrase was rigidly restricted to sayings attributed to Jesus and, conversely, absent from all New Testament statements about his significance suggests that, like Paul and John of Patmos, the Palestinian Christians did not find the phrase useful for talking about the meaning of Jesus for faith. They did not perceive the phrase as a title bearing significant content.

It appears, therefore, that the phrase was not seen as a mysterious title begging for interpretation. This conclusion does not absolutely preclude the possibility that *bareh de-enasha* (or a similarly complex form) constituted the phrase attributed to Jesus, but it tips the scales of probability in favor of a simpler form.

3. *Bar enasha.* The material from Qumran suggests that the Palestinian dialects of Aramaic in the first century were beginning to confuse the absolute and emphatic states of the noun; the final aleph (the equivalent of the definite article) is frequently attached to nouns where the context would suggest an anarthrous usage. It has been proposed that this process had advanced to the point that the two states were indistinguishable.

This seems to exaggerate the extent of the confusion.[74] It is probable, therefore, that the bilingual translators who established *ho huios tou anthrōpou* as the standard rendering of the phrase had before them *bar enasha* and felt that the force of the final aleph ought to be represented by the definite articles in Greek. Would this mean that they perceived the phrase as a title laden with important christological content? Apparently not, for the reasons given above concerning the postulated *bareh de-enasha*.

These same considerations challenge the validity of the third proposal of the six listed above, namely, that the underlying Aramaic term was genuinely ambiguous, capable of being perceived as titular by some and as nontitular by others. In view of the frequency with which the emphatic state was substituted for the absolute, a first-century Palestinian would not always be certain whether the final aleph in *bar enasha* should be taken seriously or not. In some contexts there could be genuine ambiguity. If *bar enasha* were used in the Aramaic version of Mt. 4:4 // Lk. 4:4, for example, the reader would be unsure whether the text meant, "A man shall not live by bread alone," or "Humanity shall not live by bread alone"—or was Jesus perhaps referring to himself as "the Son of man"?

One of the strongest proponents of the third proposal is M. Black. In a recent article he has reaffirmed his conviction that the emphatic form *bar enasha* could have served in first-century Palestine both as the apocalyptic title in an Aramaic version of the Similitudes of Enoch and as the self-referring idiom documented by G. Vermes.[75] Black illustrates his hypothesis by reference to Lk. 12:8f. (Mt. 10:32f.), where he finds a double entendre: "it is self-referring, as Matthew clearly understood by substituting the first person, but at the same time it has eschatological overtones. It is here an exclusive self-reference to Jesus as present Son of Man, but also as the One destined to take up the traditional role of the Son of Man Messiah, but as Advocate as well as Judge, on the day of Judgment."[76] In a footnote Black suggests that this possibility of double entendre makes most of the Son of man sayings "parabolic."[77]

It must be remembered that Black is discussing what he regards as Jesus' ipsissima verba. Our concern at this point is rather with the post-Easter stage of the Aramaic tradition. Would the sayings have appeared

74. See chapter 1, n. 82. Beyer, *Die aramäische Texte vom Toten Meer*, p. 518, maintains that *ho huios tou anthrōpou* must represent an underlying emphatic form, *bar enasha*. For Beyer, *bar enasha* constitutes an unambiguous allusion to Dan. 7:13, "der (aus Dan 7,13 bekannte) *bar enash,* das *bar nash* genannte Wesen" (ibid.).

75. Black, "Aramaic Barnasha and the 'Son of Man,' " especially p. 203.

76. Ibid., p. 203.

77. Ibid., p. 206 n. 5.

ambiguous to Palestinian Christians? Black would undoubtedly agree that the Son of man sayings were transmitted precisely because they were perceived as statements Jesus had made about himself. That is, the tradents experienced no uncertainty about the denotation. What about the connotation? Did the phrase appear to them *both* as a self-referring idiom (which, presumably, could have been similarly employed of himself by Peter or any other male follower of Jesus) and as a traditional messianic title used by a competing eschatological sect, the group that produced the Similitudes of Enoch?

Here we must draw a distinction between theoretical possibilities of double entendre and the way language actually functions. One of the titles given to the Son of man in the Similitudes is "the Righteous One." In Aramaic this title would have been *Saddiqa*.[78] If, as Black assumes, the final aleph was already being used in many instances where the absolute state was required, a contemporary reader would not be immediately certain whether the phrase meant "a righteous man" or "the Righteous One." From the context of the Similitudes, however, the reader would gather that the term was meant as a name or title, and there would henceforth be no double entendre. From the Book of Acts we can infer that Aramaic-speaking Christians applied the same title to Jesus (7:52; 22:14). Now, if we were to postulate that a saying had been attributed to Jesus in which he referred to himself as *saddiqa*, would Palestinian Christians have perceived a double entendre therein? Would it have been for them a "parabolic word" in which Jesus spoke of himself as "a righteous man" (i.e., one righteous man among others) and at the same time hinted that he was "the Righteous One," using a title with "eschatological overtones"? This would be an improper inference, based on a failure to consider the pragmatic way language functions. In the transmission of the postulated saying, the "weak" meaning would be quickly discarded in favor of the "strong" one (unless it too could be exploited theologically).

We can infer, therefore, that if *bar enasha* functioned both as a theologically neutral idiom of self-reference and as a theologically loaded eschatological title, the former would quickly be forgotten in the transmission of the Aramaic sayings. No ambiguity would be perceived. *Bar enasha* would have been treasured as an important tool for talking about the meaning of Jesus. The evidence, however, suggests that this was not the case (see the preceding discussion of *bareh de-enasha*). There is no theological exploitation of *ho huios tou anthrōpou* in early Christian literature except

---

78. See, e.g. *Targum Neofiti* Ex. 9:27 (Diez Macho, *Neophyti 1*, vol. 2, p. 55).

in the Fourth Gospel, where the "title" is employed not with reference to the Danielic figure but as a means of referring to the incarnate state of the Word-become-flesh (see chapter 4).

Of the six possibilities listed above, the three nontitular proposals remain to be discussed. The fourth has been forcefully presented by M. Casey and B. Lindars, the fifth and sixth by R. Bauckham and G. Vermes, respectively.[79]

Despite the initial attractiveness of Casey's hypothesis and Lindars's variation of it, both must be rejected as far as the Aramaic tradition is concerned. Whatever the conclusions reached in the next chapter regarding Jesus' use or nonuse of the phrase, we can be certain that the Aramaic-speaking Christians who transmitted (and probably added to) the tradition of Son of man sayings did not perceive the phrase as generic, referring to men in general or to a class of persons among whom the speaker includes himself. For the tradents the phrase was not indefinite but definite. Whatever its spelling and pronunciation, the Aramaic expression underlying *ho huios tou anthrōpou* was understood as referring exclusively to Jesus.

This can be tested by reference to Lk. 12:8f. Both Casey and Lindars maintain that this logion circulated in Aramaic with *bar enasha*.[80] Neither is willing to concede that *bar enash(a)* can here have been used in a non-generic way. Lindars is unequivocal: because of the generic nature of the idiom, we must paraphrase, "All those who confess me before men will have a man to speak for them (i.e., an advocate) before the judgment seat of God."[81] This reference to an advocate is not to be taken literally, however; it is a Christian's own public confession of Jesus that will function as advocate. Hence, there is no need to identify the advocate with Jesus. "But the irony of the idiom with *bar enasha* requires this too. Metaphorically speaking, Jesus will be there at the judgment to give the appropriate testimony. But this side of the matter must not be overemphasized."[82] The Greek translators obscured the subtlety of the idiom by using a phrase that could refer to Jesus only.

It must be objected that Lindars does not in this instance take *bar enasha* generically but as the equivalent of an indefinite pronoun—that is, as illus-

---

79. Casey, *Son of Man*; Lindars, *Jesus Son of Man*; Bauckham, "The Son of Man: 'A Man in My Position' or 'Someone'?" and Vermes, "The Use of *bar nash/bar nasha* in Jewish Aramaic." See also Bietenhard, "Der Menschensohn."

80. Casey, *Son of Man*, p. 194, supplies a possible Aramaic reconstruction; on p. 232, he argues for its generic meaning. Cf. Lindars's English translation of his reconstructed Aramaic saying (*Jesus Son of Man*, p. 53).

81. Lindars, *Jesus Son of Man*, p. 54.

82. Ibid., p. 56.

trative of the fifth proposal.[83] Casey, while giving the same impression in his earlier treatment, strives valiantly in a recent article to preserve a generic understanding: "At Lk. 12:8f. the general level of meaning assumes that other people will stand and witness for or against the people of Jesus' own environment in accordance with their basic attitude to his ministry."[84] He suggests that other faithful followers of Jesus may be implied as the future advocates in this generic statement.[85] Like Lindars, Casey is emphatic that *bar enasha* as a generic idiom includes Jesus but cannot refer to him exclusively.

This position seems to misconstrue the force of the logion in question. Matthew appears to be fully justified in regarding the two parts of each half of the double logion as directly correlative. The person who will serve as advocate or accuser is not a third party but the very one who has been confessed or denied.[86]

The generic interpretation of Mt. 11:19 // Lk. 7:34 must likewise be rejected. It is an unsuccessful tour de force to argue that *bar enasha* is here a "generalizing expression" that implies the existence of other people who ate and drank among tax collectors and sinners.[87] Awareness of the existence of such persons is irrelevant to the understanding of this statement, which is perfectly intelligible without it. The logion contrasts two individuals, both described as God's messengers by means of the idiomatic use of the Aramaic antecedent of *ēlthen*. While one is explicitly named, the other is identified simply by *bar enasha*. It is possible to take the expression as *indefinite* here, as Lindars in fact does by employing the English indefinite pronoun "someone" ("someone else").[88] It is a misuse of the English word to call this use of *bar enasha* "generic."[89]

The fifth possibility, most recently championed by Bauckham, thus has much in its favor. It is entirely credible that in the earliest *bar enasha* sayings attributed to Jesus, the Master was represented as speaking of himself indirectly by means of a phrase that meant "someone," the deno-

---

83. Lindars is justly accused by Bauckham, "The Son of Man," p. 26, of confusing "generic" and "indefinite." In his response to Bauckham, Lindars claims that "the idiom of the generic article" "specifies an individual, but leaves his identity ambiguous," as in Lk. 12:8f. ("Response to Richard Bauckham," p. 39). While strongly resisting Bauckham's proposal, Lindars in fact capitulates to it!
84. Casey, "Aramaic Idiom and Son of Man Sayings," p. 235.
85. Ibid., p. 236.
86. See "The argument based on Lk. 12:8f." in the first half of this chapter.
87. Casey, "General, Generic, and Indefinite," p. 40.
88. Lindars, *Jesus Son of Man*, p. 33.
89. In any language every common noun is generic; each one connotes all members of a class and can be used to denote any single member, but it is semantically misleading to suggest that the latter is a *generic* use of the noun.

tation of which was to be grasped by his hearers from the context.[90] "Jesus would be referring to an unidentified 'someone,' but those who fully understood his meaning would infer that the 'someone' was himself."[91] In support of this proposal Bauckham urges the advantage that future sayings would not have to be excluded a priori because of their restricted (non-generic) reference to Jesus.[92] If it could be shown that Jesus referred to the future in an allusion to Dan. 7:13 employing this oblique self-reference, it would then, Bauckham argues, be possible to explain the "quasi-titular" Greek translation, *ho huios tou anthrōpou*. Bauckham postulates that Jesus avoided *hahu gabra*, the customary self-designation, because it was a fixed circumlocution for "I"; in the *bar enasha* sayings Jesus wished to avoid an explicit self-reference. In some cases the hearers would have little difficulty perceiving the self-reference, but in others the indefinite phrase would leave them puzzled, as perhaps at Lk. 11:30.[93]

Two caveats must be raised against this excellent proposal. First, despite its advantages over the generic understanding of Casey and Lindars, Bauckham's likewise fails to explain adequately the Greek rendering. In his very brief treatment it was not possible for him to justify his conjecture that the "quasi-titular" Greek phrase derives from Jesus' use of *bar enasha* as an allusion to Dan. 7:13. Until he has successfully overcome Casey's objections to this traditional British hypothesis, we should continue to take seriously the probability that the Danielic allusions in the Gospels are secondary.[94] We are then left wondering why a term perceived by the Aramaic tradents as meaning "someone" should not have been rendered by *tis*, *anthrōpos*, or perhaps *anthrōpos tis* (cf. Lk. 10:30; reversed in Jn. 5:5) or *anēr tis* (Acts 5:1; 8:9; reversed in Acts 3:2).

Second, while the possibility of genuine ambiguity in the original Aramaic of Lk. 11:30 cannot be excluded a priori, no support for such a conjecture can be found in the extant Greek versions and their Gospel contexts. That is, the narrative settings uniformly presuppose clarity of

90. Pace Casey, this use is attested; cf. Vermes, "The Use of *bar nash/bar nasha* in Jewish Aramaic," pp. 319ff. In the anecdote about R. Kahana, which is claimed by Casey as illustrating the generic idiom, the use of *bar enash* is indefinite, not generic. The statement does not require that there be a class of persons who are despised by their mother but honored by another wife of their father; it raises a question about a specific case (ibid., p. 322). Casey, "General, Generic, and Indefinite," p. 50, insists that there are no examples of *bar enash* where the reference might be to some other individual. But that is precisely the point of this anecdote. R. Jochanan is justified in assuming that Kahana is using *bar enash* with respect to someone else. It is not a semantic error that Jochanan has made but a contextual one.
91. Bauckham, "The Son of Man," p. 29.
92. Ibid.
93. Ibid., p. 30.
94. Casey, *Son of Man*, especially chap. 8.

denotation for the phrase. The Synoptic Gospels provide not the slightest suggestion that anyone was ever puzzled by Jesus' use of the term.[95]

These two considerations prompt us to take another look at the sixth proposal, that of G. Vermes. Although his construal of the evidence can be criticized, Vermes seems to be closer to the truth than Casey, Lindars, and Bauckham in his insistence that the Aramaic phrase was capable of serving as a circumlocution for "I."[96] Unfortunately, none of the many examples he cites from rabbinic sources satisfactorily proves his case, as his critics have been quick to point out.[97] The phrase itself was indefinite, and only from the context could one determine—as in any other language— whether the speaker meant to refer *also* to himself in a general statement about men or the genus ("I'm not afraid—a man has to die sometime"), *especially* to himself ("I had to sell the house to pay for my wife's surgery. A man has to do what he has to do"), or *exclusively* to himself ("Can't a man have any peace around here?"). It is not the phrase that renders the self-reference obvious but the context.

That Aramaic-speaking Christians did not perceive the phrase as generic, including others potentially in its scope as Casey and Lindars urge, or referring to an unspecified "someone" as Bauckham proposes, is adequately demonstrated by the consistent choice of *ho huios tou anthrōpou* as its Greek equivalent. The articles indicate that the tradents regarded the Aramaic phrase as referring to a single individual, Jesus.

Some attempt to evade this conclusion by means of the hypothesis of mistranslation. In chapter 1 we looked briefly at Casey's proposal that the Aramaic idiom was so idiosyncratic to Aramaic that it was impossible to render it accurately in the receptor language. If Casey is correct, the translators ought to have employed a suitable paraphrase, just as he himself has attempted in his English renderings. Since Jesus, according to Casey, wished to make general statements in which he was included, there was no justification for translating his phrase *bar enasha* as an appellative. Aramaic-speaking Christians, for whom Casey's idiom was presumably a commonplace, should have translated it with the simple *anthrōpos* or, if they wished to be more literal or more poetic, *huios anthrōpou* (cf. Jn. 5:27) and thus have been faithful to Jesus' intention. Casey objects that the translators

95. The special problem presented by Jn. 9:36 and 12:34 has been examined above in chapter 4.

96. In addition to Vermes's article cited in n. 79, see his *Jesus the Jew*, p. 168, and "The 'Son of Man' Debate."

97. Casey, *Son of Man*, pp. 224–27, and literature there cited; Lindars, *Jesus Son of Man*, pp. 20–24. See also Casey, "General, Generic, and Indefinite," pp. 21ff. Vermes, *Jesus and the World of Judaism*, p. 91, lists opponents.

could not omit the articles, because "that would produce a general statement which would not clearly refer to Jesus."[98] But on Casey's hypothesis
that was precisely what Jesus intended—to make a general statement in
which he was included only by contextual implication! The anarthrous
translation would perfectly represent his intention, as do Casey's English
renderings employing the indefinite article.

The consistent use of *ho huios tou anthrōpou* in rendering the phrase
attributed to Jesus suggests very strongly that the tradents did not perceive
Jesus' intention as Casey does. The Aramaic-speaking church treasured
the Son of man sayings precisely because they were regarded as statements Jesus made about himself alone.

Lindars assumes that the underlying phrase, *bar enasha*, employed the
final aleph as the Aramaic equivalent of the generic article. The Greek
rendering is thus "a much too literal translation of the Aramaic."[99] He
concedes that *ho huios tou anthrōpou* would not be recognized as generic
in Greek, "so that *all* the gospel sayings do in fact treat it as an exclusive
self-reference, and therefore virtually as a circumlocution for the first person."[100] He proposes that Dan. 7:13 must have played a role in the translators' choice; *ho huios tou anthrōpou* may thus represent "a deliberate,
interpretative translation."[101]

This view is presented even more emphatically by G. Schwarz, who
insists that the Greek rendering falsely interprets the tradition; the way the
phrase functions in the extant Greek sayings cannot be taken as determi-
native, "weil es mit dieser Wendung nachweislich falsch ins Griechische
übersetzt worden ist."[102] He consequently finds it necessary to emend the
Greek texts extensively in order to recover the original sayings. Most critics will be appalled by the violence with which the defenseless Synoptic
sayings are made to fit his Procrustean bed.[103]

Lindars, Schwarz, and others who resort to the theory of mistranslation
inspired by Daniel must explain why precisely *this* mistranslation was
consistently selected instead of a formulation that would more obviously
refer to Daniel, and why the Greek tradition does not more extensively

98. Casey, *Son of Man*, p. 231. This claim is reiterated in "The Jackals and the Son of
Man," p. 14.
99. Lindars, *Jesus Son of Man*, p. 24.
100. Ibid., p. 25.
101. Ibid., p. 26.
102. Schwarz, *Jesus "Der Menschensohn,"* p. 14; cf. p. 10.
103. A particularly grievous example is Mt. 10:23, where the alleged original is presented
in German translation as follows: "Amen, ich, ich sage euch: Ihr sollt nicht lehren in den
Ortschaften Israels, bis *ich* zu euch kommen werde" (ibid., p. 156).

"Danielize" the transmitted sayings. In chapters 3–6 we found no evidence that the gospel writers were aware that *ho huios tou anthrōpou* had been created or adopted for the purpose of identifying Jesus with a figure of apocalyptic expectation. What basis, then, can be found *in the texts* for the proposal that the original translators intentionally, consistently, and unanimously mistranslated the Son of man sayings in order to render obvious to their Greek readers that Jesus was the figure foreseen by Daniel?

The hypothesis of mistranslation, finally, does not adequately account for the fact that future Son of man sayings, in which the self-reference was assumed to be patent, circulated *in Aramaic*. It was apparently possible to attribute to Jesus sayings such as Lk. 12:8f. in which he referred exclusively to his own future role by means of this idiom.

While the evidence adduced by Vermes does not seem to prove his claim that *bar (e)nash(a)* functioned as an exclusive self-reference, his inference concerning the way the phrase functions in the sayings appears correct. Is it possible to construe *ho huios tou anthrōpou* as a legitimate translation of a form of *bar enasha* that was capable of functioning in this way?

First, is it theoretically possible that *bar enasha* served both as an indefinite pronoun meaning "a man," "someone," or "anyone" in some contexts (e.g., Lk. 10:30) and in others as an exclusive self-reference without producing hopeless ambiguity? A positive answer can be given to this question on a priori grounds by means of an analogy drawn from English usage. The English word "one," in addition to being a numeral, serves also as an indefinite pronoun. It can be used in general statements of the widest possible application ("One has to die sooner or later") or in admonitions aimed at another individual ("One doesn't get anywhere by behaving *that* way"). It can be used in certain contexts to refer to a known person ("But there is one in heaven who understands our condition"). Most important for the purposes of this study, it can be used unambiguously by a speaker as a modest way of referring to herself or himself. A recent letter from an older friend requesting a letter of recommendation included the explanation, "Who knows one better than you?" The idiom is not very common.[104] It is not always as unambiguous as in the sentence just quoted, but usually the context permits an intuitive grasp of the speaker's meaning. If an elderly

104. I have the impression that it was more often used in my parents' generation. My children would perhaps be startled by it, had they not heard their grandfather use it. For him it was a characteristic habit of speech, indicative of modesty and reserve. For a careful linguistic study of contemporary British usage of "one," see Kathleen Wales, " 'Personal' and 'Indefinite' Reference: The Users of the Pronoun *One* in Present-day English."

woman declares, "One wishes the pension were a little larger," it is not difficult to surmise that she is not making a statement about pensioners in general but is employing restrained language to give expression to her feelings about her own straitened circumstances.

What Vermes's helpful collection of *bar nash(a)* passages indicates is that the Aramaic expression, like the English "one," could be used in a wide variety of situations. In some instances the self-reference, even if intended by the speaker, was not at all obvious (see the incident involving Rab Kahana and his teacher), whereas in others there would be little uncertainty.[105] When Jacob of Kefer Nibbarayya asked R. Haggai, "Should *bar nash* be scourged who proclaims the word of scripture?" it is to be assumed that he is not really interested in discussing the possible fate of all scriptural exegetes but his own situation, as Vermes properly insists.[106] It is the context, however, that assures this correct understanding. Vermes's next illustration suggests not an exclusive self-reference but a generic use. R. Ze'ira, after discovering that the local butcher would not sell him meat without administering a lash, complained, "Rabbis, how wicked is the custom of this place that *bar nash* cannot eat a pound of meat until he has been given a lash!"[107] R. Ze'ira is, of course, particularly concerned about his own mistreatment, but the phrase *bar nash* is used in a general statement, since he refers to what he (mistakenly) regards as a custom. His observation assumes that every *bar nash* will be treated in the same way in this wicked village.

What Vermes's examples suggest, then, is the possibility that an Aramaic speaker could use the phrase in a variety of ways and that his hearers would usually catch the intended nuance from the specific context. An exclusive self-reference might be more difficult to detect with certainty, but if a speaker were known by intimate friends or disciples to employ the idiom frequently out of modesty or reserve, this use would be more readily recognized. Similarly, those familiar with the tradition of Jesus' sayings, in which he was represented as frequently referring to his vocation and destiny in this modest and reserved way, would have little difficulty in distin-

---

105. *J. Ber.* 5c, as cited by Vermes, "The Use of *bar nash/bar nasha* in Jewish Aramaic," p. 322. Commenting on a similar passage, N. Perrin suggests: "Here 'son of man' is being used in reference to the speaker himself, although this use seems to be no more than could be the case in English with 'one' " (*Rediscovering the Teaching of Jesus*, p. 120 n. 1). Casey, *Son of Man*, p. 212, insists that if Jesus had used *bar enasha* as a simple self-reference, he would have produced a linguistic innovation, whereas nothing in the Synoptic Gospels suggests this. Here I am assuming that the modesty idiom did not constitute an innovation, but was simply one possible use of the indefinite *bar enasha*.

106. Vermes, "The Use of *bar nash/bar nasha* in Jewish Aramaic," p. 321.

107. *J. Ber.* 5c, as translated in ibid.

guishing the different intentions of the phrase in such sentences as *"Bar enash(a)* came eating and drinking and they say, 'Behold, a glutton and a drunkard . . .' " (Mt. 11:19) and *"Bar enash(a)* went down from Jerusalem to Jericho and fell among brigands" (Lk. 10:30). In the one case the phrase would easily be perceived as a self-reference, and in the other just as quickly recognized as the equivalent of an indefinite pronoun.

If the tradition had attributed to Jesus the statement *"Bar enasha* must die," Palestinian Christians might have inferred that a self-reference was intended, because of the central importance to their faith of the passion story, but unless the statement's context were provided, it would be possible to take it as a general statement, as Casey proposes.[108] That is, without elaboration the statement is truly ambiguous. It is very unlikely, however, that Palestinian Christians would have understood it as Casey suggests, namely, *both* as a general statement about human destiny *and* as a declaration about Jesus' own passion. They would have intuitively searched for some hint that one or the other was intended. For this reason we should probably infer that the postulated logion was never transmitted in splendid isolation but in association with other sayings or, as we in fact have it, in an elaborated form that includes allusions to the Passion.

The validity of Vermes's proposal depends, of course, on the possibility of explaining satisfactorily why *ho huios tou anthrōpou* was chosen to represent the modesty idiom in Greek. We have seen that theories of mistranslation do not seem justified. Is it possible to avoid the conclusion that the Greek rendering must be viewed as a very immodest representation of the modesty idiom? In the Greek form of the sayings Jesus appears to many researchers to be giving himself an exalted title, whatever its meaning.

It is important for us to realize that it does not seem to have appeared as imposing to early Christians as it does to modern scholars. The primary evidence for this has been presented in the preceding chapters and need not be repeated. The form of the Greek phrase is indeed identical with the form used for such titles as "the Son of God" and "the King of the Jews," but the form itself was not titular. It was more frequently employed nontitularly in such phrases as "the son of the carpenter" (Mt. 13:55), "the man of God" (2 Tim. 3:17), and "the son of perdition" (Jn. 17:12). In view of the way the phrase "son of man" is used in Ezekiel, early Christians would not have been inclined to assume that Jesus was making an immodest claim when referring to himself in this way. The bilingual translators

108. Casey, *Son of Man*, p. 229; cf. p. 232.

did not think they were attributing a "title of majesty" to Jesus, and their Greek readers did not infer that this had been their intention. The translators' choice of *ho huios tou anthrōpou* apparently did not mislead anyone until the emergence of the history-of-religions school in nineteenth-century Europe!

We must still ask, however, whether the Greek phrase with the two articles is a defensible translation of the modesty idiom. Would it not have been better to render it as *huios anthrōpou*? Casey correctly points out that translators, when faced with the problem of rendering an idiom into a language in which there is no proper equivalent, sometimes content themselves with providing a very literalistic translation.[109] It has often been assumed, therefore, that the underlying Aramaic phrase possessed the final aleph, and that this was represented in Greek by the use of two articles.[110]

As far as I can determine, Greek possessed no modesty idiom comparable to the Aramaic one, just as French and German (for example) do not have an exact equivalent of the English use of "one" as an exclusive self-reference. It was just as impossible to translate the idiom into Greek as it is to translate "Who knows one better than you?" into French or German. In this connection, it should be noted that Paul's use of *anthrōpos* in 2 Cor. 12:2 is *not* a parallel in the strict sense. Paul uses ordinary language, not a special idiom, in order to speak of himself in this indirect way, and for this reason his statement can be readily translated into any other language. Had Paul employed the postulated idiom in an Aramaic letter, he could have written more directly, yet still modestly, "Fourteen years ago *bar enasha* was caught up to the third heaven. . . ." His recipients could have surmised that he was speaking modestly about himself, not about another man.

The decision to employ definite articles in the Greek translation was probably prompted by something other than the presence of the final aleph and the translators' despairing literalism, however. Had they been translating the phrase into Latin, there would have been no difficulty in this regard, since Latin possesses no definite article; they would undoubtedly have written *filius hominis*, the rendering later employed in the Old Latin and Vulgate versions. If they chose to use this unusual Latin phrase when translating *bar enasha* in "*Bar enasha* came eating and drinking . . ." but not in "*Bar enasha* went down from Jerusalem to Jericho . . . ," it would be because the self-reference implied in the original would be more clearly indicated if the Aramaic phrase were more literally rendered. That is, in statements attributed to Jesus in which he spoke about himself, the

109. Ibid., p. 230.
110. E.g., Lindars, *Jesus Son of Man*, p. 24.

phrase, while not a name, nonetheless functioned in much the same fashion as does a name (i.e., in identifying a specific individual). While not capable of reproducing the modesty idiom, *filius hominis* by its distinctiveness would far better preserve the designative function of the Aramaic phrase than would the simple *vir* or *homo* (or *homo quidam*).

Assuming, then, that *filius hominis* constituted a satisfactory Latin equivalent, why did the translators not employ a similarly anarthrous phrase in Greek, *huios anthrōpou*? If consistently employed, it might have worked just as well as *filius hominis* in the Latin versions except for one significant drawback, as illustrated in Jn. 5:27. Because Greek, unlike Latin, does have a definite article, the absence of the article gives a noun or nominal phrase the appearance of indeterminacy. In Jn. 5:27 *huios anthrōpou* is correctly perceived not as a "name" for Jesus but as an indefinite phrase ("because he is a son of man").

In Greek, as in most languages, proper names are considered definite in themselves and do not require the use of an article. The article is nevertheless frequently used with names in Greek, as in contemporary German ("Wo ist der Peter? Kommt die Sabine mit?"), perhaps further to emphasize their definiteness. In Matthew's genealogy, for example, the name of each progenitor, when given in the accusative, is preceded by the article (Mt. 1:2–16), and the article is found also with the nominative of the names of Jesus and John in 3:13–15. It was not unnatural, therefore, for the Aramaic-speaking Christians to render the modesty idiom into Greek using a phrase with articles, whose definiteness would clearly suggest that, namelike, it was intended to point to a single individual. It would not be immediately recognizable as a self-reference, as would have been the case had the translators chosen to use *houtos ho anthrōpos*, "this man," but it literalistically reproduced the idiom. Greek-speaking Christians who became familiar with the Son of man sayings would soon have no difficulty with the term. They would have perceived it, as do contemporary readers of the Gospels in a modern language, as a name Jesus frequently used in statements about himself. They understood its function, even though the nuance of modesty was blurred or lost in the translation. They apparently gave as little thought to the phrase's "content" as do most of their modern successors.

Conclusion

Concerning the Greek stage of pregospel Son of man sayings, it has been argued in this chapter that Bultmann's observation is fully justified: the Greek tradents betray no awareness of an apocalyptic myth concerning the heavenly Son of man. In the second half of this chapter it has been insisted that the same holds true of the Aramaic-speaking tradents, who transmitted nonapocalyptic sayings along with apocalyptic ones without perceiving any tension between the two groups as far as their employment of "the Son of man" is concerned. For this reason it is impossible to establish the priority of one group over the other relative to this post-Easter stage of the tradition.

In terms of form and function, it was inferred that the Aramaic expression was, as most scholars have assumed, *bar enasha* and that this phrase was capable of functioning in some contexts as a modesty idiom, whereby a speaker referred to himself exclusively.

It must be emphasized that this conclusion is based on nothing stronger than inference. As many have pointed out, there is no unambiguous philological evidence in support of the proposal that *bar enasha* sometimes served as an exclusive self-reference.[111] On the other hand, there is no philological evidence whatsoever, ambiguous or otherwise, for the opposing proposal that *bar enasha* could sometimes function as a recognizable apocalyptic title. Given this state of affairs, the proposal to be received is the one that is least conjectural, that is, the one based on a series of inferences that is less vulnerable to attack than the inferences and assumptions of the opposing view. Readers must decide how persuasive is the case that has here been presented.

111. See Bauckham, "The Son of Man."

8 | JESUS

In chapter 7 it was argued that the inclusion of both apocalyptic and nonapocalyptic *bar enasha* sayings in the Jesus tradition indicates that the post-Easter Aramaic-speaking church did not regard *bar enasha* as an apocalyptic title. For these Christians the phrase had denotative rather than connotative force; it referred to Jesus exclusively when used in sayings attributed to him but communicated nothing about his status in the divine plan.

Is there any basis for inferring *discontinuity* between this post-Easter understanding and Jesus' own use? Should we accept Bultmann's proposal that Jesus himself prophesied the imminent coming of the heavenly Son of man, using *bar enasha* (or some variant), but that this titular use was forgotten by post-Easter followers who reinterpreted that phrase as a nontitular self-designation?[1]

Many considerations tell against such a proposal. In the first place, on a priori grounds continuity is more probable than discontinuity; the burden of proof rests on those who would assert the latter, and there seem to be no cogent arguments in its favor. Second, if Jesus' followers clearly remembered that he had predicted the coming of an angelic redeemer with whom he did not identify himself, we should expect to find a "correction" in the sayings tradition affirming Jesus' identity as the Son of man (just as Enoch is explicitly identified in 1 En. 71:14), but none is extant. Third, if the earliest Christology issued from this identification, it is inexplicable why no relic of the alleged confessional use of "the Son of man" has been preserved in the resurrection narratives, the archaizing speeches of Acts, pre-Pauline formulas, or the Apocalypse. Here the argument from silence must be given its due.

1. It must be remembered that Bultmann himself attributed this "forgetting" to the transition to the Hellenistic church; see *Theology*, vol. 1, p. 30.

Fourth, nothing in the Gospels suggests that Jesus proclaimed the coming of the Son of man to nonfollowers; as noted in chapter 7, there is no missionary use of the term, as should be expected on Bultmann's hypothesis. Fifth, the alleged authentic sayings in which Jesus announces the arrival of a supposedly well-known apocalyptic figure are remarkably colorless as far as apocalyptic features are concerned. Sixth, the titular use of *bar enasha* is purely conjectural; there is no concrete evidence in its support, and weighty linguistic considerations tell against it.[2] If Jesus had referred to the heavenly redeemer, he could have employed a complex form, such as *bareh de-enasha*, but there would then have been no reason to confuse self-reference uses of *bar enasha* with the titular use of the complex phrase in the Aramaic transmission of authentic and secondary sayings; the two uses would have been kept distinct both in the Aramaic tradition and in subsequent Greek translations. The consistent use of *ho huios tou anthrōpou* strongly suggests that Aramaic Christians attributed only one use to Jesus.[3]

Another kind of discontinuity must be briefly considered. Is it possible that Jesus' use of *bar enasha* was genuinely ambiguous, as Matthew Black claims, and that the original double entendre was forgotten after Easter?[4] But which half of the double entendre was forgotten? It was argued in chapter 7 that if "strong" and "weak" meanings had both been available, the latter would have been soon abandoned in favor of the former. The presence of "earthly" sayings in the Aramaic tradition, however, suggests that it is the transcendent, apocalyptic connotation that has been forgotten. There is no explicit theological exploitation of the term. Is this probable in a church that fervently prayed *Marana tha*?

In the absence of cogent arguments to the contrary, therefore, it is legitimate to assume that, if Jesus used the term at all, he used it as a modest self-reference, just as the subsequent Aramaic tradition understood it. But did Jesus use the term?

If we are correct in inferring that *bar enasha* did not function in the Aramaic Son of man sayings attributed to Jesus as an apocalyptic title, whether borrowed from Jewish apocalyptic circles or created by Jesus as

---

2. Cf. Casey, "Aramaic Idiom and Son of Man Sayings," p. 233: "The general improbability that *barnash(a)* would be selected for use as a messianic title is wholly supported by the empirical data: we do not have satisfactory evidence that any social group did as a matter of fact take this generally unlikely step." See also Bauckham, "The Son of Man," p. 27.

3. The same argument holds if the distinction were one of oral emphasis rather than of orthography. If the followers of Jesus perceived an important difference between *bar enashá* and *bar enásha*, they would surely have striven to preserve this distinction in divergent Greek translations.

4. Black, "Aramaic Barnasha and the 'Son of Man.'"

an allusion to Dan. 7:13, but rather as a modesty idiom, there remains no reasonable basis for denying its use to Jesus. Since there seems to have been no theological exploitation of the term until the writing of the Fourth Gospel, there is no reason to believe that its application to Jesus was first adopted after Easter.[5] Put conversely, it is inherently more probable that this strange third-person discourse was initiated by Jesus himself than that it was imposed upon him by believers for whom it had no theological significance.

This probability, however, by no means renders authentic all the sayings in our Greek Gospels in which the phrase *ho huios tou anthrōpou* is found. It is very likely that many of these are secondary, at least in their present form. It is even possible that *all* the extant sayings are secondary in this sense. What is being claimed here is that all the secondary sayings, however numerous they may be, are ultimately modeled on genuine sayings in which Jesus spoke about himself by means of this characteristic idiom.

No attempt will be made in this final chapter to examine anew each of the many Son of man sayings in the Gospel tradition for the purpose of assessing for each one the probability of authenticity. Our goal will be more modest. Are there sayings in our extant Gospels for which a credible claim to authenticity can be made?

Bultmann taught us to be exceedingly cautious about statements attributed to Jesus in which he is represented as speaking about his present role, anticipated suffering, and future destiny. This is as true for the "I" sayings as for those employing "the Son of man." In each case we may be dealing with post-Easter prophetic deliverances concerning the meaning of Jesus, such as we find in the Apocalypse (e.g., 1:17f.; 22:16).[6] There is, however, no a priori reason to deny that Jesus did on occasion speak about himself and his mission, as other prophets and religious teachers had done. The evidence suggests that he used both first-person and third-person language for this purpose. Consequently it is possible that some "I" sayings may have begun as "Son of man" sayings, and vice versa.

Mt. 11:19 // Lk. 7:34

In chapter 7 it was argued that the double logion, which in both Matthew and Luke is attached to the parable of the children in the marketplace, originated in Aramaic. It was noted that some scholars find it

---

5. Contra Käsemann, *New Testament Questions of Today*, p. 114.
6. Bultmann, *History*, p. 163. Cf. Boring, *Sayings of the Risen Jesus*, p. 129.

difficult to believe that the Aramaic version contained the self-designation "the Son of man." A. J. B. Higgins, for example, argued that an original "I" saying has been modified by the substitution of *ho huios tou anthrōpou*, regarded by Higgins as a title of majesty that would not have been used by Jesus of himself during his earthly life.[7]

There is no a priori reason for rejecting this suggestion. Assuming that Matthew is dependent on Mark, we have clear evidence at 16:13 that the author has substituted *ton huion tou anthrōpou* for the *me* found at Mk. 8:31. It is not at all impossible that an earlier version of Mt. 11:19 read: "I came eating and drinking. . . ." But is it probable?

J. Jeremias maintained that this substitution happened frequently. After comparing Son of man sayings with similar sayings couched in the first person, he enunciated the rule that, where such parallels exist, the Son of man version of the saying should be viewed as secondary.[8] It is important to note the presupposition underlying this proposal. Jeremias assumed that *ho huios tou anthrōpou* and its Aramaic antecedent both functioned for early Christians as "a messianic title derived from Dan. 7:13."[9] In the preceding chapters this assumption has been challenged. The absence of theological and confessional exploitation of the term strongly suggests that it had denotative rather than connotative force for those who transmitted and added to the stock of Son of man sayings. Thus while *ton huion tou anthrōpou* is secondary to *me* at Mt. 16:13, we found no pressing *theological* reason for Matthew's substitution, and the First Evangelist does not hesitate to remove the phrase at 16:21 (cf. Mk. 8:31).

There are many statements in the Gospels in which Jesus is represented as speaking to his audience in the first person. The tradents apparently felt no pressure to convert the majority of these into third-person language. Consequently, if it is necessary to enunciate a rule about the secondary formation of Son of man sayings, it will be contrary to Jeremias's: *We should assume that it was more natural for Greek tradents to convert Son of man sayings into "I" sayings than vice versa, and the creation of new Son of man sayings was likely to occur only where the tradition provided clear models.*[10]

---

7. Higgins, *Jesus and the Son of Man*, pp. 122f. See also Bornkamm, *Jesus of Nazareth*, pp. 229f.

8. Jeremias, "Die älteste Schicht." Jeremias's proposal seems not to have won many converts.

9. Ibid., p. 165; cf. his *New Testament Theology*, p. 261. Jeremias assumed that *bar enasha* was ambiguous, serving both as an apocalyptic title and as a generic expression ("One came who did eat and drink," *New Testament Theology*, p. 262). A similar position is maintained by Seyoon Kim, *"The 'Son of Man' " as the Son of God*, pp. 32–36. For arguments against this assumption, see chapter 7.

10. Cf. Borsch, *Christian and Gnostic Son of Man*, pp. 1–28.

When we compare Matthew and Luke with Mark, for example, it looks as
if the additional passion sayings have been formulated with *ho huios tou
anthrōpou* rather than first-person language precisely because of the powerful models provided by Mark (e.g., Mt. 26:2; Lk. 17:25 is based on the
same model, although it employs a resumptive *auton* rather than repeating
the idiom itself from the preceding line). The textual glosses of Mt. 18:11
and Lk. 9:56 are modeled on (if not simply repetitions of) Lk. 19:10, which
itself (assuming it is secondary) may have been modeled on Lk. 7:34 // Mt.
11:19. On the other hand, the Gospels contain a number of similar sayings
employing "come" and first-person language (e.g., Mt. 5:17; 9:13; 10:34).
Future sayings were probably formulated with even greater regularity in
Son of man form, since there were so few "I" sayings of this type in the
gospel tradition (in contrast to the relative frequency of future "I" sayings
in the Apocalypse).

Especially significant in this regard is the evidence provided by the important future saying found both in the double tradition (Lk. 12:8f.; cf. Mt.
10:32) and in Mark (8:38). Although we have this saying in two rather
different Greek versions, in both cases first-person language has been
preserved in the first clause. Although *ho huios tou anthrōpou* was for the
Greek tradents not an apocalyptic title but a "name" that could be used
just as appropriately of the earthly Jesus as of the heavenly Lord, there
was apparently no temptation to alter the saying to a more symmetrical
form by substituting *en tō huiō tou anthrōpou* for *en emoi* in the first clause.
Instead we have in Matthew's version clear evidence of the opposite tendency; symmetry is achieved by substituting first-person language for "the
Son of man" in the second clause of each half of the logion.[11]

In the absence of specific evidence to the contrary, therefore, it is
methodologically sounder to presuppose continuity between the Greek
form of Mt. 11:19 // Lk. 7:34 and its Aramaic antecedent. We shall proceed
on the assumption that the saying circulated in Aramaic with *bar enasha* as
the subject of its opening clause.

Can we go further and infer that the double logion as a whole constitutes
an authentic utterance of Jesus? Several considerations have been raised

11. In *Rediscovering the Teaching of Jesus*, pp. 187–91, Perrin claimed that this was not
originally a Son of man saying, arguing that a passive had been used in both clauses, for
which Matthew substituted "I" language and Luke "the Son of man." Lindars, *Jesus Son of
Man*, pp. 52f., proposed that Luke found "I" in his source and substituted "the Son of man"
under the influence of Mk. 8:38. The Markan logion provides independent evidence, however, that the common ancestor of the Q and Markan versions probably had *bar enasha* in the
second clause. Cf. Boring, *Sayings of the Risen Jesus*, p. 166 and n. 91; Kümmel, "Das Verhalten Jesu gegenüber und das Verhalten des Menschensohns," pp. 214f.

against its genuineness. It is claimed that the past tense verbs (*ēlthen*, "came") indicate a later perspective: the saying looks back on the careers of John and Jesus as completed wholes.[12] This judgment is supported by appeal to Bultmann's general principle that sayings in which Jesus speaks of himself and his mission should be regarded with the greatest suspicion.[13] While Bultmann himself considered the possibility that the logion may have been uttered by Jesus using *bar enasha* generically ("a man"), so that only the mistranslation *ho huios tou anthrōpou* may be secondary, Vielhauer insisted that the title is original and that the saying must consequently be seen as having been created after Easter as a christological statement.[14] An early-church perspective is perceived by Wanke in the saying's pessimism regarding the possibility of converting Israel to faith in Christ.[15]

Bultmann's historical skepticism regarding the "I" sayings attributed to Jesus is justified in principle, but, as Bultmann himself comments, "There are no possible grounds for objecting to the idea that Jesus could have spoken in the first person about himself and his coming; that need be no more than what befits his prophetic consciousness."[16] With regard to Mt. 11:19 // Lk. 7:34, therefore, the case should not be decided in advance on the basis of Bultmann's methodological skepticism. We must ask instead: Is this logion more credible as a product of the early church or as an authentic saying of Jesus?

To begin with, it must be emphasized, against Vielhauer, that the saying in itself, apart from its context in a post-Easter collection of sayings and/or the Gospels of Matthew and Luke, need not be seen as looking back on Jesus' career as a completed whole. As Jeremias points out, *ēlthen* renders an Aramaic idiom meaning "intend" or "have as one's task."[17] Jeremias is supported by E. Arens, who found additional rabbinic instances of the idiom, including the (later) formula, "the Scripture comes to teach. . . ."[18] To this we can add the observation that, whether based on the Aramaic idiom or not, the Greek verbs meaning "come" are frequently used metaphorically in the New Testament. When we read in Mt. 21:32 that "John

---

12. Bultmann, *History*, p. 155; cf. Vielhauer, "Jesus und der Menschensohn," p. 164; Lührmann, *Die Redaktion der Logienquelle*, pp. 29f.; Kloppenburg, *The Formation of Q*, p. 112.
    13. Bultmann, *History*, p. 153.
    14. Vielhauer, "Jesus und der Menschensohn," p. 165.
    15. Wanke, *"Bezugs- und Kommentarworte" in den synoptischen Evangelien*, p. 40.
    16. Bultmann, *History*, p. 153.
    17. Jeremias, "Die älteste Schicht," p. 167; cf. Colpe, "Ho huios tou anthrōpou," TDNT 8, p. 431 n. 238.
    18. Arens, *The* **ēlthon**-*Sayings*, p. 267.

came to you in the way of righteousness," we recognize that the verb functions very differently than if the statement read "John came to you from Galilee." In the same way we read about the necessity of *skandala* "coming," where our idiom would use the verb "to be" ("there will necessarily be offenses"). In Mt. 11:19 // Lk. 7:34, as in Mt. 21:32, "came" means "make a public appearance" or "emerge as a public figure." Because both John and Jesus were regarded as prophets, we can suspect that in these passages "came" is roughly synonymous with "sent" (cf. Jn. 1:6; Mt. 15:24); they have been sent by God with a prophetic commission to fulfill.

Given this function of *ēlthen*, it can be argued that the creator of the saying, whether Jesus or a member of the post-Easter church, assumed the perspective of the time of John's ministry, not a postmortem point of view. The saying attributes to John's contemporary opponents a statement in the present tense: "They *say*, 'He *has* a demon' "; they do not look back upon his completed ministry with the judgment, "He *had* a demon." This, of course, does not suffice to prove that the saying originated during John's ministry, but it should caution us against assuming that the saying necessarily looks back at that ministry from a much later date. The same perspective is reflected in the second half of the double logion, where Jesus' detractors are represented as speaking in the present tense (*legousin*): "Behold, a glutton and a drunkard. . . ." The interjection "Behold" (*idou*) is normally used in direct discourse with reference to a current rather than a historical state of affairs (cf. Mt. 12:47, 49).

If "the Son of man" is not here a christological title, Vielhauer's main objection to authenticity is overcome. Wanke's suggestion that pessimism regarding the mission to Israel reflects a later date can be dismissed when the double logion is treated independently of its present context; in itself the logion refers to the resistance of an unspecified number of opponents, not to the response of the people as a whole. Is it possible, however, that the logion never had a separate existence but was created precisely for its present context, that is, that it was fashioned as a "commentary word"? In this case, the parable will have been understood as illustrating the Jewish-Christian conviction that, whether God's messengers bring good news or bad to Israel, the response is rejection. The double saying may have been made to make this meaning more explicit.

This is not an impossible explanation of the logion's origin, but it is improbable. It is unlikely that a Christian Jew concerned about the mission to Israel would have chosen to refer to John the Baptist. Since Jesus was remembered as having offered to his people both threats of judgment and promises of redemption, his activities could be seen as illustrating both the piping and wailing of the parable; there was no need to introduce an allusion to a rival figure. Moreover, as E. Schweizer has emphasized, it is hardly credible that this rival figure would be presented as Jesus' equal; unlike most other allusions to John in the Gospels, there is here no subordination of John to Jesus—he is not reduced to being simply a witness to the Messiah.[19] If, however, this postulated commentator had nonetheless felt it necessary to allegorize the parable by reference to two contrasting figures, it is most unlikely that he or she would have gone beyond noting that John and Jesus, despite the diversity of their messages, had both been rejected. What would have motivated the commentator to introduce the uncomplimentary and unedifying report of the slanderous charge against Jesus?

Since none of the objections to authenticity are persuasive, and since the logion makes no theological point beyond observing that two of God's contemporary messengers are being slandered by some in Israel, there is no justification for regarding it as secondary.

If it is authentic, what does it tell us about Jesus? It confirms the picture we receive from various narratives in the Gospels that portray Jesus as reclining at sumptuous banquets (e.g., Mk. 2:15; Lk. 7:36). Jesus was no ascetic; he was open to the charge, although here greatly exaggerated, of enjoying food and wine in "bad company."[20] If the use of *bar enasha* here is also authentic as argued above, we learn from the logion that Jesus used this modest self-reference when alluding to the prophetic task he shared with John.

Lk. 12:10 // Mt. 12:32

In attempting to determine the point of origin of this logion in the tradition, our first decision must be concerning its relationship to Mk. 3:28f. Do these derive from a single saying or from different ones?

Since the time of Wellhausen it has been commonly argued that the Markan and Q versions represent divergent renderings of a single Aramaic saying employing *bar enasha*. Wellhausen postulated an intermediate common ancestor in Greek employing *tō huiō tou anthrōpou* in the dative

19. Schweizer, "Der Menschensohn," p. 200.

20. Daube, *Appeasement or Resistance*, pp. 25f., argues forcefully that the charge raised against Jesus is that he is the "disobedient son" of Dt. 21:20, "whose crime consists of a general, calculated, incorrigible defiance of those in authority, the feasting and drinking being only its most visible mark." While this claim may be true, it cannot be certainly demonstrated, since the logion contrasts Jesus' behavior with that of John the Baptist, who "came neither eating nor drinking."

("Everything can be forgiven the son of man"). To avoid confusion, Mark changed this generic expression to its plural equivalent, "the sons of men," while the Q tradition altered the structure of the clause so as to make "the Son of man" the object of the slander rather than the recipient of forgiveness ("Everything against the Son of man can be forgiven").[21]

This proposal is not convincing, because the Greek phrase *tō huiō tou anthrōpou* could hardly have been taken by anyone in the early church as a generic expression.[22] That is to say, if Harnack's common ancestor is to be conceivable, the divergence must have occurred at the Aramaic level and have involved *bar enasha*. In this case, however, the Q version becomes improbable. Wellhausen and his followers ask us to believe that a post-Easter Aramaic tradent, familiar with both the generic use of *bar enasha* and Jesus' use of the term as a self-designation, chose the more difficult interpretation, namely, that the logion declared that sins committed against the now-exalted Jesus were forgivable while sins against the Spirit were not. As Fiebig observed decades ago, such a translation error is theoretically possible but hardly probable.[23]

Because the point of the logion is to establish a contrast between forgivable and unforgivable forms of slander, it is probable that the first half of the saying, like the second, referred to the *object* of slander. The Markan version, by spoiling the symmetry, characterizes itself as secondary in relation to the Q version.[24] If a common *Vorlage* is to be presupposed, Tödt may well be correct in surmising that Mark (or his source) was scandalized by the Aramaic antecedent of the Q version, which seemed to suggest that blasphemy against the church's exalted Lord was forgivable.[25]

Gundry, however, cautions us against too quickly assuming a common origin; the variations are sufficiently numerous and linguistically significant to warrant the supposition of separate but similar sayings.[26] Because of the uncertainty of the relationship with Mk. 3:28f., we are justified in examining Lk. 12:10 independently of the possibility that Mk. 3:28f. may represent a reformulation.

This move, however, does not relieve us of the necessity of asking whether Lk. 12:10 constitutes a mistranslation of an Aramaic saying in which *bar*

---

21. Wellhausen, *Einleitung in die drei ersten Evangelien*, p. 67; cf. also Bultmann, *History*, p. 131.
22. Cf. Boring, "The Unforgivable Sin Logion," p. 275.
23. Fiebig, *Der Menschensohn*, p. 62.
24. Contra Boring, "The Unforgivable Sin Logion," p. 278.
25. Tödt, *Son of Man*, p. 120. Such a response would result from Mark's (or his predecessor's) knowledge of the denotation of "the Son of man"; we need not concur with Todt's understanding of the connotation of the term.
26. Gundry, *Matthew*, p. 239.

enasha was used generically ("Whoever speaks a [slanderous] word against a human being can be forgiven, but whoever blasphemes the Holy Spirit will not be forgiven"). Attractive at first sight, this proposal raises more problems than it solves. In the first place, we are asked to believe that the Aramaic tradents of the sayings of Jesus treasured a logion that was nothing but an axiom of Jewish religious life. Everyone knew that it was infinitely more serious to blaspheme God (or God's Torah, or God's Spirit) than to speak ill of other humans. Even if such a truism were credited to Jesus, however, can we believe that any Aramaic-speaking Christian would have "corrected" it by reinterpreting *bar enasha* as Jesus' self-designation and thus translating it as *ton huion tou anthrōpou*? What could possibly impel the novel interpretation that blasphemy against Jesus, now honored as heavenly Lord, was more forgivable than blasphemy against the Spirit, which the risen Jesus had poured out on his church?[27] In considering this question, we must remember that the early Christians were not much interested in historical reconstruction; it would not occur to them to create and attribute to Jesus a statement that was more relevant to his time than theirs. Assuming that *bar enasha* could be taken in either way, it is entirely improbable that a translator would have selected the more difficult alternative on the assumption that Jesus had referred exclusively to his earthly career, not his heavenly estate.

If the saying is not the mistranslation of an Aramaic saying, should it be viewed as the creation of a Greek-speaking Christian who was unaware of the ambiguities of *bar enasha*? This possibility cannot be arbitrarily dismissed, since the presence of an Aramaism in the idiom "speak a word against," while urged by M. Black, is not clearly demonstrable.[28] It could be hypothesized that the Greek saying was not composed as an independent word of warning but as a gloss on the Beelzebul narrative (just as the glossator of Mt. 18:11 wished to comment on the parable of the lost sheep and the accompanying logia). But why would such a commentator create the first half of the saying, which in fact is in tension with the story as we have it in its three Synoptic versions (Mk. 3:22–27; Mt. 12:22–30; Lk. 11:14–23)? The point of the narrative is that in slandering Jesus, his opponents are in fact slandering God's Spirit. A glossator can conceivably have created something like Mk. 3:28f., but hardly the Q version. Would it ever have occurred to one of Paul's converts to propose to the church that

---

27. Cf. A. Y. Collins, "The Origins of the Designation of Jesus as 'Son of Man,' " p. 399.
28. Black, *Aramaic Approach*, p. 195, is opposed by Kloppenborg, *Formation of Q*, p. 57 n. 59, who points to a similar expression in Plato's *Apology* 37B.

Anathema Iēsous was more forgivable than *Anathema Pneuma Hagion* (cf. 1 Cor. 12:3)?

These considerations, together with the probability that "speak a word against" was an idiom more prevalent in Aramaic than in Greek, tip the scales in favor of an Aramaic origin for the saying. In view of the difficulties encountered above in postulating a generic use of *bar enasha* in the Aramaic logion, we will further assume that in this earlier version too, Jesus was represented as speaking of slander directed against himself. Since it is improbable that any early Christian would have created such a saying, the best explanation of its origin is that it is a "hard saying" deriving from Jesus himself.

If authentic, what does it reveal concerning its creator? It suggests that Jesus carefully distinguished between ad hominem attacks and challenges to his claim of Spirit empowerment. Assuming that Mt. 5:38–48 is largely authentic, we can infer that Jesus was prepared to pray for personal enemies but saw no point in praying for those who witnessed his victory over the evil spirits of Satan's kingdom but stubbornly refused to acknowledge that it was the presence of God's Spirit that made this success possible. By calling good evil, they put themselves beyond the pale of divine forgiveness.

Lk. 12:8f. (Cf. Mt. 10:32f.)

In our consideration of the possible authenticity of this logion, we will presuppose conclusions reached at earlier points in this study, namely, that the double logion circulated in Aramaic, with first-person language in the first clause and *bar enasha* in the second clause of each half, and that *bar enasha* functioned as an idiom of self-reference.[29] It ought, therefore, to be treated as more nearly related to the "earthly" sayings than to the apocalyptic logia, inasmuch as it refers to a future role of Jesus rather than to an apocalyptic role of a heavenly redeemer and/or heavenly judge.[30]

Attempts have been made to demonstrate the inauthenticity of the logion on form-critical grounds. Käsemann, for example, opposed Bultmann's

29. At no point in its early history was the saying perceived as distinguishing between Jesus and "the Son of man," not even with reference to two periods of activity of the same person, as urged by Vielhauer, "Jesus und der Menschensohn," p. 146; he cites G. Iber's "Überlieferungsgeschichtliche Untersuchungen zum Begriff des Menschensohns im Neuen Testament," p. 55. Unfortunately, this dissertation was not available to me.

30. Boring, *Sayings of the Risen Jesus*, p. 278 n. 92, suggests that the Son of man will function both as judge and as Paraclete/guarantor, as in Revelation.

supposition of authenticity by describing the logion as a "sentence of holy law," a form attributable to prophets in the early church.[31] It is moot whether the saying is adequately described in this way.[32] Even if we accept Käsemann's form-critical analysis, however, it by no means follows that the saying must on that account be secondary.[33] Jesus himself was also an eschatological prophet; if early Christian prophets made use of the form, there is no a priori reason for excluding the possibility that they derived the form from Jesus or, more precisely, that they followed Jesus in borrowing the form from the Old Testament—an excellent model is provided by 1 Sam. 2:30.[34] The issue of authenticity, therefore, must be decided on the basis of the logion's content and implied background.

Many have argued that the saying cannot have been created until after Easter because it presupposes a situation of legal persecution.[35] There can be little doubt that persecution provided motivation for the cherishing and transmission of the saying. The complex in which it has been preserved in Matthew 10 has been shaped by the persecution experience of Jewish Christians who have attempted to convert other Jews to faith in Christ.[36] This setting does not, however, require that the saying originated in post-Easter persecution.

In the first place, the language of the logion does not imply *legal* persecution. No evidence has been discovered in support of the common assumption that confession of faith in Jesus as the Christ constituted a crime in Palestinian Jewish law.[37] If Jewish-Christian missionaries were occasionally (not regularly!) hailed into court and punished with flogging, it was probably on a charge of breach of peace, although our evidence at this point is unsatisfactory.[38] There is no evidence that rank-and-file Christians

31. Käsemann, "Sätze heiligen Rechtes im Neuen Testament"; for the English translation, see Käsemann, *New Testament Questions of Today*, pp. 66–81.

32. Kümmel, "Das Verhalten Jesu gegenüber und das Verhalten des Menschensohns," pp. 221f., surveys criticisms that have been made of Käsemann's thesis.

33. Borsch, *Christian and Gnostic Son of Man*, p. 18, points to Mk. 11:25f.; Mt. 6:12f. par.; Mt. 5:7; Lk. 6:37f.

34. Cf. Käsemann, *New Testament Questions*, p. 77.

35. E.g., Vielhauer, "Gottesreich und Menschensohn," p. 70. See also his "Jesus und der Menschensohn," p. 144: "Da in den beiden Nachsätzen unleugbar eine himmlische Gerichtsszene geschildert wird, muss in den beiden Vordersätzen eine irdische Gerichtsszene gemeint sein. Der forensische Charakter von Lk 12,8f kann nicht bestritten werden."

36. Hare, *Persecution in Matthew*, pp. 96–114, especially p. 101.

37. Contra Burkill, "The Competence of the Sanhedrin," p. 80: "It is quite possible . . . that St. Mark's account of the nocturnal trial before the sanhedrin (14:55–65) is basically a reflection of the fact that certain Christians had been put to death at the order of the Jewish authorities for committing blasphemy in identifying the crucified Jesus with the promised Messiah." Cf. Hare, *Persecution in Matthew*, pp. 25–29.

38. See Hare, *Persecution in Matthew*, pp. 43–46.

in Jewish towns in Palestine were subject to arrest and trial on account of their faith, and it is unlikely that they were subjected to excommunication.[39]

The persecution that Aramaic-speaking Christians faced was much more informal. The more outspoken among them had to face verbal and physical abuse (cf. Mt. 5:11, 39), estrangement from their families (10:34–37), and social ostracism (Lk. 6:22).[40] There were many informal situations, consequently, in which Christians could find themselves required to confess or deny a relationship to Jesus. Instructive is the coupling of the two verbs "confess" and "deny" in Jn. 1:20, where there is no question of a legal context. The paradigm for refusing to "confess" is, of course, the narrative of Peter's denial, which is also informal rather than forensic (Mk. 14:66–72 par.; Jn. 18:25–27).

Second, as Kümmel points out, the forum before which the confessing and denying are to take place is simply *tōn anthrōpōn*, that is, human beings in general.[41] This means, of course, that we can no longer limit the confessing situation to the post-Easter era of the church.[42]

No gospel narrative, Synoptic or Johannine, suggests that Jesus' disciples were subject to violent persecution during his lifetime, but we have every reason to believe that their allegiance to Jesus aroused the hostility of others. On a priori grounds alone, it is to be expected that those who abandoned their families and occupations to join the itinerant prophet-exorcist were the objects of public ridicule and abuse. If the consensus that Mt. 5:39 is dominical is justified, we can surmise that it may have been addressed in part to disciples who had been publicly insulted on account of their folly in following Jesus.[43]

It is sometimes objected that Jesus cannot possibly have made so grandiose a claim. Teeple, for example, proposed: "If a saying makes salvation depend upon loyalty to Jesus' person, it can hardly be a genuine logion of Jesus."[44] Such an opinion appears to be unjustified. Surely one of the least contested sayings of Jesus is the incredibly harsh declaration "Follow me,

---

39. Despite the thrice-repeated claim of the Fourth Gospel (9:22; 12:42; 16:2). In the absence of corroborative evidence, it is better to take these verses as representing either unfulfilled predictions or a local practice unknown elsewhere. In view of Matthew's particular interest in persecution, his omission of excommunication is inexplicable if such was a widespread policy. See ibid., pp. 48–56.

40. Ibid., pp. 53–58.

41. Kümmel, "Das Verhalten Jesu gegenüber und das Verhalten des Menschensohns," p. 218.

42. Cf. ibid.

43. Bultmann, *History*, p. 105, includes Mt. 5:39b–41 among sayings that he regards as "characteristic of the preaching of Jesus."

44. Teeple, "The Origin of the Son of Man Christology," p. 222. Similarly Lindars, *Jesus Son of Man*, p. 53, but rejected on p. 54.

and let the dead bury their own dead" (Mt. 8:22; cf. Lk. 9:60).[45] This can be understood only as the utterance of a man who was absolutely convinced of the importance of his cause and its divine origin. The same attitude is displayed in the parable of the two builders, with which the Q sermon ends (Mt. 7:24–27; Lk. 6:47–49): eschatological salvation depends on strict adherence to *Jesus'* words.[46]

Did Jesus anticipate a heavenly role as witness at the judgment? Nothing in his cultural world inhibited such an expectation.[47] Indeed, dominical sayings whose authenticity is seldom questioned attribute this function to others: "The queen of the South will arise at the judgment with this generation and condemn it" (Mt. 12:42 // Lk. 11:31; similarly "the men of Nineveh," Mt. 12:41 and Lk. 11:32). Lindars is therefore fully justified in asserting of Jesus: "Naturally, insofar as he thought of the divine judgment in realistic terms, he would expect to be there, and, as God's spokesman, to have an important position in the proceedings."[48] The emphasis, for Lindars, is not on Jesus' status but on his function in the divine economy: the response to Jesus is of ultimate importance, "not because Jesus holds a formal eschatological position, but because it is his own teaching from God which is at stake."[49]

Nothing in the logion precludes a post-Easter origin, but this is rendered unlikely by the use of *bar enasha* in the second half of each part (assuming, with Lindars, that the earliest antecedent of Lk. 12:9 contained *bar enasha*).[50] Since the postulated Christian prophet would have been familiar with sayings such as Mt. 11:19 // Lk. 7:34, in which Jesus speaks of his present activity using *bar enasha*, why would he or she have used the idiom in the second clause only? Poetic symmetry would be better served by using *bar enasha* in both clauses. It cannot be maintained that the creator used the term in the second clause only because *bar enasha* was felt to be particularly appropriate as a designation for Jesus' postmortem existence: in this case it would have been fitting to use the phrase in the first clause as well, since, from this later perspective, the new oracle was a word of the heavenly Lord and concerned a Christian's confession or denial of this exalted Christ, not the earthly Jesus. It would have been more natural, however, for the creator to use first-person language in both clauses, especially if he or she

45. Hengel, *The Charismatic Leader and His Followers*, pp. 3–15.
46. Cf. Kümmel, "Das Verhalten Jesu gegenüber und das Verhalten des Menschensohns," p. 223.
47. Cf. Schweizer, "Der Menschensohn," pp. 193f., 205.
48. Lindars, *Jesus Son of Man*. p. 57.
49. Ibid., p. 56.
50. Ibid., p. 53.

were a prophet like the author of the Apocalypse (". . . I will confess his name before my Father and before his angels," Rev. 3:5).

This alternation of first-person and third-person language is more readily understandable if the logion is authentic. Jesus is likely to have felt a greater need for the modesty idiom in the second clause than in the first, whereas a post-Easter prophet would be unlikely to make such a distinction on his behalf. As illustrated in the line from the Apocalypse just quoted, early Christian prophets felt no need to attribute modesty of speech to their risen Lord.

If the logion is essentially authentic, what does it reveal concerning its author? It is not to be regarded as the utterance of a megalomaniac. Nor should it be treated as a christological statement in any direct sense; it does not give us Jesus' own definition of his rank and status in God's plan of salvation. It does, however, betray Jesus' profound, yet modest, conviction concerning his central importance in God's evolving eschatological drama. To deny him, Jesus informed his followers, was to deny oneself a place in the kingdom God was inaugurating through him. To shrink from confessing him among those who were rejecting him was equivalent to denying that God had chosen to act in and through him. It was not so much loyalty to his person that Jesus demanded of his followers as loyalty to his vision of God's activity. In the imminent denouement of the great drama, he would witness for and against the disciples who had witnessed for and against him.

Mt. 8:20 // Lk. 9:58

Bultmann hypothesized that this saying originated as a secular proverb about the human condition: "Man, homeless in this world, is contrasted with the wild beasts."[51] Even the postulation of such a proverb is problematic, since it is so manifestly false; in every human culture humans create shelters for themselves. Even the nomads of Nabataea had more sumptuous accommodations than the foxes (or jackals!) and birds. Even if we were to assume the existence of so pessimistic a proverb, however, its application to Jesus would be farfetched. Does the reformulated saying wish to proclaim that the Messiah shares the universal, natural homelessness of men and women in contrast to the animals, whose resting places are provided by God?

---

51. Bultmann, *History*, p. 28; cf. p. 98.

Much more credible is the proposal that the implicit contrast is between the speaker and other humans: Most people have far better homes than foxes and birds, but this human is homeless.[52]

It is objected that this cannot have been an utterance of Jesus because it is contradicted by what we know of his life; the Gospels frequently place him in a home in Capernaum.[53] There are two obvious answers to this objection. In the first place, it appears that during one or more periods of his ministry, Jesus was truly an itinerant, if not a fugitive (Lk. 13:31–33); such a saying could reflect his sense of homelessness at such times. Second, we ought not to assume too quickly that the statement was intended to be taken at its most literal level. After all, even a fugitive Jesus could lay his head down on a stone like his ancestor Jacob (Gen. 28:11). It is therefore possible that the utterance refers figuratively to the rejection he experienced from family, neighbors, and religious leaders.[54]

P. Hoffmann concedes that, apart from its use of the apocalyptic title "the Son of man," he sees no reason to question the saying's genuineness and proposes that it was perhaps originally an "I" saying.[55] Many who are convinced that "the Son of man" functioned in earliest Christianity as an apocalyptic title resist proposals that seek to understand the saying by eliminating any consideration of the title's contribution to it. To Higgins, for example, the logion is clearly secondary; "Our saying reads like a preacher's exhortation concerning discipleship of Jesus the Son of man. As Jesus on earth was rejected by his people and wandered homeless, so must the disciples expect to be."[56] This is not an impossible proposal, but once the identification of "the Son of man" as an apocalyptic title has been given up, there is no particular reason for ascribing the saying to a Christian preacher rather than to Jesus. As Casey points out, if *bar enasha* is an indirect way of referring to Jesus, it becomes harder to conceive of the saying as the product of the early church.[57]

Casey and Lindars find here another example of the generic use of *bar enasha*. In this instance, according to Lindars, the term refers not to men or humans in general but to that class of persons indicated by the context, namely, Jesus and his prospective disciples. "The generic article specifies

52. Cf. Zahn, *Matthäus*, p. 356.

53. Cf. Teeple, "The Origin of the Son of Man Christology," p. 235, and Vielhauer, "Jesus und der Menschensohn," p. 161.

54. Cf. Marshall, "The Synoptic Son of Man Sayings in Recent Discussion," p. 340f.

55. Hoffmann, *Studien zur Theologie der Logienquelle*, p. 92 n. 46. Similarly Colpe, "Ho huios tou anthrōpou," TDNT 8, p. 433.

56. Higgins, *Jesus and the Son of Man*, p. 126.

57. Casey, "The Jackals and the Son of Man," p. 13.

an individual, but leaves his identity ambiguous. It could be a self-reference (the one, i.e. myself, whom you wish to follow) or it could be the disciple himself (the one who follows me)."[58] The irony is lost, Lindars objects, when *bar enasha* is treated simply as a self-reference. Similarly, Casey proposes that "the saying will clearly have referred to the whole company of disciples who were accompanying Jesus."[59] In response to Lindars, R. Bauckham points out that it is by no means obvious that " 'the generic usage is *essential* to the purpose of the saying.' . . . If 'the Son of man' were an exclusive self-reference . . . it would still be a perfectly adequate reply to the disciples' words in Mt. 8:19 // Lk. 9:57."[60]

Those who are not convinced that *bar enasha* was completely nontitular ask: But if the saying is authentic and the phrase has no theological meaning, why did Jesus use it here? It cannot be said in response that the saying makes an exalted claim and consequently indirect language was chosen for modesty's sake. As far as can be determined from the saying itself and its present context in the Gospels, it could just as well have been formulated in first-person language, as is the case in other discipleship sayings (e.g., Mk. 1:17; 2:14; 8:34). On the other hand, Vermes may be correct in surmising that *bar enasha* is employed in reference to "humiliation, danger or death" as well as in statements calling for modesty.[61] Here God's ultimate messenger alludes to the shame of rejection at the hand of those who should have welcomed him. To become his disciple is to share his shame.

Lk. 11:30 (Cf. Mt. 12:40)

It is possible that an earlier form of this logion was uttered by Jesus as a statement about his prophetic ministry. Caution is demanded because of the probability that the exceptive clause ("except for the sign of Jonah," v. 29) is a secondary addition to an earlier version in which Jesus was represented as declaring unequivocally, "No sign shall be given to this generation" (cf. Mk. 8:12).[62] On the other hand, the exceptive clause may have been added by a tradent precisely for the purpose of reconciling the refusal of a sign with another, independent "sign" logion in which Jesus compared his God-authorized prophetic ministry with that of Jonah. There seem to be no strong reasons for denying such a logion to Jesus.

58. Lindars, "Response to Richard Bauckham," p. 38.
59. Casey, "The Jackals and the Son of Man," p. 10.
60. Bauckham, "The Son of Man," p. 25.
61. Vermes, "The Use of *bar nash/bar nasha* in Jewish Aramaic," p. 327.
62. Cf. Edwards, *Sign of Jonah*, p. 80.

If this saying is authentic, the *bar enasha* idiom was presumably chosen by Jesus for modesty's sake. Here he makes the stupendous claim that he is the ultimate expression of God's will-to-save prior to the impending judgment (Nineveh was to be destroyed forty days after Jonah's appearance).

Mk. 2:10

Once it is conceded that *bar enasha* does not function as an apocalyptic title in Mk. 2:10, it is possible to attribute the saying to Jesus, while acknowledging that demonstration of its authenticity is impossible. If uttered by Jesus, was *bar enasha* here used generically, as maintained by Casey and Lindars?[63] It would almost seem that Matthew so understood it, in view of his redactional conclusion: "And they glorified God, who had given such authority to *men*" (9:8). Given Matthew's understanding of *ho huios tou anthrōpou*, however, as presented in chapter 5 above, this view is most unlikely. The alteration in v. 8 can be readily understood without postulating that Matthew was aware of the multiple functions of the underlying Aramaic phrase.[64]

The possibility of a generic use cannot be categorically denied. That is, our knowledge of Jesus and his socioreligious context does not permit us to assert that Jesus claimed to be the only person to whom God had delegated authority to forgive sins. The Prayer of Nabonidus discovered among the Dead Sea documents refers to a Jewish exorcist who pardoned the sins of Nabonidus.[65] The question is moot, however, because there is no need to infer the generic use. While the opponents in the narrative regard it as blasphemy for anyone to claim such authority, Jesus' response focuses not on the issue of whether there are others who claim it but on his own claim: "But that you may know that *bar enasha* has authority to forgive sins on earth. . . ."

If this is indeed a genuine instance of Jesus' use of the modesty idiom, its appropriateness is obvious, requiring no comment.

The Passion Sayings

If *bar enasha* was an idiom employed by Jesus when speaking of his vocation and destiny, we may expect it to appear in statements in which

---

63. Casey, *Son of Man*, pp. 228f.; Lindars, *Jesus Son of Man*, pp. 44–47.
64. This point is maintained also by Lindars, *Jesus Son of Man*, p. 46.
65. The relevant portion of the text is translated by Vermes, *Jesus the Jew*, p. 67.

he spoke about his death. It is not improbable that Jesus anticipated a violent death. Herod's execution of John the Baptist must have revived the old belief that true prophets are persecuted by Israel. Jesus apparently expected that the kingdom of God would be established in the near future but disclaimed any knowledge of its date.[66] While he instructed his followers to pray for its coming (Mt. 6:10), he had to reckon with the possibility that he would suffer violence before the kingdom arrived.

Unfortunately, general considerations of this kind are of almost no help when it comes to dealing with the Son of man passion sayings. While it is possible that Jesus predicted his own demise in a statement employing the *bar enasha* idiom, this does not enable us to identify any of the extant sayings as authentic, since all can be regarded as products of early Christian reflection on the passion and resurrection narratives.[67]

It can, however, be argued with some cogency that behind all the passion sayings in Mark and their derivatives in Matthew and Luke lies at least one pre-Markan logion that served as a model for the very different Johannine version (Jn. 3:14; cf. 8:28; 12:34), since there is insufficient evidence in support of the view that the Fourth Evangelist was dependent on Mark.[68] Despite the intense efforts of many careful scholars, however, no consensus has emerged concerning the shape and content of the postulated pre-Markan saying. There is no certainty that it originated in Aramaic.[69]

It would be fruitless at this point to review the extensive debate regarding which of the Markan sayings has the best claim to represent the earliest version.[70] We must rest content with a more modest goal. Is it likely that the earliest passion saying, one anterior to both Mark and John, derived from Jesus himself rather than from post-Easter reflection on his death?

There is little that can be urged in favor of a positive answer to this question except the presumption that it would be more natural for a Christian creator of such a saying to attribute first-person language to Jesus rather than this unusual third-person idiom. The employment of *bar enasha* is not adequately justified by the hypothesis that the Danielic figure "one like a son of man" was perceived as representing the suffering saints of the

---

66. I regard Mk. 13:32 as a "hard saying" that probably preserves a genuine reminiscence, even though the present formulation employing "the Son" as a title for Jesus may well be secondary.

67. Cf. Wrede, *Messianic Secret*, pp. 82–100; Schweizer, "Der Menschensohn."

68. Pace Barrett, *John*, pp. 34–37. Black, "The Son of Man Problem in Recent Research and Debate," p. 317, proposes that Jn. 3:14 may be closer to the earliest formulation than any of the Markan sayings.

69. See n. 43 in chapter 7 above.

70. See chapter 6 above.

Most High (Dan. 7:13f., 25–27).[71] We have argued in chapter 7 that there is insufficient evidence that the Aramaic phrase behind *ho huios tou anthrōpou* was regarded as a title referring to the Danielic vision. Moreover, the connection between the exalted figure of Dan. 7:13f. and the suffering of the saints is tenuous in the extreme unless a corporate understanding of the figure is adopted. In this case, however, there is no validity in the suggestion that the passage speaks of the suffering of a specific individual called "the Son of man." Nor can this proposal be rescued by arguing that later uses of the Danielic scene in 4 Ezra and 2 Enoch attest the concept of a suffering Son of man, since they borrow certain features of the servant of Deutero-Isaiah.[72] Even if this last claim could be defended, it does nothing to support the association of the Danielic "son of man" with suffering, since the later writings do not borrow the motif of *suffering* from either Isaiah 40–55 or Daniel 7!

If we are justified, therefore, in postulating that the earliest model for the Son of man passion sayings was provided by Jesus himself, we can infer that his use of *bar enasha* was prompted by the feeling that indirect language was appropriate when speaking of one's own death.[73] If he declared that *bar enasha* must be killed, he was undoubtedly referring to divine necessity. He may have believed that his death was prophesied in Scripture, but we have no means of inferring that he had a specific passage in mind; he may have simply been giving expression to a profound conviction that whatever happened to him was in accordance with God's plan.

It cannot be demonstrated that Jesus clearly and firmly taught that his death was to have saving power (Mk. 10:45), because the post-Easter church should otherwise have been unanimous in its interpretation of the cross. C. H. Dodd's startling claim, "The Jerusalem *kerygma* does not assert that Christ died *for our sins*" has been reaffirmed by J. Roloff, who identifies three different ways of interpreting Jesus' death in the early church.[74]

One of the earliest, the "contrast-schema," whose *Sitz im Leben* was the mission to Israel, emphasized the resurrection: "You crucified, but God raised" (Acts 2:23f.). Here Jesus was presented as the suffering Righteous One par excellence, with no reflection on the soteriological effect of the

---

71. Moule, *Phenomenon*, p. 83; Hooker, *The Son of Man in Mark*, pp. 27–30; Barrett, *Jesus and the Gospel Tradition*, pp. 41–45. This position is critiqued by Casey, *Son of Man*, pp. 39, 205.

72. Jeremias, *New Testament Theology*, p. 272.

73. Cf. Vermes, *Jesus the Jew*, pp. 181f.; examples from rabbinic literature are provided on p. 164.

74. Dodd, *The Apostolic Preaching and Its Developments*, p. 25; Roloff, "Anfänge der soteriologischen Deutung des Todes Jesu." Roloff cites Dodd in p. 39 n. 2.

crucifixion. A second pattern, which Roloff calls the "salvation-historical-causal," emphasizes that Christ's death was the fulfillment of Scripture. This understanding is reflected in two different sets of passion announcements: (1) Mk. 8:31a; 9:12b; Lk. 17:25; and (2) Mk. 9:31a; 14:41c; Lk. 24:7. He argues that in this second interpretation the Scriptures referred to are primarily the psalms about the suffering righteous one that are alluded to in the passion narrative and *not* Isaiah 53, insisting, correctly, that the use of *paradidosthai* does not demonstrate a reference to the latter. It was only through reflection on the meaning of the Lord's Supper, Roloff proposes, that the third schema, "Christ died for us," developed. The antecedent of Mk. 10:45 and Lk. 22:27 originated as an interpretation of the Last Supper tradition; Jesus' "service" was understood as manifested supremely in his sacrificial death. Mk. 10:45b, according to Roloff, probably never had a verbally corresponding line in the antecedent of Lk. 22:27, but it finds its narrative equivalent in the context.[75] He concedes that, in view of the uncertainty concerning the authenticity of the extant forms of the bread and cup words, it cannot be insisted that Jesus himself interpreted his dying as a service performed on behalf of his followers or "the many," but he urges that it was in any case a very early interpretation, and one that was in continuity with Jesus' attitude toward sinners.[76]

R. H. Fuller's recent proposal that authentic elements in the passion sayings can be identified by eliminating those phrases that reflect the passion narrative, kerygma, and liturgy is worthy of further consideration.[77] On this basis he accepts shortened forms of Mk. 9:31, 14:21, 14:41, and 10:45 as genuine.

For the purposes of this study it is sufficient to urge the possibility that Jesus spoke of his anticipated death in indirect language employing the *bar enasha* idiom. It is unlikely that any consensus can be achieved regarding the precise Aramaic formulation of such an utterance.

The Apocalyptic Sayings

If *bar enasha* was used by Jesus as a modest self-designation, it is unlikely that any of the apocalyptic Son of man sayings are authentic. They conform so closely to the expectation of Jesus' Parousia that soon prevailed in the post-Easter church that all can be readily explained on

---

75. Roloff, "Anfänge der soteriologischen Deutung des Todes Jesu," p. 59.
76. Ibid., pp. 62f.
77. Fuller, "The Son of Man: A Reconsideration," pp. 212f.

this basis.[78] To put it the other way, if any of these sayings are authentic, it will be impossible to demonstrate this fact, since they can be more easily understood as church products than as statements of Jesus; in no instance is Jesus represented as predicting both his resurrection after a violent death and his Parousia, or promising that *bar enasha* will come again.

Leaving this heuristic problem aside for the moment, we may ask: If Jesus anticipated his postmortem vindication by God, including the right to testify against disloyal disciples (Lk. 12:8f.), did he also expect to play a role in the restoration of Israel? I can think of no sufficient reason for excluding this possibility if, as seems probable, he regarded himself as Messiah.[79] On the other hand, Jesus seems not to have been an apocalyptist; he seems not to have indulged in detailed descriptions of the denouement of history. C. H. Dodd may well be correct in his surmise that, if Jesus spoke at all about a postmortem return, it may have been couched in such vague terms as we have in Jn. 14:28, "I go away, and I will come to you"; this ambiguous statement, Dodd proposes, was interpreted as a reference to the resurrection by some and as an allusion to an apocalyptic Parousia by others.[80]

If Jesus anticipated a postmortem fulfillment of his messianic role, did he conceptualize it with the help of Dan. 7:13f.? As T. F. Glasson and J. A. T. Robinson have argued, it would be more natural to draw on this text as a prediction of Jesus' heavenly vindication, since it says nothing about a coming on the clouds from heaven to earth.[81] Since early Christians were able to overlook such exegetical difficulties (cf. Rev. 1:7), this must have been possible for Jesus as well. Nor can we deny this possibility by appeal to Jesus' sanity. Early Christians apparently did not believe that they were attributing madness to Jesus when they credited him with such statements as Mk. 14:62 and 13:26.

Did Jesus at his trial predict his future messianic role by way of an allusion to this text (Mk. 14:62 par.)? It should be granted that this is

78. Schweizer, "Der Menschensohn," p. 192; Glasson, "Theophany and Parousia," pp. 265f.; Wrede, *Messianic Secret*, p. 220.

79. We can now regard the caution urged by Wrede and Bultmann as excessive. Several recent studies have reopened the question in important ways. It is erroneous to reason that Jesus could not have held together the ideas of messiahship and suffering because Judaism had no conception of a suffering Messiah. If Jesus regarded himself as the Lord's Anointed and became convinced that he would suffer a violent death, the second conviction would not obliterate the first. His theology would surely have adjusted the one to the other: "If I am Messiah, and if I must die, God must have so determined." See Leivestad, "Jesus—Messias—Menschensohn."

80. Dodd, *Historical Tradition in the Fourth Gospel*, pp. 413–20.

81. Glasson, *The Second Advent*, pp. 63–68. Cf. J. A. T. Robinson, *Jesus and His Coming*, pp. 44f.

theoretically possible. Since the vision of Daniel 7 appears to predict the restoration of Israel, it would be natural for one who viewed himself as Messiah to see himself referred to in the "coronation" of the "one like a son of man." It is not legitimate, however, to convert this possibility into a probability without more evidence than we now possess. By comparison with the simpler narrative in Jn. 18:19, 24, the Markan account of a formal trial before "the whole Sanhedrin" (14:55) appears very tendentious; it can scarcely be taken as a transcript of the pretrial hearing at which the high priest and his advisers prepared the case to be presented to Pilate.[82] The whole scene should probably be viewed as the product of Christian imagination.

What must be insisted upon, however, is that even if it could be demonstrated that Mk. 14:62 represents an authentic utterance of Jesus, this would not demonstrate that his use of *bar enasha* was due to his appropriation of the Danielic text. Where we have any measure of confidence that we have a fairly reliable translation of an authentic saying, as in Mt. 11:19 // Lk. 7:34 and Lk. 12:8f., *bar enasha* functions as a modest self-reference, and not as an apocalyptic allusion. This generalization would remain true even if it could be demonstrated that the lightning logion, Mt. 24:27 // Lk. 17:24, represents a genuine saying. The Aramaic antecedent of our two Greek versions must have spoken of the coming or the day of *bar enasha*, but, as was argued in chapter 7, the phrase would not have been perceived by Jesus' hearers as a title meaning "the heavenly figure described by Daniel." Even if it were linguistically possible for the phrase to function as an apocalyptic title in some other Aramaic-speaking sect (a conjecture, let us remember, that has not yet been substantiated), Jesus' use of it as a modest self-reference in the sayings examined earlier in this chapter would dictate how his hearers would perceive it in the lightning saying.

On the whole, it seems more probable that Jesus never spoke unambiguously of a postmortem return to the scene of his prophetic career. We have good reason to believe that he did speak often and in diverse ways of the coming of the kingdom of God and taught his followers to pray for it. It is therefore possible that a number of gospel sayings about the coming of the Son of man originated, as did Mt. 16:28, as logia concerning the coming of the kingdom (cf. Mk. 9:1). Surely Matthew was not the first

82. See especially Donahue, *Are You the Christ?* and Juel, *Messiah and Temple*. A valuable older study is Winter's *On the Trial of Jesus*, especially pp. 27–43. The authenticity of Mk. 14:62 is not guaranteed by the fact that it constitutes an unfulfilled prediction; Christians would have perceived it (whatever its origin) as still to be fulfilled; cf. Glasson, *The Second Advent*, p. 61.

Christian theologian to appropriate kingdom sayings for Parousia teaching. Perhaps the lightning saying is an earlier example of this tendency.

Theological Epilogue

The purpose of this book has been historical rather than theological. Its intention has been to establish, if possible, the earliest use of the phrase "the Son of man" in the gospel tradition. It has been concluded that at no stage of the tradition did this term serve as a christological title with a clear theological content. In Luke and John, as in the subsequent era of the Apostolic Fathers, it was used as a way of referring to the humanity of Jesus. In Matthew and Mark it functioned as a mysterious "name" employed by Jesus of himself, but its connotation was apparently of little concern. By a series of inferences it was concluded that the originator of this strange linguistic idiom in the gospel tradition was Jesus himself. In those few Son of man sayings that raise the fewest doubts concerning authenticity, Jesus refers to his own vocation and destiny in third-person language, employing *bar enasha* as a modest self-reference. As far as we can tell from the way these sayings were transmitted in the early church, the linguistic power of the phrase was denotative only; it pointed to the speaker without conveying anything about his self-estimate. That is, Jesus' use of *bar enasha* communicates nothing to us about "Jesus' own Christology," except that he regarded modesty in speech as an appropriate form of behavior.

For many readers this conclusion, whatever its historical merits, will be so disappointing theologically that they will be inclined to reject it. Reacting to the similar proposals of Vermes, Casey, and Lindars, Morna Hooker writes:

> The phrase cannot be a messianic title—yet the theory which interprets it as such at least offers a reason for its use; the view that it was an acceptable self-designation offers a plausible explanation as to *how* Jesus could have used it of himself—but fails to explain *why* he should have employed a colorless phrase which has no particular function.[83]

That is, she assumes that the phrase must have had theological content, or Jesus would not have used it. Accordingly she believes that "Any satisfactory solution to the problem of the Son of man must demonstrate not only why Jesus was thought to be referring to himself but also how the term came to be interpreted as denoting a figure who exercised superhuman

83. Hooker, "Is the Son of Man Problem Really Insoluble?" p. 159.

authority and who would play a central role in the future as judge."[84] The present study has attempted to show that, while the term did indeed *denote* such a figure, this was not its *connotation*. It was regularly employed in sayings attributed to Jesus in which he spoke modestly of his vocation and destiny. It was therefore not unnatural that secondary sayings about Jesus' future role as judge should employ such indirect language, modeled on the authentic saying found in Lk. 12:8f.

Nothing of essential importance has been lost if we are no longer able in good conscience to attribute to Jesus the creation and use of a special title by which he marked himself off as the to-be-vindicated suffering servant of Dan. 7:13f., as Hooker urges.[85] It is enough if we can say that we have good reason to believe that the historical Jesus saw his own suffering (i.e., his anticipated rejection and violent death) as a function of his uncompromising obedience to God and thereby interpreted that suffering as fulfilling a positive role in God's plan. He may have interpreted his suffering by reference to the songs of the suffering servant of Deutero-Isaiah. The few references to these passages in the gospel tradition do not strongly encourage such a view, however. He may have appealed to Dan. 7:13f. in support of his conviction that God would vindicate him, but again the supporting evidence is very weak.[86] It is not essential, however, that he should have done so.

Perhaps this nontheological interpretation of "the Son of man" may help us respond to the instructive criticism of Leander Keck delivered at the Trondheim meeting of the *Studiorum Novi Testamenti Societas*.

> Probably no other factor has contributed more to the current aridity of the discipline [of New Testament Christology] than this fascination with the paleontology of christological titles. To reconstruct the history of titles as if this were the study of christology is like trying to understand the windows of Chartres cathedral by studying the history of colored glass. In fact, concentration on titles finally makes the christologies of the New Testament unintelligible as christologies and insignificant theologically.[87]

Keck rightly insists that our christological study should be guided by the recognition that Paul's most important statements about the meaning of Jesus for faith do not involve titles.[88]

---

84. Ibid., p. 165.
85. Ibid., pp. 165–68; cf. her *The Son of Man in Mark*, p. 191.
86. Cf. Casey, *Son of Man*, pp. 157ff.
87. Keck, "Toward the Renewal of New Testament Christology," p. 368. See also Leivestad, "Jesus—Messias—Menschensohn."
88. Keck, "Toward the Renewal of New Testament Christology," p. 369.

If the conclusion of this book is accepted, and it is no longer claimed that the earliest Christians were able, in the light of Easter, to conceive of his return in power and glory by identifying him with a heavenly figure called "the Son of man," how did the belief in the Parousia arise? This is a history-of-ideas question that deserves more attention than can be given it in these closing lines, but the removal of a false solution to the problem should not be greeted with alarm. There is no need to find a history-of-religions antecedent. Faith in the Parousia must surely have been an almost automatic reflex to the Easter experience on the part of those who were convinced that Jesus was the Lord's anointed. Since God had confirmed Jesus' messiahship by raising him from the dead, it was certain that he would return in the power of God to complete the Messiah's task. An analogy was perhaps provided by the anticipated return of Elijah to judge Israel (Liv. Pro. 21:3), but even such a "precedent" was unnecessary. How the expectation of the Parousia came to be couched in Old Testament language about the coming of Yahweh is another issue.[89] Here it is sufficient to note that the classic passage 1 Thess. 4:16f. makes no allusion to Daniel 7 or to any apocalyptic passages dependent thereon. The earliest Christians clearly had no need to resort to the Danielic text in order to articulate their faith in the Parousia. If it was later added to their arsenal of proof texts, as in Rev. 1:7 and Mk. 13:26 and 14:62, this was a perfectly natural development, but the claim that Dan. 7:13f. was the cornerstone of belief in the Parousia is not supported by the evidence.

Some contemporary Christians would find it reassuring if it could be confirmed by historical study that Jesus himself was the author of the belief in his glorious return. It is not impossible that he intimated to his followers, "I go away, and I will come to you" (Jn. 14:28).[90] It is not necessary, however, that he should have done so. Christian faith in Jesus is based ultimately not on what can or cannot be demonstrated to have been Jesus' estimate of his role but on the world-shattering event of the resurrection.

89. Glasson, "Theophany and Parousia."
90. Ibid., p. 267, citing Dodd, *Historical Tradition in the Fourth Gospel*, pp. 413–20. See note 80 above.

BIBLIOGRAPHY

Achtemeier, Paul J. " 'He Taught Them Many Things': Reflections on Marcan Christology." *CBQ* 42 (1980): 465–81.

———. *Mark*. 2d ed. Proclamation Commentaries. Philadelphia: Fortress Press, 1986.

———. "The Origin and Function of the Pre-Markan Miracle Catenae." *JBL* 91 (1972): 198–221.

———. "Toward the Isolation of Pre-Markan Miracle Catenae." *JBL* 89 (1970): 265–91.

Alford, H. *The Greek Testament*. 5th ed. 4 vols. London: Rivingtons, 1863.

Allegro, J. M., and A. A. Anderson. *Qumran Cave 4, Discoveries in the Judean Desert*. Vol. 5. Oxford: Clarendon, 1968.

Allen, W. C. *A Critical and Exegetical Commentary on the Gospel according to S. Matthew*. 3d ed. Edinburgh: T. & T. Clark, 1912.

Appel, Heinrich. *Die Selbstbezeichnung Jesu: Der Sohn des Menschen*. Stavenhagen: Beholtz'sche Buchhandlung, 1896.

Arens, Eduardo. *The elthon-Sayings in the Synoptic Tradition*. Göttingen: Vandenhoeck & Ruprecht, 1976.

Augustine. *The City of God*. Trans. M. Dods. 2 vols. Edinburgh: T. & T. Clark, 1872.

Badham, F. P. "The Title 'Son of Man.' " *ThT* 45 (1911): 395–448.

Baldensperger, W. "Die neueste Forschung über den Menschensohn." *TRu* 3 (1900): 201–10, 243–55.

Bammel, Ernst. "Erwägungen zur Eschatologie Jesu." In *StEv* III, ed. F. L. Cross, pp. 3–32. Berlin: Akademie Verlag, 1964.

———. "Mt. 10,23." *SST* 15 (1961): 79–92.

———. "The *Titulus*." In *Jesus and the Politics of His Day*, ed. Ernst Bammel and C. F. D. Moule, pp. 353–64. Cambridge: Cambridge University Press, 1984.

Barr, James. *The Semantics of Biblical Language*. London: Oxford University Press, 1961.

Barrett, C. K. *The Gospel according to St. John*. New York: Macmillan, 1955.

———. *Jesus and the Gospel Tradition*. Philadelphia: Fortress Press, 1968.

Barth, Gerhard. "Matthew's Understanding of the Law." In *Tradition and Interpretation in Matthew*, ed. G. Bornkamm, G. Barth, and H. J. Held, pp. 58–164. Trans. Percy Scott. Philadelphia: Westminster Press, 1963.

Barth, Karl. *The Doctrine of Creation. Church Dogmatics* III/2. Trans. H. Knight et al. Edinburgh: T. & T. Clark, 1960.

———. *The Doctrine of Reconciliation. Church Dogmatics* IV/2. Trans. G. W. Bromiley. Edinburgh: T. & T. Clark, 1958.

Bauckham, Richard. "The Son of Man: 'A Man in My Position' or 'Someone'?" *Journal for the Study of the New Testament* 23 (1985): 23–33.

Bauer, Walter. *A Greek-English Lexicon of the New Testament and Other Early Christian Literature.* Trans. W. F. Arndt and F. W. Gingrich. Chicago: University of Chicago Press, 1956.

Beare, Francis W. *The Gospel according to Matthew.* San Francisco: Harper & Row, 1981.

Bernard, J. H. *A Critical and Exegetical Commentary on the Gospel according to St. John.* 2 vols. Edinburgh: T. & T. Clark, 1928.

Best, Ernest. *The Temptation and the Passion.* SNTS MS 2. Cambridge: Cambridge University Press, 1965.

Beyer, K. *Die aramäischen Texte vom Toten Meer.* Göttingen: Vandenhoeck & Ruprecht, 1984.

Bietenhard, Hans. " 'Der Menschensohn'—*ho huios tou anthrōpou.* Sprachliche und religionsgeschichtliche Untersuchungen zu einem Begriff der synoptischen Evangelien. I. Sprachlicher und religionsgeschichtlicher Teil." In *Aufstieg und Niedergang der römischen Welt* II.25.1, ed. W. Haase, pp. 265–350. Berlin: De Gruyter, 1982.

Black, Matthew. *An Aramaic Approach to the Gospels and Acts.* 3d ed. Oxford: Clarendon Press, 1967.

———. "Aramaic Barnasha and the 'Son of Man.' " *ExpTim* 95 (1983–84): 200–206.

———. "The Eschatology of the Similitudes of Enoch." *JTS,* n.s., 3 (1952): 1–10.

———. "Jesus and the 'Son of Man.' " *Journal for the Study of the New Testament* 1 (1978): 4–12.

———. *The Scrolls and Christian Origins.* London: Nelson, 1961.

———. "The Son of Man Problem in Recent Research and Debate." *BJRL* 45 (1962–63): 305–18.

———. "The Throne-Theophany Prophetic Commission and the 'Son of Man.' " In *Jews, Greeks and Christians: Essays in Honor of William David Davies,* ed. R. Hamerton-Kelly and Robin Scroggs, pp. 57–73. Leiden: Brill, 1976.

Blair, Edward P. *Jesus in the Gospel of Matthew.* New York: Abingdon, 1960.

Blank, J. *Krisis.* Freiburg: Lambertus, 1964.

Bonnard, Pierre. *L'Évangile selon Saint Matthieu.* Neuchâtel: Delachaux & Niestlé, 1963.

Boobyer, George H. "Mark II,10a and the Interpretation of the Healing of the Paralytic." *HTR* 47 (1954): 115–20.

———. *St. Mark and the Transfiguration Story.* Edinburgh: T. & T. Clark, 1942.

Borgen, Peder. "God's Agent in the Fourth Gospel." In *Religions in Antiquity: Essays in Memory of Erwin Ramsdell Goodenough,* ed. J. Neusner, pp. 137–48. Leiden: Brill, 1968.

Boring, M. Eugene. *Sayings of the Risen Jesus: Christian Prophecy in the Synoptic Tradition.* Cambridge: Cambridge University Press, 1982.

————. "The Unforgivable Sin Logion Mark III 28–29/Matt XII 31–32/Luke XII 10: Formal Analysis and History of the Tradition." *NovT* 18 (1976): 258–79.

Bornkamm, Günther. "Die eucharistische Rede im Johannes-Evangelium." *ZNW* 47 (1956): 161–69.

————. *Jesus of Nazareth.* Trans. I. McLuskey and F. McLuskey, with James M. Robinson. New York: Harper & Row, 1961.

————. "Vorjohanneische Tradition oder nachjohanneische Bearbeitung in der eucharistischen Rede Johannes 6?" In his *Geschichte und Glaube*: Zweiter Teil. Gesammelte Aufsätze, Band IV, pp. 51–64. Munich: Kaiser Verlag, 1971.

Bornkamm, Günther, Gerhard Barth, and Heinz Joachim Held. *Tradition and Interpretation in Matthew.* Trans. Percy Scott. Philadelphia: Westminster Press, 1963.

Borsch, Frederick H. *The Christian and Gnostic Son of Man.* SBT, 2d ser., 14. Naperville, Ill.: Allenson, 1970.

————. *The Son of Man in Myth and History.* Philadelphia: Westminster Press, 1967.

Bousset, Wilhelm. *Kyrios Christos.* Trans. J. E. Steely. Nashville: Abingdon, 1970.

————. *Die Religion des Judentums im späthellenistichen Zeitalter.* 3d ed. Ed. H. Gressmann. Tübingen: Mohr, 1926.

Bowker, John. "The Son of Man." *JTS*, n.s., 28 (1977): 19–48.

Braun, François-M. "Messie, Logos, et Fils de l'homme." In *La Venue du Messie,* by É. Massaux et al., pp. 133–47. Paris: Desclée de Brouwer, 1962.

Broer, Ingo. "Das Ringen der Gemeinde um Israel: Exegetischer Versuch über Mt 19,28." In *Jesus und der Menschensohn: Für Anton Vögtle,* ed. R. Pesch, R. Schnackenburg, and O. Kaiser, pp. 148–65. Freiburg: Herder, 1975.

Brown, John P. "The Form of 'Q' Known to Matthew." *NTS* 8 (1961–62): 27–42.

Brown, Raymond E. *The Gospel according to John.* AB, vols. 29, 29a. Garden City, N.Y.: Doubleday, 1966.

Bruce, Alexander B. "The Synoptic Gospels." In *Expositor's Greek Testament,* ed. W. Robertson Nicoll, vol. 1, pp. 3–651. London: Hodder & Stoughton, 1912.

Bruce, Frederick F. "The Oldest Greek Version of Daniel." In *Instruction and Interpretation,* by H. A. Brongers et al., pp. 22–40. OTS 20. Leiden: Brill, 1977.

Bultmann, Rudolf. "Die Frage nach der Echtheit von Mt. 16:17–19." *TBl* 20 (1941): 265–79. Reprinted in *Ex.,* pp. 255–77. Tübingen: Mohr, 1967.

————. *Die Geschichte der synoptischen Tradition.* Göttingen: Vandenhoeck & Ruprecht, 1921. Trans. J. Marsh, *History of the Synoptic Tradition.* Oxford: Blackwell, 1963.

————. *The Gospel of John.* Trans. G. R. Beasley-Murray, R. W. N. Hoare, and J. K. Riches. Philadelphia: Westminster Press, 1971.

————. *Theology of the New Testament.* 2 vols. Trans. K. Grobel. New York: Scribner's, 1951.

Burkill, T. A. "The Competence of the Sanhedrin." *VC* 10 (1956): 80–96.

Burton, E. D. *Syntax of the Moods and Tenses in New Testament Greek.* 3d ed. Chicago: University of Chicago Press, 1900.

Calvin, John. *Institutes of the Christian Religion.* Ed. J. T. McNeill, trans. F. L. Battles. 2 vols. Philadelphia: Westminster Press, 1960.

Caragounis, Chrys C. *The Son of Man: Vision and Interpretation.* Tübingen: Mohr, 1986.

Casey, P. Maurice. "Aramaic Idiom and Son of Man Sayings." *ExpTim* 96 (1984–85): 233–36.

———. "General, Generic, and Indefinite: The Use of the Term 'Son of Man' in Aramaic Sources and in the Teaching of Jesus." *Journal for the Study of the New Testament* 29 (1987): 21–56.

———. "The Jackals and the Son of Man." *Journal for the Study of the New Testament* 23 (1985): 3–22.

———. "The Son of Man Problem." *ZNW* 67 (1976): 147–54.

———. *Son of Man: The Interpretation and Influence of Daniel 7.* London: SPCK, 1979.

Catchpole, David R. "The Answer of Jesus to Caiaphas (Matt. xxvi.64)." *NTS* 17 (1971): 213–26.

———. "The Poor on Earth and the Son of Man in Heaven: A Reappraisal of Mt. 25:31–46." *BJRL* 61 (1979): 355–97.

———. "The Problem of the Historicity of the Sanhedrin Trial." In *The Trial of Jesus: Cambridge Studies in Honour of C. F. D. Moule,* ed. E. Bammel, pp. 47–65. London: SCM Press, 1970.

———. "The Son of Man's Search for Faith (Luke XVIII 8b)." *NovT* 19 (1977): 81–104.

———. "The 'Triumphal' Entry." In *Jesus and the Politics of His Day,* ed. Ernst Bammel and C. F. D. Moule, pp. 319–334. Cambridge: Cambridge University Press, 1984.

Ceroke, C. P. "Is Mk 2,10 a Saying of Jesus?" *CBQ* 22 (1960): 369–90.

Charles, R. H. *The Apocrypha and Pseudepigrapha of the Old Testament in English.* 2 vols. Oxford: Clarendon Press, 1913.

———. *The Book of Enoch.* Oxford: Clarendon Press, 1893.

Chevasse, C. "Not the Mountain Appointed. Studies in Texts: Mt. 28:16." *Theol.* 74 (1971): 478.

Collins, Adela Yarbro. "The Origins of the Designation of Jesus as 'Son of Man.' " *HTR* 80 (1987): 391–407.

Collins, John J. "The Son of Man and the Saints of the Most High in the Book of Daniel." *JBL* 93 (1974): 50–66.

Colpe, Carsten. "Ho huios tou anthrōpou." TDNT 8, pp. 400–477.

———. "New Testament and Gnostic Christology." In *Religions in Antiquity: Essays in Memory of Erwin Ramsdell Goodenough,* ed. J. Neusner, pp. 227–43. Leiden: Brill, 1968.

Colwell, Ernest C. "A Definite Rule for the Use of the Article in the Greek New Testament." *JBL* 52 (1933): 12–21.

Conzelmann, Hans. *Die Apostelgeschichte.* Tübingen: Mohr, 1963.

———. *The Theology of St. Luke.* Trans. G. Buswell. New York: Harper, 1960.

Cope, O. Lamar. "Mt. xxv.31–46 'The Sheep and the Goats' Reinterpreted." *NovT* 11 (1969): 32–44.

———. *Matthew: A Scribe Trained for the Kingdom of Heaven.* CBQ MS 5. Washington, D.C.: Catholic Biblical Association of America, 1976.

Coppens, Joseph. "Le Fils de l'homme dans l'évangile johannique." *ETL* 52 (1976): 28–81.

Cortis, J. B., and F. M. Gatti. "The Son of Man or the Son of Adam." *Bib* 49 (1968): 457–502.

Creed, J. M. *The Gospel according to St. Luke.* London: Macmillan, 1930.

Dahl, Nils A. "The Atonement—an Adequate Reward for the Akedah? (Ro 8:32)." In *Neotestamentica et Semitica: Studies in Honour of Matthew Black,* ed. E. Earle Ellis and Max Wilcox, pp. 15–29. Edinburgh: T. & T. Clark, 1969.

———. "The Johannine Church and History." In *Current Issues in New Testament Interpretation: Essays in Honor of Otto A. Piper,* ed. W. Klassen and G. F. Snyder, pp. 124–42. New York: Harper & Bros., 1962.

Dalman, Gustav. *Die Worte Jesu.* Leipzig: Hinrichs'sche Buchhandlung, 1898. Trans. D. M. Kay, *The Words of Jesus.* Edinburgh: T. & T. Clark, 1902.

Daube, David. *Appeasement or Resistance, and Other Essays on New Testament Judaism.* Berkeley and Los Angeles: University of California Press, 1987.

———. *The New Testament and Rabbinic Judaism.* London: Athlone Press, 1956.

Davies, William David. *The Gospel and the Land.* Berkeley: University of California Press, 1974.

———. *Paul and Rabbinic Judaism.* London: SPCK, 1948.

———. *The Setting of the Sermon on the Mount.* Cambridge: Cambridge University Press, 1964.

Delcor, Mathias. *Le Testament d'Abraham.* Leiden: Brill, 1973.

Dibelius, Martin. *Die Formgeschichte des Evangeliums.* Tübingen: Mohr, 1919.

———. *Jesus.* Trans. C. B. Hedrick and F. C. Grant. Philadelphia: Westminster, 1949.

Diez Macho, A. *Neophyti 1.* 5 vols. Madrid: Consejo Superior de Investigaciones Científicas, 1968–78.

Dinkler, Erich. "Petrusbekenntnis und Satanswort: Das Problem der Messianität Jesu." In *Zeit und Geschichte: Dankesgabe an Rudolf Bultmann zum 80. Geburtstag,* ed. E. Dinkler and H. Thyen, pp. 127–53. Tübingen: Mohr, 1964.

Dion, H.-M. "Quelques traits originaux de la conception johannique du Fils de l'homme." *ScEc* 19 (1967): 49–65.

Dodd, C. H. *The Apostolic Preaching and Its Developments.* New York: Harper & Row, 1962.

———. *Historical Tradition in the Fourth Gospel.* Cambridge: Cambridge University Press, 1963.

———. *The Interpretation of the Fourth Gospel.* Cambridge: Cambridge University Press, 1954.

Donahue, John R. *Are You the Christ? The Trial Narrative in the Gospel of Mark.* Missoula, Mont.: Society of Biblical Literature, 1973.

Dunn, James D. G. *Baptism in the Holy Spirit.* Naperville, Ill.: Allenson, 1970.

———. *Christology in the Making: A New Testament Inquiry into the Origins of the Doctrine of the Incarnation.* Philadelphia: Westminster Press, 1980.

———. *Jesus and the Spirit.* Philadelphia: Westminster Press, 1975.

———. "John VI—a Eucharistic Discourse?" *NTS* 17 (1971): 328–38.

Dupont, J. " 'Vous n'aurez pas achevé les villages d'Israël avant que le Fils de l'homme ne vienne' (Mat. x.23)." *NovT* 2 (1958): 228–44.

Dupont-Sommer, A. *The Essene Writings from Qumran.* Trans. Geza Vermes. Cleveland: World Publishing, 1962.

Edwards, Richard A. *The Sign of Jonah in the Theology of the Evangelists and Q.* SBT, n.s., 18. Naperville, Ill.: Allenson, n.d.

Elbogen, Ismar. *Der jüdische Gottesdienst in seiner geschichtlichen Entwicklung.* 2d ed. Frankfurt: J. Kauffmann, 1924.

Ellis, E. E. *The Gospel of Luke.* NCeB, vol. 42. London: Nelson, 1966.

Emerton, John A. "The Origin of the Son of Man Imagery." *JTS,* n.s., 9 (1958): 225–42.

Eusebius. *The Ecclesiastical History.* Trans. K. Lake and J. E. L. Oulton. 2 vols. Vol. 1: London: William Heinemann; New York: G. P. Putnam's Sons, 1926. Vol. 2: Cambridge: Harvard University Press; London: William Heinemann, 1942.

Farmer, William R. *The Synoptic Problem.* New York: Macmillan, 1964.

Fenton, John C. *Saint Matthew.* PGC. Baltimore: Penguin Books, 1963.

Fiebig, Paul. *Der Menschensohn: Jesu Selbstbezeichnung.* Tübingen: Mohr, 1901.

Fitzmyer, Joseph A. "Another View of the 'Son of Man' Debate." *Journal for the Study of the New Testament* 4 (1979): 58–68.

———. *The Gospel according to Luke I–IX.* AB, vol. 28. Garden City, N.Y.: Doubleday, 1981.

———. "Methodology in the Study of the Aramaic Substratum of Jesus' Sayings in the New Testament." In *Jésus aux origines de la christologie,* ed. J. Dupont, pp. 73–102. Leuven: Leuven University Press; Gembloux: Duculot, 1975.

———. "The New Testament Title 'Son of Man' Philologically Considered." In his *A Wandering Aramean: Collected Essays,* pp. 143–60. Missoula, Mont.: Scholars Press, 1979.

Flender, H. *St. Luke: Theologian of Redemptive History.* Trans. R. H. Fuller and Ilse Fuller. London: SPCK, 1967.

Foakes Jackson, F. J., and Kirsopp Lake. *The Beginnings of Christianity.* Part 1, *The Acts of the Apostles.* 5 vols. London: Macmillan, 1920.

Formesyn, R. E. C. "Was There a Pronominal Connection for the 'Bar Nasha' Self-Designation?" *NovT* 8 (1966): 1–35.

Freed, Edwin D. "The Son of Man in the Fourth Gospel." *JBL* 86 (1967): 402–9.

Fritsch, Irénée. " '. . . videbitis . . . angelos Dei ascendentes et descendentes . . .' (Io. 1,51)." *VD* 37 (1959): 1–11.

Fuller, Reginald H. *A Critical Introduction to the New Testament.* London: Duckworth, 1966.

———. *The Foundations of New Testament Christology.* New York: Scribner's, 1965.

———. "The Son of Man: A Reconsideration." In *The Living Text: Essays in Honor of Ernest W. Saunders,* ed. Dennis E. Groh and Robert Jewett, pp. 207–17. Lanham, Md.: University Press of America, 1985.

Gaster, Moses. *Studies and Texts.* 3 vols. New York: KTAV, 1971.

Geist, Heinz. *Menschensohn und Gemeinde: Eine redaktionskritische Untersuchung zur Menschensohnprädikation im Matthäusevangelium.* Würzburg: Echter Verlag, 1986.

Giversen, S. *Apocryphon Johannis.* Copenhagen: Prostant apud Munksgaard, 1963.

Glasson, T. Francis. "The Ensign of the Son of Man (Mt. xxiv.30)." *JTS* 15 (1964): 299–300.

———. *The Second Advent: The Origin of the New Testament Doctrine.* 2d ed. London: Epworth, 1947.

————. "Theophany and Parousia." *NTS* 34 (1988): 259–70.

Gould, Ezra P. *A Critical and Exegetical Commentary on the Gospel according to St. Mark.* Edinburgh: T. & T. Clark, 1896.

Grant, Robert M. *Gnosticism: A Source Book of Heretical Writings from the Early Christian Period.* New York: Harper & Row, 1961.

Grässer, Erich. "Beobachtungen zum Menschensohn in Hebr 2,6." In *Jesus und der Menschensohn: Für Anton Vögtle,* ed. R. Pesch, R. Schnackenburg, and O. Kaiser, pp. 404–14. Freiburg, Herder: 1975.

————. *Das Problem der Parusieverzögerung in den synoptischen Evangelien und in der Apostelgeschichte.* Berlin: Töpelmann, 1957.

Green, H. Benedict. *The Gospel according to Matthew.* London: Oxford University Press, 1975.

Grundmann, Walter. *Das Evangelium nach Lukas.* 2d, rev. ed. Berlin: Evangelische Verlagsanstalt, [1961].

Gundry, Robert H. *Matthew: A Commentary on His Literary and Theological Art.* Grand Rapids, Mich.: Eerdmans, 1982.

————. *The Use of the Old Testament in St. Matthew's Gospel, with Special Reference to the Messianic Hope.* Leiden: Brill, 1967.

Haenchen, Ernst. *Der Weg Jesu.* Berlin: Töpelmann, 1966.

Hahn, Ferdinand. *The Titles of Jesus in Christology.* Trans. H. Knight and G. Ogg. London: Lutterworth Press, 1969.

Hamerton-Kelly, Robert G. *Pre-existence, Wisdom, and the Son of Man: A Study of the Idea of Pre-existence in the New Testament.* SNTS MS 21. Cambridge: Cambridge University Press, 1973.

Hare, Douglas R. A. "The Lives of the Prophets." In *The Old Testament Pseudepigrapha,* ed. James H. Charlesworth, vol. 2, pp. 379–99. Garden City, N.Y.: Doubleday, 1985.

————. *The Theme of Jewish Persecution of Christians in the Gospel according to St. Matthew.* SNTS MS 6. Cambridge: Cambridge University Press, 1967.

Hare, Douglas R. A., and Daniel J. Harrington. " 'Make Disciples of All the Gentiles' (Mt. 28:19)." *CBQ* 37 (1975): 359–69.

Harnack, Adolf von. *Marcion: Das Evangelium vom fremden Gott.* Leipzig: Hinrichs, 1921.

Harner, Philip B. "Qualitative Anarthrous Predicate Nouns: Mark 15:39 and John 1:1." *JBL* 92 (1973): 75–87.

Hay, David M. *Glory at the Right Hand: Psalm 110 in Early Christianity.* SBL MS 18. Nashville: Abingdon, 1973.

Hay, L. S. "The Son of Man in Mark 2:10 and 2:28." *JBL* 89 (1970): 69–75.

Hengel, Martin. *The Charismatic Leader and His Followers.* Trans. J. Greig. New York: Crossroad, 1981.

Hennecke, E., and W. Schneemelcher. *New Testament Apocrypha.* Trans. and ed. R. M. Wilson. Philadelphia: Westminster Press, 1963.

Hertz, Joseph H. *The Authorized Daily Prayer Book.* Rev. ed. New York: Bloch Publishing, 1961.

Higgins, A. J. B. *Jesus and the Son of Man.* Philadelphia: Fortress Press, 1964.

————. "Jewish Messianic Belief in Justin Martyr's *Dialogue with Trypho.*" *NovT* 9 (1967): 298–305.

————. *The Son of Man in the Teaching of Jesus.* Cambridge: Cambridge University Press, 1980.

Hill, David. *The Gospel of Matthew.* NCeB. London: Oliphants, 1972.

Hoffmann, Paul. *Studien zur Theologie der Logienquelle.* Münster: Aschendorff, 1972.

Hooker, Morna D. "Is the Son of Man Problem Really Insoluble?" In *Text and Interpretation: Studies in the New Testament, Presented to Matthew Black,* ed. E. Best and R. M. Wilson, pp. 155–68. Cambridge: Cambridge University Press, 1979.

————. *The Son of Man in Mark.* London: SPCK, 1967.

Horstmann, Maria. *Studien zur markinischen Christologie.* Münster: Aschendorff, 1969.

Hoskyns, E. C. *The Fourth Gospel.* Ed. F. N. Davey. 2d ed. London: Faber & Faber, 1947.

Iber, G. "Überlieferungsgeschichtliche Untersuchungen zum Begriff des Menschensohns im Neuen Testament." Diss., Heidelberg, 1953.

Irenaeus. *The Writings of Irenaeus.* Trans. A. Roberts and W. H. Rambaut. ANCL, vol. 5. Edited by A. Roberts and J. Donaldson. Edinburgh: T. & T. Clark, 1869.

Jeremias, Joachim. "Die älteste Schicht der Menschensohn-Logien." *ZNW* 58 (1967): 159–72.

————. "Die Berufung des Nathanael." *Angelos* 3 (1928): 2–5.

————. *New Testament Theology: The Proclamation of Jesus.* Trans. J. Bowden. New York: Scribner's, 1971.

————. *The Parables of Jesus.* Rev. ed. Trans. S. H. Hooke. New York: Scribner's, 1963.

Johnson, Sherman E. "The Gospel according to St. Matthew: Introduction and Exegesis." In *IB,* ed. George A. Buttrick, vol. 7, pp. 231–625. New York: Abingdon-Cokesbury Press, 1951.

Johnston, George. *The Spirit-Paraclete in the Gospel of John.* SNTS MS 12. Cambridge: Cambridge University Press, 1970.

Juel, Donald. *Messiah and Temple: The Trial of Jesus in the Gospel of Mark.* Missoula, Mont.: Scholars Press, 1977.

Käsemann, Ernst. *New Testament Questions of Today.* Trans. W. J. Montague. Philadelphia: Fortress Press, 1970.

————. "Sätze heiligen Rechtes im Neuen Testament." *NTS* 1 (1954–55): 248–60.

Kearns, Rollin. *Vorfragen zur Christologie.* 2 vols. Tübingen: Mohr, 1978–80.

Keck, Leander E. "Toward the Renewal of New Testament Christology." *NTS* 32 (1986): 362–77.

Kertelge, Karl. "Die Vollmacht des Menschensohnes zur Sündenvergebung (Mk 2,10)." In *Orientierung an Jesus,* ed. P. Hoffmann, N. Brox, and W. Pesch, pp. 205–13. Freiburg: Herder, 1973.

Kim, Seyoon. *"The 'Son of Man' " as the Son of God.* Tübingen: Mohr, 1983.

Kingsbury, Jack D. *The Christology of Mark's Gospel.* Philadelphia: Fortress Press, 1983.

————. "The Figure of Jesus in Matthew's Story: A Literary-Critical Probe." *Journal for the Study of the New Testament* 21 (1984): 3–36.

————. *Matthew: Structure, Christology, Kingdom.* Philadelphia: Fortress Press, 1975.

————. *The Parables of Jesus in Matthew 13*. London: SPCK, 1969.

Kinniburgh, Elizabeth. "The Johannine 'Son of Man.' " In *StEv* IV, ed. F. L. Cross, pp. 64–71. Berlin: Akademie Verlag, 1968.

Klausner, J. *The Messianic Idea in Israel*. Trans. W. F. Stinespring. New York: Macmillan, 1955.

Klein, M. L. "The Messiah 'That Leadeth upon a Cloud' in the Fragment Targum to the Pentateuch." *JTS*, n.s., 29 (1978): 137–39.

Klijn, A. F. J., and G. J. Reinink. *Patristic Evidence for Jewish-Christian Sects*. Leiden: Brill, 1973.

Kloppenborg, John S. *The Formation of Q*. Philadelphia: Fortress Press, 1987.

Klostermann, Erich. *Das Lukasevangelium*. 3d ed. Tübingen: Mohr, 1975.

————. *Matthäus*. With the collaboration of Hugo Gressmann. Tübingen: Mohr, 1909.

Knibb, Michael. *The Ethiopic Book of Enoch*. Oxford: Clarendon Press, 1978.

Koester, Helmut. *Synoptische Überlieferung bei den apostolischen Vätern*. Berlin: Akademie Verlag, 1957.

Kohler, K. "The Origin and Composition of the Eighteen Benedictions, with a Translation of the Corresponding Essene Prayers in the Apostolic Constitutions." In *HUCA*, voi. 1, pp. 387–425. Cincinnati: Hebrew Union College, 1924.

Kümmel, Werner Georg. "Eschatological Expectation in the Proclamation of Jesus." In *The Future of Our Religious Past: Essays in Honour of Rudolf Bultmann*, ed. James M. Robinson, pp. 29–48. Trans. C. E. Carlston and R. P. Scharlemann. New York: Harper & Row, 1971.

————. *Promise and Fulfilment: The Eschatological Message of Jesus*. Trans. D. M. Barton. SBT 23. Naperville, Ill.: Allenson, 1957.

————. "Das Verhalten Jesu gegenüber und das Verhalten des Menschensohns: Markus 8,38 par und Lukas 12,8f. par Matthäus 10,32f." In *Jesus und der Menschensohn: Für Anton Vögtle*, ed. R. Pesch, R. Schnackenburg, and O. Kaiser, pp. 210–24. Freiburg: Herder, 1975.

Kysar, Robert. *The Fourth Evangelist and His Gospel*. Minneapolis: Augsburg, 1975.

Lachs, Samuel T. "Rabbi Abbahu and the Minim." *JQR* 60 (1969–70): 197–212.

Lagrange, Marie Joseph. *Évangile selon Saint Matthieu*. 3d ed. Paris: J. Gabalda et Fils, 1927.

Landes, George. "Mt. 12:40 as an Interpretation of 'The Sign of Jonah' against the Background of the Book of Jonah and Other Texts." In *The Word of the Lord Shall Go Forth: Essays in Honor of David Noel Freedman in Celebration of His Sixtieth Birthday*, ed. C. L. Myers and M. O'Connor, pp. 665–84. Winona Lake, Ind.: Eisenbrauns, 1983.

Leaney, A. R. C. *A Commentary on the Gospel according to St. Luke*. New York: Harper, 1958.

Le Déaut, Roger. "Le substrat araméen des Évangiles: Scolies en margie de l'*Aramaic Approach* de Matthew Black." *Bib* 49 (1968): 388–99.

Leivestad, Ragnar. "Der apokalyptische Menschensohn ein theologisches Phantom." *ASTI* 6 (1968): 49–105.

————. "Exit the Apocalyptic Son of Man." *NTS* 18 (1972): 243–67.

————. "Jesus—Messias—Menschensohn: Die jüdische Heilandserwartungen zur Zeit der ersten römischen Kaiser und die Frage nach dem messianischen

Selbstbewusstsein Jesu." In *Aufstieg und Niedergang der römischen Welt* II.25.1, ed. W. Haase, pp. 220–64. Berlin: De Gruyter, 1982.

Levey, Samson H. *The Messiah: An Aramaic Interpretation.* Cincinnati: Hebrew Union College Press, 1974.

Lietzmann, Hans. *Der Menschensohn.* Freiburg: Mohr, 1896.

Lindars, Barnabas. *The Gospel of John.* NCeB. London: Oliphants, 1972.

———. *Jesus Son of Man.* London: SPCK, 1983.

———. "Re-enter the Apocalyptic Son of Man." *NTS* 22 (1975): 52–72.

———. "Response to Richard Bauckham: The Idiomatic Use of Bar Enasha." *Journal for the Study of the New Testament* 23 (1985): 35–41.

———. "The Son of Man in the Johannine Christology." In *Christ and Spirit in the New Testament: In Honour of C. F. D. Moule,* ed. B. Lindars and S. S. Smalley, pp. 43–60. Cambridge: Cambridge University Press, 1973.

Linton, O. "The Trial of Jesus and the Interpretation of Psalm CX." *NTS* 7 (1961): 258–62.

Luedemann, Gerd. *Paul, Apostle to the Gentiles: Studies in Chronology.* Trans. F. Stanley Jones. Philadelphia: Fortress Press, 1984.

Lührmann, Dieter. *Die Redaktion der Logienquelle.* Neukirchen-Vluyn: Neukirchener Verlag, 1969.

Luz, Ulrich. *Das Evangelium nach Matthäus.* Part 1: *Mt 1–7.* Zurich: Benziger Verlag; Neukirchen-Vluyn: Neukirchener Verlag, 1985. Trans. W. C. Linss, *Matthew 1–7: A Commentary.* Minneapolis: Augsburg, 1989.

———. "The Secrecy Motif and the Marcan Christology." In *The Messianic Secret,* ed. Christopher Tuckett, pp. 75–96. London: SPCK; Philadelphia: Fortress Press, 1983.

McNeile, Alan Hugh. *The Gospel according to St. Matthew.* London: Macmillan, 1915.

Maddox, Robert. "The Function of the Son of Man in the Gospel of John." In *Reconciliation and Hope: New Testament Essays on Atonement and Eschatology Presented to L. L. Morris on His Sixtieth Birthday,* ed. R. Banks, pp. 186–204. Grand Rapids, Mich.: Eerdmans, 1974.

Major, H. D. A., T. W. Manson, and C. J. Wright. *The Mission and Message of Jesus.* New York: Dutton, 1938.

Manson, T. W. *The Teaching of Jesus.* Cambridge: Cambridge University Press, 1931.

Marsh, John. *The Gospel of St. John.* Baltimore: Penguin, 1968.

Marshall, I. Howard. *Commentary on Luke.* New International Greek Testament Commentary. Grand Rapids, Mich.: Eerdmans, 1978.

———. "The Synoptic Son of Man Sayings in Recent Discussion." *NTS* 12 (1966): 327–51.

Martitz, W. von. "*Huios* in Greek." TDNT 8, pp. 334–40.

Martyn, J. Louis. *History and Theology in the Fourth Gospel.* New York: Harper & Row, 1968.

Marxsen, Willi. *Mark the Evangelist.* Trans. R. A. Harrisville et al. New York: Abingdon, 1969.

Meeks, Wayne A. "The Man from Heaven in Johannine Sectarianism." *JBL* 91 (1972): 44–72.

———. *The Prophet-King.* Leiden: Brill, 1967.

Meier, John P. "Nations or Gentiles in Mt. 28:19?" *CBQ* 39 (1977): 94–102.
———. *The Vision of Matthew.* New York: Ramsey; Toronto: Paulist Press, 1979.
Merkel, Helmut. "The Opposition between Jesus and Judaism." In *Jesus and the Politics of His Day,* ed. Ernst Bammel and C. F. D. Moule, pp. 129–44. Cambridge: Cambridge University Press, 1984.
Mertens, A. *Das Buch Daniel im Lichte der Texte vom Toten Meer.* Würzburg: Echter Verlag, 1971.
Metzger, Bruce M. *A Textual Commentary on the Greek New Testament.* London: United Bible Societies, 1971.
Meyer, H. A. W. *Critical and Exegetical Handbook to the Gospel of John.* 2d ed. Trans. W. Urwick and F. Crombie. 2 vols. Edinburgh: T. & T. Clark, 1879.
Michaelis, Wilhelm. "Joh 1,51, Gen 28,12, und das Menschensohn-Problem." *TLZ* 85 (1960), cols. 561–78.
Michel, Otto. "Der Abschluss des Matthäusevangeliums." *EvT* 10 (1950): 16–26.
Milik, Josef T. "Problèmes de la littérature Hénochique à la lumière des fragments Araméens de Qumran." *HTR* 64 (1971): 333–78.
Moloney, Francis J. "The End of the Son of Man?" *DR* 98 (1980): 284–86.
———. *The Johannine Son of Man.* Rome: Las, 1976.
Montefiore, Claude G. *The Synoptic Gospels.* 2 vols. London: Macmillan, 1927.
Moore, A. L. *The Parousia in the New Testament.* Leiden: Brill, 1966.
Moule, C. F. D. *An Idiom Book of New Testament Greek.* Cambridge: Cambridge University Press, 1953.
———. "The Individualism of the Fourth Gospel." *NovT* 5 (1962): 171–90.
———. "Neglected Features in the Problem of 'the Son of Man.' " In *Neues Testament und Kirche: Für Rudolf Schnackenburg,* ed. Joachim Gnilka, pp. 413–28. Freiburg: Herder, 1974.
———. *The Origin of Christology.* Cambridge: Cambridge University Press, 1977.
———. *The Phenomenon of the New Testament.* SBT, 2d ser., 1. London: SCM Press, 1967.
Müller, Karlheinz. "Menschensohn und Messias. Religionsgeschichtliche Vorüberlegungen zum Menschensohnproblem in den synoptischen Evangelien." *BZ* 16 (1972): 161–87; 17 (1973): 52–66.
Müller, Mogens. *Der Ausdruck "Menschensohn" in den Evangelien: Voraussetzungen und Bedeutung.* Leiden: Brill, 1984.
Müller, Ulrich B. *Messias und Menschensohn in jüdischen Apokalypsen und in der Offenbarung des Johannes.* Gütersloh: Mohn, 1972.
Muraoka, Takamitsu. "The Aramaic of the Old Targum of Job from Qumran Cave XI." *JJS* 25 (1974): 425–43.
———. "Notes on the Aramaic of the Genesis Apocryphon." *RevQ* 8 (1972): 7–51.
Nickelsburg, George W. E. *Resurrection, Immortality, and Eternal Life in Intertestamental Judaism.* Cambridge: Harvard University Press, 1972.
Noack, B. *Das Gottesreich bei Lukas: Eine Studie zu Luk. 17,20–24.* Lund: Gleerup, 1948.
Odeberg, H. *The Fourth Gospel.* Amsterdam: Grüner, 1968.
———. *Third Enoch.* Cambridge: Cambridge University Press, 1928.
O'Neill, John C. *Messiah: Six Lectures on the Ministry of Jesus.* Cambridge: Cochrane Press, 1980.

Pamment, Margaret. "The Son of Man in the First Gospel." *NTS* 29 (1983): 116–29.

Peel, Malcolm L. *The Epistle to Rheginos*. Philadelphia: Westminster Press, 1969.

Perrin, Norman. "The High Priest's Question and Jesus' Answer (Mark 14:61–62)." In *The Passion in Mark: Studies on Mark 14–16*, ed. Werner H. Kelber, pp. 80–95. Philadelphia: Fortress Press, 1976.

———. "Mark 14:62: The End Product of a Christian Pesher Tradition?" *NTS* 12 (1965–66): 150–55.

———. *A Modern Pilgrimage in New Testament Christology*. Philadelphia: Fortress Press, 1974.

———. *Rediscovering the Teaching of Jesus*. New York: Harper & Row, 1967.

Petersen, Norman R. *Literary Criticism for New Testament Critics*. Philadelphia: Fortress Press, 1978.

Plummer, Alexander. *A Critical and Exegetical Commentary on the Gospel according to S. Luke*. 4th ed. Edinburgh: T. & T. Clark, 1901.

Potterie, Ignace de la. "L'exaltation du Fils de l'homme (Jn 12,31–36)." *Greg* 49 (1968): 460–78.

Preuschen, E. Origenes Werke. Vol. 4. *Der Johannes Kommentar.* Leipzig: Hinrichs, 1903.

Proksch, Otto. "Der Menschensohn als Gottessohn." *CuW* 3 (1927): 425–43, 473–81.

Quispel, G. "Nathanael und der Menschensohn (Joh 1,51)." *ZNW* 47 (1956): 281–83.

Räisänen, H. *Das "Messiasgeheimnis" im Markusevangelium*. Helsinki: Lansi-Suomi, 1976.

Rehkopf, F. *Die lukanische Sonderquelle*. Tübingen: Mohr, 1959.

Reim, Günter. *Studien zum alttestamentlichen Hintergrund des Johannesevangeliums*. SNTS MS 22. Cambridge: Cambridge University Press, 1974.

Rengstorf, Karl H. *Das Evangelium nach Lukas*. NTD 3. Göttingen: Vandenhoeck & Ruprecht, 1962.

Roberts, Alexander, and James Donaldson, eds. *The Ante-Nicene Fathers*. 10 vols. American reprint of the Edinburgh ed. Buffalo: Christian Literature Publishing, 1885–96.

Robinson, James M. *A New Quest of the Historical Jesus*. London: SCM Press, 1959.

———, ed. *The Nag Hammadi Library in English*. San Francisco: Harper & Row, 1977.

Robinson, John A. T. *Jesus and His Coming*. London: SCM Press, 1957. 2d ed. Philadelphia: Westminster Press, 1979.

———. "The 'Parable' of the Sheep and the Goats." *NTS* 2 (1955–56): 225–37.

———. *Redating the New Testament*. Philadelphia: Westminster Press, 1976.

———. *Twelve New Testament Studies*. SBT 34. London: SCM Press, 1962.

Robinson, William C. "The Quest for Wrede's Secret Messiah." In *The Messianic Secret,* ed. Christopher Tuckett, pp. 97–115. London: SPCK; Philadelphia: Fortress Press, 1983.

Roloff, Jürgen. "Anfänge der soteriologischen Deutung des Todes Jesu (Mk. X.45 und Lk. XXII.27)." *NTS* 19 (1972): 38–64.

Ruckstuhl, Eugen. "Die johanneische Menschensohnforschung, 1957–1969." In *Theologische Berichte I*, ed. J. Pfammatter and F. Furger, pp. 171–284. Einsiedeln: Benziger, 1972.

Sanders, E. P. *Jesus and Judaism*. Philadelphia: Fortress Press, 1985.

———. *Paul and Palestinian Judaism*. Philadelphia: Fortress Press, 1977.

———. "The Testament of Abraham." In *The Old Testament Pseudepigrapha*, ed. James H. Charlesworth, vol. 1, pp. 871–902. Garden City, N.Y.: Doubleday, 1983.

Schenke, Hans-Martin. *Der Gott "Mensch" in der Gnosis*. Göttingen: Vandenhoeck & Ruprecht, 1962.

Schlatter, A. *Der Evangelist Johannes*. 2d ed. Stuttgart: Calwer Verlag, 1948.

———. *Der Evangelist Matthäus*. 3d ed. Stuttgart: Calwer Verlag, 1948.

Schmid, Joseph. *Das Evangelium nach Lukas*. 4th ed. Regensburg: Pustet, 1960.

Schmidt, Karl Ludwig. *Der Rahmen der Geschichte Jesu*. Berlin: Trowitzsch, 1919.

Schmithals, Walter. *Das Evangelium nach Markus*. 2 vols. Gütersloh: Mohn, 1979.

———. "Die Worte vom leidenden Menschensohn: Ein Schlüssel zum Lösung des Menschensohns-Problems." In *Theologia Crucis—Signum Crucis: Festschrift für Erich Dinkler zum 70. Geburtstag*, ed. C. Andreson and G. Klein, pp. 417–45. Tübingen: Mohr, 1979.

Schnackenburg, R. "Der eschatologische Abschnitt Lk 17,20–37." In *Mélanges bibliques en hommage au R. P. Beda Rigaux*, ed. A. Descamps and A. de Helleux, pp. 213–34. Gembloux: Duculot, 1970.

———. *Das Johannesevangelium*. 4 vols. Freiburg: Herder, 1965–71. Trans. K. Smith et al. *The Gospel according to St. John*. 3 vols. New York: Crossroad, 1982.

———. "Der Menschensohn im Johannesevangelium." *NTS* 11 (1965): 123–37.

Schneider, G. " 'Der Menschensohn' in der lukanischen Christologie." In *Jesus und der Menschensohn: Für Anton Vögtle*, ed. R. Pesch, R. Schnackenburg, and O. Kaiser, pp. 267–82. Freiburg: Herder, 1975.

———. *Parusiegleichnisse im Lukas-Evangelium*. Stuttgart: KBW Verlag, 1975.

Schneider, J. *Doxa: Eine bedeutungsgeschichtliche Studie*. Gütersloh: Bertelsmann, 1932.

Schniewind, Julius. *Das Evangelium nach Markus*. Göttingen: Vandenhoeck & Ruprecht, 1952.

———. *Das Evangelium nach Matthäus*. NTD, vol. 2. Göttingen: Vandenhoeck & Ruprecht, 1962.

Schoeps, Hans Joachim. *Jewish Christianity*. Trans. D. R. A. Hare. Philadelphia: Fortress Press, 1969.

———. *Theologie und Geschichte des Judenchristentums*. Tübingen: Mohr, 1949.

Schulz, S. *Q: Die Spruchquelle der Evangelisten*. Zurich: Theologischer Verlag, 1972.

———. *Untersuchungen zur Menschensohn-Christologie im Johannesevangelium*. Göttingen: Vandenhoeck & Ruprecht, 1957.

Schürer, Emil. *A History of the Jewish People in the Time of Jesus Christ*. New York: Scribner's, 1897–98.

Schürmann, Heinz. "Beobachtungen zum Menschensohn-Titel in der Redequelle: Sein Vorkommen in Abschluss- und Einleitungswendungen." In *Jesus und der Menschensohn: Für Anton Vögtle*, ed. R. Pesch, R. Schnackenburg, and O. Kaiser, pp. 124–47. Freiburg: Herder, 1975.

————. "Joh 6,51c—ein Schlüssel zur grossen johanneischen Brotrede." *BZ* 2 (1958): 244–62.

————. *Das Lukasevangelium*. Part 1. Freiburg: Herder, 1969.

Schwarz, Günther. *Jesus "Der Menschensohn."* Stuttgart: Kohlhammer, 1986.

Schweizer, Eduard. "Das johanneische Zeugnis vom Herrenmahl." *EvT* 12 (1953): 341–63; reprinted in *Neotestamentica*, 371–96. Zürich: Zwingli, 1963.

————. "Der Menschensohn." *ZNW* 50 (1959): 185–209.

————. "Menschensohn und eschatologischer Mensch im Frühjudentum." In *Jesus und der Menschensohn: Für Anton Vögtle*, ed. R. Pesch, R. Schnackenburg, and O. Kaiser, pp. 100–116. Freiburg: Herder, 1975.

————. *Neotestamentica: Deutsche und Englische Aufsätze, 1951–63*. Zürich: Zwingli, 1963.

————. "The Son of Man." *JBL* 79 (1960): 119–29.

————. "The Son of Man Again." *NTS* 9 (1962–63): 256–61.

Segal, Alan F. *Two Powers in Heaven*. Leiden: Brill, 1977.

Seitz, Oscar J. F. "The Future Coming of the Son of Man: Three Midrashic Formulations in the Gospel of Mark." In *StEv* VI, ed. Elizabeth A. Livingstone, pp. 478–94. TU 112. Berlin: Akademie Verlag, 1973.

Senior, Donald P. *The Passion Narrative according to Matthew*. Louvain: Leuven University Press, 1975.

Sidebottom, E. M. *The Christ of the Fourth Gospel*. London: SPCK, 1961.

Sigal, Phillip. *The Halakah of Jesus of Nazareth according to the Gospel of Matthew*. Lanham, Md.: University Press of America, 1986.

Sjöberg, E. *Der verborgene Menschensohn in den Evangelien*. Lund: Gleerup, 1955.

Smalley, Stephen S. "The Johannine Son of Man Sayings." *NTS* 15 (1969): 278–301.

Smith, Jonathan Z. "The Prayer of Joseph." In *Religions in Antiquity: Essays in Memory of Erwin Ramsdell Goodenough*, ed. J. Neusner, pp. 253–94. Leiden: Brill, 1968.

Sparks, H. F. D., ed. *The Apocryphal Old Testament*. Oxford: Clarendon Press, 1984.

Stendahl, Krister. *The School of St. Matthew and Its Use of the Old Testament*. Lund: Gleerup, 1954.

Stone, Michael. "The Concept of the Messiah in IV Ezra." In *Religions in Antiquity: Essays in Memory of Erwin Ramsdell Goodenough*, ed. J. Neusner, pp. 295–312. Leiden: Brill, 1968.

————. *The Testament of Abraham*. Missoula, Mont.: Society of Biblical Literature, 1972.

Strauss, David F. *Das Leben Jesu kritisch bearbeitet*. Trans. from the 4th ed. of 1840 by M. Evans, *The Life of Jesus Critically Examined*. New York: Blanchard, 1860.

Strecker, Georg. "Die Leidens- und Auferstehungsvoraussagen im Markusevangelium." *ZTK* 64 (1967): 16–39. Trans., "The Passion- and Resurrection Predictions in Mark's Gospel." *Int* 22 (1968): 421–42.

————. *Der Weg der Gerechtigkeit: Untersuchung zur Theologie des Matthäus*. Göttingen: Vandenhoeck & Ruprecht, 1962.

Streeter, B. H. *The Four Gospels: A Study of Origins*. London: Macmillan, 1924.

Suggs, M. Jack. *Wisdom, Christology, and Law in Matthew's Gospel*. Cambridge: Harvard University Press, 1970.

Tagawa, Kenzo. "People and Community in the Gospel of Matthew." *NTS* 16 (1970): 149–62.

Taylor, Vincent. *The Passion Narrative of St. Luke*. Cambridge: Cambridge University Press, 1972.

Teeple, Howard M. "The Origin of the Son of Man Christology." *JBL* 84 (1965): 213–50.

Tertullian. *Against Marcion*. Trans. and ed. A. Roberts and J. Donaldson. ANF, vol. 3, pp. 271–474. Buffalo: Christian Literature Publishing, 1885.

Theisohn, Johannes. *Der auserwählte Richter: Untersuchungen zur traditionsgeschichtlicher Ort der Menschensohngestalt der Bilderreden des Äthiopisch Henoch*. Göttingen: Vandenhoeck & Ruprecht, 1976.

Thompson, G. H. P. "The Son of Man—Some Further Considerations." *JTS* n.s., 12 (1961): 203–9.

Tödt, Heinz Eduard. *Der Menschensohn in der synoptischen Überlieferung*. Gütersloh: Mohn, 1959. Trans. D. M. Barton, *The Son of Man in the Synoptic Tradition*. Philadelphia: Westminster Press, 1965.

Trakatellis, D. C. *The Pre-existence of Christ in the Writings of Justin Martyr*. Missoula, Mont.: Scholars Press, 1976.

Tuckett, Christopher. "The Present Son of Man." *Journal for the Study of the New Testament* 14 (1982): 58–81.

———. "Recent Work on the Son of Man." *ScrB* 12 (1981): 14–18.

———, ed. *The Messianic Secret*. London: SPCK; Philadelphia: Fortress Press, 1983.

Turner, N. "Testament of Abraham." In *The Apocryphal Old Testament*, ed. H. F. D. Sparks, pp. 393–421. Oxford: Clarendon Press, 1984.

Tyson, Joseph B. "The Blindness of the Disciples in Mark." *JBL* 80 (1961): 261–68.

———. "The Lukan Version of the Trial of Jesus." *NovT* 3 (1959): 249–58.

Vassiliadis, P. "The Nature and Extent of the Q-Document." *NovT* 20 (1978): 49–73.

Vermes, Geza. *Jesus and the World of Judaism*. Philadelphia: Fortress Press, 1984.

———. *Jesus the Jew*. New York: Macmillan, 1974.

———. "The Present State of the 'Son of Man' Debate." *JJS* 29 (1978): 123–34.

———. "The 'Son of Man' Debate." *Journal for the Study of the New Testament* 1 (1978): 19–32.

———. "The Use of *bar nash/bar nasha* in Jewish Aramaic." In *An Aramaic Approach to the Gospels and Acts*, by M. Black, 3d ed., Appendix E, pp. 310–28. Oxford: Clarendon Press, 1967.

Vielhauer, Philipp. "Erwägungen zur Christologie des Markusevangeliums." In *Zeit und Geschichte: Dankesgabe an Rudolf Bultmann zum 80. Geburtstag*, ed. Erich Dinkler, pp. 155–69. Tübingen: Mohr, 1964.

———. "Gottesreich und Menschensohn in der Verkündigung Jesu." In *Festschrift für Günther Dehn*, ed. Wilhelm Schneemelcher, pp. 51–79. Neukirchen-Vluyn: Erziehungsverein, 1957.

———. "Jesus und der Menschensohn: Zur Diskussion mit Heinz Eduard Tödt und Eduard Schweizer." *ZTK* 60 (1963): 133–77.

Vögtle, Anton. "Das christologische und ekklesiologische Anliegen von Mt. 28,18–20." In *StEv* II, ed. F. L. Cross, pp. 266–94. TU 87. Berlin: Akademie Verlag, 1964.

―――. " 'Der Menschensohn' und die paulinische Christologie." In *SPCIC* 1961, pp. 199–218. Rome: Pontifical Biblical Institute, 1963.

―――. "Messiasbekenntnis und Petrusverheissung." *BZ* 1 (1957): 252–72.

―――. *Das Neue Testament und die Zukunft des Kosmos.* Düsseldorf: Patmos-Verlag, 1970.

Wacholder, B. Z. *The Dawn of Qumran.* Cincinnati: Hebrew Union College Press, 1983.

Waetjen, Herman C. *The Origin and Destiny of Humanness.* San Rafael, Calif.: Crystal Press, 1976.

Wales, Kathleen. " 'Personal' and 'Indefinite' Reference: The Users of the Pronoun *One* in Present-day English." *Nottingham Linguistic Circular* 9 (1980): 93–117.

Walker, William O. "The Son of Man Question and the Synoptic Problem." *NTS* 28 (1982): 374–88.

―――. "The Son of Man: Some Recent Developments." *CBQ* 45 (1983): 584–607.

Wanke, Joachim. *"Bezugs- und Kommentarworte" in den synoptischen Evangelien.* Leipzig: St. Benno-Verlag, 1981.

Wellhausen, Julius. *Einleitung in die drei ersten Evangelien.* 2d ed. Berlin: Georg Reimer, 1911.

―――. *Das Evangelium Marci.* Berlin: Georg Reimer, 1909.

―――. "Des Menschen Sohn." In his *Skizze und Vorarbeiten,* vol. 6, pp. 187–215. Berlin: Georg Reimer, 1899.

Wendling, Emil. *Die Entstehung des Marcus-Evangeliums.* Tübingen: Mohr, 1908.

Westcott, B. F. *The Gospel according to St. John.* 2 vols. London: Murray, 1908.

Wikenhauser, A. *Das Evangelium nach Johannes.* 3d ed. Regensburg: Pustet, 1961.

Windisch, Hans. "Angelophanien um den Menschensohn auf Erden: Ein Kommentar zu Joh 1,51." *ZNW* 30 (1931): 215–33.

Winter, Paul. *On the Trial of Jesus.* 2d ed. Rev. and ed. T. A. Burkill and Geza Vermes. Berlin: De Gruyter, 1974.

Wrede, William. *The Messianic Secret.* Trans. J. C. G. Greig. Cambridge and London: Jas. Clarke, 1971.

Zahn, Theodor. *Das Evangelium des Lucas.* 3d/4th ed. Leipzig: A. Deichert, 1920.

―――. *Das Evangelium des Matthäus.* 3d ed. Leipzig: A. Deichert, 1910.

Zerwick, Max. *Biblical Greek.* Rome: Pontifical Biblical Institute, 1963.

SCRIPTURE AND ANCIENT SOURCES

BIBLE

Old Testament

Genesis
1:26f.	37
2:7	232 n.49
2:15	232 n.49
2:18	232 n.49
22	89 n.34
28:11	272
28:12	83-84, 84 n.18
28:13	84
49:10f.	33 n.19

Exodus
8:8	127
17:14	42, 238

Numbers
23:19	18

Deuteronomy
18:15-18	59
18:15	59
21:20	264 n.20
25:19	238
30:4	171, 171 n.204

1 Samuel
2:30	268
9:6-10	21 n.79
20:35	127
29:6	168 n.195

2 Samuel
7	157 n.167
12:13	50 n.5

1 Chronicles
3:24	20

Nehemiah
2:6	168 n.195

Psalms
8:6	234 n.55
21:8	168 n.195
62:13	156
76:7	71 n.55
96:13	168
110	154 n.159, 208 n.88
110:1	4, 154, 208-9, 233 n.52
118:22	196, 201
130:3	71 n.55
147:17	71 n.55

Proverbs
24:12	156

Isaiah
11	164, 172
11:1ff.	172
11:1-5	15
11:4	12, 169
11:10	172-73
11:12	172

EARLY CHRISTIAN LITERATURE

EARLY JEWISH LITERATURE

Dead Sea Scrolls

Rabbinic Literature

OTHER ANCIENT LITERATURE

AUTHORS